Popular music in
England, 1840–1914

To Veronica

Dave Russell

Popular music in England, 1840–1914

A social history

McGill–Queen's University Press
Kingston and Montreal

780.942
R96p

First published in Great Britain by
Manchester University Press
Oxford Road, Manchester, M13 9PL
ISBN 0 7190 2233 9 *hardback*

First published in Canada in 1987 by
McGill–Queen's University Press
849 Sherbrooke Street West, Montreal H3A 2T5
ISBN 0 7735 0541 5 *hardback*
Legal deposit third quarter 1987
Bibliothèque nationale du Québec

Canadian cataloguing in publication data

Russell, Dave
  Popular music in England, 1840–1914.

Bibliography: p. 292.
Includes index.
ISBN 0–7735–0541–5

1. Music, Popular (Songs, etc.) – England – History
and criticism.   2. Music – England – 19th century –
History and criticism.   3. Music – England – 20th
century – History and criticism.   4. Music and
society.   I. Title.

ML286.4.R87   1987   780′.42′0942   C87–093438–4

AL

Photoset in Linotron Plantin with Gill Sans
by Northern Phototypesetting Co., Bolton

Printed in Great Britain

Contents

Illustrations

Illustrations appear between pages 160 and 161

Preface

Britain in the Victorian and Edwardian periods was an extraordinarily musical place. The home, the street, the public house and the public park were almost as much musical centres as the concert hall and the music hall. A communal or civic event was a poor affair indeed if not dignified by music. An Italian government official visiting Britain in 1897 reported that 'there are few countries in the world where music is made the object of such enthusiastic worship. It might almost be said that music is a vital and indispensable element of English life.'

Significantly, many members of the contemporary musical establishment were unaware of this fact. Was not Britain, they argued, *Das Land ohne Musik*, possessed of a musical culture grossly inferior to that of continental Europe?[1] The so-called 'English musical renaissance' of the late nineteenth and early twentieth century, which generated so much new and exciting composition, helped alleviate their complex, but there were many who still bemoaned Britain's musical culture. Preoccupied by the country's failure to produce composers of the highest international standing, and either blissfully ignorant or deliberately dismissive of popular musical taste, they failed to perceive the depth of musical appreciation amongst the population as a whole. For some, to seek out or acknowledge the strength of popular musical life was a dangerously egalitarian act in a class-based society. It was the strength of this popular base, however, that gave British musical activity its distinctive flavour and this book, by focusing on popular music in the urban and industrial areas of England between 1840 and 1914, seeks to rescue that activity from the obscurity to which it has been consigned.

Popular music is a troublesome concept at all times, but especially so when applied to the nineteenth and early twentieth centuries. The phrase has been used in all manner of ways. It has been given a pejorative connotation by some writers and viewed as the highly commercial antithesis to some nobler 'art music' or purer 'folk music'.

Others have also stressed the commercial element as a crucial touchstone when differentiating popular music from other genres, but without the hostile overtones. Alternatively, it has been adopted as a descriptive term relating to musical form; popular music is seen to have a relatively simple verse/chorus structure whereas 'serious' music is more complex. Yet again, it has been seen as the music played by, produced by, or produced for the 'ordinary person'.[2]

These definitions, some concerned with style and form, others with the social base of musical production, are not mutually exclusive; and, apart from the first (which by positing popular as 'bad' merely substitutes prejudice for theory), they all have some validity. However, it is not possible to adopt any one of them as the ultimate definition, and a perfect, watertight definition is probably unobtainable. Neat categories such as 'popular', 'serious', 'folk' and suchlike have a habit of disintegrating when examined closely. The issue is further confused by the need to alter our terms of reference according to the specific historical situation. When dealing with the period 1840–1914 so many of the categories on which our theories are constructed, based as they are upon modern preconceptions, do not seem to apply. A late twentieth-century observer viewing Handelian oratorio or early nineteenth-century Italian opera, for example, would be unlikely to deem these forms 'popular' music, either in terms of artistic structure or social base. (There can be few more obviously middle-class gatherings than those found in a modern opera house.) Yet in the nineteenth century, both were strongly 'popular' in the sense of being watched and *performed* by working and lower-middle-class audiences, bands and choirs. Perhaps the most useful 'definition' – 'framework for study' might be more accurate – is one which gives the widest possible picture of the age we are studying. Popular music, in this work at least, refers simply to the music that was offered to, listened to and performed by the majority of the population. The working classes, who remain, however defined, always the largest grouping in the Victorian period, inevitably become the focal point of much of what follows.

There have been remarkably few serious histories of popular music. Until relatively recently, historians of working-class life – for the most part concerned chiefly with organised labour in the shape of trade unions and political parties – and historians of music, interested essentially in the composer and his art – ignored the area almost totally. Most of the literature concerning popular music of all types came traditionally from outside academic circles': some of it, like J. F. Russell and J. H. Elliot's *The Brass Band Movement* (1936), is perceptive, informative and still unsurpassed; most of it is anecdotal and inaccurate. Reginald Nettel in his various studies and Eric Mackerness in his *A Social History of English Music* (1964) were almost the only scholars to take the subject seriously. Fortunately the mini-revolution in historical and musicological scholarship in the last decade, which has caused such a widening of focus and interest, has altered this picture considerably. The music-hall in particular is attracting the attention of numerous students and it cannot be long before something akin to a 'definitive' history of the halls can be assembled.[3]

Nevertheless, much remains to be done and this book is intended to help fill some of the gaps. The range of topics covered is deliberately broad. Most writers to date have usually been concerned with only one element of the musical configuration, but there is much to be gained from a broad, contextual view. At its most basic level, this work provides a synthesis of the existing literature (both popular and academic) on the music-hall, the brass band and the choral society in particular, adding supporting or critical notes based on primary research where possible. Alongside this, previously neglected topics such as the 'Music for the people' movement, touring opera companies and amateur orchestral societies are brought into the discussion, thus emphasising the diversity of popular musical experience. Perhaps most important of all, I have attempted to construct a genuine *social history of*, rather than a mere *social background to*, popular music. As much of the writing which has already been produced has not been the work of specialist historians, some attempts to place music in its socio-economic setting have been vague and misleading. Above all, even writers such as Mackerness, have offered a one-dimensional view whereby social and economic factors create a superstructure within which music operates, largely ignoring music's potential, in turn, to shape and structure the society that had created it. A key element in what follows – in fact perhaps the dominant element – moves toward a broader picture through an investigation of the way in which ideas and experience gained through various forms of popular musical activity influenced popular political life.

'England' rather than 'Britain' forms the core of the study, not out of any intended slight to Scotland, Wales and Ireland, but simply because their distinctive musical traditions deserve detailed assessment of a type not possible in a book such as this. The text is strongly coloured by West Yorkshire sources (a reflection both of the location of my initial research and my place of residence). It is important to appreciate that Yorkshire enjoyed a remarkably developed musical culture and care must be taken not to assume similar levels of musicality everywhere else in the country. At the same time Yorkshire was far from unique. The concentration on urban, industrial music partly reflects an inability to give adequate treatment to the 'rural folk' tradition, but is also intentional. We know far less about the Black Dyke Mills Band or the Leeds Philharmonic Society than we do about folk-song and its collectors and singers in Edwardian Sussex and Somerset. I trust the ghost of Cecil Sharp will not haunt me for my omission.

Decisions about chronology were relatively straightforward. The 1840s were an obvious starting point: the Knighting of Henry Bishop in 1843, the first Briton to be so honoured for his services to the art; the emergence of the singing-class movement; Novello's first cheap music publications; the appearance of the railway as a factor in musical life: these and many other features show this as a decade when music at all social levels took on a new importance. At the other end of the time-scale, although, as will be seen, there were considerable changes in the structure of popular music from about 1906, 1914 was a watershed in musical life as in all aspects of existence.

What follows, after a general 'picture setting' chapter, divides into three sections which reflect the three broad categories of popular musical activity that existed between 1840 and 1914. The first investigates that generated by the moral crusaders, philanthropists, educationalists and reformers who sought to use music as a method of instilling certain habits of mind and body into the English working classes. There then follows a study of the musical forms produced by entrepreneurial effort, focusing mainly on the music-hall. The third section centres on the music and musical institutions produced by the 'community'. This section is by some way the longest, a conscious emphasis intended to illustrate the popular capacity for *making* as well as consuming music. There is a danger that, by focusing too much on institutions such as the music-hall, historians may unwittingly depict the working classes as mere recipients of, rather than co-partners in, the process of cultural production.

Writing this book has been a chastening experience. In no way does it masquerade as a definitive history. Certain areas of musical life have not been examined, and almost every paragraph could tolerate further detailed exploration.[4] Within ten or fifteen years, while some of the broad argument may remain, many points will, hopefully, have been refined and altered by future scholars. If this work succeeds in stimulating this further research and providing a framework for it, it will have served a useful purpose. If it alerts people to the depth of nineteenth-century popular culture and to the artistic potential of those whom early Victorians called the 'common people', it may have done a great deal more.

Many of the ideas in this work first took shape while I was undertaking postgraduate research at the University of York, and my debt to my supervisor, Jim Walvin, is a massive one. His encouragement from the mid-1970s onwards has been a great spur. My debt to other members of the academic community is less direct. This book was largely conceived and drafted while I was a schoolteacher, and thus most of the help I received from fellow students of popular music came from their writings rather than through personal contact.

Writing in such conditions was useful in one crucial sense, for in the periods snatched from Bismarck and the Balkans and other (usually more interesting) topics, I came to feel increasingly like some latterday character from Craik's *In Pursuit of Knowledge Under Difficulties* or Smiles's *Self-Help*, albeit a vastly more privileged one. This led to a gradual realisation of the level of sacrifice required of those members of the nineteenth-century working class who wished to make music. I hope readers will, therefore, forgive the extent of my enthusiasm for those 'popular musicians' who feature in Part 3. The final stages of writing have been eased by working in the School of Historical and Critical Studies at Lancashire Polytechnic, where staff and students have, by dint of encouragement, argument and criticism, given me an even more intense interest in this subject.

The staff of many libraries and archives have given me much valuable help, most notably those at the British Newspaper Library at Colindale, and the British Library. Special thanks, however, are due to the staff of Bradford Local History and Archives departments. Their guidance and interest over a long period shows what a difference dedicated staff make to a library. An army of typists has grappled with my handwriting. I am grateful to Anne Hitchen, Alison Horsley, Lynne Rowley, Theresa Smith and, above all, Ann Hamer, who produced an excellent final copy, for their perseverance. Barbara and Martin Douglas have given me houseroom and encouragement over many stays in London and John Banks at Manchester University Press has been helpful and reliable throughout. Finally, to express a hackneyed but apt sentiment: without my wife, Veronica, there would not have been a book at all.

P. Bailey (ed.), *Music Hall: The Business of Pleasure* and J. Bratton (ed.), *Music Hall: Performance and Style* (both Open UP, 1986) were published as this book was going to press, and I was therefore unable to make use of these valuable publications.

Dave Russell
School of Historical and Critical Studies
Lancashire Polytechnic

Acknowledgments

I would like to thank the following for permission to use photographs and other illustrative material: the Guildhall Library, London (nos. 1, 2); the British Library (nos. 3, 9, 10, 11); Manchester City Libraries (nos. 4–7); Pudsey Civic Society (no. 8); Leeds City Libraries (nos. 12–15).

Photographs 9–11 are reproduced with the permission of the *British Bandsman*; the photograph of William Atkinson first appeared in *The Strad* and is reproduced here by permission of Granada Publishing.

Chapter 1

Introduction: music and society

It seems useful at this stage to provide an outline of the main patterns of popular music between 1840 and 1914, and the one offered here concentrates especially upon size, geography, class and gender. Many of the points touched on will be explored in detail later. There then follows a sketch of the contemporary historical setting giving a partial explanation for the emergence of these particular patterns.

Three key processes, *expansion*, *diversification* and *nationalisation*, can be identified operating within the field of popular music during this period. There was clearly a huge expansion in musical activity of all types, as even the most random set of statistics illustrates. The number of 'musicians and music masters' recorded in the census returns increased from nineteen thousand in 1871 to forty-seven thousand in 1911. In 1856 there were perhaps only half a dozen brass band contests in England, yet in 1896 there were over two hundred and forty, and, by 1913, a crowd estimated at between seventy and eighty thousand could be attracted to the Crystal Palace National Band Championships. In 1840, a piano was luxury item: by 1910, it has been estimated, there was one piano for every ten to twenty of the population.[1] By 1900, there were more institutes of musical education, music journals and musical societies than at any previous time in the nation's history. The pace of expansion seems to have been broadly similar across the whole field of musical life: steady from about 1845 to 1875, rapid from that date and reaching a peak in the 1890s. This decade was arguably the high-water mark of the popular musical tradition that typified the period 1840–*c*. 1920. Dozens of new choral societies emerged, particularly in the North and Midlands, encouraged by the new competitive festival movement. The piano became an ever more common feature of working-class homes, the music-hall industry began to reach more deeply into the ranks of the middle-class audience and to thrust into the middle-sized provincial communities it had previously ignored. From this time on, the peculiar musical configuration of nineteenth-century England was in stagnation and, eventually, decline.

The second half of the century saw not merely growth, but diversification as new styles, genres and institutions emerged. The transformation of musical life in Bradford in the West Riding of Yorkshire underlines this point well. In 1840 the town's musical activity was centred on a sizeable group of local musicians whose main love was the performance of sacred music, and who sustained the local chapel choirs, a choral society and a number of 'clubs'. There were occasional concerts in the few available public halls and a growing number of singing-salons based on town centre public houses. Bradford was certainly musical at this time, but within relatively confined traditions. By 1900 the area within five miles of the town centre boasted almost thirty choral societies, some twenty brass bands, an amateur orchestra, six concertina bands, a team of handbell-ringers, two music-halls and a number of venues offering Saturday evening 'popular concerts'. The local theatre had at least one annual visit from a leading opera company and had begun to feature the musical comedies so much a novelty within the late Victorian musical environment. As early as 1887, a social investigator noted that the piano, in the past a 'rarity . . . may now be found almost in house-rows'.[2] The West Riding, as already stated, may well have been somewhat untypical, but most English communities will have shared in the enjoyment of the new types of musical experience that the period produced.

The process of 'nationalisation' whereby most areas of England developed an increasingly similar, unified popular culture, has been less widely commented upon than the two themes outlined above and needs more detailed attention. This process should not be exaggerated, and indeed the need for geographical precision when describing musical life is a key theme of this book. Informed contemporaries were aware that strong regional variations existed. W. J. Galloway, writing in 1910, observed that, 'it is as true as it is curious that natural aptitude for music is found in very diverse degrees in different parts of the country'.[3] The word 'aptitude' may not be accurate, but local tastes and opportunities certainly varied. The music-hall industry, for example, was essentially centred in cities and large towns and, above all, in London. For all its strength in the provinces, the industry looked to the capital for the greatest levels of support and for so many of the new trends and developments. Community-based music, however, in the form of choirs and bands, was far more a product of the small towns and industrial villages of the Midlands and Northern England. Significantly, the largely London-orientated musical establishment took until the Edwardian era to appreciate this fact and it required a provincial musician, Edward Elgar, to make it known to them. In 1904, during the course of a letter to Canon Gorton, organiser of the Morecambe Music Festival which Elgar had just attended and where he had been greatly impressed by the quality of the working and lower-middle-class choirs, the composer made an eloquent observation upon the geography of popular music:

It is rather a shock to find Brahms's part-songs appreciated and among the daily fare of a district apparently unknown to the sleepy London press: people who talk of the spread of music in England and the increasing love of it rarely seem to know where the growth of the art is really strong and properly fostered. Some day the press will awake to the fact, already known abroad and to some few of us in England, that the living centre of music in Great Britain is not London, but somewhere further north.[4]

There were also smaller-scale examples of local variation. In the late nineteenth century Durham pitmen sang or listened to the songs of their local bard Tommy Armstrong (1848–1919), a collier/songwriter from Tanfield who specialised in songs of mining life which were often in local dialect and shot through with local references. These songs would have been largely unknown to, for example, the weavers and miners of the Holme Valley in West Yorkshire, who would have preferred the much-prized songs associated with their local beagle hunt.[5]

Nevertheless, while allowing for clear local patterns it is undeniable that the period after about 1840, and particularly from the 1870s, saw an increasing unification of taste and repertoire encouraged above all by the railway, the music-hall industry, music publishers and, to a lesser extent, the expanding state education system. Music-hall artists toured the country performing virtually the same repertoire at each venue. New compositions spread rapidly across the country, becoming part of a genuinely national culture. Five hundred thousand sheet-music copies of Sullivan's 'The Lost Chord' were sold between 1877 and 1902, while Lady Hill's 'in the Gloaming' sold 140,000 copies in the 1880s. Henry Round's arrangement of Donizetti's *Lucrezia Borgia* was used at almost one-fifth of the two hundred and forty brass band contests held in 1896.[6] Although local traditions could survive, they were, as in the case of the coster songs of the London music-hall, often either absorbed into the national popular culture or destroyed by it.

Throughout the period, English musical life, particularly at institutional level, was organised broadly along class lines. Although the various forms of popular activity could show subtle variation – the brass band, for example, drawing its strength from the skilled and semi-skilled working classes, the choral society from the skilled working and the lower middle classes – popular music was essentially the music of the great majority of the population: those who, even by 1900, earned less than £200 a year and left school at the end of the elementary stage.

For many observers higher up in the social order, the social base of popular music gave sufficient grounds for confident dismissal of its artistic value. Art, therefore, gave the middle and upper classes another opportunity to claim superior status over subordinate classes. At its most extreme level, such an attitude led to the view that working-class taste was little short of moronic, a belief eloquently expressed by the Reverend Haweis in his influential *Music and Morals*: 'Music is not to our lower orders a deep-rooted need, a means of expressing the pent-up and often oppressive emotions of the heart, but merely a noisy appendage to low pastimes.'[7] The more humble the social base of the musical organisation in question, the more divorced it was from accepted musical values, the more likely it was to suffer. The attitude of the musical 'establishment' to the brass band illustrates the point well. Undervaluation of working-class musical sensitivity was especially pronounced before about 1875, as the following extract from the *Yorkshire Orchestra* in 1868, illustrates.

Our bandsmen are all mechanics; some of them, no doubt fine specimens of humanity – rough, hardworking, honest fellows – deserving our highest admiration as mechanics, *but lacking the refinement of feeling or the ability to become efficient musicians*. The greatest delight many of them have is to wear a grand military uniform, so that they may parade in the streets at night, followed by a large crowd (usually composed of all the tag-rag and bobtail of the town) when 'bang' (goes the big drum, immediately followed by a terrific crash of nasty, coarse, brassy sounds, enough to terrify into fits our little ones, who are frequently awoke out of the first sleep by these noisy, thoughtless, brassy men.[8]

Even after this date, as bands become better known to 'respectable' audiences, criticism was voiced, sometimes by authorities who, although supposedly sympathetic to the working classes, could adopt a decidedly prejudicial tone. John Spencer Curwen, son of the 'inventor' of the tonic sol-fa sight-singing method and himself a devotee of the crusade to bring music to the poor, dismissed what was arguably the major vehicle for popular musical education in industrial England with the following observations:

It is much to be regretted that these brass bands do not tone down their blare by the addition of flutes, clarionets, oboes, etc., making a properly balanced military band. A good authority tells me that it is not the difficulty of learning the instruments of the wood band which stands in the way of this reform so much as the British love of noise.[9]

It is worth noting that, despite the forays of Holst, Elgar and others in the band world after 1918, establishment attitudes did not change particularly rapidly. As late as 1927, *Grove's Dictionary of Music and Musicians* made no mention of the brass band movement, while several distinguished inter-war critics and educationalists, including Percy Scholes, Landon Ronald and Peter Warlock, were all genuinely surprised to discover the extent and quality of the movement.[10]

It is not possible to discuss here contemporary criticism of music-hall, folk song, the concertina and many other aspects of musical life. Popular music, like so many aspects of contemporary popular social life, attracted many barbs. Great care, however, must be taken with such middle-class testimony when recreating the history of popular music, as much of it is nothing more than class prejudice. Undoubtedly, levels of popular musical achievement were not always high. It is equally certain, however, that some remarkable accomplishments can be found in every sphere of popular musical life. The quality of much Victorian and Edwardian popular music must not be hidden from us by the ignorance and partiality of those contemporaries who could not accept that an artistic temperament was not the prerogative of an exclusive minority.

While it is clear that music did reflect the class patterns of the age, it must not be assumed that popular musical institutions adhered rigidly to these patterns. As will be seen, individuals *could* cross class boundaries in order to pursue their musical interests and in some quarters were actively encouraged to do so. Even more strikingly, the *repertoire* of the period was very often not class-specific. There was a vast middle ground that became common property. *Il Trovatore*, which in the late twentieth century may be pigeon-holed as a cultural product for the middle class, was known not only to fashionable audiences in London, but to the gallery in countless provincial theatres, brass bandsmen (many of whom could, according to one source, whistle parts of it from memory), and, albeit in markedly altered form, to the urban poor, who had it drummed into their consciousness by countless barrel organs. Similarly Sullivan's 'Lost Chord', again perhaps 'bourgeois' according to current preconception – well, was there a man, woman, child or beast who *couldn't* whistle it from memory? Alternatively, the 'plebeian' music hall song increasingly found its way into middle-class drawing rooms from the 1890s.

Certainly, at the poles of the contemporary repertoire, there were clear taste publics and sub-cultures. Chamber music, for example, remained the preserve of the 'intellectual' middle class, while the pit-songs of Tommy Armstrong stayed in their original social locales. Moreover, the same music in a different social setting could carry markedly different social connotations and meanings. Donizetti, enjoyed by a popular audience at a Carl Rosa or Moody-Manners production in Blackburn, did not have the élan of Donizetti at Covent Garden, while the singer of a rural folk-song might invest it with a meaning far removed from that given to it by a middle-class collector.[11] Nevertheless, by the end of the nineteenth century something very close to a mass musical culture had emerged in England, a sharing of common taste across a broad social range.

One noteworthy aspect of this sharing is the extent to which popular musicians and audiences drew upon what we tenuously call 'art music'. Many contemporaries, even those sympathetic to the working classes, were totally unaware of this. William Morris, for example, painted an all-too-persuasive picture of a populace driven to mass philistinism by industrial capitalism: 'over many parts of Britain the common people have forgotten what a field or flower is like, and their idea of beauty is a gas-poisoned gin palace or a tawdry theatre.'. On a further occasion, when discussing music specifically, he claimed that 'what the 'unsophisticated' person takes to is not the fine works of Art, but the ordinary, commonplace, banal tunes which are drummed into his ears at every street corner.'[12] Academic literature, until extremely recently, has shown a similar belief in the exclusion of the working class from the arts. Relatively modern works of sociology and musicology claim that the working class 'were shut out from official 'high culture' by the barriers of class, money, literacy and education', that they inhabited a 'musical desert' and 'grew up with no contact with the world of high culture except perhaps the language of the Authorised Version of the Bible'.[13] In fact, through the people's concert, the concert-hall, the music-hall, the choral contest, the brass band performance and other routes, Handel, Wagner and Donizetti, to name but three, were known to many 'ordinary people': vaguely by some, intimately and expertly by a significant minority. It would clearly be fanciful to claim that, for example, once-weekly exposure to ten minutes of Rossini arranged for a five-piece orchestra in a music-hall gave people a genuine stake in 'high culture'. Nevertheless, it seems likely that a greater popular base for art music existed between 1840 and 1914 than before or since, despite the efforts of schools and arts councils. Well-intentioned sponsorship is no substitute for a genuine popular appetite.

Partly as a result of the willingness to move beyond a simple class-based musical diet, the nineteenth century, especially in its later stages, saw the emergence of a remarkably catholic taste amongst both professional and amateur musicians. Sensing that much music was, to an extent, common property, individuals felt free to range widely. Leslie Stuart (real name Thomas Barrett), composer of music-hall favourites such as 'Lily of Laguna' and the musical comedy *Floradora*, was also for a period during his song-writing career, organist at Salford Cathedral and promoter of 'people's concerts' in Manchester which featured many of the 'popular classics' of the day. This one figure spanned a huge section of the musical spectrum. Similarly, Frederick Cowen wrote oratorios, symphonies and parlour ballads. Lionel Monckton, the most prolific of musical comedy composers, was a devotee of Wagner. Amateur and semi-professional musicians showed similar eclecticism. Harry Mortimer played operatic selections, marches and hymns with Luton Red Cross Band, but also accompanied music-hall artists, including Marie Lloyd, at the local theatre. One member of the Bradford Festival Choral Society liked both Handel and Vesta Tilley, the music-hall male impersonator![14]

The 'general public', who, unlike the musical community, were paying for their musical experiences and therefore might be expected only to afford more defined taste, in fact accepted some interesting mixtures. A popular concert in Bradford in 1871 featured the music-hall star The Great Vance, Miss Newbould, a local soprano and the Halifax Glee and Madrigal Society; in 1897 visitors to the Bournemouth Winter Gardens could have heard the municipal orchestra

follow Mendelssohn's *Ruy Blas* with a medley of Albert Chevalier's
coster songs.[15]

A further explanation for this breadth of taste is to be found in the
nature of much of the actual music. Most musical genres had similar
unifying elements. Above all, much music was sentimental in the
broadest sense. Richard Hoggart had an uncle who described such
songs as 'Bless This House' as 'music that makes you want to give
your money away'.[16] This seems a particularly apt description for
these tear-jerkers that can be found at every level of Victorian and
Edwardian musical life, whether it be 'Home Sweet Home', 'My Old
Dutch', 'Spare The Old Mud Cabin', many hymns and almost any
stirring choral music. Perhaps this sentimentality was rooted in the
religious spirit of the period, which generated the need to make music
which created noble thoughts. Moreover, most music was *melodic*.
For the majority of the population music and melody seem synonymous, and in the period 1840–1914 composers from Bishop to Harry
Lauder gave their audiences and performers strong melodies. These
two common elements did much to stimulate this shared musical
culture.

In some senses, the sexual divide was greater than the class divide
in Victorian and Edwardian popular music. Women's role in the
brass band movement was almost totally a subservient (if vital) one –
cakes and teas were to be made for fêtes, uniforms cleaned, meals
prepared in good time for rehearsals and so forth. Even by 1914
women seem to have been in a minority in music-hall audiences and
working-class women appear to have frequented concerts far less
often than their menfolk. There was, however, a greater range of
opportunities provided for women by music than by most other
leisure forms. Piano playing (a mixed blessing for many) and choral
singing were probably the two pursuits most closely associated with
women, although neither was the exclusively 'female' pastime that it
– piano playing especially – is sometimes assumed to have been. For
the talented (or lucky) few, music offered women a chance to build a
career. Performers such as the music-hall singers Marie Lloyd and
Vesta Tilley, or the musical comedy star Gertie Millar, were amongst
the first women from working-class backgrounds to become national
figures in this country. It is, however, significant that this breakthrough could only occur in a field of entertainment where the commodity being marketed was as much female sexuality as musical
talent.

A wide range of factors coalesced to help create this distinctive popular musical culture. Historians of music have, perhaps inevitably, concentrated upon overtly 'musical' and 'artistic' factors when examining Victorian and Edwardian music. Undoubtedly, the stimulus provided by such things as the much-discussed production of cheap sheet music, the musical competition, the hire-purchase system for musical instrument purchase and so forth was critical, and such features will be described at length in later chapters. However, it is hard to see such factors exerting influence, or indeed existing at all, without key social and economic changes establishing a climate in which such 'musical' factors could operate.

The most crucial single influence was beyond doubt industrialisation which, during the period encompassed by this book, wrought major changes at every level. Above all, it changed England's human geography dramatically and called into being a new set of social relationships. The demands of industry (coupled with the growth in population) produced an increasingly urban environment. The 1851 census revealed for the first time a clear majority of English people living in towns rather than in rural areas, and by 1881 almost 40 per cent of the population of England and Wales lived in the six great 'conurbations' of London, South East Lancashire, the West Midlands, West Yorkshire, Tyneside and Merseyside.[17]

The greatest hardships generated by industrialisation and urbanisation belong to the period before 1850 and indeed after about 1875 the working classes probably began to profit materially from Britain's industrial strength. However, even after this date there was still much to activate the working-class movement which had been forged in the political and economic crises after 1790. The English working class in general was never to be revolutionary and until the last two decades of the nineteenth century was largely untouched by socialism, or indeed by theoretical doctrine of any form. From about 1850 until the 1880s, a type of consensus existed in the political arena, best expressed by the marriage of classes and interests that made up the Liberal Party. From the 1880s, the growth of unionism amongst the unskilled, the appearance of socialist organisations and the growth of independent labour gave a more combative flavour to the popular political movement, although in comparison with the mass political activities of the period 1815–1848, the events of the late Victorian and Edwardian eras often appear essentially defensive; an acceptance of the system rather than an attempt to alter it. For all its supposed political and theoretical 'peculiarity' when compared with equivalents in some European countries, however, the English working class still had both sufficient cutting edge and distinctive culture to disturb the middle classes. With their political and economic ambitions largely satisfied by the 1832 Reform Bill and the fiscal policies of successive governments from 1841 onwards, the middle classes were forever glancing uneasily over their shoulders at the class which some of their leaders had flirted with and then abandoned in the 1840s.

It was impossible for popular musical life to avoid the impact of such change. Certainly not all the guiding factors stemming from industrialisation were the result of the grand sweeps of history outlined above. At a more modest level, for example, the substantial growth of the lower middle classes, especially the clerk, the commercial traveller and associated occupational groups, had clear significance. Clerks, who formed only 0.7 per cent of the population in 1851 but 3 per cent by 1911 as both the state and industrial capitalism increased their specialist needs, made a considerable contribution to contemporary musical life.[18] David Lockwood, in his pioneering *The Blackcoated Worker*, noted the 'wider achievements which many clerks prized – in painting, music, history, literary composition'.[19] Their presence, whether it be in the ranks of the choral or orchestral society, or at a somewhat less exalted level in the stalls or lower gallery in the music hall, was a dynamic one. Similarly, the massive growth of cheap rail travel from the 1840s boosted popular musical life. It is inconceivable that such events as the Belle Vue and Crystal Palace band championships, which involved the transportation of thousands of competitors and spectators distances of up to three hundred miles, could have developed without the railway. The armies of music-hall performers, opera singers and concert artistes that constantly crossed and recrossed the country were likewise virtually dependent upon the railway network for their existence.[20]

It would seem, however, that musical life after 1840 was altered most profoundly by the processes outlined above whereby England became an increasingly urban, class-conscious society, but one in which material gains gradually permeated downwards. A student of folk music would perhaps contend that the processes of urbanisation should be seen as destructive, eating away at the social and economic structures that had nurtured the staple music of the rural poor. It is undeniable that the virtual cessation of rural song creation from about 1850 owed much to the impact of the new structures and rhythms of

changing society.[21] However, while allowing for its capacity to undermine certain cultural forms, it is tempting when looking across the
whole period to 1914 and at a broad range of musical life to see
urbanisation in a more positive light. Above all, it created the large
market for music upon which so many institutions were dependent.
The creation of the multi-million-pound music-hall industry would
have been impossible without the existence of large centres of population. Choral societies would never have attained their eventual size
or influence without the support of large communities. Again, the
specialist music shop would have had no place in a rural community.

Of equal significance was the emergence of a class-based society in
industrial England. This influenced popular music in two ways.
Firstly, music reflected class structures very clearly. (As will be seen,
however, music was not simply a reflector, but could have a dynamic
influence of its own.) The pattern described earlier, whereby musical
life reflected class division yet allowed for some movement of both
people and repertoire between classes, was very much a product of the
nineteenth-century class system, which was both clearly defined, and
capable of flexibility. Individuals could make both permanent progress up the social scale and, more typically, form temporary liaisons
with their supposed 'inferiors' or 'betters' either through politics, as
happened in the Liberal Party, or, more usually, through leisure.[22]
The second contribution of the class-based society on popular music
was that middle-class concern about the political and social problems
generated by the emergence of distinctive and, to many minds,
suspect working-class cultural patterns led to a major expansion of
musical provision expressly for the working class. This theme receives
detailed attention in section one, but needs acknowledgement at this
juncture. Certain elements of popular musical life – the singing class,
some brass bands, the people's concert – were in part born out of fear
of the problems created by industrial society.

Gradually, industrialisation did bring benefits to some members of
the working classes, two of which, time and money, deserve the
greatest attention.[23] The expansion and formalising of leisure time
that took place from the mid-nineteenth century were two of the key
social changes of the industrial age. Between 1850 and 1914 large
sections of the skilled and semi-skilled working class gained considerable reductions in their hours of work as a result either of parliamentary legislation or the threat or actuality of industrial action.
Generalisation about this topic is difficult because of regional and

occupational differences, but by 1914 a working week of between fifty and sixty hours had become the norm as the brutal work regimes of the early industrial phase were brought under control. The new leisure time was usually in the evenings after seven and, particularly from the 1870s, on Saturday afternoons from two. It was the creation of these distinct periods of free time into which leisure pursuits could expand, rather than the increase in free time in absolute terms, which proved so vital to the development of popular music and of course, to all forms of popular recreation. Evenings provided the focal point for music-hall and concert performances and the expansion of these forms in the second half of the nineteenth century was undoubtedly due to people's increased ability to attend. Saturday afternoon became the favoured time for the musical competitions and contests which were to become such a central element of musical life.

However, this new leisure structure would have been of little value unless accompanied by increased wealth. Again, from about mid century, sections of the English working class began to enjoy an improvement in financial status, and by the 1890s there was even, for a significant minority, a relative prosperity. The most important developments took place between 1876 and 1896, the years of the 'Great Depression', when the combined effect of a slight increase in actual wage rates and a 40 per cent decrease in prices, resulted in a national rise in real wages of 66 per cent. As with discussion of increased leisure time, beneath such bland generalisation lies immense regional and occupational variation, countless individual stories of hardship and poverty caused by economic depression, ill-ness, unemployment and industrial dispute, and, at the bottom of society, a sizeable group whom beneficial economic change by-passed altogether. But the basic picture is clear: sections of the working class had an increased economic capacity for musical enjoyment. Both community-based organisations and the capitalist leisure industry were to benefit.[24]

While increased financial opportunity and free time have for some time been seen as central to the expansion of popular recreation, religion has often been seen as its inevitable enemy.[25] Undeniably, certain aspects of recreational life – the public house, gambling, cock-fighting and bloodsports in general (apart from foxhunting, a favoured sport of the rural clergy) – were victims of constant criticism and crippling attack from certain religious quarters. Popular music did not escape, the music-hall, especially in its early period, becoming a target for the most virulent attacks.[26] Nevertheless, the growth of the music-hall industry was hindered only occasionally by religious opposition and in general the whole field of popular music benefited positively from the prevailing religious atmosphere of Victorian England. Music, because of its association with religious ceremony and its supposed ability to civilise and humanise, was known to Victorians as the 'sacred art'. Its performance was encouraged by a succession of Christian philanthropists and missionaries throughout the period, who maintained the accepted wisdom of the day that music could 'with Orphean magic raise in perfected beauty the towers of the City of Man'.[27] Singing classes and people's concerts were the most obvious beneficiaries of such a mentality, but most forms of music received encouragement. One major reason why music was so popular in Victorian, and perhaps, to a lesser extent, in Edwardian times, was that it was suited to the needs of an overtly religious society.

The choral movement probably gained more from this situation than any other element of popular musical life. Its repertoire, firmly grounded in cantata and oratorio, provided 'respectable' society, be it patrician or plebeian, with rational entertainment steeped in sacred sentiment. Handel's *Messiah* became the object of special devotion. Writing in 1888, William Spark, the Leeds Borough organist, claimed that the work 'has done more to educate musical taste, unclasp the hands of charity, and unfold the mind of God to man, than any other composition, save the Bible itself'. His contemporary F. J. Crowest agreed, claiming that: '*The Messiah* has probably done more to convince thousands of mankind that there is a God above us, than all the theological works ever written'.[28] Obviously, attitudes towards the sacred repertoire varied according to individual standpoints. While many would have agreed with the choral singer who believed 'there's nothing to beat *Messiah* for real truth', others would have seen attendance at or performance in a choral concert as merely a social duty, a chance for public display of righteous behaviour, or a pleasant substitute for more strenuous devotional activity.[29] But from whatever position it was viewed, the choral concert was the ideal musical vehicle of the age and it is hardly surprising that the emergence of the choral society was one of the primary features of nineteenth-century musical history.

The religious sensibilities of early and middle Victorian England did not survive the century unscathed. In the final decades of the

century, a more 'liberal' theology took root in all but the most evangelical denominations. As the fear of hell and damnation receded,
pleasure (often an object for intense suspicion in the earlier period),
was increasingly regarded as an acceptable, even valuable experience.[30] Initially, this new attitude had a liberating effect upon many
areas of popular musical life. The religious mores of high Victorian
England had protected many forms of music from those attacks so
frequent in other areas of popular recreation, and fostered 'suitable'
musical institutions. The changes of late century now encouraged a
much wider process of musical expansion. Church and chapel choirs
were viewed increasingly not as mere aids to religious observance, but
as a source of entertainment to the local community.[31] Moreover, the
concert-hall, the performance of the travelling opera company and
even the more salubrious music-halls were now permissable sources of
entertainment for many. It is hard to imagine the frivolous musical
comedies of Lionel Monckton or even the work of Gilbert and Sullivan enjoying success in the emotional climate of 1840–1875. It is
harder still to imagine fourteen Yorkshire church and chapel choirs
singing, as they did at Batley Town Hall in 1895, Psalm 95 for prizes
of £6, £4 and £2![32] Clearly a great social and musical change had taken
place. Only in the years immediately preceding the Great War did
many observers realise that these changes were a prelude to a decline
in religious observation and increase in secularisation, a situation
fraught with difficulty for certain areas of popular musical life,
especially the choral movement.

Part 1

Control: music and the battle for the working-class mind

Chapter 2

Music and morals, 1840–1880

To most middle-class Victorians it was axiomatic that music should be more than a mere artistic experience or a form of amusement. John Spencer Curwen's assessment of his father's tonic sol-fa sight-singing method illustrates clearly the overtly moralistic approach to music so common in the nineteenth century.

The method was the indirect means of aiding worship, temperance and culture, of holding young men and women among good influences, of reforming character, of spreading Christianity. The artistic aspect of the work done by the sol-fa method is indeed less prominent than its moral and religious influence.[1]

Certainly, there were clear signs of an 'art for art's sake' mentality emerging from the late nineteenth century onwards. In 1907 a London schools inspector attacked the Tonic Sol-Fa Association for its refusal to accept 'the modern way of looking upon music not merely as an appendage of religion, or drink, or teetotalism, but as an artistic force valuable for its own sake'.[2] However, holders of the 'modern' view – mainly professional musicians whose artistic preoccupations transcended social deliberations – were still in a minority. In the same year as the inspector made his remark, a Bradford shoe manufacturer defended a proposed series of free chamber music concerts on the decidedly practical grounds that they would limit the excesses of local courting habits by clearing the streets 'of the young life of the city . . . no one can pass along Market Street and Manningham Lane without feeling that something should be done to correct the evil influences of these parades'.[3] The view of music as an object of social utility and balm for society's many evils remained extraordinarily common until at least 1914.

Such a view was by no means a Victorian invention but it was in the second half of the nineteenth century that it reached its apotheosis. It was not confined to music, as the arts and leisure pursuits in general were often treated in like manner. Music, however, was always a particularly popular component in the various schemes whereby reformers sought social and moral regeneration through 'rational recreation'. Through its supposed capacity to touch the emotions, music was uniquely suited to the task of shaping men's thought and actions. Moreover, many contemporaries stressed the close relationship between music and religion. As early as 1834, when contemporary discussion of music's powers was only in its infancy, the journalist George Hogarth made a forceful case for popular choral music in a description of the weaving communities of Yorkshire.

The spirit of industrious independence maintains its ground among them in spite of the demoralising progress of pauperism and poor laws; they are religious in spite of the spread of infidelity; and they love their families and friends, in spite of the attractions of the beershop. All this, of course, is not universally the case, but its general truth, to a remarkable extent, will be doubted by no one who has lived among and known the people of this neighbourhood. The power to which these effects are, in a very considerable degree, to be ascribed, we hesitate not to affirm, is SACRED MUSIC.[4]

Fuelled by such confident pronouncements, a mass of activity which embraced singing classes, temperance bands, popular concerts and music festivals arose all over the country.

Throughout the period up until 1914, much of this 'music for the people', as later Victorians eventually christened it, centred on the middle-class wish to destroy the potentially 'dangerous' elements within working-class culture and to create a respectable, self-reliant, collaborationist working class.[5] It is significant that although music for the people was a constant feature of the recreational landscape from the mid-nineteenth century onwards, it was particularly prominent in the mid-1840s and early 50s, and again in the 1880s and early 1900s, all periods during which the propertied classes exhibited intensified concern about the political behaviour of the lower orders. While it would be over-simplification to see every musical project emanating from a middle-class source as a direct attempt at political control, it is clear that fear of political unrest generated heightened interest in working-class culture and its reform.[6]

The aspects of popular culture under attack varied according to circumstance. The period 1840 to 1914 saw relationships between classes and the issues which structured these relationships change considerably, and music for the people reflected these changing pre-occupations. Before moving on to explore the detailed history of musical provision it is worth picking out the two main themes that structured it. At the heart of the earliest attempts to provide 'decent' popular musical recreation was the desire to limit the place of drink in working-class culture. The 1820s and 1830s were worrying decades for observers of working-class social life. A supposed *per capita* increase in the consumption of spirits (in reality merely the result of more effective legislation against smuggling), combined with an equally chimerical rise in crime rate to stimulate a serious questioning of the role of the public house.[7] In particular, reformers were anxious to break the ever-strengthening connection between the publican and popular entertainment. By the 1840s it was only too apparent that public house singing-saloons and concert-rooms were an established feature of urban popular culture, and complaints about them became a commonplace of contemporary investigative literature. In 1844 Leon Faucher discovered that one Manchester public house concert-room 'collects in this manner, one thousand persons, every evening until eleven p.m. On Sundays, to diminish the scandal, religious hymns and sacred music are performed upon the piano and organ.' Five years later Samuel Smith, a Bradford textile dyer, magistrate and music-lover, was saddened to discover that 'on a Saturday night, wherever there was a sound of music to be heard, however offensive and contaminating the atmosphere might be, there a crowd of people was collected'.[8] The need to combat these places, particularly the music-hall industry they spawned and the drink trade in general, remained a dominant theme until the very end of the century. Then, as new problems arose and as the consumption of alcohol showed signs of decline (consumption per head of the population fell from the late 1870s onwards), fear of the consequences of demon drink receded a little.[9]

Equally pervasive, and perhaps longer-lasting, was the belief that by bringing together people from different backgrounds music could act as a social cement, a bridgehead between antagonistic social classes. This argument was at its firmest in the middle of the century. In 1857 John Hope Shaw, a Leeds solicitor and active moral reformer, told the audience at a local 'people's concert' that: 'It was impossible that all classes of society could mingle with each other week after week, as at these concerts, without feeling their mutual regard for each other strengthened and confirmed'. As the period progressed, the rhetoric became less assertive but the message remained the same. Writing in 1909, a commentator observed the social benefits of the competitive music festival:

The competitive festival movement is responsible for much socialism, although of a very different kind from that conventionally associated with the word. A festival brings into pleasant contact people of all classes who, in the ordinary course of events, would probably not be on speaking terms.[10]

The belief in music's efficacy as a social healer had taken deep root.

Not all the activity generated by this amalgam of homespun, quasi-philosophical theory was positive, however. Recreational reformers had two basic courses of action open to them: direct repression or the provision of alternatives (the first of these was preferred by some throughout the period). Music-halls and singing-saloons, particularly in the period up to 1830, were threatened regularly at the annual licensing session, when local magistrates reviewed their fitness to continue in operation. The Alexandra Hall in Gateshead was closed by magistrates in 1871 after an unspecified 'unseemly performance' and its successor, the People's Concert Hall, had initially to struggle hard in the period up to 1880, were threatened regularly at the annual nience and annoyance to the neighbourhood'. They were particularly enraged by the proprietors' inventive tactic of issuing tickets to Sunday-school children at a penny a head.[11] The Star, Bolton, along with its progeny the Museum Music Hall, was the victim of a long-running campaign which enjoyed brief success in 1872 when the magistrates removed its licence, only to rescind the decision after a strong counter-protest.[12] The London County Council gained itself a reputation as a stringent authority, backed as it was by the 1878 Board of Works Act which gave it the capacity to shut down halls that failed to meet fairly rigorous fire and safety regulations. A number of small London halls fell foul of this Act in the 1880s, to the pleasure of reformers and of managers of larger halls who must have gained additional business as a result.[13] In time, however, even the larger halls were to be threatened. In 1892, in one of the most celebrated incidents of music-hall history, Mrs Ormiston Chant, a leading moral reformer, opposed the renewal of the London Empire's licence on the grounds that its promenade was frequented by prostitutes. The LCC stopped short of refusing renewal but agreed that a screen should be erected around the promenade bar so that the prostitutes could not be seen by the respectable element of the audience. The screen was erected, but then duly demolished by a group of bohemian blades, including the young Winston Churchill, who were angered by such prudish interference with their pleasure.[14] What constituted hooliganism when perpetrated by the poor was merely justifiable high spirits when carried out by their superiors.

Direct attack clearly produced only limited results and many critics of popular recreation showed a sensible willingness to produce alternative forms. Thus rational recreation was born. Probably the earliest attempts to harness music to the service of popular improvement were made by industrial entrepreneurs. The first generation of industrial workers had to be taught new work codes and disciplines if the capital expenditure of the employers was to bring the hoped-for level of profit. The old pre-industrial work patterns – irregular bursts of relatively intense activity punctuated by spells of inactivity to allow for drinking, sport and holidays – had to be replaced. Most industrialists resorted to threats, fines, and, for the children, corporal punishment.[15] Others, especially those from certain Nonconformist backgrounds, augmented or supplanted these methods with more sophisticated approaches. It was in this type of industrial environment that music was most likely to be used as a method of creating a rapport between capital and labour. Besses o'th' Barn Village band, founded in 1818, was originally sponsored by three members of the Clegg family, representatives of the local cotton manufacturing industry. The Quaker London Lead Company supported bands at at least three of their remote mining villages in North Yorkshire and Durham between 1820 and 1825. Robert Owen's factory children were taught singing at New Lanark, and John Strutt founded an orchestra and choir at his textile mill in Belper. (Strutt was so concerned that his musicians might leave to become music teachers that the orchestral members had to agree to work for him for a minimum of seven years.)[16] Perhaps the most impressive musical configuration of all was that encouraged by Samuel Greg at his factory village of Bollington between the opening of the mill in 1832 and 1840, when he gave this proud description to factory inspector, Leonard Horner:

Our music and singing engage many of both sexes – young and old, learned and unlearned. We have a small glee class that meets once a week round a cottage fire. There is another, more numerous, for sacred music, that meets every Wednesday and Saturday during the winter and really performs very well, at least I seldom hear music that pleases me more. A number of men have

formed a band with clarionets, horns, and other wind instruments, and meet
twice a week to practice, besides blowing and trumpeting nightly at their own
homes. A few families are provided with pianos and here I believe all the
children of the household play on them. The guitar is also an instrument not
unknown among us, and to these may be added sundry violins, violoncellos,
serpents, flutes and some sort of thing they call a *dulcimer* . . . and when you
remember how few families we muster – not more than seventy or eighty – you
will think with me that we are quite a musical society.[17]

Music was not, of course, the sole element in such industrialists'
attempts to instill correct habits in their workforce. Owen's achievements at New Lanark need no further amplification here, but all the
other companies noted above played their part in the move for a more
thoughtful approach to early industrial relations.[18] Strutt insisted on a
limited amount of schooling for hands under twenty, Greg provided a
reasonable level of living accommodation for his workers, and both
built chapels. That entrepreneurs utilised music in their schemes
needs some explanation. Initially, at least, it was not so much a
reflection of music's accepted value as a vehicle of control – such a
belief was as yet in its infancy and these men were helping to give it
credence – as an indication of the industrialist's own musical interest.
Strutt, for example, came from an extremely musical Derbyshire
family. Similarly, John Foster of Black Dyke Mills, Queenshead
(later Queensbury) near Bradford, whose firm produced the most
famous brass band of all time, had played the French horn in a local
village band. William Lister Marriner, a Keighley worsted manufacturer whose works band enjoyed some success in the later nineteenth
century, was a keen cornet player and his works band evolved from a
private band he had founded in 1844.[19] The list could be extended
considerably. The decision of these men to make music a part of their
paternalist machinery must to some extent have been influenced by
their love of the art.

These initiatives were vital, not merely because they were amongst
the first but because they created the principle of industrial sponsorship of working class-music, which was to become so important
later in the century. However, at the time they appear to have gone
largely unnoticed and do not seem to have inspired much imitation.
There were a few attempts to utilise music in schemes of moral
regeneration, such as William Hickson's singing classes in the Smith-
field district of London in the later 1830s, but it was not until the
1840s that music for the people really gained national prominence
with the appearance of 'sight-singing mania'.[20]

'Sight-singing', 'sol-faing' or any of the other names that were used by contemporaries refers essentially to methods of teaching people to sing music at sight without recourse, at least initially, to the complexities of traditional musical notation. Most nineteenth-century practitioners based their notation on the gamut, in use since medieval times, whereby each note was given a name (doh, ray, mi, and so forth) instead of its 'correct' term (C, D, E or whatever). It was believed that, apart from simplifying matters, such a system gave people a far greater understanding of the relationship between notes and it was this that made singing at sight much easier.[21] The 'mania' of the period 1841–c. 1844 was looked back on with great affection by Victorian writers. A contributor to the *Musical Times* in 1887 remembered how,

with curiosity excited everywhere, and hopes flattered on all hands, the desire to study music spread like a wave over the country, affecting secluded hamlets, as well as conspicuous cities. Few were exempt from its influence. Young and old went sol-faing, and even the prejudices of class were in many cases broken down by a common desire to sing with understanding.[22]

Some historians of music have perhaps interpreted such nostalgia a little too literally. Eric Mackerness has claimed that sight-singing 'aroused [a] thirst for music'. Similarly, Dr Bernard Rainbow argues that 'the public of England and Scotland at large found themselves infected with an enthusiasm to learn to sing which these islands had never previously experienced'.[23] The implication in such statements is that the sight-singing experiments of the 1840s largely produced the popular music-making tradition in this country. Such a view is exaggerated. An enthusiasm for popular musical activity had long been established in many parts of the country and, indeed, the working-class choristers of Yorkshire and Lancashire were already noted for their excellence. Moreover, some writers claim a novelty for these sight-singing schemes that is not justified. The 'Old English' or 'Lancashire' notation, a form of sol-fa, had been used by many northern choristers from the middle of the eighteenth century and possibly earlier, and continued in use in some parts of the country until this century.[24] The originality of the 1840s lay in the transformation of what had previously been a purely musical activity into a moral crusade led by middle-class reformers and philanthropists seeking to use music as a force for social regeneration.

The 'mania' occurred in the early 1840s for a number of interconnected reasons. Continued industrialisation was producing an environment which was hostile and frightening to many middle class observers, who perceived large working-class communities which were intemperate, ill-educated, ill-disciplined and increasingly prey to the public house and the singing-saloon. Perhaps most worrying of all was Chartism, the largest political mass-movement the nation had seen, which was still recovering from its defeats in 1839–1840, but nevertheless an awesome reminder of the potential power that the working class wielded.[25] Three men, Joseph Mainzer, John Hullah and John Curwen, preached a musical and social message that was perfectly suited to this troublesome age. By the mid 1840s a network of singing classes inspired by their separate but complementary efforts had been established, often with middle-class assistance. Here significant numbers of working men and women gathered to sing glees, national songs, hymns and other generally 'improving' music.

Joseph Mainzer (1801–1851) is the least well-known to a twentieth-century audience, but in the 1840s he was probably the most celebrated of the three. Born in Germany, the son of a butcher, he was in turn choirboy, mining engineer and trainee priest before rejecting Roman Catholicism and embracing political radicalism in the 1830s. He eventually settled in Paris, devoting himself to music journalism, the composition of political opera (he produced two, *Triomphes de la Pologne* and *La Jacquerie*, both of which failed) and teaching artisan singing-classes. Forced to flee to England by the attentions of the Orleanist police in 1841, he immediately began propagating the idea of moral reform through music in his publication *The National Singing-Class Circular* which in July 1842 became *Mainzer's Musical Times and Singing-Class Circular*. He also published a sight-singing textbook *Singing For The Million*, which he claimed sold 200,000 copies within six months.[26] He emphasised from the outset the two dominant themes of temperance and class collaboration in language that was almost millenial.

The time is hastening when the soldier and the sailor, the plodding labourer and the dusky artisan, will forsake the pothouse and the gin-palace for the singing-school, and so become raised in the scale of civilisation – raised in the scale of humanity.

He promised 'mutual sympathy and good-will among classes, who in the existing state of society, are too much alienated and estranged from each other'.[27] Such phrases soon seduced the propertied classes.

Within a year of his arrival, he and the band of disciples which he rapidly gathered had established at least eighteen classes within a twenty-mile radius of Manchester, which always seems to have been his most fertile region. By December 1842 a network of classes had been established in London and classes had emerged in at least thirty centres elsewhere in the country, ranging from Bath to Newcastle.[28] Interested employers and reformers went to considerable lengths to support Mainzer. A group of Bolton millowners closed their premises early to enable some 1,500 workers to attend singing classes. The proprietors of the Katesgrove Ironworks in Reading provided a free room, equipment and tuition, although workers who had agreed to attend and failed to do so were fined.[29] In March 1843, the élite of Leeds worked hard to attract Mainzer to Yorkshire, until then untouched by his mission. Charles Wicksteed, a Unitarian Minister, president of both the local Mechanics Institute and the Literary and Philosophical Society, wrote a letter asking him to visit Leeds signed by almost every eminent citizen of the town. Lectures were then arranged in the Mechanics Institute and the prestigious East Parade Chapel, and Mainzer was given almost celebrity status by local society and the press. His visit was not in vain, as by July 1843 a Yorkshire Working Men's Singing Association had been founded.[30]

John Hullah (1812–1884) had like Mainzer begun his musical career as an operatic composer and, like Mainzer, had failed, despite having the youthful Charles Dickens as librettist on *The Village Coquettes*, which ran briefly in 1836 at St James's Theatre.[31] In 1840, he was engaged by Dr James Kay, secretary of the Committee of Council on Education which had been set up in the previous year to ensure efficient use of central government's first tentative support of elementary education. Kay had recently undertaken a European tour in order to study educational methods and had been impressed by the artisan singing-classes operated in Paris by Mainzer's rival, Guillaume Wilhem. Seeing music as a method of making the British 'industrious, brave, loyal and religious people', Kay asked Hullah to take responsibility for music teaching at Battersea Teachers Training College, which Kay had been instrumental in establishing.[32] In 1841 Hullah began singing-classes 'for the instruction of Schoolmasters of Day and Sunday-schools in vocal music' at Exeter Hall in London, and in April of the next year he showed off the fruit of his labours when a choir of some 1,500 sang in the hall at a choral concert.[33] Soon, Hullah's pupils were returning to various parts of England (one gains the impression that Hullah had his greatest support in the south) carrying his technique and sharing his and Kay's belief in music's capacity to reform society.

The third of the triumvirate came from a very different background from the others. John Curwen (1816–1880) was not a musician, and indeed appears to have known very little about music when he began his sight-singing work. Less well-known in the 1840s than the other two, he in fact made the greater contribution in the long run because of the technical superiority of his system. Born in Heckmondwike in Yorkshire, he became a Congregationalist Minister and originally turned to sight-singing as a method of improving Sunday-school singing. Finding 'traditional' notation difficult to understand and even harder to teach, he approached Miss Sarah Glover of Norwich, a noted musical educator, for guidance in 1841. Miss Glover's *Scheme to Render Psalmody Congregational*, published in 1835, formed the basis of Curwen's work. From 1844 at his Chapel in Plaistow, London, and later, through his contributions to Cassell's *Popular Educator*, Curwen began the training of musical crusaders. [34]

To some extent, the early 1840s represented a false start. Both Mainzer and Hullah's systems, based on the 'fixed doh' principle (doh was always C) proved incapable of dealing with more complex music, and interest in their classes levelled off. Chartism, the public houses and singing-rooms remained, and middle-class reformers, although broadly happy with the sol-faists efforts, began looking for another miracle cure for society's ills. Nevertheless, some important achievements remained. Curwen's more flexible tonic sol-fa method endured and, as will be seen, made a solid contribution to amateur music-making in the second half of the century. Thousands of people gained some form of musical tuition (which they may or may not have used in the future) by attending the innumerable classes run by Curwen's trainees in Mechanics Institutes, temperance halls, Sunday-schools and the like. Most important of all, however, the singing-class movement had proved remarkable propaganda for the course of music. The idea that music had a valuable social purpose was now no longer merely the belief of certain reformers and educationalists; it was a truism. From the middle 1840s a scheme of rational recreation that did not include music, was no scheme at all. [35]

Having established to their satisfaction the value of working-class involvement in musical life, it was inevitable that reformers should continue to experiment within the musical field. Their next product was the 'people's concert'. By the mid-nineteenth century concerts were a firmly established feature of social life in most European centres.[36] Even a moderately-sized English provincial town such as Leeds or Manchester could expect to enjoy thirty to forty public concerts a year. In general, with admission prices rarely falling below two shillings and never below one, regular attendance was a financial impossibility for the majority of the working classes. Social reformers, fired far more by moral than artistic considerations, set out to remedy the situation. It is not clear when the first 'People's Concerts' began, but it is likely that the series begun by the Glasgow Total Abstinence Society in spring 1843 was among the first. Gradually English cities followed suit. In 1844 a popular concert series began in Lord Nelson Street, Liverpool, which became a model for others to follow, while in the following year Birmingham Corporation arranged for the Town Hall organ to be played one evening a week from 7.30–9.30 for the benefit of the labouring classes, who were to pay 3d for the privilege.[37] By early in the next decade regular cheap concerts had been established in Manchester, Sheffield, Leeds, Oldham, Huddersfield, Bradford and Halifax, and doubtless also in other locations. While the 'people's concert' was initially a feature of urban *industrial* England, occasional ventures were organised in smaller towns and villages.[38]

The exact motives behind the concerts varied from area to area. Those organised by the Leeds Rational Recreation Society between 1852–1859 began as a direct response to the popularity of the Leeds Casino, where, according to the outraged Reverend A. M. Stalker, an audience of some seven or eight hundred could be found nightly 'gazing with zest on scenes, and listening with delight to sounds, which to us at least, were both humiliating and appalling'.[39] Others were a generalised counter-attack against the social, moral and political evils of early industrial society. It is significant that the people's concert was at its most popular between about 1849 and 1854, the years when it became clear that the Chartist threat was greatly diminished and economic stability increasing. The concerts formed part of the great sigh of middle-class relief as they sought to rebuild harmonious class relationships – if indeed these had ever existed. Most concerts were organised in a similar manner. The 'season' lasted from approximately October to March and concerts were usually weekly in larger centres, less frequent in smaller ones. Although termed 'people's concerts', they were never intended as performances for the working class alone. The concerts were specifically designed to unite different classes in at least the same building, if not in the same sections – the middle classes occupied the reserved seats and side galleries, the working class the gallery. Whilst maintaining hierarchy, the concerts symbolised community and shared experience. At a more basic level, the middle classes were essential to the schemes' finances, as they paid one shilling admittance and therefore subsidised the cheaper 6d and 3d seats, which were intended for the 'humbler mechanic'.[40]

The music was usually of what contemporaries called a 'miscellaneous' nature, involving a mixture of Italian, English and occasionally French opera, as well as glees, ballads and respectable comic song drawn largely from the repertoires of Samuel Lover the Irish composer and John Liptrot Hatton, an English composer and singer who enjoyed quite considerable fame in the mid-Victorian period. The following programme offered by the Leeds Rational Recreation Society in April 1853 is fairly typical, although Hatton's presence in the performance meant the inclusion of a greater amount of his material than was usual. His appearance indicates that some concert promoters attempted to provide entertainment of a very high standard.

Madame D'Anteny	'Son Vergin Vezzosa' from *I Puritani*	Bellini
Madame D'Anteny	'Sing Not Thy Song To Me Sweet Bird'	Glover
Madame D'Anteny Mr Hatton	'La Ci Darem La Mano' from *Don Giovanni*	Mozart
Madame D'Anteny Miss Brown	'Sweet Sister Fay'	Barnett
Mr Hatton	'The Little Fat Man'	Hatton
	'Day and Night'	Hatton
	'O Ruddier Than The Cherry'	Handel
Leeds Madrigal & Motet Society	'Sailors Beware'	Hatton
Miss Brown	'O Preserve & Bless The Queen'	Wallace

In the largest towns, such as Liverpool and Manchester, there might have been some orchestral music as well.[41]

It is significant that most concert organisers used the standard repertoire of the period and made little or no attempt to encourage either the performance or the composition of songs with a specific 'moral' message. Moreover, they showed a relatively casual attitude towards the songs performed. The Leeds concerts, supposedly dedicated to the undermining of the public house, regularly featured Signor Delavanti (who, despite his Italianate pretensions, came from Rochdale!) singing Hatton's 'Simon the Cellarer', a hymn to the delights of alcohol if there ever was one.

> Old Simon the Cellarer keeps a large store,
> of Malmsey and Malvoisie,
> And Cyprus, and who can say how many more?
> For a chary old soul is he,
> A chary old soul is he.
>
> Of Sack and Canary he never doth fail,
> And all the year round there is brewing of ale;
> Yet he never aileth, he quaintly doth say,
> While he keeps to his sober six flagons a day.
>
> But ho! ho! ho! his nose doth show,
> How oft the black jack to his lips doth go.
> But ho! ho! ho! his nose doth show
> How oft the black jack to his lips doth go.[42]

Essentially, the organisers were simply concerned with providing a 'correct' environment. Music *per se* was a force for the good of the lower orders, provided it was heard in the presence of their social superiors and 'in an atmosphere of moral purity suitable to the proper enjoyment of such a gift'.[43]

In a small number of towns and cities, local philanthropists were not merely content with the production of concerts but sought to build concert-halls to house them in. The St George's Halls in both Liverpool and Bradford, the concert-hall in Leeds Town Hall (all opened in the 1850s, and the Colston Hall, Bristol (opened in 1867), were all to some extent intended as 'people's music halls'.[44] St George's Hall, Bradford, the earliest of these projects, was the brainchild of Samuel Smith, whose unhappiness about the state of popular music in the area has already been noted. In a speech made in 1851, on the day the foundation stone was laid, he outlined his vision.

Here may we oftimes see the young men and old, with their wives and daughters, and sisters, listening with deep and rapt attention to the soul-inspiring strains of music, or to the fervid eloquence of some gifted teacher, going to their several homes elevated and refreshed, rising in the morning to their daily toil without headache and regret.[45]

"Most of our wealthy citizens took shares" in the company Smith
floated, and a neighbouring warehouse under construction at the same
time was lowered and St George's redesigned and made higher so that
the munificence of the millocracy could be seen clearly. In September
1853 the building opened with the first Bradford Triennial Music
Festival. Many workers were given time off to view the new building
and its inhabitants, but few of them could get into the concerts, for
which minimum cost of entry was 3s. 6d., unless their employers gave
them free tickets. The gap between the theory and practice of rational
recreation was never more clearly stated.[46]

  Although problems of this type arose regularly, at least in general
the reformers were pleased with their efforts. Working men and their
families attended in far greater numbers than expected and several
organisers claimed that they could have filled the hall with a purely
'popular' audience. Occasionally the working class let the philanthropists down through their lack of etiquette. The *Halifax Guardian* was
clearly angry after a concert in 1854. A man in the gallery had called
out 'That's true!' during a rendition of 'Home Sweet Home' and the
audience cheered in agreement! Worse was to come.

We are sorry again to refer to the objectionable mode which the occupants of
the gallery especially, adopted to signify their approval, or when demanding
an encore. The committee had issued printed notices strictly prohibiting
whistling, but somehow the whistling on Monday evening was more shrill and
piercing than ever! More effectual measures *must* be adopted to abate the
nuisance in future. And we may as well add that it would be an advantage to
the rest of the audience, if certain mothers would in future allow their babies
to have the powers of their lungs tested at home, and put to bed at a very early
hour on a Monday evening especially those who have premonitory symptoms
of the croup![47]

In general, however, a picture of contentment was painted by most
observers and organisers. An investigator from the *Morning Chronicle*
in 1849 was pleased to note during his visit to Manchester how
selections from Handel, Meyerbeer, Rossini and Bishop were
'listened to with the most reverent silence, and then applauded to the
echo by an assemblage of between two or three thousand working men
and women . . . who took up nearly the entire area of the Free Trade
Hall'. Moreover, the organisers believed that their message was penetrating. The Leeds audience were informed on one occasion that
many of the 'artisan class of the town . . . had expressed the obligation
they were under to the founders of the society for the opportunity

afforded them of gratifying their musical aspirations, apart from the demoralising influence of the Casino and the beer-house'.[48]

By the end of the 1850s music was firmly established as a method of promoting the public good. Much less fuss was made by its supporters in the following two decades, partly because the argument for music had been won, but perhaps also because a less strident tone could be adopted in this the 'age of equipoise' when class relationships entered a relatively peaceful phase.[49]

Nevertheless, the amount of musical activity that the rational recreationists generated undoubtedly increased, although to avoid repetition, it will only be dealt with very briefly here. The brass band movement continued to benefit from the encouragement both of individual benefactors and organisations dedicated to moral improvement. It was in this period, for example, that certain bands became closely associated with the temperance movement. Temperance organisations like the Band of Hope also began to publish selections of temperance songs, thereby providing one of the earliest examples of an attempt by reformers to create a specialist repertoire rather than relying on existing 'standard' material. It has to be said that the results were usually dire by any standards:

> 'Tis cocoa, cocoa, a steaming cup of cocoa
> 'Twill warm your hands and cheer your hearts,
> I tell what I think;
> Like cocoa, cocoa, we ought to make life's yoke, oh,
> As pleasant bright and good for all, as this refreshing drink.

Any musical charm was inevitably battered into submission by the banality of such lyrics. One can sympathise to a point, however; after all, does anything rhyme with 'cocoa'?[50]

During this period, too, the Curwenite tonic sol-fa movement continued its work, with impressive results. A newspaper, *The Tonic Sol-Fa Reporter* (1855), eventually the *Musical Herald* from 1889, a college (1862), and a music publishing house (1867) gave the sight-singing movement a structure and organisation that it had never attained in the 1840s. By the late nineteenth century, tonic sol-fa had been extended to meet the needs of instrumental performers as well as singers, and by the 1890s Curwen's methods had been more widely adopted in English elementary schools, thus extending his influence still further. Perhaps the greatest compliment to his work was the existence at the end of the century of over five hundred forms of notation devised by imitators.[51]

In this period of quiet steady progress, there was perhaps only one major development, which was important because it offered a pointer to future trends. This was most noticeable in the people's concerts. From the 1860s onwards, such concerts were increasingly the creation of either astute local businessmen (a point to be developed later) or paid representatives of the municipality and less the work of individual philanthropists. In the larger towns and cities, philanthropic effort was increasingly supplemented by the efforts of municipal organists as more and more towns erected town halls furnished with magnificent organs. The weekly concerts featuring the Liverpool municipal organist W. T. Best (1826–1897) were extremely well attended (by the Edwardian period annual attendance at the twice-weekly concerts given by his successor was over fifty thousand) and gained a national reputation for musical excellence. Best and his compatriots were laying a crucial foundation for later years.[52]

Chapter 3

Music and morals, 1880–1914

The period from about 1880 saw both a great revival of public debate over the 'music for the people' movement and a broadening and altering of its scope and aims. Certainly many of the tried and trusted features were still present, and the old clarion calls for class unity and moral regeneration were still strong. In December 1883, Viscount Folkestone of the London-based People's Entertainment Society stated the Society's intention 'to cultivate a taste for good, high-class amusement among the poorer classes in the hope of withdrawing them from lower places of resort, to introduce an element of brightness into their lives, and to establish a better feeling between the different classes by bringing them into clear contact with each other'.[1] His sentiment is that of the 1840s and 1850s, as was that of the countless vicars, industrialists, doctors, MPs, lords and ladies called upon to speak at brass band teas, choral concerts, competitive festivals and other musical events. The term 'control', used as a convenient descriptive umbrella for the schemes under discussion in this section, is still valid for this period.

Yet, although the continuities will be obvious in what follows, there were also many changes which would benefit from brief discussion before entering into more detailed investigation. There are three themes which emerge most clearly. Most obviously, a variety of new approaches were tried in the period after 1880, many of them involving a determination to *take* music to the working class rather than merely provide an entertainment which it was hoped would attract a popular audience. Alongside this there was, especially after 1900, a far greater emphasis placed upon the quality of musical experience being offered, and a genuine attempt to broaden popular cultural horizons. This was partly a corollary of the third point, touched upon already; a decline in the involvement of local notables in musically-orientated philanthropy (and probably in philanthropy of all kinds) and an increase in the part played by socially-aware amateur musicians of more humble social status and professional musicians, often working under municipal auspices. Increasingly, music was to reach the people through the agencies of the local state, the municipal concert and the elementary school.[2]

The 1880s witnessed a great resurgence of middle and upper-class philanthropic activity in all forms, as the relative stability of the third quarter of the century was disturbed by the return of more aggressive class-based politics, therefore renewing concern about the dangerous classes. From about 1879, concert series, lectures and classes appeared in most larger cities and, to a greater extent than previously, in smaller towns. A series of people's concerts were held in Cambridge, partly organised by the young Cecil Sharp, then a mathematics student at Clare College. In 1881 concerts were promoted in Bridgewater, including a full performance of *Judas Maccabeus*, at which the audience of almost 1,500 consisted 'very largely of brickyard labourers and artisans, many of whom stood all evening, and were, nevertheless, more quiet and attentive than some who occupy a higher social position'. Amongst the first ventures to gain attention in this new period of enthusiasm were the popular concerts organised in 1879 by the Mayor of Birmingham, Jesse Collings. One of the principle figures in provincial Liberalism, it may be that Collings organised this particular concert series as much to gain political advantage and/or to win attention for Birmingham as for more traditional reasons. Collings's concerts were unusual in that they were free, the tickets being distributed in batches to employers all over the city. The following year Collings established the Birmingham Musical Association, which provided concerts priced at 6*d* and 3*d* and aimed eventually to provide a permanent orchestra, a school of music and a music library. In the first year average attendance at the association's concerts was over 2,500. Collings's work was widely discussed in journals such as the *Musical Times* and in the national press, and seems, along with the London-based People's Concert Society, to have acted with a catalyst effect similar to that of the Liverpool concerts of 1844. Organisations such as the Kyrle Choir and the People's Entertainment Society in London, the Ancoats Recreation Committee in Manchester, the Musical Guild in Nottingham, or individuals such as J. G. Meakin in Hanley, the Ford Sisters in Leeds

and many others, again strove for a musical and social millenium.[3]
New approaches were much in evidence.

Most noticeable at the organisational level was the attempt to go out
to the working classes, especially the poorest sections. The mid-century concerts had succeeded in reaching the upper working class, but
it is doubtful if they penetrated any lower. The lack of finance, of
suitable clothing and of interest, a result of an educational and cultural
background which retarded (and still does) lower working-class
involvement in so many aspects of popular recreation and culture, was
clearly evident in the musical sphere. Late Victorians sought to
correct this. The People's Entertainment Society and the Kyrle
Society, the latter founded by Octavia Hill's sister Miranda, pioneered this with a move toward holding concerts in areas such as
Lambeth, Westminster and Battersea, usually in local halls, churches
or chapels. Some were free, others involved a nominal entrance fee.
The Kyrle Society also held performances in hospital wards and
workhouses. Both societies, assumed, not always correctly, an
extremely low level of musical sensitivity amongst their audiences and
reinforced their concerts with singing and instrumental classes as a
means of increasing musical appreciation. By July 1883 the Battersea
branch of the People's Entertainment Society performed sacred
selections sufficiently well in a concert at Bolingbrooke Hall to wring
praise, albeit restrained, from the *Musical Times*. 'As both band and
choir are exclusively composed of mechanics, factory hands, and men
employed on the river, the performance was in the highest degree
creditable'.[4]

By the 1890s the attempt to reach the poorest resulted in the
inevitable step of reformers, almost in imitation of street musicians,
taking their music into the streets, yards and courts of 'darkest
England'. The 'court and alley' concert, as this type of event became
known, probably originated in Manchester in 1895, although there
may have been earlier examples.[5] But once again it was from
Liverpool that perhaps the best publicised venture came. These
concerts were the brainchild of H. Lee J. Jones, founder of the
Liverpool Food Association, an organisation devoted to the distribution of free food to very poor children and invalids. On a July evening
in 1897 some four hundred 'curiosity-struck' residents attended the
first venture, after having first washed out the court and decorated the
windows with tissue-paper flags. By 1899 Jones and his supporters –
some one hundred and fifty people took part in these concerts over the

period from 1897 – had the organisation and approach thoroughly
worked out. Hand-bills advertising the event were distributed in
advance. These stressed that the concerts were free, that the performers had no connection to any church, chapel or political party,
and that previous fortunate recipients had thoughtfully washed out
the court, provided chairs and kept children quiet! On the evening of
the concert a platform and a piano would be pulled by a horse into the
chosen street, and, armed with only their music, a rope to keep people
off the platform and 'about 2 lbs of chloride of lime to antidote any
immediately disagreeable effluvia', the performers would begin.
Sacred tunes, patriotic songs, comic songs, violin solos 'such as
'Home Sweet Home', Scottish and Irish selections, mandolin and
banjo solos and selections from *The Bohemian Girl* and *Maritana* were
the staple fare of the concerts, which the organisers believed to be
extremely popular.[6]

Similar experiments were tried in other cities. In Sheffield the
council gave a small grant to enable the concerts to take place,
supplementing them with penny concerts in local halls in the winter,
while in Bradford the Free Church Council enlisted local chapel
choirs to tour slum districts. The *Yorkshire Observer*, describing a
concert in George Court, 'one of the poorest quarters of Bradford', by
the Eastbrook Methodist Choir, claimed that:

Everybody was rapt in attention, and so great was the interest that a heavy
shower of rain went almost unheeded. . . . When at the end of the programme, the audience had the opportunity of joining in the well known hymn
'Lead Kindly Light', the court was made to ring again with the hearty sound
of voices.[7]

What these concerts illustrates is not merely a new approach to
providing music for the people, but the emergence of a new style of
philanthropy. In the mid nineteenth century the middle classes
financed and patronised the concerts and used them as a platform to
promulgate their ideology. Many of the late Victorian and Edwardian
musical reformers shared the fears of earlier generations, but they
approached the problem with far less condescension and with far
greater willingness to take part. They went to the people and sometimes performed for them, appreciating that harmonious class relationships and a more 'civilised' working class would emerge only if the
middle classes made compromises and showed good faith, rather than
believing that massive social change could flow from pious hopes
expressed on the platform of a civic hall.[8]

This new way of looking at the problems of the poor and their music also had artistic repercussions as many philanthropists, especially those from musical backgrounds, combined their moral mission with a genuine attempt to raise musical standards. The public pronouncements of the later Victorian and Edwardian period often laid far greater emphasis upon music than had been the case in the 1840s and 1850s, or was still the case within the tonic sol-fa movement. From the 1880s, and especially during the Edwardian period, many organisers attempted to break from the tradition of miscellaneous collections of glees, songs and overtures in order to produce programmes which had, in their opinion, greater artistic merit. Reinforcing, and indeed eventually dictating, this change was the increased involvement of professional musicians in people's concerts. In the earlier period a committee was established, a secretary elected and, with some help from the local, often amateur, musical world, a programme would be devised. Now, many towns had available a new generation of professionals – private music teachers, professors in local colleges and conservatoires, borough organists, school teachers – all, for artistic, social or commercial reasons, anxious to impart their riches to the community.

Not all popular concerts from the late nineteenth century onwards were innovatory; financial restraints, conservatism and a low expectation of popular taste on the part of some organisers ensured that the miscellaneous form continued. In a number of towns, however, concerts were produced which were dramatically different from any previous venture. Some of the most impressive events were those backed by a degree of municipal patronage. As has been seen already, municipal participation in popular musical life had its tentative beginnings in the middle of the century with the appointment of borough organists. From the 1890s, 'music on the rates' increased in scope, especially in seaside towns and in urban areas influenced by progressive Liberalism and the emerging socialist movement. 'Music for the people' in a resort like Bournemouth or Eastbourne had a distinctive connotation, usually referring to the entertainment of middle-class visitors in the summer and the resident 'retired' population in the winter. Bournemouth in particular, under the guidance of Dan Godfrey who contrived to turn a twenty-five-piece military band into a forty-eight-strong symphony orchestra between 1893–1903, gained a national reputation as a musical centre, and therefore gave a boost to the basic concept of rate-supported music.[9] The most expensive scheme was initiated by the London County Council, whose Parks and Open Spaces Committee allowed its musical director, Carl Armbruster, £12,500 per annum to provide concerts in London parks. By 1910 Armbruster had organised three bands (two miliary, one string) in the permanent employ of the council, and each season he hired as many as ninety other army and civilian bands, usually for weekly engagements. Manchester and Sheffield operated similar, if smaller-scale, schemes. Even these smaller projects are crucial to the long-term history of the arts in Britain, as they helped formalise the concept of municipal sponsorship, so important to the maintenance of musical and artistic life in general throughout the twentieth century.[10]

None of these municipal enterprises was more striking to contemporaries than the Leeds City Orchestral concerts in 1902–1910. The concerts were initiated by Herbert Fricker, borough organist since 1895. Fricker had made previous unsuccessful attempts to supplement the town hall organ concerts, but in 1902 he persuaded the Liberal Council – albeit at an extremely low level of finance – to help support a series of orchestral concerts run on strictly 'educational' grounds. Fricker, who appears to have been inspired almost totally by musical rather than social considerations, felt that the local population was limited in its taste and he sought 'to select a few of the somewhat as yet unbeaten paths, and to provide, I hope, many a pleasant and instructive evening for the benefit of the masses'.[11]

Building a symphony orchestra out of local professionals and the better amateur orchestras and using the best of the numerous local choral societies, he gave a bold and ambitious lead. The following programme, given in February 1904 and featuring the Leeds Symphony Orchestra and the Armley Choral Society, illustrates an entirely new conception of the people's concerts, a far cry from 'Simon the Cellarer'.

From the Bavarian Highlands	Elgar
March and Chorus from *Tannhäuser*	Wagner
Overture *Prometheus*	Beethoven
Gypsy Suite	Percy Godfrey
Two movements from 'New World' Symphony	Dvorak
Violin Concerto in G minor	Bruch
Two melodies (op. 34)	Grieg
Variations on *Three Blind Mice*	Josef Holbrooke
Introduction to Act III, *Lohengrin*	Wagner[12]

The works by Percy Godfrey and Josef Holbrooke indicate Fricker's determination to provide a forum for English composers. In the 1904–05 season Ralph Vaughan Williams conducted his *Heroic Elegy*, and two years later Havergal Brian was engaged to conduct his *English Suite*. On a further occasion, an entire concert was given over to works by contemporary English composers.[13] Fricker made much use of this thematic approach, with concerts devoted to the work of one composer or one style as a regular feature; Wagner nights were particularly popular, usually attracting full houses. Wagner appears to have been the most regularly-performed composer during the eight years, a reflection not merely of Fricker's but of the public's taste at this period. Tchaikovsky, Mendelssohn, Beethoven, Sibelius and Edward German were also strongly represented.

The problem for advocates of municipal music was that they were engaging in a political as well as an artistic mission. (Generally, the seaside resorts were spared political confrontation as a party consensus operated, viewing music as 'one of the most effective commercial assets to the town').[14] They were attempting to extend the scope of the local state and to finance aspects of social life previously left to voluntary organisations. Sections of the Liberal party and almost all of the Conservative Party opposed this process utterly. Fricker's concerts fell victim, despite all their quality. Leeds Council had only given minimal levels of financial support, providing the town hall free, defraying the cost of lighting and occasionally meeting minor financial deficits. Fricker had been constantly forced to raise the price of admission in order to combat the lack of municipal enthusiasm. Free seats had been provided in the first season, but these were quickly abolished, 1*d* and then very quickly 2*d* becoming the cheapest rate. By 1908 only sixty 2*d* seats were provided in a hall with a capacity of over two thousand.[15] The dramatic reduction in cheap seats was in fact the first reaction to the demands of the newly-elected Conservative administration, which took power in autumn 1908, and was dedicated to a dramatic restriction in public expenditure. Alderman Wilson, the new council leader, made his view of municipal support for the arts abundantly clear.

This is the time when we cannot afford luxuries such as these grants for music and pictures. We are not going to put up the rates if we can possibly avoid it. Moreover, as regards these grants for municipal concerts, I do not think it is part of the duty of the corporation to enter into competition with the normal amusement caterers. . . . The Conservative Party are pledged to economy, and we are going to 'set about' it as it has never been 'set about' before.[16]

Despite a heated local newspaper correspondence – featuring 'Disgusted', 'Disgusted the Second' and 'Still more Disgusted' – Wilson successfully ended a grant of £500 to the art gallery and one of similar size to the bands in the parks committee, and refused to meet the current deficit incurred by the orchestral concerts.[17] At the end of the 1908–09 season, therefore, municipal involvement ended, although a private guarantee fund was established, the concerts ceased altogether after one more season. In the 1840s and 1850s the local élite had abandoned political differences and were united by the idea of the power of music, hoping that it might reinforce a political and social system that was under challenge. By 1910 the grandees of the industrial communities had long abandoned the scene of their triumphs for extensive estates in the south and west of England. They left their cities in the hands of men for whom the management of party politics was now the major priority. For the moment, music, now less a symbol of community and more a weapon in a party struggle, had lost some of its attractions.

All the new developments in the 'music for the people' movement of the late nineteenth century and onward so far examined have concerned the people's concert. More influential, however, at least in terms of spreading performance skills, was the competitive music festival. The movement was intimately connected with the name of Mary Wakefield and although she never attempted to claim responsibility for its development, there is no denying her enormous influence. Born in Kendal in the Lake District in 1853, the daughter of a Quaker businessman, Miss Wakefield was a lady of much musical ability, considerable financial means and radical sensibility. Unable, because of her family's religious beliefs, to pursue as secular a career as that of a professional singer, she was nevertheless allowed to study singing under Randegger in London in the 1870s, and she sang regularly at amateur and philanthropic concerts both in London and the provinces. After her father's death in 1889, she appears to have remained largely in Kendal, devoting herself to various political, artistic and musical pursuits. A friend and devotee of Ruskin, who was from the late 1870s a near neighbour at Coniston, she was also an active supporter of the suffragette movement. The music festival can be seen as a compounding of her love for music with her social and political philosophy.[18]

In 1884 she contributed an article entitled *Amateur Music as it Should be* to the *Musical Times*, emphasising the need to spread musical taste amongst the widest possible audience. The inspiration for the article appears to have been a stay with Sir Henry Leslie, a leading choral trainer and conductor who had since 1880 organised a musical competition at Oswestry, based on the principle that competition was fundamentally a vehicle for musical education, and not an excuse for prize-hunting and self-glorification (the two prime characteristics in his view of the Welsh eisteddfod). Inspired by Leslie's example and anxious to put the sentiments expressed in her article into practice, she gathered three local quartet parties one day in August 1885 on the tennis court at 'Sedgwick', the Wakefield family home, where, in a spirit of friendly competition, each sang Stephen's 'Ye Spotted Snakes.'[19] From this modest beginning, the Sedgwick Festival (renamed the Westmorland in 1900 and eventually the Mary Wakefield Choral Competition after her death in 1910), grew in size and scope and fuelled a national movement.

By 1900, at least sixteen festivals existed, all more or less modelled on the Westmorland meeting. In 1904, a meeting convened by Miss Wakefield at the London home of Dowager Lady Beauchamp resulted in the establishment of the Association of Musical Competition Festivals, and over thirty festivals were affiliated. By 1914 there were some seventy-five festivals in England, of which thirty-nine were affiliated to the AMCF.[20] Many of the early festivals had been clustered in the north-west of England, close to Miss Wakefield's initial experiment, but by the end of the period almost every community in the country was within relatively easy travelling distance of a competition. It is impossible to measure the exact numbers involved in these festivals, although in 1906, when some fifty festivals were in existence, it was estimated that about 60,000 competitors had taken part.[21] The emphasis was always on choral music, but sections for solo instruments, piano and amateur orchestras were added to some events. The major festivals, such as those at Blackpool and Morecambe, which as prominent resorts had the capacity to deal with the large number of visitors involved, eventually expanded to cover several days. By 1910 the Blackpool Festival encompassed fifty-nine sections and five days.[22]

Obviously there was much local variation, but many festivals shared a common style of organisation to ensure that musical education rather than simple competition should predominate. Many competitions were open only to choirs from the immediate locality to prevent established societies simply moving from festival to festival in search of glory. 'Open' classes were instigated in some events, however, notably those at Blackpool and Morecambe, and to win these was the ambition of the major choirs of the period. Certificates and medals were given in preference to cash prizes, detailed assessments of each choir was made by the judges to facilitate improvement and many festivals ended with a combined concert, in which the various competitors submerged their competitive instincts in united song. 'The co-operative movement adapted to musical requirements' was Miss Wakefield's personal depiction of the festival, while Dr William McNaught, the government's Chief Inspector of School Music and one of the prime movers of the competitive movement, called it 'a school of music, and not a school of glory'.[23] The efforts of the organisers were discussed, reinforced and advertised at length in the *Musical Times* in particular, and from 1908 Novello published a supplement to the *Musical Times* and its sister publication the *School Music Review*, entitled the *Competition Festival Record* and dedicated entirely to the movement's progress.

Perhaps because of the heavy involvement of professional musicians and educationalists, the festival movement placed a far greater emphasis upon its musical mission than any other aspect of Victorian and Edwardian philanthropy through music. Its national spokesmen constantly stressed the educational value of their work; 'good' music was being disseminated, an audience for serious music being created, choral and, to a lesser extent, orchestral technique improved, and an opportunity given to provincial conductors to gain experience and to raise their standards. There was a particular emphasis upon improving musical life in rural areas, where, according to the composer Hubert Parry, people's minds were often 'troubled and dull'.[24] At least twenty of the competitions scheduled for 1914 were aimed at small rural communities largely untouched by previous schemes of musical enlightenment and indeed by many other aspects of popular musical culture.

While musical deliberations were uppermost at national level, social ones were never entirely absent. Miss Wakefield's comments about the value of the festivals as a force for class cohesion has already been noted, and these were echoed by several of her colleagues. There was a pleasant absence of the cruder 'popular control' theories concerning such things as drink, manners and street life amongst the leading spirits in the movement, although these sometimes crept in at local level. A small number of festivals were actually organised by bodies dedicated to social and moral reform, including the Burnley branch of the Girls Friendly Society, Leicester YMCA and the Northamptonshire Sunday School Union.[25] There was also perhaps in the organisation of certain festivals an element of the amalgam of musical enthusiasm and paternalistic control that typified the brass band movement. A number of festivals, especially rural ones, were organised by 'leading' families, a good example being the Wensleydale and Swaledale 'tournaments of song' created by the Hon. Amias Lucien Orde-Powlett. There can be no denying Orde-Powelett's genuine commitment to 'propagating and fostering a love of music among the humbler classes', as the *Yorkshire Post* obituary notice put it. The writer noted that:

In not a few cases he has given personal tuition to lads showing a gift for music, and has himself defrayed the cost of instruments and books . . . he was highly delighted when one of his former proteges – a son of a former stationmaster at Leyburn – qualified as mus. bac. [*sic*] at Oxford, and subsequently became doctor of music.[26]

However, the local farmers, tradesmen and artisans who made up the Dales musical community must have been acutely aware that he was also a son of the third Lord Bolton, one of the premier landowners in North Yorkshire. Significantly, the phrase 'tournament of song' has a somewhat feudal ring about it. Even as open-handed a figure as Orde-Powlett was, through his musical patronage, reinforcing the dominant position of his class.[27]

But it would be misleading if the final words on this topic were given to the political dimension of the festivals, for it is above all for their musical contribution that they should be remembered. Choirs were brought into existence, especially in rural areas, which would almost certainly never have begun but for the festivals. In this sense they really did add to the foundations of popular musicality. Moreover, by providing a large 'market' for composers and by raising the standard of choral technique to arguably the highest level it had ever attained in this country, they called into being a body of part-songs by Elgar, Bantock, Delius and others which would otherwise have never been written. The festival movement was a critical part of the English 'musical renaissance'.

Addressing the committee of the Worcestershire Festival in 1910,

the music critic Ernest Newman claimed that the festival movement
was doing what music in English schools had singularly failed to do:
developing an appreciation of serious music amongst as broad an
audience as possible and therefore creating a larger audience for
musical performance.[28] In fact it is doubtful whether such lofty
artistic ambition had ever figured in the imaginations of the architects
of English school music. School music, along with that organised by
the municipality, was the one aspect of 'music for the people' that did
not stem from private sponsorship. Nevertheless, it was rooted in
similar socio-moralistic premises. Before about 1840, the study of
music in schools – then essentially in the control of either the Anglican
National Society or the Nonconformist British and Foreign Schools
Society – was almost non-existent, and indeed Lord Brougham's
suggestion in 1835 that the rudiments of vocal music might be taught
in National Schools was regarded as somewhat eccentric.[29] The
efforts of Kay and Hullah in the 1840s improved the situation, and
from this point onward there were always a number of teachers
entering the profession who were at least partially qualified in the
teaching of music. But the scope, quality, and indeed the actual
existence of school music was still almost entirely dependent upon the
whim of individual teachers, and there were undoubtedly many
schools in which music had no place in the curriculum. Only a state
education system, many within the musical establishment came to
believe, could establish the unified, directed musical policy necessary
to establish a vigorous musical culture throughout the nation.

The anger of this musical establishment was considerable on
discovering that music was not to receive a subsidy under the terms of
the 1870 Education Bill, which 'brought state into action in education
as never before'.[30] William Forster, the minister responsible, was
apologetic but defended the decision by explaining that a lack of
suitably qualified inspectors (a factor illustrative of the extent to
which music had been ignored in the public schools where many of the
inspectorate had been educated) made the exclusion of music from
grant aid unavoidable. Eventually, after pressure from the music
profession, it was decided in 1871 that any state elementary school not
including music on its syllabus would lose 1s per child. This rather
negative measure marks the establishment of music in the state school
curriculum, and although both central government and its representatives at local level sometimes showed great reluctance to regard
music as a subject of any importance, it laid the basis for development

in succeeding decades.[31]

Initially, a heavy emphasis was placed on vocal music. Its great appeal to both educationalists and many music specialists lay in its cheapness, and above all its value as a vehicle for moral education. The philosophy of 1840 was still dominant, which was hardly surprising given that the Chief Inspector for school music from 1872–1881 was Hullah.[32] The 1870s found pupils in Durham pit-village schools singing 'Hurrah, Hurrah for England' and 'Work Hard, Help Yourselves'.[33] The *School Music Review*, begun by Novello in June 1892 and an invaluable source of material, claimed in its initial editorial that: 'The innocence of the recreation provided by song, and the beneficial influence an early taste for music may exert upon the choice and character of the amusements of the people, cannot be seriously disputed'. Later in the year, an HMI speaking at a school music conference argued that, 'a good song, with rousing and healthy words, would be likely to remain in children's memories and have a beneficial effect upon their characters'. He suggested six suitable song categories, including 'war songs and patriotic songs of other nations', comic songs such as 'North Country Lass' and 'Oak and the Ash', and, rather oddly, 'wine and love songs'.[34] Sacred music was performed far less than many would have liked as it was strictly discouraged by the Education Code, which sought to ensure that state schools were non-denominational.

From the early 1890s there was a strong attempt to introduce folk-song into the school music repertoire, which reflected the increasing interest in folk music amongst sections of the musical community. The Folk-Song Society was founded in 1898 and the period between 1903 and 1912 proved particularly productive for song collection.[35] The campaign to introduce these newly-'discovered' works into schools was again to some extent overlaid with moral arguments, albeit of a more sophisticated type than those noted earlier. Many collectors were influenced by various levels of radical, and sometimes socialist, thought and believed that by giving children supposedly uncontaminated products of rural culture they would help cleanse them from the impurity of city life.[36] Folk-songs did find their way increasingly into the classroom, although the claims made for them were often countered. The *School Music Review* adopted a fairly tolerant view toward folk-songs, despite the essentially hostile position of the editor, W. G. McNaught, but believed that far too much was expected as a result of their adoption, as the following satirical review of a folk-song collection by Sydney H. Nicholson shows:

the naughty boy should not be caned or given an imposition; he should be
made to learn say *The Bay of Biscay* and if that fails *The Spotted Cow* (no. 88
in the above book), and moral regeneration will set in, especially we should
say if the song is transposed down a tone, as it is difficult to be moral in the
high key in which it is written.[37]

The magazine also doubted the supposed healthiness of the songs
attacking 'their frank vulgarity in which quality they compete
successfully with the much abused beery, music-hall song'.[38] In the
years immediately before 1914, when the debate over music in education moved increasingly from a moral to an artistic basis, there was
further criticism that the songs, normally learnt by ear and sung in
unison, were damaging the quality of sight-reading and part-singing.
The appointment of Arthur Somervell as Chief Music Inspector in
1901 proved something of a defeat for the folk school, as Somervell
was a fierce proponent of 'national songs', composed British pieces of
the seventeenth and eighteenth century. He encouraged Charles
Stanford's production of the *National Song Book* (1906) which was to
have huge sales.[39]

At first singing was taught largely by ear, but from the early 1880s
pressure was exerted on the government by the musical establishment
to encourage teaching by note, which could involved traditional staff
notation or sol-fa. After much debate, it was agreed in May 1883 that
schools teaching by note would receive 1s per pupil, those by ear only
6d. As the following table shows, this financial incentive had a dramatic effect.

School departments in England and Wales
and their methods of singing instruction

	Staff notation	Tonic Sol-fa	Ear
1884	2,396	6,773	18,593
1891	2,362	15,153	11,833[40]

By 1891, 60 per cent of children in English and Welsh elementary
schools were being taught from one form of notation or another and
were singing to a high enough standard to gain the full government
grant. The long-awaited musical millenium was, it seemed, at hand.

From the very end of the nineteenth century, progress appeared
also to be made in the instrumental sphere as ambitious schools and
authorities moved beyond teaching just vocal music. The main school
instrument was the violin. William McNaught had seen an estimate

claiming that 10 per cent of English children were receiving school violin tuition.[41] It owed its prominence partly to its convenient size and partly to the commercial skills of Messrs Murdoch and Company who, by 1909, claimed to have supplied violins to some 400,000 pupils in over five hundred schools over an eleven-year period.[42] Based on a method begun at All Saints National School, Maidstone, in 1898, and therefore known as the 'Maidstone System', the technique employed by Murdoch and other companies was simple and effective. They provided a violin on hire purchase, at the rate of 3d per week, and then arranged for teaching facilities at a further 3d a week.[43] The system undoubtedly helped foster the growth of school orchestras – which often comprised violins and little else – that flourished in many schools from the early twentieth century. A National Union of School Orchestras was established and claimed to have 100,000 affiliated pupils by 1906. There were also attempts in some schools to introduce piano lessons, but the expense of obtaining instruments was simply too great for this to become widespread.[44]

Obviously, the expense involved to parents restricted the degree of instrumental tuition. In an extremely thorough investigation of instrumental music in Bradford schools, McNaught discovered that in four of the Bradford board schools almost half the pupils were learning an instrument (significantly, 60 per cent of the girls were learning as opposed to 30 per cent of the boys). In schools attended by poorer children, 'the percentage learning instruments is, as may be expected, very low – sometimes in the boys schools as low as one per cent. The obstacle to instrumental instruction is entirely one of pounds, shillings and pence, and more especially pounds.'[45] While the children of the lower middle and upper working classes – for these were the children who attended the four schools he surveyed – might find intrumental tuition a possibility, the poorest were excluded.

There were undoubtedly schools where, despite all the reforms and monetary incentives, little enthusiasm for music existed. The voluntary schools, which remained outside the state system until 1902, were not affected by much of this musical activity until that date, and even then the quality of their musical life was dictated by the wishes of individuals. Overall, however, there had been an impressive expansion of musical life affecting a large number of the school population. Many contemporaries believed that this in turn had improved the depth and quality of the nation's musical traditions. For the *School Music Review*, the progress in school music since 1870 'was a central

factor in the great, we are almost tempted to say phenomenal, progress the nation as a whole has made in music during the last thirty
years'. Again, in 1910, the magazine seized on a statement by a
marine bandmaster that Yorkshire and Lancashire possessed
between them 4,000 brass bands involving 60,000 men. 'It is true',
the magazine argued, 'that they did not learn to play brass instruments [at school] but they acquired an elementary knowledge and
practical skill that formed a foundation upon which later study was
built.'[46]

There is impressionistic evidence that suggests such a link between
the growth of state education and the progress of general popular
music. The arrival of state education in 1870, with the resultant vast
increase in sight-singing after 1880, coincides with the great expansion in choral activity in this period. To a lesser extent, there is a connection between the development of the amateur orchestral society
and the increase in violin tuition.[47] Furthermore, the development of
skills not connected in any obvious way with music, such as basic
literacy, were an advantage to those seeking to enhance their musical
life. Choral music in particular became more approachable if the
libretto could be read with ease.

However, the picture is not so clear as it first appears. Formal
music teaching, either because of the poor standard (few schools had
a specialist) or because the recipients were not ready for what they
received, may have destroyed the musical potential of some of the
children. An inspector commented at a conference in 1892 that
certain secondary school teachers had attempted to introduce music
beyond their pupils' grasp and had 'put them off'. A miner with no
vocal ability could still remember with horrible clarity, when writing
in the 1970s, the voice tests of over half a century earlier. It was hard
work for the 'grunters', he recalled, most of whom, like himself,
abandoned music as soon as they could.[48] Many who might later have
developed a talent for instrumental, if not vocal, music were lost in
this way. Again, music might have suffered from the general anti-
intellectualism which could be bred by schools. In his excellent
history of the working men's club, John Taylor has documented the
swing away from 'intellectual' to 'social' pastimes at the clubs in the
1890s. He suggests that the new school-attending generation felt no
need for the autodidactism of their forebears who had been denied
educational opportunity. Music, through its association with school,
may well have been regarded by some as an unsuitable recreational

pursuit, and whether individuals regained or developed a taste for it at a later date would depend upon their future circumstances.[49]

Alongside this, even those who enjoyed music at school might never utilise their skills on leaving. There was, to borrow from the language of the nineteenth-century Roman Catholic Church, a considerable 'leakage' between the school and the organised musical society. There were numerous counter-attractions, especially for boys. One writer, later to become a devoted musical enthusiast, recollects how of the twelve boys who had begun to study the violin at his village school he was the only one still playing four years after the commencement of their lessons. Even he 'found billiards and other frivolities far more attractive than music' for a period after leaving school, but was tempted back into the musical fold after hearing a friend perform a Chopin nocturne.[50] When a pupil did want to continue his or her studies, there was not always a suitable (or inexpensive) teacher available. A few councils offered the opportunity to continue musical education under the auspices of their evening classes. However even in such places as Leeds, where by 1896 seven singing classes, as well as piano and violin classes and an Old Scholars Choral Society had been established, such moves barely scraped the surface.[51]

In general, supporters of state musical education were too fond of believing that a region's extreme musicality came as a direct result of the 1870 Education Act, and that the skills imparted in school had lasting significance. They ignored the possibility that it was society that was influencing education, rather than the other way round. It is significant that school music was at its strongest in those areas which already possessed a highly developed musical culture. On numerous occasions schools in the West Riding of Yorkshire, and especially the textile district, were chosen by the educational establishment either as a testing ground for its ideas or as examples to be emulated. Bradford, for example, was chosen for trials of new government-inspired test-pieces and songs in 1905, on account of its generally high reputation. Great Horton Board School in Bradford, where the headmaster T. P. Sykes, took responsibility for school music, received great praise over the years in the *School Music Review*, as did Hanson Boys School in the same city, with its 36-strong orchestra trained by the school's music teacher and local brass band trainer James Brier.[52] Music in Huddersfield and Leeds was also picked out for praise on a number of occasions.[53] Conversely, the limitations of school music in an unsuitable musical environment are well illustrated by the fact that London,

where ninety-three per cent of schoolchildren sang well enough from
notation to earn the full 1s grant in 1891, had arguably the most
stunted amateur musical tradition in the country.[54] Complaints about
the poor quality of and the problems of gaining members for its bands,
orchestras and choral societies were legion. It may well be that school
music only had a long-term effect upon local musical life where
teachers were building on the foundations established by earlier
generations of music enthusiasts. In general, the theorists of school
music were too anxious to impose their own standards and taste, when
they might have benefited from a more careful listening to and
working with the popular musical culture that already existed. Only
in the more egalitarian social and educational atmosphere of the later
twentieth century has such a position become possible.[55]

Socialism and radicalism

While the majority of schemes for the provision of music to the
working classes were under-pinned by an essentially conservative
ideology, the defenders of the established order were not alone in
viewing music and the arts in general as forces which could shape the
minds of the labouring population. There were individual socialists
and progressives involved in many of the schemes discussed so far,
although, in general, their viewpoint was subsumed by the wider
aspirations of the organisations they served. However, a separate
socialist-radical element did exist within 'music for the people'.

Criticism of conditions, employers and even governments had formed the stuff of numerous broadsides and folk-songs from the seventeenth century and probably even earlier, and the nineteenth century
(especially before about 1870) was to see an enormous addition to such
literature. What was novel about the nineteenth century was the
emergence of an organised popular political movement which deliberately used music as a weapon. At the most sophisticated level, the arts
in general were seen as a liberator of human potential, thereby opening minds to more progressive political philosophies.[56] More simply,
songs and anthems carried the messages of organised labour to the
rank and file. This could be done remarkably effectively as in the
dialect piece, *Dialogue between Peter Fearless and Dick Freeman*, a
song associated with the Durham pit strike of 1831. Peter explains to
the doubting Dick the value of union membership and gradually wins
the argument.

Wey, Peter, aw begin to see things right plain,
For wor maisters they care for nowt else but gain.
Then its only in reason worsels to protect,
And to mak them pay smartly for any neglect.[57]

Political ideas could also be transmitted totally ineffectively in the ponderous, pseudo-Byronic hymns and anthems that radical composers and poets continued to produce, despite a profound and obvious lack of enthusiasm amongst their intended audience.[58]

A further use for music was for it to be performed in such a location or context as to challenge dominant perceptions of 'suitable' behaviour and attitude. This is most clearly illustrated by the Sunday bands issue of 1856. The Victorian Sunday, serious, non-commercial and devotional, came under forceful attack from a number of directions in the mid-1850s.[59] One of the most purposeful campaigns was fought by the secularists. Secularism – which covered a broad spectrum of opinion, but which might be crudely defined as the belief that religion was at best mere irrelevant speculation and that man might be better occupied in promoting worldly good rather than in worship – was never a mass movement. Its foremost historian suggests a following of perhaps 100,000 at its height, but accepts a core membership a fraction of that size.[60] In 1856, however, seculalist leaders found themselves spearheading a popular cause. In May of that year Sir Benjamin Hall, the commissioner of Woods and Forests, allowed a series of Sunday band concerts to be held in London. It was estimated that on 4 May 140,000 people attended the three concerts on offer. The strong Sabbatarian lobby, already concerned by the campaign for Sunday opening of the British Museum and the Crystal Palace (begun in the previous year by the radical MP Sir Joshua Walmsley) immediately mobilised and, via the Archbishop of Canterbury, persuaded the Prime Minister Palmerston to ban future concerts.[61]

There was a strong secularist counter-attack, with concerts rapidly organised in London and several provincial centres. Eighty-six thousand were reputed to have attended in Victoria Park London, 15,000 on Newcastle's Town Moor, and a similar number on Woodhouse Moor in Leeds.[62] For all of May and much of June the issue dominated the provincial press and generated a fierce debate between those making 'a practical protest against the proceedings of those who, in an unwise spirit of puritanical gloom, seek to prevent the people from enjoying even the most innocent recreation on the

Sunday', and their enemies anxious to avoid 'the curse of the continental sabbath'.[63] Gradually the issue died down, although the
secularist National Sunday League organised concerts in London the
following summer and similar provincial ventures kept the issue
simmering throughout the period to 1914.[64] The sacred art was
clearly a double-edged weapon.

It was in the late nineteenth and early twentieth century that music
reached its apotheosis as an instrument of radical politics. It owed this
status to the late Victorian socialist revival. The period from 1880 saw
the emergence of several important bodies influenced by socialist
philosophy, but it was amongst the cluster of northern provincial
organisations, the Independent Labour Party, the Labour Church
and the *Clarion* newspaper, with its phalanx of recreational offshoots,
that music was most carefully nurtured. Dedicated to 'the making of
socialists', they found music well suited to their task. Socialist songs
were sung during leafleting campaigns, and it was an unusual gathering that was not enlivened by music.[65] Concerts were regularly
organised by various socialist bodies. Some were decidedly functional, designed to raise money for suitable causes. Huge crowds
could be attracted to such events as at Dewsbury in 1897, where an
estimated 20,000 heard the Penrhyn choir who were raising money for
striking quarrymen at the Penrhyn Slate Quarries, Bethesda, North
Wales. Other concerts were merely educational, such as the chamber
concerts featuring Mozart, Mascagni, Haydn and Chopin introduced
by Bradford Labour Church in 1895.[66]

Mere 'passive' attendance at concerts was not enough, however,
and music making was widely encouraged. The choir, relatively cheap
to run and well suited to communicating specific ideas and slogans,
was the favoured institution although a small number of socialist
orchestras and brass bands were formed. It was within the *Clarion*
movement that choral music received the greatest encouragement.
The *Clarion* newspaper had been founded by Robert Blatchford in
Manchester in 1891.[67] Blatchford was a skilled populariser and he
used the paper to advertise socialism as offering a genuinely alternative lifestyle. The Clarion cycling clubs, rambling clubs, camera clubs
and many others that he and his supporters encouraged were intended
both to generate a concept of socialist fellowship and to liven up a
socialist movement which Blatchford saw as being far too earnest. His
brother Montagu ('Mont Blang' to *Clarion* readers) was the originator
of the Clarion's musical life. In autumn 1894 he wrote a series of

articles in the newspaper stressing the value of vocal music and outlining the work of a choir he had started earlier in the year amongst socialists and 'fellow-travellers' in his native Halifax.[68] In the following year the Clarion Vocal Union was established to oversee the activities of the three or four choirs that had emerged partly as a result of his missionary zeal.

By 1910 at least twenty-three choirs or Clarion Vocal Unions were in existence, mainly in Yorkshire and Lancashire. They attended meetings and rallies and, as their standards rose, gave concerts. In 1898 an annual competition was inaugurated. Montagu Blatchford had initially been hostile to the competitive ideal, claiming that artistic considerations were too often abandoned in favour of performing works of 'length and difficulty'.[69] Gradually, his view softened as he came to view contests as an exercise in musical education and fellowship. By the early 1900s the annual competition had matured into an affair of some importance with two regional qualifying heats and a final taking place alternatively in Lancashire and Yorkshire. Several choirs developed a taste for contests and entered events beyond the Clarion orbit. The Keighley Clarion Vocal Union were regular attenders at Yorkshire competitions, and on one occasion showed extreme dissatisfaction with the decision of the judge (Mary Wakefield) to place them fourth of four. In this instance at least, the competitive ethos clearly outweighed the yearning for fellowship and education.[70]

Blatchford, with some assistance from the *Clarion*'s music correspondent Georgina Pearce, built a rudimentary socialist philosophy of music upon the work of the vocal unions. It owed little to 'scientific' socialism and was at times merely a rewording in socialist language of the traditional 'rational' arguments outlined in previous sections. At the most simple level, music was simply a means of brightening the movement. 'Come!' exhorted Blatchford, 'we want some broad, humanising interest to brighten the dingy round of our struggling party, some more genial and cheering amusement than political speeches and contested elections; and where can you find a more cheering, harmonising, inspiring force than choral music well sung?'[71] More important, music could provide moral and political education. As well as raising the intellectual horizons of the individual and thus helping to 'make socialists', choral music in particular gave an active lesson in fellowship. 'It is a lesson in discipline and socialism of the most convincing sort. It shows the interdependence of each on

all; the necessity of each member doing a given duty in a given way at
the proper time to the instant, and gives an exultant feeling of precision, unity, and power that would raise and dignify a tailor's
dummy.'[72] Moreover, according to another member of Yorkshire's
socialist fraternity, the socialist choir could serve as: 'a first promise of
what enjoyment may be obtained from life, when under the socialism
which these choirs are using their voices to promote, all men and
women have leisure to devote to intellectual pleasures'.[73] Socialists of
the late nineteenth and early twentieth centuries, like the pioneers of
Methodism a century and a half earlier, strove to sing themselves to
paradise.

A further – although generally non-socialist – radical element was
added by the choirs from within the Co-operative movement. The first
Co-operative choirs appear to have begun in the middle 1890s. They
were most common in the movement's heartland in Lancashire and
West Yorkshire, although by the later Edwardian period choirs were
appearing in other areas, notably London and the North-East. Their
activities centred on the provision of music at Co-operative Festivals,
fairs and meetings, although the best choirs also gave public performances. There was also a competitive aspect to their singing, with
national and regional championships commencing in the late 1890s.
The choirs were often of considerable size – the Huddersfield Choir
numbered one hundred and forty in 1899 with another one hundred
and ten in training in a singing-class – and the best obtained extremely
high standards, capable of performing some of the most demanding
part-songs of the period.[74]

Both Clarion and Co-operative choirs seem to have made extensive
use of tonic sol-fa, which was a neat subversion of a weapon forged to
defend, not to reshape, capitalism.[75] (Musical as well as orthodox
literacy was perhaps a dangerous skill!) It is significant that the choirs
use of tonic sol-fa, which was a neat subversion of a weapon forged to
defend, not to reshape, capitalism.[75] (Musical as well as orthodox
concerts, even in the recitals to an already committed audience, the
repertoire of both Co-operative and Clarion choirs remained remarkably similar to that of non-political choirs. Certainly, they adopted a
number of pieces which were radical in tone either because of the text
or because of historical connotation. These included Adolphe Adams'
'Comrades', a setting of a poem *Les Enfants De Paris*, although this
was also popular with other non-political choirs, 'The Marseillaise',
'The Red Flag' and Carpenter's 'England Arise, the Long, Long

Night is Over'. Furthermore, the annual Clarion competition and concert usually featured a specially-commissioned political work. Many of these early pieces were produced from within the movement, like Montagu Blatchford's socialist hymn 'Hark, a New Song Rising', written for the Manchester meeting of 1906.[76] By 1914, however, professional composers with radical sympathies were commissioned to compose material. The concert in that year featured a motet by Rutland Boughton, *The City*, 'embodying the composer's vision of the ideal city', and *1910* by the feminist composer Ethel Smythe, dedicated to the women's suffrage movement.[77] The co-operative movement too produced a certain amount of propagandist material with stirring titles such as 'Brothers in Co-operation' (to the tune of 'Men of Harlech'), 'Hope of Ages', 'Sons of Labour' and 'Forward All Ye Workers'.[78]

In general, however, the dearth of suitable 'socialist' songs, together with a belief remarkably similar to that held by more traditional schools of reform through music, i.e. that the act of performing and its social context mattered more than the music performed, led to orthodox programmes. The 1904 Clarion contest and concert was well within the mainstream of the Edwardian choral tradition. Buck's 'Hymn to Music', Caxton's 'Ode to Spring', King's 'Soldier, Rest' and Elgar's 'O Happy Eyes' and 'Weary Wind of the West' formed the contest pieces, while at the combined concert the audience was offered:

'Judge Me O God'	Mendelssohn
'Hunting Song'	Mendelssohn
'Song of the Vikings'	Fanning

Similarly, in the Co-operative contest at Grimsby in 1907, the closing concert comprised:

'Moonlight'	Fanning
'Come to me, Gentle Sheep'	H. Cowen
'Sleeping Leaves'	A. J. Caldicott
'Break, Break'	MacFarren
'In this Hour of Softened Splendour'	Pinsuti

The advent of socialism was to have some eminent, if unwitting, handmaidens.[79]

Assessment 1840–1914

As has already been seen, many contemporaries believed that their schemes had made an extremely effective contribution to the rebuilding of working class culture. As the period progressed, the working classes appeared to be ever further integrated into the existing system and music received its share of the praise.

Obviously many of the wilder claims and statements of success, including some of those noted in foregoing sections, were grossly exaggerated. They are also revealing, as if (as sometimes appears to be the case) reformers felt that by organising some half-dozen concerts they were leaving an indelible impact upon the social fabric, such claims illustrate forcibly the inability of many middle-class crusaders to comprehend the magnitude of their task. In certain ways, their efforts were almost certainly counter-productive. Many working people must have realised that mainstream music for the people, especially around mid-century, operated according to rules laid down by the propertied classes. Concerts were a good idea, but not on a Sunday. Sacred music was a powerful aid to industry and morality, provided that it was not heard in a public house. There was also the strong patronising element so resented by many Victorian and Edwardian working men. Here was 'culture', a much easier asset to share than political equality or industrial wealth, being distributed like alms to the deserving poor. Perhaps most critically of all, much philanthropically-inspired musical life merely underlined for the working classes the class basis of society. The whole concept of a 'people's concert', for example, implied a second-class citizenship in an artistic and a social sense; if there were 'people's' concerts, then this implied that there were others, to which the working classes could not go.[80] It is similarly hard to believe that such musical events had more than marginal influence upon the institutions they were supposed to undermine. It took a century of social change to challenge the place of drink in popular culture, and, as has been eloquently pointed out by Brian Harrison, the direct efforts of reformers formed only one aspect, and not always a very successful one, of that challenge.[81]

It is equally improbable that socialist-inspired ventures had quite the miraculous effect that some seemed to expect. Indeed some contemporaries and recent historians have suggested that recreational institutions such as the Clarion vocal unions might have *reduced* the effectiveness of the radical challenge by deflecting the participant's attentions away from more obviously political struggles and engagements.[82] At least, as Montagu Blatchford had hoped, music made the socialist movement a more colourful one.

Nevertheless, despite the 'modest activity and utopian rhetoric' which was such a common feature of rational recreation in all its guises, and despite all these disclaimers, there were undoubtedly many small yet significant ways in which the efforts of reformers may have helped create the type of society they yearned for.[83] This is clearly most apparent in the case of those committed to defending contemporary society. There was, for example, always a possibility that some working men would take the rhetoric of middle-class philanthropy at face value and accept the claim that social progress and improvement was happening for everybody. Often, however, the changes that occured through musical activity did not arise in the way that the reformers expected. An example of this, and one of great significance, was their belief that they *were* influencing popular lifestyles. They were pleased by the levels of working-class attendance at the various ventures throughout the period and were encouraged by the standard of behaviour – whistling and unruly children apart! It was perhaps in this way – especially in the earlier period – that 'music for the people' did influence class relationships. Although it was presumed that it was the working classes who were to have their preconceptions challenged, it was the middle classes who found these events socially educative. Audiences at cheap concerts, brass bandsmen and choristers at competitive festivals helped persuade some of their 'betters' in the localities, just as the 1851 Crystal Palace Exhibition had done on a national scale, that the lower orders were not after all beyond redemption and indeed gave cause for optimism.

It is also possible that music and musical events may have encouraged or reinforced the adoption of particular ideological standpoints, something which, of course, applies equally to the music of those seeking to challenge capitalist society as to that produced by its defenders. Perhaps, for example, 'Touch Not the Cup', 'Hurrah, Hurrah for England' and other such material did have an influence upon some minds. Probably more significant, however, was the emotional impact of certain types of musical experience. Music is for many people a powerful emotional stimulant. John Wesley firmly believed that his religious conversion in 1738 owed much to exposure to sacred music – which explains, to a degree, his later emphasis upon

music in Methodist work.[84] The exact nature of the music performed
may well have had little direct relationship with its ideological influence. After all, music intended for a specific purpose or a specific
location could take on entirely new dimensions when sung in a
different context. Hymns and music-hall songs could become
working class battlecries, as they did in 1891 when strikers at Bradford's Manningham Mills sang, 'Crown Him Lord of All', 'Sweet
Beulah Land', 'The Tally Man', 'His First Wife' and a musical
mélange that is well known to pantomime admirers', before strike
meetings.[85] In the same way, it may be that a Haydn symphony, a
Henry Russell ballad, a Chopin nocturne – irrespective of any ideological statement intended by the composer or 'discovered' by historians – could reinforce socialism at a Labour Church concert,
temperance at a Rechabite festival or patriotism at a Boer War rally.
The emotional aura engendered and the concomitant lumps in
throats, shivers down spines and tears down cheeks reinforced
whichever ideological standpoint the listener happened to embrace.
The contemporary belief that music *per se* mattered, rather than any
particular form of music, was perhaps well founded.

Whatever their social and political achievements – and it must be
admitted that much of what has just preceded is highly speculative –
there can be no doubt that politically-motivated musical projects did
have important musical implications. Some attempt has already been
made to assess each element as it has been discussed, but general
points remain to be made. Above all, such projects increased enormously the amount of music available in nineteenth and early
twentieth-century England. This was of the greatest importance in
those areas not possessed of a strong pre-existing musical culture.
Singing-classes in London and other large urban centres and choirs
fostered by the festival movement in rural areas brought about
hitherto unexperienced levels of musical participation and helped
make the habit of music-*making* a truly national one. Obviously, the
people reached by philanthropic institutions were not always those
aimed at by the organisers. The lower middle classes must have
benefited considerably from the cheap rates at concerts such as those
run by Leeds council in the early years of the twentieth century. Even
the richer elements of society made some gains. The 'people's concert
halls' of the 1850s and 1860s rarely functioned in their intended
manner, becoming instead the focus for all manner of entertainment,
including the 'carriages at eleven' concerts to which the upper middle

class came often as much to display wealth and enjoy subtle distinctions of social status as to appreciate the music. Nevertheless, it is clear that the 'common people' made substantial gains from the innumerable schemes on offer.

In the last analysis, the greatest achievement of the Curwens, Wakefields, Frickers, Blatchfords and others was to reinforce the process begun in the 1840s, whereby music became the most acceptable, the most respectable of the arts. By persuading the nation of the social value of music, they ensured its health in an age when all arts were viewed in the light of morality, and, therefore, helped create the atmosphere which made English people between 1840 and 1914 arguably the most musically-inclined in the nation's history.

Part 2

Capitalism: entrepreneurs and popular music

Chapter 4

The popular music industry

The favourable musical climate of Victorian England offered numerous opportunities for the fertile imagination of the entrepreneur. Old musical institutions were restructured and new ones born as the music 'industry' came of age. Obviously, the music-hall represents the greatest achievement of this period and it is the halls, and more especially their influence upon contemporary social and political attitudes, that form the core of this section. But the music-hall was only part of a great span of entrepreneurial musical activity ranging from the musical and organisational simplicity of a street musician's performance to the complexity of a London concert, and initially this section explores some of these neglected but important areas of popular musical experience.

Street music

Street music was not a novel feature of Victorian and Edwardian life; ballad chanters, fiddlers and others had long been part of English street life. Nor was it the sole preserve of the petty capitalist. Many of the louder performances came from Sunday school scholars celebrating chapel anniversaries, brass bands collecting funds and even socialists spreading their message. But in London and the larger provincial cities, street music was essentially a highly competitive branch of the musical economy. It differed from the other elements studied here in one fundamental aspect; the street musician was often – although by no means always – *forcing* his music upon the public. One could choose whether to see George Leybourne or the Carl Rosa Opera Company, but the efforts of a one-armed piccolo player were more likely to be imposed than demanded! At present, relatively little is known about numbers, the background of performers or their mode of operation, although Henry Mayhew has bequeathed us some details of activity in London in the 1850s. He found some 1,250–1,500 musicians and singers, ranging from the glee singers who called at middle-class houses and offered to provide concerts, by which they could earn twenty-five shillings a week, to those sad figures for whom possession of a musical instrument was merely a thin veil for mendicancy! One assumes that most practitioners were either born into the trade or were travelling theatre musicians or orchestral musicians fallen upon hard times. In the lower reaches it was clearly a hazardous pursuit. In 1857 an itinerant singer called Mary Naseby was found hiding in the grounds of a Halifax manufacturer's house, having lived solely on water for eight days.[2]

There is sometimes a tendency to think that all nineteenth-century street musicians were foreign, mainly either members of the ubiquitous German bands or Italian organ grinders. Certainly the German bands, usually some six to twelve in number and originating initially from the Black Forest, were a feature of a typical English summer.[3] They often returned home for the winter, unlike the equally populous grinders who were more likely to establish permanent bases. A colony developed in Clerkenwell, on the fringe of the City of London, around the street-organ and piano workshops of two leading makers, Joseph Canova and Luigi Villa, and some provincial towns and similar centres.[4] Street musicians undoubtedly *claimed* to emerge from every conceivable ethnic background, as Frederick Crowest observed:

We meet in our streets Jews and Turks, Hindoos and Laplanders, Germans, Poles, Italians and motley groups and specimens of our own nationality, playing, grinding, blowing, beating, scraping, thumping, plucking, rubbing all sorts of instruments of real torture and we pay them for it.[5]

It is, however, probable that the majority were in fact British, masquerading under exotic disguises and titles in order to increase their attraction. A sense of musical inferiority even pervaded the street!

The street musicians' instrumentation was even more bewildering and varied than their ethnic origin, assumed or otherwise. Zithers, piccolos, banjos, concertinas, one-string fiddles and even tumblers of water, as well as the better-known barrel-pianos, barrel-organs and the brass instruments of the German bands, were used in innumerable combinations, often producing music of a surprisingly wide range. The repertoire of the more skilful performers embraced quadrilles and waltzes, music-hall favourites and even operatic selections. Popular Italian opera was certainly a feature of the barrel-organ and barrel-piano repertoire. Standards varied enormously, some performers being little more than extortionists.

> When we are out pitching, the first place for us is where there is anybody sick . . . we are sure to play up where the blinds are down . . . we don't move for less than a bob, for sixpence ain't enough for a man that's ill.[6]

However, most made some pretence at giving value for money and some were probably extremely accomplished musicians.

Street musicians elicited remarkably varied responses. The artist John Leech was reputed to have been driven from his home in Brunswick Square to the quieter suburb of Kensington by the incessant noise of the local performers.[7] Its sternest enemies were prepared to use the law on occasions, especially in London. In 1864 the MP and brewer Michael Bass launched a strident campaign enthusiastically publicised by *Punch* and backed by many eminent London literary figures and professional men who believed, with some justification, that musicians were deliberately disturbing their work so that they would have to be handsomely paid to go away. He successfully introduced an Act of Parliament giving London magistrates the power to impose a 40 s fine or three days imprisonment if a musician refused to move on, although it is unclear how effectively this legislation operated.[8]

However, street music, although often complained about in respectable circles, generated only rarely the virulent opposition that met so many aspects of popular recreation and even the early music-halls. Street music, unlike the halls, was in no way connected with the drink industry and gave visible and simple pleasure, especially to the children of the very poor. (This is not to suggest that street musicians only operated in poorer districts; the best practitioners were normally found in suburban quarters where financial reward was greatest.) It was amongst the lower working classes that performances seemed most appreciated and it was this aspect of street music that made it tolerable even to as choleric and idiosyncratic an observer of popular musical life as the Reverend Haweis, who, in his *Music and Morals*, recorded his views with considerable feeling.

> I bless that organ-man – a very Orpheus in hell! I bless his music. I stand in that foul street where the blessed sun shines, and where music is playing. I give the man a penny to prolong the happiness of these poor people, of those hungry, pale and ragged children. . . .'[9]

Thirty years later, in Edwardian Salford, the organ-grinder maintained his function as entertainer of the poor, bringing the music that allowed the local children the opportunity to dance.

A barrel organ called Tuesdays and Saturdays; children danced solo in a kind of private ecstasy. Only top persons and a few avowed Christians renowned for their clean doorsteps and 'amen' faces kept aloof from it all.[10]

It is probable that the popular appeal of the professional street musicians encouraged the 'court and alley' concert movement of the late nineteenth century and early twentieth century. Perceptive performers appreciated that, while visiting a concert-hall or even a music-hall may have been a rare and untypical form of lower working-class musical experience, they were used to music being brought to them and were thus more likely to be 'reached' in this way. Thus street musicians made an important if unintended contribution to the development of middle-class philanthropy. Far more importantly, they added to the musical and social experience of the poor. It would perhaps be unrealistic to argue that the street musician with his operatic selections allowed the poor any real share in the art music tradition of the period, but he certainly gave them glimpses of music otherwise largely out of their reach, and, above all, a taste of 'private ecstasy'. Street life for many would have been infinitely poorer without the street musicians' contribution.

Concerts

While Victorian street music was essentially an intensification of a pre-existing cultural form, the appearance of concerts aimed at a broad-based, ticket buying audience was a new phenomenon. The public 'concert' had, by the late eighteenth century, become dominated, at least in London, by the nobility. The period from the end of the Napoleonic Wars until 1848 witnessed what the premier historian of concert development, William Weber, has described as an 'explosion' in concert life throughout Europe as the middle classes, anxious for social and cultural respectability, began to attend in large numbers.[11] What appears to have happened from about 1845 was an extension of this process as new types of popular concert, which on occasions could reach well into the ranks of the working class while still holding attraction for the upper middle classes, emerged.

These new concerts ranged from those which, like Charles Hallé's

Manchester concerts established in 1858, concentrated on art music and charged a minimum 1*s* admittance, to the more miscellaneous, 'lighter' concerts so common in provincial towns from the 1850s and 1860s, at which prices could fall as low as 6*d* or even 3*d*.[12] Many of these early, cheaper concert series were essentially an entrepreneurial extension of the people's concerts established by middle-class philanthropists. Like the music-hall proprietor, the concert promoter was adept at dressing his product in the trappings of rational recreation, offering 'people's concerts' at 'people's prices'. Uplifting entertainment was offered for the people with a small profit for the organiser, who was typically either a small businessman seeking to diversify, or a music teacher or musical accessory dealer advertising his skills, pupils or stock.

Fairly typical were the concerts begun in 1877 by Liverpool piano dealer William Lea which featured, alongside a programme similar to that of the Leeds Rational Recreation Society mentioned earlier, the 'improving' ballads of a local Baptist chapel organist, William H. Jude. (His speciality was an overture for piano and harmonium in which he played both instruments!)[13] Over the course of the century, a number of professional entertainers emerged aiming specifically at the 'respectable', 'improving' concert sector. Most famous perhaps were Mr and Mrs German Reed who, from the 1850s until Mr German Reed's death in 1888, set out to provide 'dramatic amusement for that class of society which was reluctant to visit theatres'.[14] The Nigger Minstrel Troupes, so popular from 1857 (the year of the Edwin P. Christy troupe's first British tour), also enjoyed connotations of 'respectability'.[15] This type of concert, musically miscellaneous, 'improving' and funded by small businessmen, went on throughout the country and the period until at least 1900, and was probably more typical of popular concert-going experience than the mainly London-centred events, such as August Mann's Crystal Palace Saturday concerts (1855–1901) or the less art music orientated Monday 'Pops' at St James's Hall (1858–1898), previously concentrated upon by historians.

Arguably, nobody did more to encourage the habit of concert-going amongst the working and lower middle classes and to make other potential concert promoters appreciate that a popular audience existed, than the conductor/promoter Louis Jullien.[16] An outline of his career reads like a caricature of the most vivid Victorian romantic fiction. Born in France in 1812, he came to England in 1840, where he established a series of promenade concerts at Drury Lane based on an amalgam of 'quality' art music and spectacular dance music. A Mendelssohn symphony or a Mozart aria could rub shoulders quite comfortably with his own quadrille *Les Echos du Mont Blanc*. Charging a minimum entry of 1s, unusually low for the period, he made a number of tours in Britain, gaining both notoriety and acclaim for his brand of showmanship. His jewelled baton would be handed from a silver tray into his white gloves by a servant; he might seize an instrument from a performer and add to the climax of a performance; he once used four brass bands in Beethoven's Fifth. He went bankrupt in 1848, suffered several more financial disasters, including a spell in a French debtor's prison, attempted suicide, and eventually died in 1860. Beneath the showmanship Jullien made a highly significant contribution to English popular music. In 1859 the magazine *The Musical World* referred to him as a 'musical Luther' and although the parallel is a little over-dramatic, it points up his importance as a populariser and educator. His orchestra contained some outstanding soloists, notably the cornet player Herr Koenig, and early generations of brass bandsmen travelled considerable distances to hear and learn from Jullien and his men. In 1850 three members of a Keighley band walked the twenty-mile round trip to Bradford in order to attend a Jullien concert. Other businessmen were not slow to exploit the audience potential he had helped to expose.[17]

Working-class attendance at concerts, especially concerts devoted to art music, is hard to quantify, but at least in the larger provincial centres, it was certainly higher than has often been assumed. Attendance often involved considerable self-sacrifice. William Hopkinson, a Bradford factory-worker, regularly saved his dinner-money in the 1850s and 1860s in order to see concerts at the St George's Hall. Fifty years later a writer in a Bradford socialist newspaper commented that there were many weavers who rarely missed a good concert 'though they can often ill afford it'.[18] The majority of the working-class people attending may well have been members of the local musical community, bandsmen and choristers anxious for inspiration and education. Certainly, the keen discrimination of the popular sector was often commented upon by promoters. Charles Hallé's son, writing in 1896, noted the large working-class contingent 'standing packed together in great discomfort as I have often seen them . . . listen[ing] for hours, and evidently with much appreciation' at his father's Manchester concerts.[19] While it would be ridiculous to argue that concert-going became a central feature of popular social life in the nineteenth century and very early twentieth century, it is valuable to appreciate the variety of musical experience open to those members of the lower middle and working classes who actively sought it.

One of the best-supported forms offered by provincial concert promoters was opera. Touring opera companies with grandiose titles made increasingly regular visits to provincial centres from the 1840s and 1850s. In 1856, three companies visited Sheffield alone. By the late nineteenth century, well over a dozen companies existed. The most important of these was the Carl Rosa Opera Company; to elderly provincial opera-lovers, the company is almost a synonym for opera. Karl August Nicolaus Rose was a German violinist who, after the death of his opera-singer wife, dedicated himself to the presentation of opera in English. From their opening performance in 1875 until Rose's death in 1889, the company was most closely associated with Drury Lane. But after Rose's death it became essentially a touring company adding, after a Balmoral recital in 1893, 'Royal' to its title. Its major rival was the Moody-Manners Company founded in 1898 by Rose's bass singer Charles Manners and his wife Fanny Moody.[21]

There was undoubtedly a popular audience for operatic tours. Much of our specific evidence for working-class attendance is again drawn from the Northern manufacturing districts and concerns dedicated members of the local musical community. The choral trainer and conductor Henry Coward, then an apprentice cutler, was a regular opera-goer in Sheffield in the 1860s; 'innumerable sixpences went into the pay-box of the local theatres when opera companies visited the town' claims his biographer.[22] Brass bandsmen, especially soloists, were, as will be seen later, close followers of operatic visits. But it is clear that opera reached an audience beyond the absolutely committed musical enthusiast. Admission prices were lower than for 'serious' concerts, with even the Carl Rosa Company, generally held to be the most expensive company, allowing gallery prices as low as 6 d on occasions. A week's engagement, a common duration in a provincial town, at these prices would not have been possible without substantial penetration into the lower middle and upper working class audience. Some of the smaller companies charged even less and were prepared to visit very small towns. J. W. Turner's English Opera Company, for example, performed in the Yorkshire textile town of Yeadon for three consecutive nights in 1890. Even allowing for the presence of a substantial 'millocracy' in the surrounding villages, this would not have been economically viable without patronage from the 'cheaper seats'.[23] Companies like Turner's helped make opera an important element in contemporary popular music.

This emerges strikingly from the autobiography of the music critic and cricket writer Neville Cardus. Cardus, especially in his cricketing works, was prone to exaggeration and glorification and we should be aware of this tendency when using his musical reminiscences.[24] Nevertheless, the picture he creates of late Victorian and Edwardian Manchester corroborates much evidence from more 'objective' sources. Cardus, the illegitimate son of a laundress, spent his childhood in relative poverty, but

I remember that my mother and my aunt Beatrice would sing me to sleep with melodies from *Norma*, which is a fact significant of much of the general musical background of the period.

Bellini's melodies had been learnt both at local pantomimes, where producers often used popular operatic arias, and in the gallery of the Theatre Royal.

The old touring companies actually made opera a popular entertainment for the masses. . . . Every autumn the Theatre Royal in Manchester was crowded each night and on Saturday afternoons for the Carl Rosa Opera Company. . . . There was little musical atmosphere about it all, no doubt, and the productions were palpably 'stock' – a segment of Venusburg would turn up tomorrow night in Seville, while the noses of the high priests in *Aida* were never sufficiently coptic. The point is that there were opportunities in the provinces of England of those days, to get acquainted with opera if you happened to be poor to the point of poverty.[25]

The repertoire was based largely upon the popular British and Italian operas. *Bohemian Girl*, *Maritana*, *The Lily of Killarney*, and *Il Trovatore* were perhaps the most commonly performed works, although *Faust*, *Carmen* and, from the mid-1890s, Mascagni's *Cavalleria Rusticana*, were also extremely popular. New works were regularly included, however, either from the stock of new compositions or in the form of revivals. Mozart, Gluck and Beethoven all appeared in the repertoire of the larger companies. The Carl Rosa performed at least fifty-five works in its tours between 1890 and 1914.[26]

In the period after 1900, the touring companies appear to have experienced a contraction. A musical centre like Bradford could have expected three, perhaps four, week-long visits from two or three different companies in the 1890s. Although one or two new companies, such as Joseph O'Mara's, appeared in the years immediately before 1914, after 1900 Bradford and similar towns could expect for the most part only an annual visit from Carl Rosa.[27] This contraction may well have been due to the problem of meeting increased expenditure, although competition from other genres such as musical comedy may have played a part. The Carl Rosa Company survived until 1958 when it was absorbed by Sadler's Wells, but the other companies mostly failed completely to survive the Edwardian age. Never again has opera attained the place in popular musical life that it held in the nineteenth century.[28]

Musical comedy

Although there is not space here to dwell upon musical comedy, it still seems necessary to make a few brief comments, partly because such an important feature of musical life from the 1890s onwards cannot go unmentioned, but mainly because such comments might inspire the much needed study that musical comedy deserves. Its 'artistic' limitations and the obsession with glamour and frivolity, manifest in so many plots, may have alienated potential observers, but it was a musical form that generated a huge following and, for this reason alone, simply cannot be ignored by scholars.[29]

The origin of musical comedy offers a fine example of the creation of a cultural product out of economic necessity. In 1892 George Edwardes, manager of the Gaiety Theatre, home of many successful burlesque productions, found himself forced by the death of his leading actor Fred Leslie and the illness of leading lady, Nellie Farren, to experiment with new ideas and new talent. The result was *In Town*, a mildly satirical view of London life, with a very loose storyline but featuring up-to-minute clothing fashions, something which caught the attention of the press. The show originally opened at Edwardes's second theatre, the Prince of Wales, but quickly moved to the Gaiety where it enjoyed sufficient success to encourage Edwardes to commission a second venture, *A Gaiety Girl* by Sidney Jones and Owen Hall. This was the first work to be termed a 'musical comedy'. Between 1894 and 1896, Gaiety shares rose from 3 s to £1 as musical comedy established itself as a vital new feature of London theatre life.[30]

The key distinguishing features of musical comedy were light-heartedness and modernity. Script writers deliberately avoided the historical settings so beloved by writers of burlesque and operetta, concentrating on contemporary realism, although, beginning with Sydney Jones's *The Geisha* (1896), there was also something of a vogue for exotic settings. In general, plots were slight, featured simple class stereotypes and showed great interest in the social habits of the rich. (*A Gaiety Girl*, for example, was set at a Windsor Castle Garden Party and on the Riviera), while the music was only loosely rooted in the overall structure.[31] It was not until the appearance of Lionel Monckton's *The Arcadians* in 1909 that audiences were offered a musical comedy in which plot, music and characters were fully integrated. The Gaiety was always the centre of musical comedy production and its chorus girls gained celebrity status. No fewer than twenty-three Gaiety girls married into the aristocracy.[32]

Superficially, the musical comedy appears to have belonged to middle-class, semi-bohemian London and George Edwardes to some extent directed his early productions at this sector. In the increasingly liberated religious and moral climate after 1890, however, musical comedy was accepted quite happily by provincial audiences which often included strong working and lower-middle-class elements. The popularity of selections from musical comedy amongst brass bands and their audiences, discussed in Chapter nine, suggests that in fact these works were a central element in Edwardian popular taste. There are many possible avenues of investigation for potential students of musical comedy – the source of musical inspiration, the relationship with the music-hall, the marketing of star performers like Gertie Millar – but a vital task must be an exploration of the link between the 'message' of musical comedy and contemporary political behaviour. At first sight, these light, escapist, glamorous concoctions would appear to offer a decidedly conservative, de-radicalising world-view to the ever growing popular audiences. Detailed study is needed to ascertain whether such a view is accurate or merely simplistic speculation.

The music-hall: origins and development of an industry

Significant as the development of all the features discussed so far might be, they pale into insignificance when compared with the emergence of the music-hall industry, the growth of which is surely one the most striking features of nineteenth-century history. Here was both the most highly organised sector of the entertainment industry to date and a prefiguration of the mass entertainment business of the twentieth century. It is possible to overstress music-hall's place in Victorian and Edwardian musical life. Richard Middleton has recently referred to it as 'the principal source of musical entertainment for most urban working and lower-middle-class people in the second half of the century'.[33] Even as carefully-worded a claim as this is hard to substantiate. It might be true of London, where by the 1890s some fourteen million tickets were being sold annually, but in most other urban areas there were numerous other musical forms absorbing people's attentions to just as great an extent. Nevertheless, the music-hall was a vital element of the period and deserves detailed study. The remainder of this section offers a survey of the industry's development and analysis of the music-hall song as a reflector and shaper of popular social and political attitudes.[34]

The name 'music-hall' can be used in at least three separate ways; to describe a certain performance style, an entire section of the entertainment industry, or an individual building. The last usage is particularly awkward and seems to have foxed contemporaries as well as historians. Where does a public house singing-saloon end and a music-hall begin? For this reason, no accurate count of halls can be made. It was essentially from the singing-saloon that music-halls emerged, although in the provinces the travelling theatre, and, in London, the pleasure gardens and the bohemian song and supper-rooms, all contributed, both in terms of physical space and personnel.[35] We look in vain for the very first hall. The honour of being music-hall's founder traditionally passed to Charles Morton, a publican born in Hackney in 1819, who purchased the Old Canterbury Arms, Upper Marsh, Lambeth in December 1849. He instituted concert performances on three nights a week in the building and these became so popular that on 17 May 1852 he opened a concert-hall built on the adjacent bowling green, thus separating the entertainment from the public house. Within a few months the 6d refreshment cheque chargeable for liquid refreshment once inside was replaced by a simple admission ticket. The music-hall, so runs the story, had been born. It is, however, difficult to see what exactly Morton had done to deserve the epithet 'Father of the Halls' garlanded upon him in his old age, other than to advertise his venture in dramatic ways, (in 1855 and 1856, he fell foul of the 1843 theatrical legislation by performing dramatic sketches in the hall. *The Times* reported the case and Morton immediately pressed his advantage by placing an advertisement in the paper), and to enjoy the benefits of a long life, capped by the publication in 1905 of *Sixty Years Stage Service*, a fascinating but hagiographic biography. By outliving his rivals he absorbed much of the credit for their achievements.[36]

In fact, most of Morton's achievements appear to have been preceded either elsewhere in London or in the provinces. The type of concert performance he began in 1849 was already extremely common in London. Indeed, the principle of public house concert-room entertainment was already so well established in the capital by the 1840s that the artists had their own benevolent society.[37] In the provinces, especially Lancashire and Yorkshire, similar developments were taking place several years before Morton's initiative, as publicans turned to new methods of entertainment to stave off the threat of competition from the newly created beerhouses. Thomas Sharples opened the concert room in the Star, Bolton, as early as 1840. A picture-gallery, museum and menagerie were later added, and the hall could eventually accommodate a thousand people. A contemporary writer estimated a nightly attendance of three to four thousand in Bolton's singing-saloons.[38] The *Morning Chronicle* survey of 'Labour and the Poor' discovered what was almost a concert-room industry in Liverpool in 1849.

The attention of the stranger who walks through the streets of Liverpool can scarcely fail to be directed to the great number of placards which invite the public to cheap or free concert-rooms. Of all shapes, sizes and colours to attract the eye, they cover the walls of the town, and compete with one another in the inducements which they offer to the public to favour with its patronage the houses which they advertise.

A police return given to the *Chronicles*'s investigator recorded that in August 1849 thirty-two public houses offered concert room entertainment, the largest hall holding some four hundred people and possessing moving scenery. Some two hundred and eighteen performers, paid between six shillings and £2 a week, earned their living in these rooms.[39] Birmingham (where one publican reputedly spent £800 on an organ to accompany the sacred music that the law stipulated could be the only form of music allowed on a Sunday), Manchester, Sheffield, Leeds, Bradford and other smaller towns all possessed a strong concert-room tradition.[40] Even the building of a hall separate from the public house, seen by many as Morton's particular contribution, was not original. Richard Preece, licensee of the Grapes in Southwark, had established the Surrey Music Hall in a separate building some years before Morton commenced operation.[41] Far from music-hall originating from one man's novel idea which then spread out across England from the capital, publican-entrepreneurs all over the country were setting up similar institutions at the same time, each one poised to develop and expand according to local social and economic circumstance.

These singing-saloons and proto-music-halls went under a variety of names, with 'concert-room', 'concert-hall', and 'music-hall' as the most popular. By the 1860s the term 'music-hall' appears to have won the day. The phrase was not a particularly common one before 1850, but where it was used, it had connotations that made it extremely attractive to a group of entrepreneurs anxious to make their brand of popular entertainment respectable. The term either referred to an upper-class concert-hall or, perhaps more significantly, was used by rational recreationists to describe a place of elevating entertainment for the people. Not for the first time, the nascent entertainment industry stole its enemies' clothing.

The early proprietor-publicans were skilful propagandists in this sense, forever underlining, through their museums, picture galleries, reading rooms and public pronouncements, the 'educational' aspect of their work. In 1851, for example, Joseph Hobson, owner of the Leeds Casino, an early music-hall under extreme attack from local religious spokesmen, defended himself thus. Was not the working man, he asked,

more beneficially, more properly, and less harmfully employed, when listening to such music and innocent entertainments as I can afford to provide and he pay for . . . than he would be drinking and smoking in some taproom, talking politics until he becomes a Chartist or a rebellious democrat dangerous to society, or discussing religious topics until schism, heresy, or even Deism is the consequence?[42]

In the battle for survival, this acute sense of self-preservation was crucial. So, too, was the attitude taken by the 'establishment'. Until the very late nineteenth century, as has already been seen, the majority of middle-class observers had little praise for the music-hall. Nevertheless, while accepting its weaknesses and problems, many realised that it was not as black as painted and may have even possessed a few virtues. It is apparent from the reports of both the 1866 and 1892 select committees on Theatrical Licences and Regulations that senior policemen were aware, from the reports of their constables who regularly patrolled the halls, that prostitutes *did* use certain halls for business, but felt that, provided the halls were not rampantly disorderly and badly managed, this was not a serious problem. Sir Richard Mayne, the Chief Commissioner of the Metropolitan Police in 1866, indeed argued that such open prostitution made police work much easier and the standard of morality higher than if it had taken place in secret.[43] Similarly, many police representatives and magistrates firmly believed that the music-hall limited the excesses of working-class drinking. The chief magistrate of Bow Street Police Court told the 1866 committee that, 'I know there is scarcely ever a case of drunkenness from any of the music-halls'.[44] A number of commentators claimed that this resulted from the presence of so many family groups. An institution which kept the lower orders and their more exuberant social superiors in reasonable order and under the watchful eye of the law was clearly worth tolerating.

During the 1860s a music hall 'business' began to crystallise, given confidence by the establishment's tolerance and underpinned by an increasingly stable and prosperous economy. Increased prosperity both generated the regular employment necessary for regular attendance by the working-class element of the audience, and encouraged the search for novel and rewarding vehicles for investment amongst wealthier sectors. London saw only slow development immediately after the opening of the Canterbury, but its success, along with that of Wilton's (1856) and Weston's (1857) encouraged emulation. By 1866 London possessed thirty-three halls with an average capacity of 1,500 and an average capitalisation of £10,000.[45] Some of these halls, especially those sited in the West End, were extremely sumptuous and elaborate structures, others were bleak and barn-like. A parallel growth took place in the provinces. The appearance of the Princess Palace and White Swan Varieties in Leeds (1864 and 1865), Day's in Birmingham, Pullan's in Bradford (1869) and the Tyne Concert Hall in Newcastle (1861), to name only a few of the large halls that were emerging, meant that by the end of the decade the population of most major English towns had access to at least one example of this new element in popular social life.[46] These provincial developments need stressing, for although London was always the true focus of music-hall life, there had been a tendency amongst historians to neglect regional halls. It is highly significant that the first music-hall journal, *The Magnet*, published in Leeds from 1866, was concerned with the *provincial* music hall business.[47]

The appearance of *The Magnet* was only one feature of the

professional paraphernalia which accompanied this expansion in bricks and mortar. In 1858 the first agency appeared under the management of Ambrose Maynard. Two years later the London Music Hall Owners Protection Society was founded, followed in 1865 by the performers' tentative equivalent, the Music Hall Provident Society. Above all, the music-hall 'star', an individual performer with a defined stage persona, was beginning to emerge.[48] By the end of the decade it was obvious to all but the most virulent opponents that music-hall was an established feature of Victorian life.

It is tempting to see the music-hall industry's trajectory from this point in fairly simple terms. First, the industry became more truly national, as halls were opened in the middling-sized communities previously neglected. There had often been short-lived halls in such places, but permanent sites developed from the 1880s onwards. The pattern of building in the West Riding textile district might serve as a useful model for comparative research on this topic in other areas. The two largest towns, Leeds and Bradford, had established halls by the 1860s. The next largest communities, Huddersfield and Halifax, both with populations of about 100,000, had to wait until the 1880s for their first halls, while the 'third level' towns, Dewsbury and Keighley with populations of 30,000 and 50,000 respectively in 1901, waited until the early 1900s.[49] This 'nationalisation' process was aided by the growth of provincial touring – dating back to the 1860s, but increasingly common from the 1870s – undertaken by the leading London-based and managed stars.[50] At the same time, the structure of the business began to alter. From the 1880s the smaller halls, particularly those in London, began to disappear under a joint attack from the opposition of licensing authorities and competition from larger, more heavily-capitalised halls.[51] By the 1890s the drink trade within the halls was increasingly less important financially, and the entertainment itself became the main purpose of the industry. In the late 1890s the industry witnessed the development of provincial syndicates, of which Oswald Stoll's Empire circuit was the best-known. In the years to 1914, these syndicates erected immense 'Theatres of Variety' dedicated increasingly to the ideal of 'family entertainment'.[52] Music-hall moved from being a local, slightly risqué, largely class-based business in the hands of individual entrepreneurs, to a more centralised, increasingly respectable mass entertainment industry.

This brief outline is broadly correct. But the general picture does

obscure some continuities. The large chains did not have it all their
own way. In the provinces a small number of halls did remain in
private hands, while other managements formed themselves into
smaller, localised syndicates. In 1913, the Provincial Entertainment
Proprietors and Managers Association was founded to defend the
interests of individual owners against the more powerful circuits.[53]
Perhaps most significant of all, a brand of small-scale music-hall,
virtually indistinguishable from the concert-rooms and halls of the
1850s and 1860s, continued to exist into the opening of the twentieth
century. The advertising columns of *The Magnet* suggest that singing-
rooms in Manchester, Bradford, Barnsley, Halifax and Stalybridge
had all succeeded in evading the wrath of the licencing authorities
until at least 1902. Five of the Bradford saloons had between three and
five 'turns' on the bill and were organised very much upon 'traditional', that is early Victorian, music-hall lines. The larger saloons had
a raised platform:

With a benignant and smiling chairman in close proximity. . . . All the rooms
were extensively patronised, the company being composed chiefly of the
artisan class, and including a fair number of women, many of whom had
evidently dropped in on their way home after doing the Saturday shopping.
Seated round small tables, with their various beverages in front of them, their
behaviour was almost without exception above reproach; and the chairman,
assisted by his insistent hammer and a persuasive and bland demeanour, had
comparatively little difficulty in preserving order.[54]

One could be excused for imagining that this was written in 1852 and
not 1902. The Bradford concert-rooms did not survive the January
licencing session of that year, when the chairman of the licencing
committee, S. P. Myers, a leading local Liberal and temperance
reformer backed by a new and enthusiastic chief of police, took away
over thirty music licences. *The Magnet* mourned the end of the
singing-saloons, but the *Music Hall and Theatre Review*, representing
the new generation of entrepreneurs, did not seem concerned, imply-
ing that such places were now superfluous.

The custom of concerts or sing-songs at public houses is an old one, dating
from the times when many of the towns in Yorkshire, Lancashire and the
Midlands were without a recognised Palace or Empire of Varieties. Now,
thanks to the enterprise of Messrs Moss and Thornton, and other gentlemen
interested in amusements, no such reproach can be laid. . . .

Perhaps the writer had forgotten the parentage of the new halls, but we should not forget how long the traditions of the mid-century persisted.[55]

Social structure

Many writers, past and present, believe that the music-hall was a distinctly working-class institution. Its earliest historians, C. D. Stuart and H. J. Park, writing in 1895, saw it as a cultural product of 'the great proletariat'. More recently, in his pioneering *Sweet Saturday Night* (1967) the novelist Colin MacInnes argued that music-hall songs: 'were chiefly written by, and sung by, working-class men and women for working class audiences'.[56] Such a view, which finds echoes in some academic writing, is dangerously simplistic, making too many assumptions about singer, songwriter (to whom we shall return later) and audience. Greater accuracy on this point is essential, not simply because it will lead to a clearer picture of Victorian popular music, but because if music-hall songs are to be analysed, then a full grasp of their social context is required.

Many singers *were* from working-class backgrounds. George Leybourne (actually Joe Saunders) was initially a factory mechanic, Herbert Campbell an engineer at the Woolwich Arsenal, Bessie Bellwood a rabbit-skinner, Harry Lauder a miner. Nevertheless others, including the Great Vance (Alfred Stephens), Charles Coborn and Albert Chevalier, came from lower-middle or middle-class families. It is probable that, overall, there may have been a slight preponderance of working-class performers, but equally probable that the collective biography of the profession that someone will surely produce before long will show a far more complex situation than is often assumed.[57]

In the same way, a too simplistic view of the audience's composition must be avoided. A cultural form that embraced provincial halls which were often no more than concert-rooms, as well as the palaces of London's West End, and that changed so fundamentally between 1850 and 1914 and enjoyed certain regional idiosyncrasies, cannot be easily characterised.

Certain general patterns do emerge, however. A substantial proportion of the audience, perhaps even a majority in some halls, were under the age of twenty-five. This had been the case from the outset. A large number of attenders at Liverpool's concert-rooms in the 1840s were boys aged between fourteen and sixteen. Peter Bailey has pointed out that lists of casualties after accidents at Dundee in 1865 and Manchester in 1868 suggest a strong presence of twelve–eighteen year olds, at least in the gallery. Audiences tended to be male-dominated, although there was always a female element which appears to have increased considerably from the 1890s with the increase in matinee and early evening performances.[58]

In class terms, the backbone of the audience was probably always the upper working class and the lower middle class. The poorest sections of the community were largely excluded, as they were from so much else, not simply by lack of cash for entry and for drink once inside, but by lack of respectable clothing. This was perhaps especially important in towns where there was only one hall aiming at a broad audience and where an individual's dress was likely to be compared with that of a fairly wide social group. The social investigator C. B. Hawkins noted this problem of dress in the music-hall in his study of Edwardian Norwich. But even in larger cities, the poor may well have been excluded. H. Lee J. Jones, one of the founders of the Liverpool court and alley Concerts, claimed in 1899 that: 'I think quite two-thirds of the poor of Liverpool never go near music-halls; at any rate, by no means as a rule. Their almost sole 'music-hall' is the Italian organ. . . .'[59] Perhaps only in London, where the cheapest seats could cost only 2d compared to the normal 6d, were the lower working class able to attend in sizeable numbers. The sheer size of London made it possible for music-halls to be established almost for specific sections of the population, a factor noted by a contributor to *Harper's New Monthly Magazine* in the late nineteenth century.

London music-halls might be roughly grouped into four classes – first the aristocratic variety theatre of the West End, chiefly found in the immediate neighbourhood of Leicester Square; then, the smaller, less aristocratic West End halls; next, the large bourgeois music halls of the less fashionable parts and in the suburbs; last the minor music-halls of the poor and squalid districts.[60]

Safe amongst their own class, 'the very lowest classes of men and boys', as the chief commander of the London police described the audience of halls in Whitechapel and Wapping in 1866, were free to attend.[61] In general, however, observers from both inside and outside the music-hall industry in London and the provinces constantly referred to 'respectable artisans', 'the better class of tradesmen', 'small traders, shopkeepers and their wives' as the distinctive element in the music-hall audience.

More problematic is the issue of middle-class attendance, especially in the earlier periods. There had always been a strong 'bohemian' element in the West End halls; indeed these halls were built and managed largely with this group in mind, with expensive seats and well-stocked bars. Ungracious critics of these halls claimed that the entertainment they offered, especially ballet, a common feature at the Alhambra and not unknown in other 'aristocratic' halls, was merely a ploy to please lascivious young swells. 'I believe that men simply go there for the pleasure of looking at the women's legs', one witness told the 1866 select committee on theatrical licences and regulations.[62] But it is possible that a more 'respectable' middle-class element did attend, albeit in relatively small numbers, almost from the outset. Certainly, music-hall managements claimed that they did. The manager of Day's Music-Hall in Birmingham believed 'a very superior class of people, manufacturers and their wives', to be amongst his clientele in 1866.[63] Apart from the obvious problem of a manager seeking to win kudos for his establishment, Birmingham's economy was based very much upon small workshops and a Birmingham 'manufacturer' might be more akin to the small tradesmen noted above, than to, for example, the more affluent manufacturer of a northern textile town. By the 1880s, music-hall journals were regularly making claims of middle-class attendance, claims which could again be dismissed as attempts at enhancing the industry's respectability were it not for the occasional reinforcement they receive from other less biased sources. The *Musical Times* argued in October 1885 that 'the supporters of the leading music-halls [were] drawn from the well-to-do or comparatively well-to-do classes'. The next month the magazine took issue with a writer in the Daily News:

the writer is mistaken if he imagines the artisan to be the chief frequenter of the halls. Philistinism chiefly flourishes among the materialised middle class, according to Mr Matthew Arnold, and the true 'Arry is removed several grades in the social scale from the working man.

This view certainly clashes with much other evidence and may well be simply another example of the idiosyncracies of *Musical Times* contributors. However, future students of the halls, particularly provincial halls, would benefit from giving closer attention to the possibility of middle-class attendance between 1850–1890 than has so far been the case.

From the 1890s there is much implicit in the evidence suggesting that significant sections of the respectable middle class 'proper' began to attend.[64] The arrival of this group into the music-hall audience was facilitated by the interaction between a changing social climate and the development of certain trends within the music-hall or 'variety' profession. The changing leisure habits amongst at least the younger sections of the middle classes in the final two decades of the nineteenth century have been widely commented upon. The nature of the exact cause, which may have been, for example, a decline in religious observance, is open to considerable debate, but the growth of women's tennis and golf, the cycling craze and even the beginning of Sunday opening at art galleries and museums in 1896 are all indicative of an increasingly relaxed social atmosphere in which the music-hall might be contemplated as a recreational form.[65] However, there was a considerable difference between an afternoon in the countryside or at the Natural History Museum and an evening at a place such as the Peckham Varieties, and obviously the acceptance of the halls by the majority of the middle class could not commence until changes within the industry had heightened its attractiveness and cleansed it of the 'immorality' that so many observers, interpreting its art in various periodicals to the middle-class public, claimed it maintained.

In this sense, the music-halls benefited from developments in other aspects of the entertainment profession. The pierrot troupes which formed a central part of middle-class seaside holiday entertainment from the 1890s leant heavily upon music-hall song and thus possibly helped persuade the audience that the music-hall was not so vulgar after all, or that the vulgarity could be quite entertaining! The panto-mime, revitalised and commercialised by Sir Augustus 'Druriolanus' Harris in the 1880s, reinforced this process by bringing the middle classes into contact, not only with the songs, but with the singers, for the stars of the pantomime season were music-hall performers. Thus Dan Leno, Herbert Campbell, Marie Lloyd and others were able to make their initial impact upon a previously neglected part of the community.[66]

A further crucial component in this process of exposing the middle classes to the halls was the one-man crusade of recitals and concerts presented by Albert Chevalier (1861–1923), which began in the early 1890s. This was not entirely original. Performers such as Harry Clifton and the Great Vance had made provincial concert tours from the 1860s. But Chevalier seems to have reached a decidedly 'superior' audience and to have gained tremendous publicity. Much has been

written about Chevalier (a character actor before he took to the halls),
both by contemporaries and by subsequent *aficionados* of music-hall,
and he seems unfailingly to have aroused extremity of opinion, either
thorough captivation or total hostility. This is not the place to add
another chapter to the saga, but it is obvious that Chevalier's sometimes comical but essentially sentimental songs of costermonger life
had considerable appeal for middle-class audiences. In Brighton 'the
cream of . . . fashionable society' and in Bradford 'the ranks of those
who make a point of seeing anything first-class which is given in the
town' flocked to see him. Dowager Lady Vernon, Mrs Asquith, Lord
Rothschild and Dean Gregory of St Paul's were amongst those who
offered him private engagements, while the prime minister Lord
Salisbury enjoyed his performance at a Trafalgar Theatre benefit
concert. The *Daily Telegraph*, noting these achievements, praised
Chevalier for 'devulgarising' the music-hall, and the *Times* gave
appreciative coverage to many of his recitals. It was perhaps the effect
of reading about the success of these recitals amongst eminent
members of society, as much as actually viewing the performances for
themselves, that helped change the attitude of 'respectable' society
towards the music-hall.[67]

In the final analysis, however, the most crucial changes had to come
from within the music-hall industry itself, for even though an increasingly receptive audience existed, it still had to be enticed into attendance. It was during the last years of the nineteenth century that
managements took up the challenge. Improvement to the decor of the
theatres, strict scrutiny of the morality of the acts and careful attention to, and cultivation of, the audience's taste were the methods
employed by management in the new 'theatres of variety'. Thus,
music-hall architecture became increasingly grandiose, featuring
increasingly either Moorish or exotic Indian style. The Empire
Palace, Nottingham, a fairly orthodox provincial hall, had pagoda
domes with grinning idols representing Krishna at both sides of the
stage and four vast elephant heads in gilt in each corner of the
auditorium, while the Liverpool Empire offered its patrons a ceiling
by Secard representing cupids floating on a bed of cloud. (Inevitably,
this produced delightful incongruity. 'Fancy having to go on and sing
'Old Kent Road' in a scene representing a Moorish palace, or the
Grand Staircase of a baronial hall', commented Chevalier.)[68] This
process of glorification and pseudo-artistic 'respectabilisation' was
accompanied by the expulsion of much of music hall's earlier bawdy

element, although Vesta Victoria's 'I Want to Play with my Little
Dick' and the 'naughty' repertoire of Marie Lloyd remained. 'The
Bradford Empire will warrant the support of all classes of society.
Nothing will be seen or heard here that will raise a blush or put
modesty to shame. Bring your wives and daughters . . .', trumpeted
Frank Allen on behalf of the Moss-Thornton syndicate at the opening
of the Bradford Empire in January 1899, clearly indicating his organisation's aspirations.[69] A Bradford choral singer, daughter of a mill
manager, remembering her Edwardian childhood, illustrates well
that Allen's message reached some ears. Here was music-hall in a form
suitable for those intimidated by the older, essentially proletarian
halls:

[I] went every week to the Alhambra to see the comics and I went to the
Empire. I never went to the Palace in Manchester Road. Yes, they had people
like Chung Lin Su you know, the conjuror and that type of act at the Empire
and you didn't get those at the Palace. I don't know who *they* got.

No longer needing to brave the elements of Manchester Road and its
counterparts, the daughters of the middle class were safe.[70]

The change within the structure of the music-hall which is most
indicative of a changing clientèle was the growth of the 'twice-
nightly' system. The identity of its originator is a matter of some
dispute, but it seems to have made fitful appearances from the 1860s,
and had become the norm at a few halls by the middle 1880s. It was
not, however, until the late 1890s that it became commonplace. The
majority of McNaughten, Barrasford and Moss-Thornton halls
adopted this system almost entirely between 1896 and the early years
of the twentieth century. Certainly, it was never as all-pervading as
some writers have suggested; in 1906 the *Variety Artistes' Time-Table*,
a publication which catalogued the whereabouts of various performers, recorded twice-nightly performances at only thirteen of the
thirty-six London halls it listed, while in the provinces, the proportion was nearer to 50 per cent.[71] Nevertheless, the fact that it had
developed even this far is of crucial importance. In the 1870s and 80s
the music-hall had probably survived largely on the financial rewards
of 'sweet Saturday night' after the decline of Saint Monday, the only
night of the week when the working class and lower middle class had
the available leisure time to enjoy a form of entertainment which
continued until eleven in the evening. The growth of the twice-nightly
system, which involved one performance usually between 6.30 p.m.

and 8.30 p.m., and the other between 9.00 p.m. and 11.00 p.m., is illustrative that a more monied and leisured element was attending the halls. Thomas Skelmerdine, a Liverpool surveyor and theatre architect, giving evidence to the 1892 Parliamentary Committee on music-halls, noted a crucial difference between the two houses in a Liverpool hall, when he claimed that those who attended the 9.00 p.m. to 11.00 p.m. house were 'rather a different grade from the 7.00 p.m. to 9.00 p.m.; they were men who have not to be up at four or five o'clock in the morning'. At the same time, he differentiated these people from the 'heavy swells' of the London West End halls, indicating that this group represented the arrival of 'orthodox', rather than the 'bohemian' element of the middle class.[72] That 'twice-nightly' became so common in the music-hall organisation is a testimony to the sizeable patronage by the middle classes, for without their support the system could never have proved a viable proposition.

The expansion of the music-hall industry between 1880 and 1914 is further indication of middle-class attraction to this form of entertainment, although, obviously, it also reflects an extension of interest among the traditional audience. In 1899, the *Era Almanack* listed thirty-nine halls in London and two hundred and twenty-six in the provinces – which only represents a gradual growth since the 1880s. By 1913, the number had escalated to sixty-four and five hundred and three respectively. The problem of definition arises again here, and it is probable that many of the *Era*'s 'new halls' were actually theatres or even cinemas offering occasional variety entertainments.[73] Nevertheless, even if the figures are scaled down to allow for this, some interesting patterns emerge. It is the location of the new halls that is particularly illuminating. London suburbia had been fully penetrated by about 1906 with halls existing not only in the predominantly working-class districts such as East Ham and Holloway, but in distinctly middle and upper-middle-class regions, such as Richmond, Ealing and Kingston. Furthermore, some form of variety had emerged in country towns, such as Harrogate, Bath, Cheltenham, Salisbury and Woking. It is hard to believe that these institutions were the sole preserve of servants and the rural working class.

The attitude of the 'respectable press' further amplifies this picture of middle-class arrival. *The Times* took an increasing interest in the music-hall from about the turn of the century, although it dealt particularly with its business affairs. It could, nevertheless, by 1910, produce a fifteen-hundred-word article tracing its history and praising it for refining its morals and improving its standards. That this august organ, which had until so recently avoided mention of the music-hall unless forced by journalistic necessity to cover some aspect of its activity, could offer such praise, reveals a considerable change in attitude. Most revealing of all, however, was its comment that: 'Theatre and music-hall appeal, not to two different publics, but the same public in two different moods'. By 1914 even the profoundly respectable *Illustrated London News* could include a picture of Marie Lloyd.[74] Between the late 1890s and 1914, the music-hall had undergone a total transformation, transcending class, and become a genuinely national cultural institution.

One observation remains before turning to the study of music-hall song. The many changes outlined here had a definite effect upon audience behaviour. Certainly, the atmosphere which was in the halls by about 1900 should not be caricatured. Although some managements would have liked it, it was never possible to engineer rows and rows of perfectly socially-mixed patrons, passively enjoying a sanitised performance. Most audiences and some performers fought back against restrictions. As early as 1877, the manager of Day's in Birmingham placed an 'injunction at the head of the programme requesting the public not to chorus any of the songs'. However, during G. H. MacDermott's massively popular visit in September of that year, 'at least three thousand out of the vast assemblage echoed his refrains'.[75] In later years, from the performer's side, artists such as Vesta Victoria and Marie Lloyd (with her famous gestures and interpretations) held the line against saintliness.

Nevertheless, the music-hall had to a large extent been tamed by management. The early halls had been noisy, 'a place of freedom and ease', where everyone in the audience, according to an American observer at the Royal Victoria, 'seemed to be on speaking terms with each and all of the performers'.[76] The atmosphere in one of Stoll's Edwardian Empires was far different; the chairman, the waiters, the tables, and much of the intimate feel that characterised the early halls would have gone. By 1900, and earlier in some cases, the halls were quieter, more sober, more decorative and more rigidly under management control than the early 'caterers', so desperate for respectability, would have thought possible. There is, therefore, much in Peter Bailey's persuasive argument that, when it came to improving the tone of popular entertainment and 'defining and enforcing socially appropriate behaviour', the commercially-inspired music-hall proprietor may well have had more success than the social reformers and rational recreationists.[77]

Chapter 5

The music-hall and its music

The music-hall was never devoted entirely to music. The advent of 'variety' in the Edwardian period produced a rash of acrobats, jugglers and strongmen as well as dogs, birds and baboons which on occasions relegated the musical element to a clear second place.[1] Sketches became increasingly common from the 1890s, and, incidentally, offer a rich source to the historian. Moreover, the music in the halls was, especially in the 1850s and 1860s and again after 1900, drawn from a much wider repertoire than is often appreciated. Something which can be referred to as a 'music-hall song' did not really emerge until the later 1860s. The earlier halls appear to have garnered singers and material from numerous areas of contemporary musical life. Supper-room songs, such as Sam Cowell's 'Villikins and his Dinah' and W. G. Ross's 'Sam Hall', some parlour ballads, and on Tyneside, at least, folk tunes, passed into the halls. The following programme from Day's Music Hall in Birmingham in October 1866, illustrates the catholicism of many early programmes.

1. Overture, including backdrop 'The New Street Station'
2. Grand garland divertissement – ballet
3. Grand selection from Bellini's favourite opera *Norma* and several other pieces.
4. Mr J. G. Forde   – Patter – comic singer
5. Gymnastic entertainment   – Brothers Ridley
6. Reading   – Mr Reuben Roe
7. Waltz   – Orchestra
8. Pantomime ballet   – "The Adventures of Lord Dunderay' including comic song and Ethiopian entertainment.[2]

Perhaps most surprising in this programme, at first glance, is the inclusion of an element of art music. Opera in particular, however, was relatively common in the early halls. Morton's use of the 'serious'

repertoire at the Canterbury is well known. The first British performance of parts of Gounod's *Faust* took place at the Canterbury in 1859.
In the spring of the same year, selections from Meyerbeer's *Dinorah*
and William Sterndale Bennett's cantata *May Queen* were performed
nightly, and glees and madrigals were a regular element of the performance.[3] This was only partly another aspect of Morton's quest for
respectability. Classical selections, overtures, glees and madrigals
featured in most music hall performances throughout the 1860s. The
'serious' component gradually declined (although it was given greater
prominence in a few variety theatres immediately before the Great
War), but it remained traditional for the evening's entertainment to
commence with an overture, often drawn from the popular English or
Italian operatic repertoire.[4] Some pieces became so common that a
writer describing the opening of the Bradford Alhambra in 1914 could
describe Rossini's *William Tell* overture as 'that most hackneyed of all
music-hall classicalism'.[5] The tiny 'corpses musicale' who inhabited
the orchestra pit at most halls could rarely do full justice to these
works. Some of the larger London halls had orchestras of more than
twenty, under professional directors, but more typical were bands of
between five and ten, often comprising semi-professionals. Some
managers and proprietors made determined efforts to raise the standard of even the smallest bands. In the 1870s William Paul, owner of
Paul's Varieties in Leicester, made each of his orchestral players give
regular solos in order both to improve quality and to prove the
individual's worth to the audience.[6] *Il Trovatore* for piano, flute,
clarinet, cornet and drums or whatever must have lost a little of its
initial charm. Nevertheless, within clear limits, the music-hall acted
as a disseminator of a limited operatic repertoire and, for a few, as a
source of musical education. The choral conductor Henry Coward in
the mid-Victorian period and the musicologist Reginald Nettel in the
Edwardian period both saw their youthful music-hall visits as a crucial
source of musical encouragement.[7]

It is generally accepted that the *Lions Comiques* of the early 1860s
were responsible for the first distinctive music-hall songs, thus leading the industry away from its original eclecticism. The *Lions
Comiques* of whom George Leybourne and the Great Vance were the
most famous, were the first great music-hall 'stars'. Crude stereotypes
of London's bohemian upper class, they were marketed with skill by
rival managers. Their early songs 'Champagne Charlie', 'Cliquot,
Cliquot', and 'Night is the Time to have a Spree my Boys' contained

many of the musical and stylistic elements that we associate with the music-hall song – a relatively limited melodic range, essential given the musical limitations of many singers and the audience's need to grasp the lyrics quickly if a rapport was to be established; a verse/chorus rather than strophic structure; the common use of waltz time and the adoption by a singer of an immediately recognisable persona which becomes his trademark.[8] By the 1870s the English music-hall song was an easily identifiable genre. From the 1890s, it was joined by the products of New York's 28th Street, 'Tin Pan Alley'. Such pieces as 'After the Ball', 'Daisy Bell' and 'Sweet Rosie O'Grady', shorter than many English pieces and with strong emphasis on a melodic chorus, began the saturation of the British market with American material.[9]

Reading music-hall songs

Thousands of songs were written, some never seeing public performance, other still firmly entrenched in late twentieth-century popular culture. It is obviously possible to deal with only a tiny proportion of this material and a limited number of themes. Three song types have been highlighted here; songs of social comment, political or, as contemporaries called them, topical songs, and patriotic songs.

At face value, music-hall songs deal far more directly with the conditions of daily existence than any form of English popular music apart from the industrial folk-song. They abound with allusions to current events and fashions and to real places (usually in and around London – Chingford, Hackney, Hendon, The Strand, Piccadilly). The vernacular was often used, enhancing the note of realism. It is hardly surprising, therefore, that both contemporaries and subsequent students of the halls have seen the songs as offering an entree into, especially, working-class lifestyles and attitudes. Following on from his assertion that music-hall was a 'working class' institution, Colin MacInnes argues that: 'We may hear in them, a *vox populi* that is not to be found in Victorian and Edwardian literature'. Some historians, while aware of the need for greater subtlety than MacInnes shows, remain convinced that the songs can unfold a genuine working-class voice. Gareth Stedman Jones, seeing music-hall as an essentially metropolitan phenomenon, argues that,

the music-hall gives us a crucial insight into the attitudes of working-class

London. But this can only be done if working-class music-hall is disentangled from its West End variant with which it is generally confused.

He then commences a stimulating analysis of the songs as reflection and reinforcement of the political culture of working class London, a culture characterised, he claims, by the 'decay of artisan radicalism, the marginal impact of socialism, the largely passive acceptance of imperialism and the throne'.[10]

For all the attractiveness of such arguments, extreme caution must be exercised both when viewing songs as the product of one class, whether nationally or regionally, and as reflections of contemporary views. The social and commercial organisation of the halls generated a far more complex situation than is sometimes allowed for. First, it is surely impossible to claim the songs as the property of an individual class. As has been shown at some length, audiences were never homogeneous, and became ever less so from the 1890s. Sharply-defined class attitudes were unlikely to emerge in such a context. Moreover, even in London, where the halls were to some extent class-based, singers performed virtually the same repertoire, irrespective of the social make-up of the audience. Frederick Anstey's description of the 'four-class' nature of London halls has already been noted. He added: 'The audience, as might be expected, corresponds to the social scale of the particular place of entertainment, but the difference in the performances provided by the four classes of music-halls are far less marked.'[11] Given the pressures placed upon performers by their constant movement between halls – from the 1860s they often 'played' three or four in one evening – and later, by the twice-nightly system, it would have been impossible to tailor each performance to the exact class-base of the audience. To confuse matters still further, many songs were finding their way into more middle-class concert halls and drawing rooms from as early as the 1870s.

Occasionally, examples can be found of material meeting clear disapproval from certain social classes, thus suggesting that it 'belonged' to other classes. In the late nineteenth century three songs dealing with poverty and hardship, 'Poor Old Benjamin the Workhouse Man', 'On Guard' and 'The Blind Collier', were all taken off at West End halls after complaints from the better seats. (As all three were written and performed by Charles Godfrey, it may be that this action says more about Godfrey and/or his style of performance than it does about the 'class' nature of songs.)[12] Furthermore, it may be that different social groups had preferences for certain types of song. In general, however, to designate songs as the product of a specific class is to over-simplify matters.

Similar problems arise when attempts are made to align songs with specific regions. Certainly, London *was* the centre of the industry, many leading performers *were* Londoners and, in the final analysis, it is probable that cockney attitudes and mentality pervaded the song literature to a considerable extent. Nevertheless, with the development of touring from the 1870s, many of the songs cited by Stedman Jones became almost as well known in West Bromwich and Workington as they did in Wapping. Once again the 'disentangling' he recommends is a virtual impossibility.[13]

The issue of song as testimony is also a cloudy one. Music-hall songs, at least those dealing with social relationships and conditions, actually impart far less information than might be expected. This stems largely from the commercial constraints placed upon the halls. Their function was to provide escape. A trade journal commented in 1887 that audiences did not want 'an idealistic performance. Their first, and indeed their only wish was to be amused.' Two years later, the *Era* ventured a similar opinion. 'The real popularity of a music-hall entertainment arises from its ease and comfort. The man who goes to a music-hall expects to be neither worried, ruffled, nor over-excited. . . .'[14] Contentious, uncomfortable topics – trade unionism, the emergence of independent labour, class conflict, pacifism – had to be excluded or dealt within a trivial or comic fashion. This may even account for the lack of songs about work (that is, 'normal' work; colourful occupations such as lighthouse-keeping got the odd mention) often commented upon by students of the halls. People went to forget their daily labour, not be reminded of it. The need to mark out a safe, non-controversial middle ground became greater as managements set out to attract a cross-class clientele. A few managers attempted direct censorship, but most artists tailored their material through professional instinct. Albert Chevalier summed up the problem that faced a performer. 'In a variety show . . . every class of person is represented, and an artist must get in touch with the whole lot of them, or nearly the whole, or his performance won't go as it should.'[15] In this situation avoidance of real-life strife and tragedy become the watchword.

A further limiting factor, as regards the songs both as a product of the working class and as presenting a picture of a past society, is revealed by a study of songwriters. Some performers, including

Chevalier, Coborn and Lauder, wrote a proportion of their own material, but the majority relied on the hundreds of writers who scribbled away for what was often pitiful financial reward. These men (female writers, although not unknown, were extremely rare) are for the most part rather faceless figures, mere names on sheet music, leaving little evidence for future generations to assess. What they have bequeathed is quite fascinating and deserving of some detailed attention, because it illustrates so forcefully how they 'produced', rather than, in any artistic or 'intellectual' manner, 'composed' songs, aiming above all else to meet a commercial need. It is highly significant that the singer-writer Charles Coborn, whose compositions included the immortal 'Two Lovely Black Eyes', considered himself 'a tradesman supplying a public want'.[16]

The major writers claimed a staggering output. G. W. Hunt, who deemed himself to be the first writer to provide words *and* music, thus engineering a break with the tradition of using existing tunes, spoke of making some 7,000 songs between the 1860s and mid-1890s. Joseph Tabrar, best known for 'Daddy Wouldn't Buy me a Bow-wow', claimed to have written 17,000 in a similar period. During one phase, he told an *Era* correspondent in 1894, he was writing thirty songs a day and selling them for one shilling each.[17] Even allowing for massive exaggeration, these individuals were certainly prolific. As already clear from Coborn's statement, they were shrewd businessmen with a clear understanding of their task. On occasions, they showed something akin to contempt for their public.

It is not the kid-gloved critics in the stalls, the eminent literary man, who do the trick for you, but the people in the pit and gallery, who are not afraid to shout their approval or disapproval. And they like simple pathos or homely humour – something to do with the wife and mother-in-law, and so on. The main thing is catchiness. *I would sacrifice everything – rhyme, reason, sense and sentiment, to catchiness. There is, let me tell you, a very great art in making rubbish acceptable.*[18]

These are the words of Felix McGlennon, a Manchester-based Scot who wrote some highly successful words and music from the late 1880s until the early Edwardian period. His output was remarkably broad, a fact which, when taken alongside the attitude expressed above, illustrates how wrong we would be to expect a consistent, working-class voice or indeed *any* class-based voice to emerge from a body of men who saw songs as mere commodities in a market-place. For the American market, he produced settings of several poems by

Thomas Davis (1814–1845), one of the key intellectual figures of the
nationalist-revolutionary Young Ireland movement of the 1840s, as
well as less overtly republican, but nevertheless nationalist, songs,
such as 'The Irish Rebel Emigrants', 'The Sword' and 'Who Fears to
Speak of '98?'. The British halls were given some lachrymose Irish
eviction songs, which will be dealt with later, motto songs such as
'Aim High', (Plenty of work brings happiness, And earns us an
honoured name') and a number of 'British Bulldog', Empire-praising
ditties. 'Leave me Comrades', 'That Ship Belongs to a Lady' and 'We
Mean to Keep the Seas', with its stirring chorus:

> We mean to keep the seas,
> Keep the seas, sweep the seas!
> We count our victories in the days of yore,
> While British sons are bred – bravely bred, nobly led,
> Victory will be ours once more

were three of his best known patriotic pieces.[19] If McGlennon's texts
are taken at face value, they illustrate perplexing ideological inconsis-
tency, a sympathy with Irish republicanism mingling with a regard for
a form of the very imperialist ethos that had helped fuel the oppression
of the Irish. In fact, an acknowledgement of the commercial mode of
much contemporary song production explains a great deal.

All this must not obscure the very considerable achievements of
some of these writers. The fact that so many songs are still in circulation illustrates the skill that went into their creation. The tune of the
'Cock-Linnet Song' is hardly a masterpiece, but it is fun to sing and
easy to grasp.[20] Not surprising that McGlennon stressed 'catchiness'.
My own predilections, are for lyrics, especially the parodies of patriotic song, noted later, and the brilliantly-contrived rhymes created by
Edgar Bateman for Gus Elen in 'If it wasn't for the 'ouses in Between',
such as:

> If yer eyesight didn't fail yer
> Yer could see right to Australia. . . .[21]

Lines like this make one hope that we never become *too* academic
about the halls, applying the methodology of structuralism or Lac-
anian psychoanalysis to T. E. Dunville's 'Bunk-A-Doodle-I-Do' or
Charles Godfrey's 'Hi-Tiddly-Hi-Ti!' Many songs have considerable
charm and appeal and should be enjoyed at face value.

The songwriters' inability to capture authentic class voices was compounded by the fact that some singers from working-class back-grounds became so far removed from their original lifestyle by the financial rewards on offer that it seems unlikely that they could compensate for the writers' failings.[22] The limitations are clear. Music-hall was an *industry*, capable of reacting in a sophisticated manner to changes in the market, and not a spontaneous popular creation. The commercial restrictions that followed from this generated a song literature which at times obscures almost as much as it reveals about Victorian and Edwardian England.

Alongside the interpretive problems emanating from the commercial basis of the halls lay a further set posed by persona and performance. Individual singers and writers had their idiosyncracies, which make it difficult, and indeed dangerous, to make generalisations based on specific songs. Marie Lloyd tended to view the problems of married life as a comic disaster, as in the still much sung 'Cock-Linnet Song', but another, more sentimental performer, might portray marriage as an enduring and enriching experience. Albert Chevalier specialised to some extent in such material, most notably in 'My Old Dutch':

> We've been together now for forty years,
> And it don't seem a day too much.
> For there ain't a lady living in the land,
> As I'd swop for my dear old Dutch.

Generalisation must be based on a broad scan of performers and repertoire. In order to extract information, it is important not to focus on just one singer or one song in the hope of finding some ultimate statement. A number of recent critics have given particular emphasis to the work of certain performers. Gus Elen, for example, who specialised in witty delineations of costermonger life, often using the exact speech patterns of his father's and grandfather's generations, is far more in vogue at present amongst academic writers on music-hall than, say, Eugene Stratton, a blacked-up American with a penchant for dramatic, if sentimental, pieces. The explanation is twofold. Elen's edgy, realistic songs are far more appealing to late twentieth-century taste than Stratton's work, while songs of London life are easier to decode than 'Lily of Laguna', 'Little Dolly Daydream' or 'I May be Crazy', the story of a negro horse thief on the run. Neither current prejudice nor superficial ease of interpretation should be allowed to interfere with the process of analysis.[23]

The issue of performance is also problematic. The historian meets words and music frozen in print, which might, during the course of performance, have carried meanings more complex than is first apparent. A gesture, a comment to the audience or a musical embellishment by the orchestra could alter messages considerably. The *lion comique* songs are a case in point. Superficially (and in my opinion, this was the intention), they appear to hymn the joys of upper-class bonhomie. However, they could also be used by the singer, with help from audience cheering and jeering at the correct moments, to satirise or complement the working-class and lower-middle-class 'swells' who aped aristocratic fashion and who were keen music-hall goers. 'Champagne Charlie' sung to south London shop-assistant 'toffs' might, partly through the singer's actions, gestures and tone, and partly through the mediation of the audience, have been a very different piece from what it appears to be a hundred and twenty years later. There is no easy solution, for historians will never be able to recapture the exact moments of communication from the limited sources available. However, the essential simplicity of the songs must have imposed clear limits upon the singer's opportunity to re-work and re-interpret his or her material. While accepting that some songs are especially difficult to read, contemporary scholars should not be too intimidated by the potential complexity of music-hall song.

One problem remains before settling to the task of actually looking at some songs: how do we know that the songs studied are in any way representative, or indeed were actually performed to any significant extent? Obviously, with all but the best-known, still-performed songs, there must always be an element of doubt, which offers yet another reason for circumspection when drawing conclusions. In general, however, songs were not published until there was clear evidence of at least fleeting popularity and, therefore, any song unearthed from any sheet-music collection can normally be assumed to have had some degree of exposure.

Despite all these hesitations, music-hall songs *do* have value as a source of testimony, provided that they are seen as purveying generalised attitudes which *may* have been held by the working class, but were by no means their sole preserve. What follows is an attempt to draw out the contemporary attitudes and beliefs which do emerge from the songs. The sections on songs of social comment and political song also include investigation of how the industry's structure influenced the treatment of certain 'awkward' social and political issues.

Chapter 6

Social and political comment in music-hall song

Music-hall songs were replete with contemporary references, even after the increased performance of the socially and geographically more indeterminate American 'Tin Pan Alley' songs from the early 1890s. Love, marriage, poverty, leisure, class and many other topics were dealt with, sometimes overtly but often more obliquely, in innumerable songs.

What emerges most forcibly from a detailed reading of music-hall song is a profoundly conservative picture of life. Key social institutions are always present, on an unchanging backdrop. The existence of a huge gap between rich and poor was accepted, and indeed at certain stages, as in the *Lions Comiques* phase of the 1860s, the spendthrift upper-class youth was held up as an object of attraction. There was nothing wrong in having money to waste.

> Champagne Charlie is my name!
> Good for any game at night my boys!
> Who'll come and join me in a spree.[2]

The social order was immutable. Some might try to escape, usually thanks to an unexpected inheritance (a common theme in music-hall song). But their escape was either shortlived, as with Harry Champion's Uncle Bill whose recently bequeathed gold watch was in reality 'old iron', or won them disapproval, like the subject of Gus Elen's 'E Dunno where 'E Are'.

> But som'ow since 'e's 'ad the bullion left
> 'E's altered for the wust,
> When I see the way 'e treats old pals
> I am filled with nuffing but disgust.

Similarly, those who transgressed the rules of marriage were rewarded with tears. In 'The German Band', one of G. W. Hunt's first successful compositions, Arthur Lloyd sang of a wife leaving him for a strolling flageolet player. Her new love deserts, however, and she resorts to 'charring' for one shilling a day. Also in the 1860s, Vance told of a husband, sitting on a Margate-bound steamer with his arm around a young girl's waist, suddenly disturbed by the unexpectedly early arrival of his family.[3] Again, in 1888 Vesta Tilley's 'The Parrot and The Parson' dealt with a parson taking advantage of his wife's absence to 'canoodle' with the cook. Unfortunately, on his wife's return, the parrot told all, the cook got sacked and the parson smacked. Many more examples could be given. Music-hall audiences were reminded most strongly that those who ducked society's conventions would suffer the consequences.

While men were 'found out' as often as women in this type of song and were forever hen-pecked, in general womens' dependency upon men and their loyalty to marriage, no matter how awful, was unquestioned. Certainly, from late century some female artists, notably Marie Lloyd with her fine clothing and her 'knowing' manner, Vesta Victoria, likewise well-attired and singing of the problems of marrying older men ('Now I have to call him Father') and the male impersonator Vesta Tilley, who deflated the social pretensions of the lower-middle-class 'swells' in her audience, gave the expanding female audience both a view of female success and a chance to laugh at men. Even in the earlier period, songs concerning supposedly sophisticated young blades tricked by clever young women were extremely common. G. W. Hunt produced a rash of such numbers in the 1870s. Overall, however, a woman's place was clearly established. Home, husband and children were what really mattered.[4]

It is worth noting here that sexual relationships were treated in a muted manner. They were not ignored as is sometimes suggested. Songs are full of references to kissing – 'spooning' was a popular euphemism. G. H. MacDermott specialised in *double-entendres* which left little to the imagination, notably in 'Jeremiah Jones' and the extremely popular 'Turn Off the Gas at the Meter' (encored six times at Day's, Birmingham, in 1877).[5] This latter piece, by John Stamford, told of a miserly Scot, one Peter McClean, who took on a maid:

> For with the old fellow,
> She'd go down to the cellar
> To turn off the gas at the meter.
>
> He'd turn off the gas at the meter,
> He'd turn off the gas at the meter,
> Every night he would go
> To the regions below,
> To turn off the gas at the meter'.

Nevertheless, the truly explicit discussion and description of sexual matters, found so often in folk-song, was absent. Couples having 'a jovial spree amongst the barley raking', a young serving maiden finding nine months after 'bedmaking' for her master that she 'could scarcely lace her stays nor tie her apron string', had no place on the music-hall stage.[6] Whether this break with earlier musical forms emanated from the stricter moral code of the age, the desire of managements for decency and respectability, or from the fact that the rural images so central to much erotic folk-song were irrelevant or incomprehensible to urban audiences is open to debate, but it is obvious that sexual as well as social life was dealt with in a conservative manner.

A strong element of parochialism represents a further strand of music-hall conservatism. Any provincial artist attempting to attain success in London was forced to offer a stereotype to their audiences. Some, like George Formby senior, with his 'Lancashire loon' character 'John Willie', had great success. His evocatively titled 'Since I Parted my Hair in the Middle' and 'Playing the Game in the West', with its final chorus line 'And I'm not going home till a quarter to ten, 'cause it's my night out, are clever depictions of a provincial innocent in the capital.[7] (This undoubtedly helped reinforce the somewhat patronising attitude towards provincials held by many Londoners.) It is significant that one of Yorkshire's top artists, Chas W. Whittle, gained his major success not with the proud 'My Girl's a Yorkshire Girl', but 'Let's All Go Down the Strand'.

Accompanying this conservatism was a deep-rooted fatalism. Life simply happened to music-hall characters: they had no control over their destiny.[8] Irate husbands, landlords and outsized wives were forever finding an unexpected moment in which to 'bonk' or 'bop' the subject of the song. Luck, as in the inheritance theme noted above, offered the only escape route. Most of the time, people 'made the best of it', as J. W. Rowley encouraged them to in 'Life is Like a Game of

See-Saw', another G. W. Hunt number.

> Some people rail against the world
> Why should they – ?
> Now I take it, just as it comes
> Because the world,
> Is what we choose to make it.

'Trust your friends' – the halls put great store on friendship – 'enjoy the present, forget the future' was often the message.

Just occasionally, audiences might be jolted a little. This was most likely in the earlier days of the music-hall industry. In this period, when halls were under independent control and were, to a great extent, class-based, a more critical element was possible. Walter Ramsay, a popular performer in Morton's early years at the Canterbury, included the recitation *Satan's Address to his Imps* in his repertoire. Satan sends out his imps with the promise of a prize for the one returning with the finest article of torture. The winner returns with the cat o'nine tails and the 1834 Poor Law Amendment Act. Similarly, according to Samuel McKechnie, writing in the 1930s, a popular music-hall song of the mid-Victorian period was 'The Daily News'. Set to the tune of 'Green Grow the Rushes' – further evidence of the musical eclecticism of the early halls – it offers a stark picture of contemporary class relationships.

> The daily news is this, my boys –
> The rich get richer every day,
> Monopolising all life's joys,
> While the poor the piper have to pay.
> French cooks and tailors for the great,
> For the small hard fare, and oft no shoes;
> And hundreds forced to emigrate –
> That's bona-fide daily news[9]

Many commentators have noted that certain Tyneside performers and singers were able to produce highly combative material in front of the relatively homogeneous audiences of keelmen, engineers and pitmen in the Newcastle halls. The songs of Joe Wilson (1841–1874) are particularly noteworthy. Songs like 'No work' and 'The Strike', both written in dialect and set to 'traditional' tunes, bring together industrial folk-songs and music-hall in powerful statements of working-class confidence and intent. 'The Strike' was written in support of workers striking for a nine-hour day at Armstrong's engineering works in 1871.

> Is nine oors an unreasonable movement?
> Is't not plenty to labour for men?
> Let them that condemned hev a try on't
> An see if they'll not alter the plan.
> An if long oors industry increases,
> Hev they found oot wi' the 'oors that *they've* tried?
> Their capital grows through wor labour,
> Wey, it's mair to their shyem, that they'll find'.[10]

We should not romanticise the early period as one of intense radicalism; Tyneside appears not to have been typical, while the most popular material of the 1860s, the songs of the *Lions Comiques*, glorified rather than criticised the upper middle classes. Similarly, one of the most popular performers of the 1860s was Harry Clifton, who specialised in motto songs, 'Paddle Your Own Canoe', 'Pulling Hard Against the Stream', and 'Work, Boys, Work and be Contented', which were bastardised Samuel Smiles.

> Work boys, work and be contented,
> So long as you've enough to buy a meal.
> For if you will but try, you'll be wealthy bye and bye,
> If you'll only put yer shoulder to the wheel.[11]

Nor should we overstress the division between the 1850s and 1860s and the late Victorian and Edwardian period. A radical strand, albeit an extremely attenuated one, was preserved by a small number of writers and performers throughout the period. But it is inescapable that as music-hall matured into an ever larger industry, radical social criticism was all but abandoned.

Glimmers of an atrophied radicalism lingered on in the later period. One important writer in this context was E. W. Rogers. It would be incorrect to claim him as a truly radical presence. His output included, for example, 'The New Policeman' which showed strong anti-alien sentiment. However, he exhibited a greater degree of social criticism than most. His 'After the Show' (1894) written for Arthur Lennard, deals with a music-hall singer's decline into poverty and alcoholism. 'Master and Man' (1892), performed by Charles Godfrey, is almost a critique of the existing social order, and indeed would be, but for the deadening of the song's impact by the inclusion of a few comical verses. The song presents a series of incidents in which the master and the man enjoy the varied benefits of their respective classes: 'The Lord Chamberlain summons the master, and the schoolboard folk summon the man'; The master shoots grouse, the man 'shoots the moon'; a policeman is assaulted, the master is fined two pounds and the man receives a month in prison.

Rogers also directed some scorn at the police force, the one form of authority to fall foul of the music-hall. The 'comic' policeman formed part of London theatre entertainment from the 1830s and was, of course, later immortalised by W. S. Gilbert in *The Pirates of Penzance*. Policemen seem to have featured in music-hall song from at least the late 1860s, when Vance launched 'Peter Potts the Peeler'. To some music-hall owners, and to some elements of their audience, the police officer was a potential or actual irritant. His presence in the halls suggested that they lacked respectability: his treatment of after-hours drinking, street-gambling and general youthful exuberance made him many enemies. The late Victorian police force were also not entirely above reproach; drinking on duty was a common problem in most provincial forces until the very late nineteenth century. It is therefore not surprising that the policeman was an acceptable target for some rather barbed criticism.[12] Rogers' two best-known 'police' songs, both from the 1890s, were 'The New Policeman', which suggested that beer and women were a policeman's greatest concerns, and his celebrated 'Ask a P'liceman', performed by James Fawn. This piece begins harmlessly with the line 'If you want to know the time ask a P'liceman', but it soon becomes clear that the 'p'liceman' has talents of dubious nature. In particular, he can use his influence to circumvent the licensing laws:

> If drink you want and pubs are shut,
> Go to the man in blue,
> Say you're thirsty, and good-natured, and
> He'll show you what to do.

> If you want to get a drink, ask a P'liceman
> He'll manage it, I think, will a P'liceman
> He'll produce the flowing pot
> If the pubs are shut or not,
> He could open all the lot –
> Ask a P'liceman.

A little revenge for many years of interference in the illicit enjoyment of the working classes.[13]

These songs represent the nearest approximation to a class-conscious, critical tone within the late Victorian music-hall song. But it is clear that such songs are rare, and are extremely muted compared with, for example, the Joe Wilson songs quoted earlier, or, even more

dramatically, with some of the Irish republican songs of the nineteenth century.[14]

In general, when the music-hall dealt with poverty and hardship, it
did so in a safe but, at the same time, essentially parasitic manner,
using tragic situations to enhance a theatrical mood. Social plight was
commonly used as a backdrop to a song to generate a scene of sadness,
sentimentality and even humour. This ploy appears at it most ingenious in Albert Chevalier's introduction to 'My Old Dutch'. Chevalier,
dressed as an aged cockney, entered arm-in-arm with his equally aged
'Donah', and walked towards a set inscribed 'workhouse'. Outside
the workhouse entrance sat a porter, who, on receiving their admittance cards, tried to take Albert's wife through one door marked
'women' and Albert through the 'mens'. Realising the horror of their
plight Albert yelled: 'You can't do this to us – we've been together for
forty years'. Exit porter and wife, and Albert moved into his immortal
song:

> I got a pal: a real old out-and-outer,
> She's a dear old gal, and I'll tell you all about her.

Gareth Stedman Jones claims this backdrop to be 'the whole point' of
the song, an attempt to point out the evils of the poor-house system.[15]
This seems a decidedly twentieth-century interpretation, given the
development of the song. Chevalier simply seems to be using a tragic
situation in order to create a mood, for the workhouse issue disappears
entirely from then on, to be replaced by a hymn to the virtues of
marital content. Singers were far more likely to blur the painful
elements of existence than to focus on them. In 'The Warden's Story',
Alf Chester sang of a white-haired mother pleading valiantly for the
jury to be lenient on her son, gone astray but determined to change his
ways. They proclaim 'not guilty'.

> Their decision I've heard was opposed to the law,
> But who cares, for that was justice I am sure.

To pretend that the late-Victorian legal system could incorporate such
a notion of moral justice is romantic to the point of fantasy.

The tragedy of rural Ireland was also ruthlessly exploited in the late
nineteenth and early twentieth centuries by a number of (mainly
Irish?) singers and writers. Evictions were made the vehicle for lachrymose ballads with fairytale endings. Tom Maguire's 'Don't Burn
The Cabin Down' (1894), performed by Pat Ricks, told of a family

about to be evicted into the snow on Christmas Eve, because they had defaulted on one rent payment while the father was away fishing, unaware of his family's plight. Miraculously, a young priest rushes in to tell them all is well as the father has returned to pay his debt. The song concludes:

> The Lord of all land-lords
> Looks down from his throne,
> Rejoice my poor woman,
> Your home is your own.

Felix McGlennon's 'Spare the old Mud Cabin' (1903) tells a similar tale of aged parents on the point of eviction saved by the timely return of their sailor son. It is sometimes possible to find criticism in these Irish songs, and indeed, their very performance at least reminded their English audience of the Irish land question. A charitable student, therefore, might view these works as an attempt to make social comment within the limited avenues available in the music-hall industry. Stylistic and commercial considerations were never far away, however. Here was tragedy, suitably presented for consumption by a mass audience.

It is significant that the major beneficiary of music-hall's social conscience was a figure who, although deserving of sympathy, hardly constituted a major element in the catalogue of late nineteenth and early twentieth-century social problems – the old soldier in the workhouse. He was a fitting choice for such a militaristic institution. The soldiers who received the deepest concern were, inevitably, the survivors from the Crimea (preferably from the Charge) and the India mutiny, campaigns supposedly representative of British pluck and fortitude at their height. The instigator of this style of song was Charles Godfrey, who, having had considerable success with a song about a derelict, entitled 'Poor old Benjamin, the Workhouse Man', and with a number of songs about the Crimea, fused the two themes. The result was *On Guard*, a dramatic 'song scena' in the first half of which Godfrey appeared as a soldier in the Crimea, standing resolutely to attention, only to be struck down by a stray bullet; and in the second as the soldier, now an old man, who hobbled into a country churchyard, sat down on a gravestone to complain of being neglected and forgotten and then lay down to die amid falling snow. (On one unfortunate occasion, the stage-manager of a northern hall misinterpreted Godfrey's instructions to 'throw down some newspaper' as a

way of creating a snowstorm, and instead of tearing it up and flutter-
ing it gently down, as Godfrey intended, simply rolled up whole
newspapers and pelted the doubtless astounded figure below.) Godfrey had enormous success. 'Many a furtive tear drops into a B & S
when Mr Charles Godfrey, in a white wig, sings the woes of the old
soldier', wrote a contemporary observer, and inevitably an enormous
volume of songs and sketches projecting similar stories and sentiment
emerged.[16]

> Wounded at Balaclava, while fighting as Englishmen do;
> Quite forgotten, left to starve, now that his eyes are dim
> That's what he did for England and England did for him.

This was the lament in *Forgotten* or *He was one of the Light Brigade*, by
George Leyton, an ex-patriot American from New Orleans, who had
served for a period in the British army. He even began a special fund
for veterans of the Crimea and the India Mutiny, financed by the sale
of his song 'Boys of the Chelsea School', which by 1912 had raised
over £3,600 – and doubtless made his song one of the most popular of
the period.[17] Obviously, there *were* old soldiers in financial difficulties, but the music-hall produced an amount of material out of all
proportion to the reality of the situation. The popularity of this stage
character should be seen not merely as an aspect of the patriotic
element of the music-hall, but as another example of music-hall
finding a highly effective way of evoking sympathy for a social problem that could appeal to the majority and offend very few.

More remarkable than the use of tragedy to serve the sentimental
balladeer, is the way that poverty, hardship and unemployment also
served to assist the *comic* singer. Thus in his 'We're Taking it in
Turns', James Fawn begins with a protestation of total poverty, a
situation which forces him to share a bed. By the second verse, he is
sharing his girlfriend and by the third, due to some miraculous
financial transformation, he is taking it in turns to get drunk on
scotch. Similarly, Wilkie Bard begins 'Troubles' with the claim that
he has been out of work for life, after which he gets punched on the
nose, loses his hat at a 'socialistic meeting' and finally falls off a bus
after a girl kisses him. Again, in Marie Lloyd's 'Cock-linnet Song', the
'moonlight flit' merely serves as a background to a song about a beery
housewife 'dilly-dallying' on the way to a new house. The comic
singer was *always* poor. A contemporary satirical song captured this
well:

> The British comic singer is a simple minded man;
> His ditties are constructed on a regulation plan . . .
> And – Broke! Broke! Broke! he's invariably broke,
> And his audience consider this a joke.
> With a reference if he can to the coming broker's man;
> But there's humour in the *fact* of being broke.[18]

These claims of poverty seem hollow when compared with songs which were genuinely dealing with the realities of working-class existence. James Fawn merely uses bed-sharing as a launching-point for a string of unrelated comic incidents. Joe Wilson's 'Keep Your Feet Still Geordie Hinney', written some thirty years earlier for a Tyneside audience, uses the same idea. However, Wilson describes the bed-sharing in a matter-of-fact manner with none of the music hall's overstatement, and builds a whole song around it.

> Wor Geordie and Bob Johnson byeth lay i' one bed
> In a little lodgin' house that's doon the store . . .

Bob's delightful dreams of his wedding to Mary, who in reality is pledged to one Jim Green, are disturbed by Geordie's thrashing feet:

> Keep your feet still Geordie Hinney, let's be happy for the neet,
> For Aa may not be se happy thro' the day,
> So give us that bit comfort, Keep your feet still Geordie lad,
> And divvent drive me bonny dreams away.[19]

Traditionally, such treatment of hardship has been explained as the 'dressing up of tragedy in comic clothing' or 'the deflection of poverty through comedy'. There is doubtless an element of truth in such an interpretation. Some members of the audience must have experienced the things they saw on the stage and felt better after laughing at them. However, to a large extent, as the quotation from 'The British Comic Singer' suggested, poverty seems to be a comic convention.

Conventions must have an historical origin. To a large extent this particular one is merely stylistic, reaching back to the tradition of the folk-song which often began either with a serious protestation of poverty and its effects, or with a simple statement establishing the singer's lower-class origins. 'I'm a poor cotton weaver as many one knows' begins 'Jone o' Grinfield', one of the best-known early industrial folk-songs. 'I am a brisk lad but my fortune is bad, And I am most wonderful poor'; 'I am a hand-weaver to my trade'; 'It's of a berisk young plough boy, he was ploughing on the main'; this list could be extended greatly.[20] It is possible that early music-hall performers *were* more likely to be from a working-class background and singing to a working audience and, therefore to carry this 'folk' tradition into the halls made sense. But by the late nineteenth century, the claims to poverty are meaningless. Therefore, care must be taken not to interpret songs too literally, as Colin MacInnes does when claiming that the 'moonlight flit' was so common a theme that 'one may guess it was a familiar experience to many of the audience'. More probably, users of this and similar themes were either merely making an empty theatrical statement, or fulfilling a function suggested by the literary critic and music hall admirer, Max Beerbohm. 'The aim of the music hall is, in fact, to cheer the lower classes up by showing them a life uglier and more sordid than their own.'[21]

Political song

Overtly political material was not a major strand of music-hall performance, which is hardly surprising given the nature of the industry. There was, however, something of a vogue for political song from the late 1860s until the early 1890s, and markedly so in the 1880s. This pattern reflects broad changes within the structure of British politics. The death of Palmerston in 1865 and the controversy generated by the reform debates of 1866–67 stimulated a revival of the two-party system that had been so weak between 1846 and 1866. It was inevitable that such change should find some reflection, no matter how shadowy, on the music-hall stage. Similarly, the 1880s was in terms of party a lively decade, largely due to the reactions to the policies of the Liberal leader Gladstone.[22] It is also possible to detect explanations from within the industry itself for the political song 'craze' of the 1880s. In the late 1870s and early 1880s G. H. ('The Great') MacDermott was arguably the premier music-hall star. As will be seen, MacDermott, beginning with his well-known 'Jingo Song' ('MacDermott's Warsong' was the published title) of 1877, included a considerable body of political material in his repertoire. Almost inevitably, aspiring singers, most noticeably Walter Monroe, Harry Rickards and Fred Coyne, imitated him, hoping for similar reward.[23]

There were three basic types of political song. At the most unsophisticated level political catch phrases and the idiosyncracies of individual politicians were used as a basis for comic song. Thus, 'I've worked eight Hours This Day', one of the singer Tom Costello's

(1863–1943) early numbers, far from being the Labour anthem its title suggests, in fact relates comic incidents resulting from an over-literal interpretation of the eight-hour day. The barber shaves only one side of a customer's face, a jockey will not race any further:

> The others may pass, let my horse eat grass,
> I won't work a half minute longer.

Suffragism offered endless fun and received great 'praise' because its arguments were taken to logical conclusions, men could in Gus Elen's words, 'get boozed at 'ome, and do no work at all'.[24]

Another popular way of harnessing politics to the needs of the performer was to use contemporary issues to generate audience participation. The Great Vance enjoyed some success in the 1860s with 'Is He Guilty?', during which he asked the audience to offer, via boos or cheers, their opinions on the questions of the day. Managements were careful, however, to prevent these performers stimulating real friction. Thus, in 1889 when, at the Trocadero, Charles Collette performed a song favouring Home Rule and thereby occasioned considerable disturbance, the manager immediately withdrew the song from the bill.[25]

What is crucial about these songs, at first sight no more than an excuse for audience exuberance, was that, with very few exceptions (Collette's was one), they were constructed to favour the Conservative Party. Certainly, the Liberal case would be stated and perhaps some hint of praise given to an individual, but Conservatives inevitably had much better treatment, were only rarely criticised and were usually the subjects of a hymn of praise in a triumphal final verse. The whole process is well illustrated by 'The Tablet of Fame', performed by Vesta Tilley and written in 1886 or 1887 by none other than Oswald Stoll. Whether or not the song reflects Stoll's political standpoint, it seems fitting that the man who perhaps did most to make the halls respectable should have produced such a song.

It deals with seven public figures – four Conservatives, two Liberals and the Queen – the numerical balance thus, from the outset, firmly in the Conservatives' favour. Gladstone and Bright represent the Liberal quota, Bright in fact receiving, by the music hall standards, a considerable acolade:

> An advocate was he, that trade be rendered free,
> In which we hardly think that he was right.
> But errors we'll forgive and wish that long may live
> Of Quakers first and best, good old John Bright.

Perhaps Miss Tilley felt safe in honouring a man aged seventy-six and at the very end of his career. But in comparison to the attitude to the Conservatives, this amounts to damning with faint praise. Salisbury was congratulated upon his brilliant diplomacy, Lord Randolph Churchill depicted, perhaps doubtfully, as a man who would 'Office forsake 'ere promises he'll break', and above all as:

> A pillar of the state, unequalled in debate,
> With intellect of excellence rare

The climax came with a eulogy to the late Beaconsfield (rarely mere 'Disraeli' in music-hall song)

> Old England now misses a former premier –
> A statesman – a hero – a man!

Gladstone enjoyed no such favour from music-hall writers and performers (until his death!): in fact, quite the contrary. Changeability and long-windedness were depicted as his major failings. 'Weather-wise Notions', written in 1889, is fairly typical.[26]

> The GOM's speeches are sensible when they're short,
> Proper use of his tongue and pen he has never been taught.
> If his views of this year you compare with the last,
> The hand of my weatherglass travels round fast,
> And points to the future as well as the past.

Above all, he was seen as the unforgiveable betrayer of Gordon and of Empire. Thus in *Salisbury and Gladstone*, composed and sung by F. V. St Clair, who advertised himself in the music-hall press as 'the leading topical singer', the final verse allowed Salisbury to answer Gladstone's comment that the Tories were too fond of war with the following riposte.

> Your policy was always too late,
> You would send out our troops when the mischief was done,
> Poor Gordon was left to his fate.
> How many brave heroes in Egypt were slain?[27]

A number of Liberal supporters believed certain music-hall entertainers to be in Conservative pay. They were most concerned by MacDermott, whose Tory songs represent the third form of political statement, pure pro-Conservative propaganda with no attempt at the balance, albeit of a limited kind, seen in the 'Tablet of Fame'. His songs included 'Master Dilke spilt the Milk' (relishing the embarrassment suffered by the Liberals as a result of a celebrated divorce scandal concerning one of their senior politicians), 'True Blues' (with its chorus line, 'W. E. G. (Gladstone) is in a state of lunacy'), as well as 'True Blues Forever', 'Not Much or It's Better than Nothing At All' and 'The Flower Our Hero Loved'. The Liberals' conspiratorial thesis is both impossible to prove and almost certainly incorrect. MacDermott simply appears to have discovered a persona which guaranteed him success, perhaps particularly in the West End halls where at one stage the 'rowdy swell and medical student' element knocked people's hats over their eyes if they were not removed at mention of Beaconsfields name.[28] Nevertheless, it is easy to see how such a theory arose.

Some historians, notably Laurence Senelick, have explained away music-hall Toryism as mere theatrical convention 'as traditional and as unquestioned as the comedian's red nose'.[29] He argues that if the sentiments were intended to be taken seriously, audiences in Liberal strongholds would not have accepted the performance of the songs as easily as they appear to have done. There is contemporary evidence to support this view. While reviewing a sketch at the Bradford Alhambra in 1914, a local journalist noted that: 'Lloyd George is blamed for everything, of course, but nobody can take the smallest offence. The Liberal Party may call it broad irony the Tory humourous exaggeration, and both can laugh heartily enough'.[30] But while music-hall Toryism did perhaps *become* a convention, at its zenith in the 1880s and 1890s, it was surely a genuine reflection of the ideological standpoint of the industry's leaders.

The Liberals at national level, and sometimes in conjunction with 'progressives' and socialists at local level, exhibited a cluster of attitudes that challenged much of the music-hall's rationale. Sections of the party were either pacifist or strongly critical of certain abrasive aspects of British foreign policy, while the music-hall fostered a confident, brash patriotism. The strong nonconformist element in provincial Liberalism gave it a tone far removed from the carefree, live-for-the moment mentality preached by the music-hall. Above all, the Liberals' attempts to control the drink trade, beginning with the 1872 Licencing Act, made the inevitable enemy of an entertainment industry born in the public house and strongly allied to the increasingly Tory brewing trade. This generalised enmity took clear shape to individual owners as Liberal magistrates in various towns at various times took action against them.[31] It is hardly surprising that the Liberals found no sympathy on the music-hall stage.

It is possible that music-hall Toryism was made easier in this period by the absence from the halls, especially in the provinces, of the Liberal, non-conformist working and lower middle class. At least one contemporary observer saw the halls as unpopular in the provinces 'with the better stamp of working men' and it is certainly difficult to see how more serious-minded, 'respectable' audiences could have enjoyed performances which they might find both morally and politically distasteful.[32] Only from the late 1890s, as religious attitudes altered and the halls set out to attract a broad audience (and consequently stage Toryism diminished as a force) could provincial Liberals succumb.

The music-hall song is clearly a limited source of comment upon the social and political life of later nineteenth and early twentieth century England. It ignored vast areas of working-class experience and used others merely as a method of setting the scene for a specific act and song. Yet, for all these weaknesses, it illustrates the great conservatism of the age. The thousands of working-class people who were happy to be entertained by these songs must have found the ideals and attitudes they offered broadly sympathetic. The picture of English society, including, but not exclusively, working-class society, that the music-hall offers us, humane, but opposed to radical change and largely accepting the existing class structure, could not have been merely the work of music-hall song and sketch writers. It reflects at least a part of the reality of Victorian and Edwardian England.

Of equal significance is the effect that these songs had upon contemporary audiences. Obviously, a mechanistic approach must be avoided. One of the most significant developments within the field of literary criticism within recent years has been the realisation that texts are open to multiple readings.[33] For the 'general reader', in particular, there can be no 'correct' interpretation. In the same way, song lyrics are open to interpretation, each member of the audience bringing his own experience to bear upon his absorption of a particular song. He might ignore some messages, fail to understand others. 'Ask a P'liceman' might be a simple, face-value comic song to one person, but a biting commentary to another who had recently brushed with the forces of law and order.

However, as has already been stated, we must not be too clever. Felix McGlennon, E. W. Rogers and the others were not James Joyces, and most music-hall songs were open to only a limited field of interpretation. Their messages were usually clear and it is hard to believe that these messages which reached such a large audience, and one which was an essentially young audience still building a view of their world, did not play a role in structuring or reinforcing many key social and political attitudes.[34]

First, it is perhaps incorrect to assume that it was only the working classes who were most open to influence. It is possible that by showing the working class to the *middle classes* in a reasonably sympathetic manner, the music-hall song played a large part in lowering class barriers. It must be remembered that there was at times a genuine fear of the working class amongst their 'superiors'. That fear must have abated a little in order for the middle class to begin attending music-halls, but, once there, what they found was a stereotyped working man or woman, which was guaranteed to comfort them further: fatalistic, a little 'boozy' perhaps, but cheerful and free from the taint of political radicalism. It was perhaps Chevalier and Elen with their costers who did the most in this respect. Chevalier played a particularly important role as he actually had an effect on an audience beyond that of the halls.

The halls may have also helped shape popular political conceptions. It is unlikely that they changed the views of those already committed to the support of radical politics, and it was probably not a large enough influence upon people's lives to alter voting alignments. What it might have done, however, both by providing an avenue of escapism and by presenting an easily-absorbed dilution of current events which excluded any discussion of 'progressive' politics and genuine class conflict, was to have consolidated conservative tendencies within the popular intellectual climate and to have directed political 'agnostics' away from a radical standpoint. Such influences were perhaps strongest in London, the heart of the music-hall industry. That the major leisure industry of Victorian and Edwardian Britain was so profoundly conservative in every sense is of some significance to the structure and development of English politics.[35]

Chapter 7

Patriotism, jingoism and imperialism

There has been considerable debate in recent decades over the popular response to the 'New Imperialism' of the late nineteenth century. Given that some contemporaries, most noticably the anti-imperialist J. A. Hobson, saw the music-hall as a profoundly jingoistic institution, it is hardly surprising that a part of this debate has focused on the halls' imperialist contribution. Some writers, usually after a decidedly cursory glance at the available materials, have minimised music-hall's role. Others, after digging deeper, have found some justification for contemporary statements. No apology is made for raising the subject in depth here.[1]

First, it is essential to appreciate the sheer weight of material dealing with war and empire in the music-hall tradition. If the old joke that World War Two was started by Vera Lynn's agent holds any grain of truth, then historians of empire should perhaps have a closer look at the men behind the careers of Fred Albert, Charles Godfrey, G. H. MacDermott, Leo Dryden, F. V. St Clair and George Leyton, to name only the best-known of those who made bellicose support for British overseas achievement a central element of their performance. More importantly, the essentially dismissive attitude of some historians, noted above, must be countered. Obviously, we must be aware of Hugh Cunningham's plea to avoid 'the rather conspiratorial version of music-hall history', which sees the halls almost as a tool of the ruling classes, foisting imperialist ideology on to a pliant working and lower middle class. It is impossible, however, to believe that such a mass of material presented by entertainers of high standing did not exert some considerable influence upon the popular imagination and that its existence illustrates a considerable enthusiasm for British Imperial exploits.[2]

There is need for precision when discussing popular attitudes to empire. Three words recur in this account: patriotism, jingoism and imperialism. Patriotism is taken to mean simply love of country. Few historians would argue that such a feeling was not present both in music-hall songs and as a general sentiment at large. 'Patriotic' is used here as a convenient shorthand to describe all songs dealing with British military and imperial activity. 'Jingoism' is defined here in the words of Hobson, as an 'inverted patriotism whereby the love of one's own nation is transformed into the hatred of another nation'.[3] 'Imperialism' is obviously a more complex term, but when applied to the popular conception of British achievement it must include some notion of the ideas of racial superiority, the civilising mission, the economic motive, the colonies as a 'family' and other ideas which informed 'serious' imperial debate. As with the specific issue of music hall 'imperialism' there is no real consensus amongst historians on the wider question of whether 'jingoism' or 'imperialism' were deeply rooted amongst the working class of Victorian and Edwardian England.[4] The evidence that follows suggests that jingoism, and perhaps even a simple imperialism, were certainly on offer to working-class members of the music-hall audience and that some, especially those open to the many other similar contemporary imperialistic influences, may have accepted them.

Depiction of Britain's military exploits and territorial expansion was hardly a new feature of either song or theatre; indeed the spectacle and the heartbreak of warfare were amongst the longest-established themes in both forms. Music-hall was at first merely feeding on established custom. From the 1850s singers referred to current foreign policy and international events. By the early 1870s, Fred Albert, fast becoming music-hall's first overtly 'topical singer', was including a considerable degree of patriotic material in his repertoire.[5] The hall's really close association with the flag appears to have begun in spring 1877 however.

In April of that year, Russia declared war upon Turkey and, despite fierce Turkish resistance, gradually gained military superiority. British fears centred on the possibility of the Russians reaching Constantinople, thus gaining direct access to the Mediterranean and challenging Britain's naval supremacy in that area. In fact, British military involvement was not required and an armistice was eventually signed in January 1878, with the Russians too exhausted and too concerned about the presence of British warships in the Sea of

Marmara to risk an attack on Constantinople. The Congress of Berlin in the summer of 1878 finally settled many of the territorial issues at stake. The conflict had massive domestic repercussions, the Liberal Party under Gladstone being anti-Turkish because of the 'Bulgarian Atrocities' of 1876 in which some 12,000 Bulgars were massacred by Turkish troops, whilst the Conservatives under Disraeli were pro-Turkish, seeing Turkey as the gallant bulwark against Russia's westward expansion, and threatening war if necessary.[6]

From the very outset of the conflict the music-hall took a firm stance fairly close to that adopted by the Conservatives. Britain would not fight unless she had to, but if Turkish sovereignty were threatened then the Navy would show the Russians a lesson. These sentiments were neatly catalogued in the most famous of the songs to emerge at this time, and probably the most famous of all music-hall patriotic songs, 'MacDermott's Warsong', or the 'Jingo Song', as it was invariably known.

> We don't want to fight, but by jingo if we do,
> We've got the ships, we've got the men, we've got the money too.
> We've fought the bear before, and while we're Britons true,
> The Russians will not have Constantinople.

Written by G. W. Hunt and probably first performed in early May 1877, the song was quickly picked up by pro-war factions within the Conservative Party, thus gaining connotations not necessarily intended at its inception.[7]

The warsong is extremely well known and has been thoroughly analysed by at least one historian. What is rarely appreciated, however, is that it was only one, albeit the most popular, of many such songs. Fred Albert launched at almost the same time 'We Mean to Keep our Empire in the East' and 'Turkey and the Bear'. Later, Harry Rickards offered 'Hats Off to the Empire' and 'The Lion Wags his Tail'; Charles Williams, 'The Congress Dinner; or Who's Going to Carve the Turkey' and Hunt & MacDermott tried to repeat their success with a second warsong, 'Waiting for the Signal'. The major commercial entertainment industry of the age was staking a strong claim to becoming an institution of informal political education.[8]

There is no firm evidence that such material increased Conservative popularity – although it can hardly have hindered it – and it cannot be argued that these songs illustrate the existence of popular support for imperialism, as there was precious little imperial sentiment expressed. However, certain points are clear. Reaction to these songs, and particular the 'Jingo Song', undermines Stedman Jones's assertion that such 'bombastic' pieces were essentially the preserve of 'the audiences of Piccadilly and Leicester Square', the upper middle class and aristocratic bohemians. In fact, MacDermott launched the piece while engaged at the Sun, the London Pavilion and the Forresters, by no means all bohemian venues. Furthermore, it featured successfully throughout his provincial tour later in the year. Patriotism merging into jingoism was clearly not class-specific.[9] Secondly, the period 1877–78, as well as launching MacDermott on the political road outlined in the previous section, more generally confirmed the 'Toryfication' of the music-hall, already beginning as a result of the licensing debate in the early 1870s. Finally, the halls' reaction to the Balkan conflict set a precedent that was eagerly maintained in the years ahead. Discussion (if that is not too high-minded a term for what took place) and celebration of Britain's world position was popular with audiences, and therefore became a key element in the years ahead. The songs of the Russo-Turkish war were rarely sung again, but they were paid the compliment of endless imitation.

Music-hall's patriotic stance changed during the period after 1878–9 responding to the changing nature and scope of warfare and to the altering international climate. One element remained constant throughout, however – praise of bravery and heroism. The titles speak for themselves: 'The Boys of the Thin Red Line', 'The Gordon Highlanders', 'Leave Me Comrades'. Such songs were often embellished by dramatic tableaux, usually involving local children and/or ex-servicemen who marched, drilled and waved the relevant flags.[10] If no current campaign existed, or if nothing spectacular was offered in one that did, past 'glories' were looked back to. The Crimean War in particular was a popular source of inspiration, and indeed the music-hall did as much as Tennyson to rescue this military disaster and give it a hallowed place in late-nineteenth-century popular mythology. Charles Godfrey's 'The Seventh Royal Fusiliers', written in 1893, was perhaps then most popular of all the items dealing with the military events of the 1850s, and told the story of a Crimean hero called Fred (apochryphal?!) who cut his way through a Cossack dam which had shut off the British water supply. It is noteworthy, if only for illustrating one of those supreme moments of bathos which the music-hall offered presumably unintentionally, and was largely overlooked by the audience: 'spade in hand, he went to do or die'.

This singling out of a specific individual typifies the music-hall's tendency during the period before the Boer War to pay tribute to a single person or act of heroism, rather than to devote its praise to the army and navy in general. Certainly, hymns of praise to the forces *en masse* did exist during the Colonial War period, but it was not until the Boer War, and even more markedly in the First World War, that the emphasis tended to move noticeably away from a paean to individuals and towards collective congratulation. This presumably reflects the increasing scope of warfare, which, by affecting an increasing number of people, tended to push the act of individual heroism into the background.

A number of writers attempted to rehabilitate the reputation of the Irish by stressing their bravery while defending the British flag. The Irishman's supposed love of fighting, a favourite topic for cartoonists and comedians, suddenly became a virtue when directed against an enemy thousands of miles from home.

> True boys, blue boys
> Don't you want a shindy with the foe?

asked Walter Monroe in Felix McGlennon's 'Irishmen Must be There'. As with its saccharine eviction ballads, the music-hall, particularly during the Boer War, when songs of Irish heroism were at their most common, may have helped temper some of the worst excesses of anti-Irish sentiment in mainland Britain.[11]

An integral part of this heroic material was the soldier's or sailor's goodbye song. These followed a standard pattern, involving either a goodbye in the homeland and then death on the battlefield, or a goodbye to the homeland from a dying hero on the battlefield. The most famous of all these, a song so popular during the Boer War that it has even given its title to a military history of the war, was 'Goodbye Dolly Gray'. It was in fact not written for the Boer War at all, but for the Spanish-American war of 1898, which ended so abruptly that the publishers exported the song to Britain in 1899, hoping to reap lost financial reward.[12] It is in this type of song that we find some of the most unashamed sentiment in all of the music-hall tradition. An irresistible example is entitled 'Just As The Sun Went Down', and tells of two dying soldiers lying next to each other, one holding a lock of grey hair and thinking of his mother, the other a lock of brown hair, thinking of his girl. Without wishing to be dismissive, it is difficult to take these 'goodbye' songs particularly seriously, and it is apparent from their tone that very few of the audience actually had relatives or friends in the positions of danger which the songs discussed. It is noticeable that a considerably more realistic, if still sentimental, note emerged in 1914, reflective once again of the scope and nearness to all of this conflict.

> 'Tis the last goodbye, you must take your place in the line,
> Go and do your duty, Jack, I'll do mine,
> I'll work for the children as a soldier's wife should do,
> And while their father is fighting the foe,
> I'll be mother and father too.[13]

More sophisticated themes were also present, however. From the late 1870s, and gathering pace through the 1880s and 1890s, songwriters stressed what might be termed a sense of 'Empire consciousness', of Britain as the 'Motherland' loved and defended by her loyal subjects. Here, abstract notions of empire were given tangibility and something which might be called 'popular imperialism' resulted. The popularity of songs with this motif partly mirrors contemporary awareness of the expansion of empire – four and a quarter million square miles were added between 1871–1900.[14] Given that many songs dwelt on the 'old' colonies, especially Australia and Canada, however, it seems likely that a further explanation lies in the changing pattern of British emigration, with emigrants increasingly choosing passages to the empire rather than the USA. The Empire, or at least parts of it, therefore impinged upon the consciousness of relatives and friends 'at home'.[15]

As early as 1879, G. W. Hunt was promising that:

> The dusky sons of Hindostan
> Will by our banner stand.
> Australia, aye, and Canada,
> Both love the dear old land.[16]

The empire was safe from foreign threat. It was in the 1890s, however, that the 'Motherland' concept became widespread and it was Leo Dryden, 'the Kipling of the halls', as he was generally termed, who did much to popularise it. His 'Miner's Dream of Home' (1891), still one of the most popular songs in the family 'sing-song' repertoire in the 1930s (by which time Dryden was destitute and reduced to busking), marked his first successful venture into this field. Certainly, the word 'Motherland' does not appear and the location of the miner as he dreams of 'The old homestead and the faces I love' is never given. But it forges a link between Britain and various outposts of Empire that he later developed more overtly in 'What Britishers are Made Of', 'Canadian Redskins', 'Great White Mother' and 'India's Reply'.[17]

The involvement of colonial troops in the Boer War gave a boost to the production of songs praising and glorifying the Empire. In a number of them, the Motherland took on a more forceful, dominant image than had previously been the case. The chorus of George Lashwood's 'Motherland, or Australia Will Be There' has what might be termed an 'expansionist' second verse:

> Motherland! Motherland!
> Though your sons have crossed the sea,
> They have spread the Empire in your name –
> Great, glorious and free,
> Plant the flag, plant the flag,
> Let the world know 'tis our dream –
> To never, never rest until
> Our Empire is supreme.

'Under the Same Old Flag' (1899) proclaimed that

> And all must show respect to Britain's Monarch,
> Where England's flag is planted and unfurled.

Felix McGlennon's 'The British Bulldogs' ('who never bark unless they mean to bite') (1901) was even more confident.

> Hail our Empire's Unity!
> Manly hearts have spread it far and wide,
> Roaming with impunity,
> Masters on the land and on the tide.

There were too, a small group of songs which hymned not merely the Empire, but the entire family of white races. Again, this illustrates that a percolation into the halls of relatively common areas of 'serious' imperial and racial debate did take place, contrary to much historical judgement. A particularly potent example of this was Charles Godfrey's 'We're Brothers of the Self-same Race'.

> Folk say, 'what will Britain do?
> Will she rest with her banners furled?'
> No! No!! No!!! When we go to meet the foe,
> It's the English-speaking race against the world.[18]

In 'John Bull's Letter Bag' (1899) F. V. St Clair gave even clearer shape to the idea of white supremacy and in doing so, produced surely the most exquisitely bad rhyme in the entire music-hall canon.

> Though they may think us 'lax-uns',
> Thank God we're Anglo-Saxons,
> And the Anglo-Saxon race shall rule the world,
> John Bull.

These songs sound so unutterrably dire, both ideologically and artistically, to the later twentieth-century ear, that it seems almost impossible to believe that they were ever performed. That they were bears witness to the skill of the singers, for even in a suitable intellectual climate, it must have taken considerable ability to communicate such lyrics with sincerity.

Alongside the sense of pride in British imperial achievement a second new element arose; xenophobia or, more properly, Germanophobia. Traditionally, foreigners were portrayed on the music-hall stage as funny, odd or idiosyncratic, but generally harmless enough. An amiable insularity was all that pervaded most comic songs, as shown by Marie Lloyd's 'The Coster Girl in Paris':

> And I'd like to go again
> To Paris on the Seine,
> For Paris is a proper pantomime,
> And if they'd only shift the 'Ackney road and plant it over there,
> I'd like to live in Paris all the time.[19]

However, from about 1890, the German nation became subject to what were, at times, vitriolic attacks. Antipathy towards Germans in music-hall song was initially centred on the supposed influx of German workers into the English labour market and, in particular, the catering trade. Then from the late 1890s, the focus shifted to the increasing economic and military threat posed by German expansion. 'The Naval Exhibition' (1891) a song by Charles Osborne for George Beauchamp, more commonly remembered for 'She was one of the Early Birds (And I was one of the worms)', is representative of the anti-immigrant song and worthy of lengthy quotation.

> And Nelson certainly fought in vain,
> To sweep the foreigners from our main;
> For down at Chelsea I declare,
> There's swarms of foreigners everywhere;
> There's German music to greet the ear
> There's German sausage and German beer;

There's German yeast in the English bread,
On German matches you're bound to tread.
In fact the management of the show
Prefers the foreigner, don't you know?
The work they didn't attempt to halve,
They hired Germans to wait and carve,
While English waiters are left to starve,
Through German competition.

During the lead up to the Boer War when anti-German feeling ran high, Wilkie Bard performed 'Hey! Are you coming Back?, which contained the following debate with a German restauranteur:

Think of the oof that you've made over here,
With your ice cream and German lager beer.
But he said, "Vell! I'm on mine homeward track
I have made some money; if I vant to make some more,
Vell then! I'm coming back."

As late as 1914, Mark Sheridan revived the German waiter joke during the patter accompanying his jaunty 'Belgium Put the Kibosh on the Kaiser'.

[*Spoken*]
He went up to the trench where he couldn't find any Germans, shouted 'waiter!', and there was two hundred and eight popped up and he shot the lot of them.[20]

These songs were all the more potent because they were fuelling a fairly hysterical campaign in favour of restricting immigration which was led by a number of newspapers, including the *Daily Mail*, *Daily Express* and *Evening News*.[21] The extent of anti-German feeling in these songs was out of all proportion to the number of Germans in the country. This particularly intense form of jingoism was perhaps a result of the German immigrant, an 'acceptable' enemy in view of the international situation touched on below and possibly a real source of competition for jobs at one stage, serving as a focus for repressed anti-semitism directed at the large number of Eastern European Jews fleeing to Britain from the late 1880s. Given their refugee status and Britain's supposed tolerance of refugees, anti-semitism was not a respectable doctrine. Germanophobia clearly was.[22]

Hostility to Germans had deeper roots than job competition, real or supposed. It was the Kruger telegram of January 1896, in which Kaiser Wilhelm II congratulated the Boers on repelling an English-led raid on the Transvaal, that turned music-hall songwriters' talents away from the issue of immigration to the wider international tensions between the two countries.[23] The telegram unleashed a storm of outraged indignation on to the music-hall stage. Arthur Lennard's 'How He Received the News' depicted John Bull's fury on receiving the 'insults'.

> John hears it, and then like a lion he roars –
> Tell the beggars I'll do as I choose!
> What – They threaten? Here! – bring out a fleet, hoist my flag!
> We'll teach them that Britons can do more than brag!"

One gentleman wrote anxiously to the *Times* asking for an invervention by the Lord Chamberlain. 'Will he not interfere to prohibit the offensive references to the German Emperor and people who are being nightly delivered from the platforms of our music halls to the natural resentment of that nation and to the disgust of every right-thinking man amongst ourselves?'[24]

Each subsequent flashpoint in Anglo-German relations produced an angry snarl from the music-hall bulldogs, culminating in the glut of songs and sketches that appeared during the height of the Dreadnought building issue in 1909. The sentiment expressed was simple – Britain had to expand her army and navy.

'Are you one of England's soldiers?' [demanded Vesta Tilley]
'Are you one of England's soldiers?
It's up to everyman to do his share'.[25]

Walter Tilbury exhorted 'Wake up Ye British', and 'Wake up England', a 'stirring call to arms', when he ran at the Empire Palace, Walthamstow. The columns of the music-hall press regularly commented that such-and-such a singer had a new 'naval song', usually with titles such as 'Build Some More, John Bull', which had been received with 'tremendous enthusiasm'. Of the fact that invasion was the logical outcome of any failure to heed its advice, the music-hall had no doubt. 'There's a foe at the Gates of England', a song by Paul Pelham, who normally composed for musical comedy rather than the music-hall, concerned an apochryphal invasion of Britain, which was successful because the 'sons of the Motherland' had 'forgotten how to fight', and the song urged them to learn again before the alien hordes arrived. 'Invasion, or Wake Up England', a sketch at one London hall, included a spectacular bombardment of London in which, as the *Era* magazine instructed: 'Aerial navigation and the dreaded "electrical forces" promised and foreshadowed as the latest methods of modern warfare, are brought forward'.[61]

When Britain declared war on Germany on 4 August 1914, the halls were ready for the foe. The first months produced a glut of exuberant songs and sketches dealing specifically with the war, the latter with stirring titles such as *Under the Flag* at the Middlesex, *God Save the Empire* at the Southampton Palace and *My Friend Thomas Atkins* at the London Colosseum. As always the halls treated war as a useful source of profit. Late in August, the *Encore* magazine carried an advertisement by one Will Edwards, who urged the profession, 'be in the swim, sing something patriotic'.[27] The management of the York Empire presented a Belgian refugee soprano, Mlle Laura Novea, accompanied by a fellow Belgian M. Gaston Neuraumont, performing 'A Long Way to Tipperary', a brilliant, if tasteless, coup, which received 'a tumultuous reception'.[28] Some voices were raised against this 'claptrap patriotism'; a letter to the *Encore* complained that 'a performer need only walk on with a flag of any country (bar two) to meet with vociferous applause' and commented that 'it is perfectly obvious that there is a certain type of artiste endeavouring to reap a profit by fostering hysteria and encouraging sentiment'.[29] Such a voice was a rarity.

The majority of songs expressed a reluctance to fight, but assumed it would be a brief war that Britain was morally entitled to win.

'There's going to be dirty weather,
For anyone who tramples on the flag',

promised 'Boys in Khaki; Boys in Blue'. The music-hall had no doubt who to blame for the outbreak of hostilities; in 'Belgium put the Kibosh on the Kaiser', Mark Sheridan, a Scottish comic singer, was particularly acidic:

> The naughty boy he spoke of peace,
> While he prepared for war,
> He stirred up little Serbia
> To serve his dirty trick,
> But dirty nights at Liege, upset this dirty Dick.

'We'll put you through the mill, Kaiser Bill', however, went even further:

> You just love to wreck and kill,
> But we'll put you through the mill,
> And we'll make you pay the bill,
> When we leave you lying still,
> Kaiser Bill, Kaiser Bill.[30]

Inevitably, the recruiting song, although not a new element in the music-hall tradition, having appeared in the Boer War and its 'Wake up, England' form after 1902, reached its zenith in 1914. Obviously, it is impossible to assess the exact influence of these songs, but they must have caused at least some stirring of conscience, for they contained very strong 'white feather' elements, with an unmistakable implication that not volunteering represented a basic failure of manhood:

> For there's not a man amongst us
> Who would show his face again,
> If he did not dare or die for those at home.

Marie Lloyd sang of the manliness of the soldier, as opposed to the civilian – a common element in these songs.

> I didn't like you much before you joined the army, John,
> But I do like you, cocky, now you've got your khaki on.

For the man who was uncertain whether he should answer England's call, the music-hall was for once, not a suitable place for escapism.[31]

By the spring of 1915 it was increasingly apparent that the short, brilliant war promised by the music-hall and most other organs of public opinion was not to be, and songs which, although still bombastic and militaristic, stressed the virtues of perseverence and determination, began to appear. Never again was the euphoric patriotism of 1914 to be repeated. Not even the music-hall could continue to glorify the most catastrophic human tragedy Europe had witnessed since the Middle Ages.

It is significant that the songs the soldiers used in the trenches were not the music-hall's recruiting anthems. They were either bittersweet laments of their plight (often obscene!), tender love songs which reminded them of those at home, like Haydn Wood's 'Roses of Picardy', or cheerful music-hall songs like Jack Judge's 'It's a Long Way to Tipperary', which was only a war song because soldiers adopted it. If nothing else, the Great War killed 'claptrap' patriotism. In 1939, the variety profession knew better than to beat the drum too loudly. Only in recent years, in an age which sees the agonies of war from the safety of its living-room, have certain sections of the media sought to revive it.

Perhaps what emerges most strongly from a reading of music-hall song is the totally *unquestioning*, confident view of Britain and her place in the world, a point dramatically underlined by a brief study of the industry's treatment of the Boer War (1899–1902). The war broke out in October 1899, the culmination of almost a century's tension between the Afrikaaners and the British government. While not an unpopular war, it provoked strong opposition from certain influential groupings within the British Isles: Pro-Boers like Emily Hobhouse and Lloyd George made their point forcibly throughout the war. It was also hardly a war to delight the British military establishment. The Boers moved rapidly onto the offensive, besieging the British in Ladysmith, Kimberley and Mafeking. These three garrisons were all relieved by mid-summer 1900, which caused much celebration in Britain, and by August the Boer armies appeared to be beaten. Refusing to admit defeat, however, they adopted guerilla tactics and frustrated the British army until their eventual inevitable surrender and the subsequent signing of the Peace of Vereeniging in May 1902. The British were forced to destroy crops and herd Boer families into concentration camps where insanitary conditions claimed 20,000 lives in fourteen months, in order to bring about their victory. Exalted reputations were tarnished. The initial Commander-in-Chief, Sir Redvers Buller, was replaced by Lord Roberts after Buller's repeated failure to lift the sieges. Four hundred and fifty thousand British troops took three years and £220 million to defeat fifty thousand Boers.[32]

Yet the music-hall's presentation of events gave only the slightest hint of the arguments and difficulties that the war created. Inevitably, the great bulk of the Boer War material came in the earlier parts of the conflict and attained its height during moments of particular euphoria, above all after the relief of Mafeking, which was celebrated in a frenzy of fervent patriotism. Collins Music-Hall, in Islington, bedecked itself with acres of bunting, while at the more aristocratic Empire, Leicester Square 'when pictures of Baden-Powell were flashed onto the screen, the scene was indescribable, the audience rising and singing 'God Save The Queen' and 'Rule Britannia'.[33]

From the outset the war was depicted as a battle of right against wrong – 'to conquer all oppression, equality to bring', 'to defend the cause of truth and right', these were typical justifications offered by music-hall singers. The Boers were seen as the instigators of the conflict. To 'quiet the arrogant Boer who first caused the row' was the avowed aim of the war according to one song.[34] There was, too, much criticism of Boer tactics. A nation unused to guerilla warfare saw it portrayed as simple cowardice. Thus in the song 'Why Are you Waiting Here?' (1899), the singer supposedly discovered a group of

Boers hiding behind a cluster of rocks. In reply to the question in the
title they replied:

> I'll tell you why – it's British pluck we fear,
> And it's safer to fight from behind a rock –
> That's why we're hiding here.

There is no doubt that after the close of the 1900–1901 pantomime
season, the amount of material dealing with the war decreased.
Obviously, this was to a considerable extent simply because the topic
had been overworked. The great wave of songs and sketches which
had greeted the war could not be maintained continuously, particularly
once it had found serious rivals in the shape of the impending
coronation of Edward VII and in the craze for impersonation of, and
songs about, the American bandleader Sousa, which became almost
an obsession of the music-hall stage in 1901. At the same time,
however, the reduction in material must also reflect something of a
loss of enthusiasm for the war. A writer in the music-hall press late in
1901 commented that the management appreciated that the audience
had come to respect the bravery of the Boer soldiers, and were thus
increasingly unwilling to see them publicly derided.[35]

It would be wrong, however, to interpret this lapse as in any way
marking a crucial shift in patriotic attitude, or to suggest, as
MacInnes does, that any 'note of disillusionment' or 'marked element
of satire' appeared in the later years of the war.[36] This falling-off
merely represents a decline in enthusiasm for this specific war, not a
fundamental re-thinking of basic beliefs. More importantly, the
music-hall was only very occasionally critical of the management of
the war, and biting attacks, of the type it is possible to see in, for
example, *Punch*, were non-existent. The government and the
administration, major targets for attack in some other areas, were
never mentioned, and the military staff were treated throughout with
enormous respect. In the early days, the tone had been ecstatic, as in
this verse on Roberts:

> And his name is Bobs, dear old Bobs,
> He is a little tradesman, who does the biggest jobs,
> He's pals with Tommy Atkins, He's chums with all the nobs.
> He's Irish! He's British! And He's Dear Old Bobs'.[37]

'Top of the Class' which appeared in 1901 said that the generals in the
South African campaign were exactly that, while F. V. St Clair's
'Cheer Up, Buller', although admitting that he may have made

mistakes, expressed anger that he had been removed from his commanding position, and promised that:

> On honour's scroll we shall
> Find Buller's name – and written 'neath,
> This soldier saved Natal.

'The Galloping Major', the only evidence MacInnes cites of the supposed disillusionment during this period, was in fact not written until 1906 (and, in fact, even this belongs essentially to the *Lions Comiques* tradition).[38] Certainly, there were mild rumblings in the Edwardian period, culminating in the music-hall's contribution to the naval race, already mentioned. In general, however, the halls remained absolutely loyal.

It is essential to avoid an over-literal interpretation of this patriotic material. Music-hall audiences contained many young males and many of the songs and sketches can be explained away as managements meeting what they perceived as their audiences' need for excitement. Moreoever, the existence of these songs does not necessarily reflect any deep level of support for the ideas they espoused. The *Era* pointed this out as early as 1885.

There is a large number of people who will applaud anything that contains a blatant reference to Britannia, our Glorious Empire, and the superiority of Englishmen (i.e. themselves) in every respect to every nation on earth. But it must not be too easily concluded, for instance, because theatrical and music hall audiences often 'shout' Conservatism that, therefore, they are exclusively, or even principally, made up of Tories.[39]

Nevertheless, the sheer weight of material must again be stressed. There is *far* too much of it for it to be the results of music-hall writers creating, rather than, at least in part, capturing, a genuine sentiment. Patriotism, broadly conceived, whether it be an interest in Empire, a hostility to Germany or a vague belief in British superiority, must have been a definite element in the consciousness of all classes between 1880 and 1914. While Henry Pelling's conclusion that 'there is no evidence of a direct continuous support for the cause of imperialism among any section of the working class' is far from controverted by this chapter, it does suggest that sections of that class possessed what might be termed 'positive acquiescence'. Of cruder jingoism, there was surely plenty.[40]

It is probable that, once again, music-hall songs shaped as well as mirrored opinion. As ever, there is need for caution. Recent writers are correct in stressing that it was perfectly possible to watch and enjoy this type of material but to ignore those messages that did not accord with the listener's own standpoint. The fact that the audience applauded the achievement of its country did not mean that it accepted all 'militaristic' or 'imperialistic' viewpoints once it left the auditorium. At the most basic level, the social standing of the soldier remained extremely low. Robert Roberts writes of how the soldier was seen as the lowest form of life by the working classes of Edwardian Salford, and if the pen of Kipling can be believed, this was a feeling that had considerable currency throughout society.

> For it's 'Tommy this, an' Tommy that, an'
> Chuck him out the brute'!
> But it's saviour of 'is country'
> When the guns begin to shoot.[41]

'Dear old Bobs' may have been the hero of the Boer War, but found little popular support for his scheme for compulsory military service, promoted in the Edwardian period. Bernard Waites sums up the situation well. The audience 'could cheer the flag, Queen and Empire, but it knew that on Imperial Tariff meant Dear Bread'.[42] There were indeed strong pockets of opinion, especially in working class radical London, that were militantly opposed to the very virtues which the music-hall stage cherished. Thus, in 1887, while the halls praised Queen Victoria in her Diamond Jubilee year to one sector of the upper working class and lower middle class, at the West Kensington Park Radical Club a group from the same milieu listened to an entertainment entitled *The Queen's Jubilee, or Fifty years of Flunkyism and What It Has Cost the People*.[43]

However, while avoiding an over-simplified interpretation, we should also be aware of the current tendency to underplay the ideological impact of music-hall patriotism. Much recent argument centres on the fact that the music-hall's excessive patriotism was parodied from within the profession, thus allowing a dissenting voice to be heard. Certainly there were parodies, and extremely funny ones too. The cleverest were either written or performed by Herbert Campbell (1844–1904), an enormous, jovial man, one of the most inventive music-hall comedians and a highly successful performer in pantomime. In his earliest parody, written by Vincent Davis, MacDermott's 'Jingo Song' became:

> I don't want to fight, I'll be slaughtered if I do,
> I'll change my togs, I'll sell my kit, I'll pop my rifle too,
> I don't like the war, I ain't a Briton true,
> And I'll let the Russians have Constantinople'.

Leo Dryden's 'Miner's Dream' was dealt with in even more devastating fashion.

> Pa was boozing nightly
> And his mother was shifting the gin,
> While the lodger was taking the old gal out
> And the old man in.[44]

Little Tich's 'One of the Deathless Army' poked gentle fun at the Territorials, the accompanying patter debunking the 'heroic', pseudo-Tennysonian style of some music-hall numbers.

And the shells lay around me in thousands and still they continued to drop. So I paid for the dozen I'd eaten and walked out of the oyster shop. And the shots they were buzzing round me, and one nearly blew off my head. There were cannons to the right of me, cannons to the left of me – so what did I do? Went in off the red'.[45]

Such parodies are an amusing antidote to the normal bellicose trumpetings; but they were hugely outnumbered by traditional, uncritical patriotic material. They did not challenge in any serious way, nor were they probably intended to challenge, the orthodox interpretation of Empire and British achievement. Neither were the singers consistent in their ideological stance. Only weeks before MacDermott's 'Jingo Song' was launched, Campbell had been singing a number in the *Grim Goblin* pantomime at the Grecian Theatre which contained a jingoistic last verse.

> The Lion quite calmly awaits the attack,
> On the Bear both his eyes he does keep,
> If he's wanted I think we shall find him all there
> And bear's grease will soon be very cheap.

Later in his career, he used a song 'What do they do with the old 'Uns?', which rued the fate of old soldiers left to die in the workhouse. When it suited, Campbell was as strident a voice as those he guyed.[46]

In the last analysis, it cannot be denied that patriotic songs had tremendous potential as political educators of the predominantly young audience. The songs projected a simple imperialism of the man in the street; they were given a sense of unity with the outpost of Empire, an acceptance of, and perhaps belief in, territorial expansion and the assumption that Britain was the world's repository of light and liberty. Similarly, war was simplified and glorified.

> Through Russian shot and Cossack spears
> We carv'd our way to glory.

or,

> A deafening cheer – a rush of men – a glint of deadly steel,
> On dash the Gordons, through the bullets run.[47]

The colourful uniforms, spectacular effects and rousing tableau finales added to the illusion. The halls' constant reference to war made armed conflict appear a law of nature, and its anti-German stance defined the future opponent. When the war came in 1914 there was the promise that 'Tommy and Jack Will Soon Be Marching Home Again'. Thus, by long-term preparation and short-term confidence-boosting, warfare was made easier to accept and pacifism, or even rational contemplation of conflict, far harder to grasp.

The music-hall's influence was enhanced by the fact that it chimed in with so many other popular influences of the age, particularly in the Edwardian era. It offered an especially effective musical augmentation to many school textbooks, the propaganda of some youth movements, certain newspapers (especially the *Daily Mail* whose predominantly lower-middle-class circulation numbered a phenomenal 984,000 by 1900), and the vast body of 'imaginary war' literature, which proliferated from the 1880s.[48] This was aimed not merely at middle-class readership, as had previous pamphlets such as the *Battle of Dorking* but at the total reading public. Explicit titles such as *The Channel Tunnel or John Bull in Danger* and *England's Peril*, reinforced the *Mail's* xenophobic attitudes, telling them of Britain in danger, of German spies, and of how a brief and glorious war was the inevitable end. Written either by propagandists, who genuinely believed that such protestations of concern about the nation's strength were necessary, or by politicians or businessmen hoping for electoral or financial gain, these stories escalated during late Victorian and Edwardian England. Fittingly, one of the most popular examples, 'The Invasion of 1910', emanated from the *Daily Mail* itself in 1906. Written by William le Cleux and H. W. Wilson, with added assistance from Field Marshall Roberts, it was heralded by sandwich-board-men in Prussian helmets marching through London, and each copy of the paper carried a map depicting the area to be 'invaded' the next day.

This type of material did much to condition men's minds, to tell them that war was normal, romantic and necessary.[49]

'Claptrap patriotism' may have died on the music-hall stage during the Great War, but the ideas it bred persisted. The halls and their allied purveyors of popular conservatism preached their message at the very moment when the power of Britain was waning, when Germany, the United States and Japan were challenging its markets, its territorial supremacy, or both. But the generation that lived to see the Empire lost, watched the colonial 'savages' (one of whom had 'aim'd his spear like lightnings dart' at Tom Costello's breast in his immortal 'Comrades') became their political equals, and that witnessed the first wave of black immigration into the heart of the white 'motherland', had been shown on the music-hall stage that their Empire was supreme, and some must have believed the tale. The failure of sections of the British population to accept fully the implications of the loss of Empire, and the concomitant failure of many to genuinely absorb the spirit of multi-racial Britain, is deeply rooted. A small part of those roots may well have been planted in the Hippodromes and Empires of eighty years ago.

Part 3

Community: the music of 'the people'

Chapter 8

The emergence of a popular tradition

Professional entertainment promoters, anxious to defend their product, were prone to see themselves as the major source of musical provision. (Some philanthropists had similar delusions.) Historians have sometimes concurred in their view. 'At the beginning of the period (1800) the working classes were making their own music, while at the end of it (1914) their music was supplied by a large, commercially-organised population of professional entertainers': so argues Nicholas Temperley.[1] However, although professionals had gained much ground by 1914, the largest single element in the popular musical life of all but the very poorest in the nineteenth and early twentieth centuries was always provided by 'the people' themselves. The bulk of this section concerns popular musical societies, the bands, choirs and orchestras so much a feature of the age. To some extent, such proportioning of material is misleading. The largest part of community-based music was heard not in concert-halls or contest arenas but in pubs, houses, streets and similar focal points. Unfortunately, this type of often informal performance left very little recorded evidence, and as is so often the case, the historian is forced to devote most space to better-documented formal activity.

Before investigating the various forms of community music, however, it is useful to examine the massive growth of the musical service industry which played such an important role in underpinning the progress of 'amateur music' in the nineteenth century.

In 1840, a music enthusiast needed great resourcefulness and patience. The fundamental prerequisites – printed music, instruments and tuition – were rare and expensive. Hours were spent copying out music; unsuitable or inadequate instruments were forced to meet all manner of musical tasks. By 1914 almost all of the musician's needs, from cheap copies of orchestral scores to bandsmen's uniforms, could be obtained with relative ease. First, as already noted, there was a substantial growth in professional musical personnel. Most of the 47,000 'musicians and music masters' in 1911 would have spent some of their professional lives teaching in some form or another, working with individual pupils or training or conducting a local choir, orchestra or band. Some of the country's premier musicians were thus involved, especially in the field of amateur choral music. The composer Frederick Cowen, for example, worked with the Bradford Festival Choral Society and was highly regarded by its members. Some professionals made their talents available to the poorer sections of the community by providing cheap class lessons at public institutions. The Mechanics Institute was especially important in this sense. Many northern choral singers, including Alfred Halstead of the Huddersfield Choral Society, a carter by profession and regarded by many as one of the finest male altos of the nineteenth century, gained their grounding in this way.[2]

The efforts of the professionals were augmented by a larger body of part-time teachers, usually musically-inclined clerks and skilled manual workers, who swelled their income by giving lessons for as little as 3d an hour to the aspiring amateurs of the neighbourhood. Their existence infuriated the professionals who worked hard to try and introduce legislation against what they saw as both a dilution of standards and a financial threat. Undoubtedly, some of the semi-professionals were barely competent (although the same criticism could be levelled at a few professionals), but many made a useful contribution to local musical life and a few were possessed of genuine ability. Many of the leading brass band trainers and conductors, for example, men such as Herbert Barker, a Bradford joiner who offered bandsmen postal tuition in musical theory, or George Wadsworth, a Holme Valley stonemason, and leading trainer and adjudicator, made an impressive contribution to popular musical culture despite humble origins and lack of formal education. Together, the professionals and their part-time rivals helped make the life of the amateur musician easier than it had ever been.[3]

Similar benefit was bestowed by developments in the music publishing industry and, in particular, by the publication of *cheap* sheet music from about the mid-nineteenth century. England, a major centre of music publishing from the mid-eighteenth century, may well have witnessed a fifty to one hundred fold increase in production between 1800 and 1914. It is estimated that if *all* sources of production, including the 'pirates' common by late century, are included, almost a million items may have been published in this period.[4]

The music publishing industry still awaits its historian and existing accounts, although valuable, have accepted rather uncritically the highly partisan accounts of music publishing which emerged in the late nineteenth century from the house of Novello. There can be no denying the company's pioneering role. Founded in 1811 by Vincent Novello and originally specialists in the publication of music for the Catholic church, the company gradually diversified under the leadership of Vincent's son J. Alfred Novello (1810–1896), who seems to have had greater and greater control from the 1830s. Absolutely crucial was his encouragement of 'cheap music'. Before the mid-nineteenth century, printed music was a luxury item and, as will be shown later, working men and women in choral and instrumental societies were forced to buy a single published copy and then laboriously (but lovingly) copy out the necessary duplicate parts. Throughout the 1840s, Novello's music was cheaper than that of rival houses, but in 1849 the decision was made to reduce the price of most publications by fifty per cent. Novello's achievement seems to have been based upon the re-introduction of the by then almost obsolete practice of printing music from movable type. The price cuts of 1849 were followed by others, less spectacular but important, throughout the 1850s and 1860s. In 1837 an edition of Handel's *Messiah* cost one guinea; by 1854 an octavo edition cost only four shillings and, by the early 1860s, this and several other major oratorios were available in a pocket-sized edition for one shilling. Serial production, the introduction of which, as in literary publishing, facilitated cheapness, further added to the company's achievements. In 1865, now controlled and about to be purchased by Henry Littleton, the firm began to publish sets of glees and part-songs at only ½d a song.[5]

This is an impressive record. However, care must be taken to not misinterpret the company's motives or to overstate its role as a propagator of musical activity. Existing histories give too much emphasis to the philanthropic aspect of music publishing. Alfred Novello and Henry Littleton *were* anxious to give music to the less affluent because they believed in its value as a bringer of solace, happiness and moral regeneration. They were also part of a highly competitive industry and were seeking to develop and exploit markets and to make money.

In all these things they were highly successful, Alfred retiring to a relatively luxurious life in Sardinia in 1857. Moreover, both the company's official historian and some later writers have been too anxious to claim that the house of Novello almost *created* some aspects of popular musical life. Even before the price cuts of 1849, 'the cheap music of the house of Novello had called classes and societies into existence which, but for the aid they furnished, *could have had no being*', claimed a company writer in 1887.[6] In fact, as will be seen, they could and did have an existence, albeit one dependent upon much hard work and sacrifice. Indeed, the argument might well be reversed: Novello would never have developed this pricing policy without the prior emergence of a strong popular choral tradition. The importance of these pricing changes was that they made the existence of the choral singer or other amateur musician a great deal more straightforward. The late-night, candle-lit copying vigils of earlier days were over and everybody was grateful. This may have made music a more attractive proposition, especially in the 1890s and after, when there were many other recreational choices available.[7] Above all, Novello and others vastly increased the amount of vocal music available: the time spent copying *Messiah* could be spent learning a new work. The revolution in publishing did not create a popular choral or any other musical tradition, but it certainly made it more varied.

A final caveat concerns the range of Novello's interests. Dr Percy Young has argued that: 'In the broadest sense it is doubtful whether any two men have ever done more for the cultivation of music 'amongst the least wealthy classes' in Britain, than did Vincent and Alfred Novello'.[8] Such a comment reflects the rather limited horizons of much British musicology. Even in 'the broadest sense', this is a hefty claim and rather hard to substantiate. Choral and vocal music were only parts of a far broader musical culture to which Novello made only minimal contribution. Charles Sheard's *Musical Bouquet*, a series of over nine thousand items encompassing music-hall songs, the ballads of Henry Russell, piano solos and operatic selections published from 1846 to 1889 was an important source for home-based music making. Similarly Hopwood and Crew, along with Sheard, probably the major Victorian music-hall song publishers, carried music-hall songs into parlours, public bars and church halls all over the country. But perhaps most significant of all, one of the major musical institutions of the 'least wealthy classes', the brass band, received no assistance from the 'traditional' companies. The history of band music publication followed an entirely separate course, featuring 'heroes' from beyond the confines of most published histories of nineteenth-century music.

Amateur wind bands began to appear from about 1815 with the first specifically *brass* bands making their appearance in the 1830s. Publication of brass band music began in a limited way almost as soon as the brass ensemble became established as a medium. The first known example of a publication specifically for brass band is *MacFarlane's Eight Popular Airs For a Brass Band*, published by R. Cocks & Co. of London in 1836. Several other houses began experimenting with band publications from about this date. Most material emerged at first from the established London firms, although in 1859 Richard Smith, an ex-menagerie musician who had realised the potential market available in the North and Midlands, commenced his *Champion Brass Band Journal* in Hull.[9]

In general, however, this published music reached only a limited section of the band movement. Instrumentation was not standardised and bands preferred to use arrangements made either by their own members, if competent, or by all manner of professionals, rather than use published material which was of limited use. The band books of Black Dyke Mills Band from 1855–1862, for example, which contain forty-three works arranged for all the various parts, are entirely in the handwriting of their bandmaster F. Galloway. Professional help could be expensive: one band faced a fee of £20 for the arrangement of a contest piece in 1875.[10]

It was not until the mid-1870s, by which time sufficient bands were using identical instrumentation to make publishing a worthwhile venture, that published band music came into common usage. In 1875 Thomas Wright and Henry Round founded a band music publishers in Liverpool. Round, like Richard Smith, was a professional musician who was constantly asked to provide arrangements for local brass bands. His response led to a successful company, still in existence today and to several imitations, most notably by Richardson and Company of Sibsey in Lincolnshire. By the late 1890s, fourteen companies were devoting at least some of their energies to band music publication.[11] Individual test pieces and shorter items produced as part of a series provided their stock in trade. Prices fell dramatically and the range and amount of music available increased considerably. For 22 *s* a subscriber to Richardson's 1895 *Cornet Journal* would have received twenty pieces ranging from unambitious little waltzes to selections from Bishop's *Don John* and Weber's *Preciosa*. These *Journal* items usually contained one copy of each main part, which would still involve some copying out, but three or four shillings would buy an entire set of printed parts for a fifteen-minute operatic selection. Brass band publishing had come of age, with only minimal assistance from the 'recognised' companies, the band movement, as so often, finding its own solutions from within and around its own relatively enclosed environment.

The other major achievement of the music publishers was the generation of a music periodical press. In the mid-nineteenth century the number of periodicals devoted entirely to music was extremely small, although growing. By 1900 there were at least forty in existence. The majority emanated from publishing houses and were often initially intended as advertising vehicles, carrying details of the parent companies' latest works. The best, however, became vital sources of debate, criticism and scholarship, a source of stimulation to the existing musical community and an invaluable storehouse for later generations of historians. Undoubtedly the best known, both by contemporaries and later generations, was the *Musical Times*, originally founded as *Mainzers Musical Times and Singing Class Circular* in 1842, before passing to Novello & Company and taking on its more familiar title in 1844. The *MT* as it was often referred to, and the *Musical Herald*, published from 1889 by Curwen & Co., were probably of the greatest significance to popular musical life, carrying as they did much valuable information and discussion on the contemporary choral movement. Although both the *Musical Times* and *Herald* professed interest in the needs of the amateur musician, both largely ignored the brass band movement which once again provided its own salvation. The late nineteenth century, that key period of musical expansion, produced three band journals all tied to a major band publishing house. Wright and Round were the first in the field with their *Brass Band News* in 1881, followed by Richard Smith and company's *British Bandsmen* in 1887 and Richardson's *The Cornet* in 1893. *Musical Progress*, published by Hawkes & Son of London from 1907, also devoted considerable space to the movement. All were monthlies, except the *British Bandsmen* which became a penny weekly in 1902. Written in a very straightforward style with little literary pretension, by contributors with such splendid *nom-de-plumes* as 'Slow-worm', 'Midlandite' and 'Shoddythorpe', these journals carried contest results, adverts, technical hints and outlines of the operas that the currently popular selections were based upon, into band rooms all over England. *Brass Band News* claimed a circulation of 25,000 as early as 1890. Although somewhat 'homely' when compared to the most sophisticated periodicals of the day, they did much to guide and stimulate the growing brass band movement.[12]

The developments within music publishing in the second half of the nineteenth century were only a part, albeit perhaps the most important one, of a larger process by which an entire music service industry was established to meet the growing musical enthusiasm of the British population. By the 1890s, makers of instruments and accoutrements regaled amateur and professional alike with their wares on a scale unknown either before or since.

The second half of the nineteenth century saw a massive expansion of musical instrument manufacture. Hire purchase, increasingly common from the 1860s, coupled with a thriving second-hand trade, made the purchase of instruments a possibility for all but the poorest members of society.

It is clear that piano ownership permeated some way down the social scale. The upper echelons of the working class were certainly buying pianos by the 1860s and by the 1880s they were extremely common in traditionally 'musical' locations. A survey of later Victorian Bradford found that '[the] instrument may now be found almost in house-rows'.[13] There is evidence of semi-skilled working class families owning pianos, but it is doubtful whether this happened on any great scale. The poorest would have been unable to contemplate purchase even given the flexibility and imagination of dealers.

The Bethnal Green firm Moore & Moore is sometimes cited as the initiator of the piano 'hire' system, as hire purchase was generally known, although other firms, notably Archibald Ramsden of Leeds, also claimed the honour. Well established by the 1860s, hire purchase was impractical for most working people until the 1880s, when dealers began to accept smaller deposits. By 1900, no deposit and 10s a month payments over three years were common. There is no doubt that until the legal position was clarified in 1895, customers could fall prey to all manner of sharp practice. The quality of the cheapest pianos was often very poor.[14] Frederick Crowest claimed that while manufacturers of cheap instruments would argue that they were 'doing humanity and the state a service in furnishing means whereby the working classes may provide themselves with pianofortes', they were actually doing the opposite with their 'gluing together of unseasoned woods and common materials [carrying] false harmonics and untrue chords into the houses of hundreds and thousands of families'.[15] There was truth in both arguments. While many purchased instruments which did little justice to the music extracted from them, the same instruments could in certain instances provide vital rudimentary skills and opportunities. By the turn of the century, opportunity for popular purchase was further expanded by an increasing second-hand market.

Fitting a piano into a working class dwelling could pose serious logistical problems. In 1906, the ten-year-old daughter of a Hull seaman was at last bought the second-hand piano – price twenty-three shillings – she had longed for.

A deposit was paid and the next day, Saturday, my two elder brothers hired a handcart and with the help of other able bodied men around at the time, unscrewed the legs and hauled the body of the piano onto the cart, what a job and 1½ miles to trundle it to 110 Day Street. The whole window frame had to be removed from the front room, where the piano was to be sat and a gentleman living opposite, being a joiner by trade, promptly offered his services in payment of a pint. So in went the piano and back went the window frame.[16]

Such a tale of sweat and ingenuity perhaps explains why new and smaller instruments appeared throughout the period as makers experimented with newly-available technical processes and inventions. With regard to popular music, the most important new arrivals were the saxhorn family – dealt with later – and the concertina. This much-maligned instrument, which collected such nicknames as the 'constantscreamer' and ''arry's worrier', was patented in 1844 by Sir Charles Wheatstone, better known perhaps for his work on the electric telegraph. A full range of concertinas developed, the largest with eighty-one keys, the smallest, the 'Anglo' with as few as twenty. Its portability and relatively low price made it an extremely popular instrument in the period after 1850. By 1910 the two largest British makers had produced almost a quarter of a million instruments between them and countless imported models, usually of the smaller varieties, were in circulation.[17]

The bulk of increased production was largely met by the expansion of firms in existence before 1840, rather than by the foundation of new businesses. In 1862, for example, there were twenty-five main makers of brass instruments, yet despite the continued growth of the band movement, there were no major additions to the list after that date. Most instrument companies were centred in London, although piano

makers could be found in most regional centres, and individual
craftsmen operated throughout the provinces. John Sharpe of Pudsey
in West Yorkshire was a noted maker of oboe reeds, J. W. Owen made
violins in Leeds in 1884, Alf Gisborne and Company built brass
instruments in Birmingham, Joseph Higham in Manchester. In
general, however, only London possessed a sufficiently-developed
repository of skills and techniques, and the rest of England remained
dependent upon it. Even as essentially provincial an institution as the
brass band looked to London as its main source of supply. Of the
twenty makers advertising in band periodicals in 1914, over half were
London-based, including both Boosey and Besson, the two with the
largest share of the market.[18]

Musical accessories as well as instruments also became far more
common as the century progressed. Manuscript paper, piano stools,
bandstands, batons, metronomes and all manner of items were produced to meet the needs of musicians. The brass band movement yet
again generated its own sub-industry, involving by 1900 some twenty
to thirty companies meeting specialist needs with such items as music
stands, 'band lamps for dark nights', balm for sore lips, trombone
slide oil, instrument electro-plating and band uniforms. There were at
least eight firms specialising in uniform production by the 1890s,
centred in London and the West Riding. John Beevers of Huddersfield was probably the first man to enter this field, establishing a
business in 1864 and building trade by riding on horseback taking
orders throughout Pennine banding country. By the late 1880s he
operated two mills largely devoted to band uniform production.
Music clearly offered the *petit entrepreneur* a rich field.[19]

Most communities of over 10,000 had at least one music-seller and
instrument dealer to market these products, with the number much
higher in the most musically-inclined areas. *Hanson's Yorkshire Musical Directory*, published in 1894, illustrates a remarkable level of
provision for the local musical community. Bradford, with a population of just under 300,000, had no fewer than forty-six music
dealers. Halifax (approx. 100,000 population) had eighteen, Batley
(30,000), four and even as small a community as Sowerby Bridge
(7,500), two. Not all of them were music specialists, some probably
doing little more than supplying a rack of current sheet music in
amongst the sewing machines, cabinets or confectionery that formed
their staple trade. Nevertheless, such figures are a powerful testimony
to contemporary musical appetites. The widespread existence of such

dealers made musical activity so much easier to contemplate. When the young Eric Coates wanted a violin, his father had no need to leave the mining town of Hucknall and travel to Mansfield or even Nottingham to find one. John Munks, organist at the concregational chapel and owner of a music and cycle shop in the High Street, willingly met his requirements.[20]

Informal music

What now follows is but a glimpse of an often rich musical culture, sadly destined to remain largely hidden from view.

The house – especially the 'parlour' if one was grand enough to possess one – was a cornerstone of popular musical life. Clearly, some houses were a great deal more musical than others. Exceptional levels of domestic performance were to be found in the weaving communities of Yorkshire and Lancashire, especially in the early and middle part of the nineteenth century. Sunday evenings were a favourite time for neighbours to gather and perform.

About fifty years ago any person going through Stanbury on a Sunday evening could have stopped to listen to the singing and playing. Pianos were not common in those days, but there were fiddles and flutes and various other instruments. In many a house, if one could have gone in, he would have heard a good concert . . . some of the houses were moderately large, and you would have seen the father and mother and children, also some neighbours, sitting round the house singing and playing. This was not done in one house only, but it was so in many cottage homes. . . . At that time the young people were not satisfied with learning a few tunes, they wished to read the music themselves. Many of them would be able to play several instruments or take their part in singing. When one was tired of singing or blowing he would take up the stringed instrument and play.

Even allowing for a little exaggeration born from nostalgia, this picture of a remote Yorkshire textile village in the 1840s and 50s indicates the levels of musical enthusiasm which could appertain.[21]

As the nineteenth century progressed, music in the home became increasingly focused on the piano and, to a lesser extent, the concertina and melodeon, instruments most common in rural areas. The piano probably encouraged solitary habits to some extent, although it was still at the centre of family and neighbourhood gatherings. As already noted, piano purchase permeated some considerable way into the working class and the instrument should not be viewed as a middle-class preserve. To some extent, however, it did have definite connotations of gender, seen by many as 'the woman's instrument'. Many middle-class guides to female etiquette stressed the emotional, moral and physical benefits that stemmed from diligent practice. The piano was undoubtedly a valuable friend when filling up the long hours of leisure foisted upon many moneyed women and, although much scorn has been cast upon their efforts in much musical litera- ture, some undoubtedly became outstanding musicians. It was also an aid to romance. The blossoming of friendship and love between the female accompanist and the young male singer was not an uncommon feature of contemporary fiction, song and popular art. However, there is plentiful evidence of men, especially working-class men, playing the piano and indeed, for many of the leading male figures in their local musical communities, the instrument was an invaluable tool.[22]

It has been frequently argued that purchase of a piano, particularly by the lower middle and working classes, was more the result of social than musical considerations. This belief finds its most detailed expo- sition in the work of Cyril Ehrlich who stresses that purchase was an act of 'social emulation'. He is clearly in agreement with the second speaker when he quotes this extract from D. H. Lawrence's *Women in Love*:

'Don't you think the collier's pianoforte . . . is a symbol for something very real, a real desire for something higher in the collier's life?' 'Yes. Amazing heights of upright grandeur. It makes him so much higher in his neighbouring collier's eyes. He sees himself reflected in the neighbouring opinion . . . several feet taller on the strength of the pianoforte and he is satisfied.'

Lawrence was not alone in appreciating this aspect of the piano's function. Frederick Crowest, writing in 1881, described the instru- ment as a 'highly respectabilising piece of furniture', while Robert Roberts, remembering working-class Edwardian Salford, termed the piano a status symbol 'of the highest significance'.[23]

However, while there is value in this line of argument, the question Lawrence's character posed surely deserves as much consideration as the answer it received. Over-emphasis upon the search for respectabi- lity obscures the existence of deep levels of genuine musical sensibility amongst the working population. The purchase of a piano was often simply another manifestation of the contemporary appetite for music, and an attempt to satisfy it. While musical and social aspirations were undoubtedly mixed in many minds, to view this phenomenon as mere snobbery oversimplifies a complex picture, and forgets a history of musical attainment on the part of working-class people which was often achieved only by dint of hard work and self-sacrifice.

Musical performances extended beyond the house into more public spaces. Singing in the street seems to have been relatively common, at least by the Edwardian period, and could assume surprisingly high standards. 'Even at the corner of the street, someone would start humming a popular tune, and soon everybody would be singing the song in real harmony', a Yorkshire miner recalled.[24] Large gatherings, especially in the provinces, were often enlivened with sing-songs as two fascinating descriptions of an Edwardian football crowd illustrate. A journalist from the *Yorkshire Observer* followed some 7,000 Bradford City supporters to an away match with Nottingham Forest:

One of the young sparks of Nottingham had brought the girl of his youthful fancy to see the match. His officious attentions to the lady were soon noticed and the crowd gave vent to a prolonged 'oh' followed by an equally long-drawn-out 'ah'. Someone squeaked in a falsetto voice, and shouts of laughter nearly brought the stand down. Then the crowd broke mightily in the chorus 'My Girl's a Yorkshire Girl' varying one of the lines as follows: 'though she's a factory lass and doesn't wear Nottingham lace'. By this time the young couple thought it time to decamp. A piccolo player came along and struck up with a lively air. Immediately the 'boys' began a rhythmic accompaniment on hand-bells, bugles and tommy-talkers. The resulting effects have never been equalled by Strauss. Not far away another Yorkshire chorus was singing a hymn tune to the strain of concertinas.

The next week, before a home game with Burnley, the Bradford crowd took time off from pelting the visiting mascot with 'volleys of orange peel, banana skins and clods of earth' in order to join a local brass band in a selection of Harry Lauder songs, with one chorus of 'I Love a Lassie' placing 'a serious strain on the permanence of the stands'. It is relatively rare to be given specific details of community song repertoire in this context (even rarer to see such a candid picture of working-class youth enjoying itself), but this mixture of hymn tunes and music-hall song does appear to have been fairly typical.[25]

Probably the most important centres for informal music making outside the home were public house, church and chapel. The organised commercial element of public house singing, in the shape of the singing-saloon, has already been dealt with, but a variety of other activities existed. The number of pubs licensed for music declined from the late nineteenth century as the temperance lobby made itself felt, but there were still many available locations. The following list of

licences in major English cities, indicative more of the relative strict-
ness of various magistrates than the musical proclivities of certain
regions, was produced for the chief constable of Bradford in 1902
during the course of an action to disallow some forty licences.

Manchester	388	Leeds	113
Bradford	361	Birmingham	44
Nottingham	286	Liverpool	38
Sheffield	114		

Obviously, not all pubs made use of their licences, but it is also
possible, especially in earlier periods, that many publicans allowed
musical events without possessing a licence.[26]

At present, more is known about rural than urban public house
music. In Suffolk, an area which has been the focus of two important
surveys, one of the more common forms of activity was the 'tune up'.
Local singers and instrumentalists gathered in the taproom of a set
hostelry and entertained each other, anyone refusing or unable to
contribute being forced to buy drinks. (The urban equivalent was
often termed a 'free and easy'.) The vast majority of those present
were male agricultural labourers, women only being invited in on
specific occasions or for certain dances and the 'respectable' classes
kept at safe distance in the parlour or saloon bar. Fiddles, dulcimers,
and after about 1900, concertinas and melodeons were the main
instruments. There appears to have been a strong tradition of song
'ownership', it being assumed that certain songs or tunes belonged to
an individual who, if he chose, could pass them on to another performer. This tradition remained strong in Suffolk and doubtless in
other areas until at least 1939 and, in attenuated form, maintains an
existence in a handful of communities.[27]

Urban pub music was far more piano-centred and possibly less
'formal', with spontaneous or semi-spontaneous sing-songs as
common practice (although they doubtless occurred in country areas
too). A contributor to the *Musical Home Journal* in 1908 noted how in
Huddersfield:

It is no uncommon thing in the local public houses to see several young fellows
suddenly rise and give a lusty rendering of 'When Evening's Twilight' or
'Here's Life and Health to England's King' or 'Who Will o'er the Downs with
Me?'. And that, be it duly set down, long before 11 p.m.[28]

Unfortunately, most views of singing before this date tend to tell us far
more about the prejudices of contemporary middle-class social

observers and investigators than they do about popular music. Surely there was more to urban public house music than diverse unspecified 'low' 'immoral' and 'imprudent' happenings?

Music in church and chapel is far too large a topic to discuss here. Nevertheless, it has at least to be acknowledged that attendance at worship, either as chorister or as member of the congregation, did much to encourage the habit of music in the period up to 1914. Obviously, the patterns of religious attendance led to the exclusion of large sections of the working class from the musical influence of organised religion. For those who did attend, apart from offering specialist choral training (a point developed later), religious attendance gave many their first regular exposure to music, helping develop a basic competence and liking that could later develop in many different directions.[29]

As the scattered hints in preceding paragraphs suggest, the repertoire favoured by singers and performers in home, street and public house varied considerably according to the family tradition, levels of musical skill, place of performance, class and/or age of the participants, the nature of the occasion and the geographical location. There must in particular have been considerable regional variation, especially in the period before about 1870, after which point the combined efforts of schools, music-halls and music publishers increasingly ironed out local idiosyncracies. Doubtless a clear difference between urban and rural repertoire existed right up to 1914, in the sense that country songs collected by Sharp and his compatriots were largely unknown to towndwellers. Recent research, however, has shown that a flow in the opposite direction, from town to country, did take place, with parlour ballads and nigger minstrel pieces, and sometimes even music-hall songs, featuring quite noticeably in the stock of such celebrated country singers as Henry Burstow of Sussex, even if such pieces were altered to suit the style and tradition of country performance. (Even part of the 'Huntsman Chorus' from Weber's *Der Freischütz* found its way into the dance music of North Yorkshire.) Such pieces were edited out of published collections by middle-class folklorists anxious to find only the 'true' musical expressions of an idealised 'folk' and disappointed to find significant traces of urban taint.[30]

Again, a broad if far from rigid class difference appertained, country folk song and music hall song remaining typical of the working class, parlour ballads of the middle class. There were though strong overlaps even here, especially after about 1885 when music-hall song became far more widely available to middle-class audiences. Moreover, there existed a range of material–hymns, the ballads of Henry Russell, Gilbert and Sullivan and the best known arias from British and Italian opera – which were there for all classes to perform.

At present, it is not possible to offer the type of detailed, statistically-rooted survey of what music was the most popular in terms of sheet music sale and suchlike given by Charles Hamm in his masterful study of American popular music, *Yesterdays*. What follows is an 'educated guess' at the pieces most frequently heard by a moderately keen listener in home and public house, who had lived throughout the period 1840–1914 and who had the advantage of living in at least a moderately-sized town where opportunities were often greatest for meeting a broad repertoire. The songs are presented in alphabetical order in order to prevent any implications of scientific inquiry attaching themselves to what is a personal and inevitably haphazard exercise (see overleaf).

Even if the specific pieces listed here may not have been *the* most popular works, they do typify the core at least of urban domestic music, a mixture of parlour ballads, operatic songs, music-hall pieces and sacred works. The list probably fails to do justice to the last category and also fails to capture the significant degree of art music that found its way into, particularly, the instrumental repertoire. More confident pianists were tackling Mendelssohn's 'Songs Without Words', the simpler Chopin nocturnes and certain Beethoven sonatas, especially the first movement of the 'Moonlight'. The *Tannhäuser* overture and the intermezzo from *Cavalleria Rusticana* were featuring in the performances of the most accomplished concertina players. Once again the distinction between 'popular' and 'high' was not closely observed, a feature illustrated even more dramatically by the popular musical societies, to which we now turn.[31]

The origins of the popular musical society

Arguably the most significant, and certainly the most lasting, features of 'community-based' music life were the brass band and the choral society. By the end of the nineteenth century literally thousands of these institutions existed, alongside a smaller but significant number of amateur orchestras, handbell teams and concertina bands. It is an

Title	Composer	Source (where applicable)	Original musical location
After the Ball	Chas. K. Harris		Music-hall
Comin' Thru' the Rye	Trad. ('The Miller's Daughter')		Concert
Daisy Bell	Harry Dacre		Music-hall
Death of Nelson, The	John Braham		Concert
Holy City, The	Michael Maybrick		Concert/Parlour
Home Sweet Home	Henry Bishop	*Clari: or the Maid of Milan*	Opera
Kathleen Mavourneen	F. N. Crouch		Parlour
I dreamt that I dwelt in Marble Halls	Michael Balfe	*The Bohemian Girl*	Opera
I'll Sing Thee Songs of Araby	Frederick Clay		Parlour
In the Gloamin'	Lady Arthur Hill		Parlour
La Pluie de Perles	George Osborne		Domestic piano
Lead, Kindly Light	C. H. Purday		Hymn
Lily of Laguna	Leslie Stuart		Music-hall
Lost Chord, The	Arthur Sullivan		Concert/Parlour
Miners Dream of Home, The	Leo Dryden		Music-hall
My Old Dutch	Albert Chevalier		Music-hall
My Pretty Jane	Henry Bishop		Concert-hall
O Ruddier than the Cherry	G. F. Handel	*Acis and Galatea*	Music-drama
Salut d'Amour	Edward Elgar		Concert/Parlour
Take a Pair of Sparkling Eyes	Arthur Sullivan	*The Gondoliers*	Operetta
Tell Me Pretty Maiden	Leslie Stuart	*Floradora*	Musical comedy
To Anthea	J. L. Hatton		Parlour
The Better Land	John Blockley		Parlour
The Three Fishers	John Hullah		Parlour
Woodman Spare That Tree	Henry Russell		Concert

illuminating commentary upon the previously narrow perspectives of all relevant branches of academic scholarship, that almost no serious study of this massive element of popular culture has taken place.

The choirs and bands of Victorian England were not the first formal amateur musical societies. Secular bodies date back to at least the sixteenth century, one of the earliest recorded being founded by Nicholas Yonge, probably a St Paul's chorister, whose house formed late in the century the daily meeting-place for a group of musically-inclined London merchants and gentlemen. By the mid eighteenth century a number of formally-constituted societies existed, such as the Madrigal Society, founded in 1741 by a group of Spitalfields artisans and weavers, the altogether more socially 'select' Musical and Amicable Society founded in Birmingham in 1762, and the Oratorio Choral Society founded in the same town in 1766.[32] In general, these bodies belonged more to the pattern of Georgian élite culture, typified by the literary and philosophical societies, than to the popular musical traditions of the next century, and therefore played only a minor part in the shaping of later choral and instrumental culture.

Probably of greater importance to the popular tradition were the choirs and bands connected to the Anglican church, and, to a lesser extent, some nonconformist sects, that had begun to emerge from the late seventeenth century. They were perhaps most common in the rural south of England and it is certainly the bands and choirs of Sussex that are best known, their history having been rescued by the work of Canon K. H. MacDermott in the 1920s and given recent scholarly shape and polish by Vic Gammon. MacDermott discovered some one hundred and twenty bands in Sussex in the period 1650–1850, most of them based on a combination of flutes, violins, cellos and clarionets. Musicians and singers were mainly recruited from 'among village tradesmen, journeymen and, to some extent, agricultural labourers'. They performed sacred (and secular) music sometimes with great skill, always with great pride and enthusiasm, in a style – an emphasis on volume coupled with nasal tone, ornamentation and slow speed of delivery were pronounced features – alien and often objectionable to 'educated' taste and markedly different from the polished manner of later bodies, but firmly placed in popular taste and custom.[33]

The majority of southern bands fell victim to a rigorous campaign around mid-century, ostensibly intended to 'improve' church music as part of the wider movement for change within the church, but underpinned in many cases by a degree of middle-class hostility toward the more humble musicians. Gammon has recently characterised the ensuing events as 'a conflict of the rich against the poor, the formally educated against the non-formally educated, the articulate against those who expressed themselves more by actions than words, élite culture against popular culture'.[34] Certainly some fierce battles were fought as clergymen attempted to introduce barrel-organs and more formally-trained choirs to replace the old order. At Amberley in Sussex, the vicar 'froze the taps' of the local public house to the old choir who had gone on strike rather than follow new directions, the choir responding by whitewashing his windows, having already 'rough musicked' him from church. In 1866 at Walsingham in Norfolk, where musical issues combined with larger social and political tensions, a newly-installed organ was blown up![35]

The exact contribution of church and chapel musicians to the formal societies of the Victorian period varied from area to area. Although, as will be seen, the Methodist musicians, more commonly found in the industrial North and Midlands, also came under attack, they appear to have survived for longer and to have been absorbed quite happily in the welter of alternative musical organisations open to them. However, in the south and probably in other rural areas, the effects of suppression were profound. Certainly, statements by the late Victorian folklorists typified by Sabine Baring-Gould's comment that the abolition of the old order 'gave the death blow to instrumental music in our villages', were exaggerated.[36] The traditions of two hundred years could not simply wither away and at least some of the instruments, personnel and skill of the old musicians were eventually transferred into the countless village bands that graced local festivals and community occasions in the second half of the century. More generally, the Anglican choral revival which followed the suppression was not all bad when viewed from a popular perspective, helping stimulate an improvement in choral technique, creating the breed of organists and choirmasters eventually so important in the training of choirs and other bodies and encouraging sheet music production by firms such as Novello. Nevertheless, while the South of England lacked the social and economic advantages necessary for a full-blown musical culture of the type which emerged in the North and Midlands, the attack on popular church music severely damaged a strong local tradition which might have either provided a complement to or, in time, become a part of, the more dignified, solemn dominant tradition emerging in the North. Deemed, like blood sports or street football, to be an uncivilised remnant of a past culture and thus removed from the protective shield that religion so often held out to music, the old school of 'Repeat and Twiddle' saw such options effectively closed.

The most significant contribution to the development of the great Victorian tradition was to come from the North. The key centres were to be the textile regions of Lancashire, West Yorkshire and, to a lesser extent, Derbyshire. As early as 1788, Charles Dibdin noted that:

I have been assured, for a fact, that more than one man in Halifax can take any part in choruses of the *Messiah*, and go regularly through the whole Oratorio by heart; and indeed, the facility with which the common people join together throughout the greatest part of the Yorkshire and Lancashire in every species of choral music, is truly astonishing'.[37]

The intense musical culture of these areas emanated from the interrelation of four factors: a relatively high population which both provided a 'market' for the talent of local musicians and placed musicians within relatively close proximity to each other; the division of the population into small, often tightly-knit communities, often based on one industry, in which voluntary bodies were often easier to organise and sustain; the presence of many philanthropic/paternalist employers keen to foster 'useful' recreation; and perhaps most important of all, the strength of nonconformity.

Methodism, above all, had deep roots in both regions and Methodists had from the outset been encouraged to sing vigorously and often.[38] Indeed, Methodism and music became synonomous. Certainly, Methodists in no way had a monopoly of local musical activity. Many other religious groups enjoyed a full musical life and by the end of the eighteenth century much music-making was interdenominational. Sunday-school anniversaries were celebrated by 'sitting-ups', concerts featuring children's choirs and adult vocalists and musicians from many different denominations. However, it is clear that very often it was Methodist success that stimulated other denominations to make more use of music in worship. Many Anglican evangelicals shared the Methodists' trust in the power of music and others accepted the need for change on the practical grounds that music, or the lack of it, could dramatically alter the size of congregations. 'It is not rashness', argued Dr William Vincent in 1790, 'to assert that for one who has been drawn away from the Established Church by preaching, ten have been induced by music'.[39] Both through its own deeds and the imitation it engendered, Methodism greatly enhanced the role of music in religious life, and in time that music was to spill over from its original setting into a wider social context, thus laying the base of a popular tradition that, to an extent, remains with us today.

Informal clubs and gatherings existed in Yorkshire and Lancashire

before the 1740s and indeed Methodists attempted to 'infiltrate' and
reform them.[40] They appear, however, to have taken on renewed life
and to have increased in number from about this period, although
exact details of size and chronology are patchy. They often had rules
and membership payments similar to those used by trade clubs, but
they differed from the societies named above and those that were to
follow in the nineteenth century in their anonymity. They were
simply 'the club', 'local singers' or 'them singing and scraping chaps'.
Musicians met for weekly and monthly practices as well as meeting at
each others' houses and in public houses whenever possible. This
musical culture was by no means the sole preserve of the 'working
class', if indeed such a phrase can be applied to the late eighteenth and
even early nineteenth century. Bradford's musical community in the
1820s included the owner of a vitriol works, the manager of a textile
factory, an artist, an attorney's clerk, an architect, the postmaster and
the local inspector of weights and measures.[41] In general, however,
the impression remains that it was the domestic outworkers, artisans
and small tradesmen who formed the backbone of local musical life.
'The common people', 'mechanics', 'workpeople': these are the contemporary phrases that are so often encountered. The social and
occupational groups who played the most significant role in the
development of working-class political culture made an equally
critical contribution to the wider social life of their communities.

If one occupational group can claim particular importance in this
stage of Northern musical life, it must surely be the hand-loom
weavers. Weaver-musicians abound in the history of this period: in
Yorkshire, Thomas Fawcett of Eccleshill, a cellist and head of a
family that has since produced thirty-six professional musicians in
four generations; David Turton, a flannel weaver of Horbury, whom,
legend has it, once tamed a charging bull with a note from his bassoon;
Tommy Aumler, a worsted weaver from Idle and singer of great
renown, who while in his cups would wander the area singing:

'Lord in Thee, Lord in Thee I have trusted;
Let me never be confounded'.[42]

Lancashire could boast James Cordwell of Swinton, one of a group of
local singers who walked a hundred and thirty miles to take part in
Handel's *Israel in Egypt* at a choral festival in Newcastle, or the
anonymous musician from Dean in the Forest of Rossendale who
reputedly linked together four looms in order to give him more time
for musical study.[43] There were the slightly larger-than-life

characters remembered by antiquarians with an eye for local colour, but in their musical enthusiasm they were typical of so many of their contemporaries. They represent a further key element of that weaver culture rescued from oblivion by E. P. Thompson, another manifestation of an intellectual current that created poets, botanists, geologists and mathematicians in such apparently unlikely settings as Pendlebury, Batley and Heckmondwike.[44]

Music was pursued with remarkable enthusiasm and resulted in considerable self-sacrifice. The weavers, with their relatively flexible work routines, would often take time off from work in order to practice, working long hours at night to make up lost cloth production. Particularly keen musicians undoubtedly followed the example of Joseph Fawcett and his branch of the celebrated musical family, who even while weaving 'would sometimes stand their music on a shelf and cast glances at it from moment to moment, whistling or singing the notes so as to get familiar with them'. Mealbreaks were also used as rehearsal periods by Joseph and his three sons. Great distances were walked in order to rehearse or play in or attend a concert. The Lancashire singers' walk to Newcastle was exceptional, but was only an extreme example of a common practice. One, admittedly semi-professional, singer, computed that she had walked 36,000 miles in the 1830s alone, in order to sing at various functions.[45]

Financial as well as physical demands were considerable, for musical instruments and sheet music were luxury items, purchase of which stretched the ingenuity of working men to considerable levels. It is not clear where instruments came from. It is possible that some were abandoned or pawned by itinerant musicians, others taken into the community by demobbed soldiers. Hire purchase, certainly used in a crude form by brass bands as early as 1855, may have existed in the earlier period, thus easing financial pressures. Some instruments were home-made. Organs were built by craftsmen of musical bent – William Jackson of Masham, North Yorkshire, minor composer and eventually conductor of Bradford Festival Choral Society, built one while still in his teens – while local cabinet makers could construct a violin or cello of considerable standard. The so-called 'Larks of Dean' ('Deighn Layrocks' in local dialect) a musical group centred on the Lancashire villages of Dean, Loveclough, Goodshaw and Lumb between c. 1760–c. 1830, possessed a number of home-produced instruments, many of them violins constructed by local weaver James Nuttall. (Some of them are still to be seen in Rawtenstall museum.)[46]

Sheet music in its turn was so expensive, with the full score of an oratorio often costing over £1, that hand-made copies were widely used, the music being copied – 'pricked' was the common term – often onto hand-ruled staves. A weaver from Huddersfield remembered how:

When any new pieces were required people subscribed and bought one copy. The blank music paper was purchased at three half pence a sheet, often fetched from places four and five miles away. The different parts were copied out. It was no uncommon thing for a person to sit up all night copying. When written, each part would be bound in brown paper and most carefully guarded and used as long as the paper would hang together.[47]

One can only begin to contemplate the feelings of Edmund Beaver, 'a labouring man' and a cellist with the Keighley Choral Society who, in 1848, inadvertently tossed the printed cello part to Haydn's *Creation* on the fire and had to find 10s 6d for a new one![48]

The musical community drew its repertoire from a broad range. Glees, part-songs, operatic overtures and even traditional dance tunes occur frequently in the remembrances of contemporaries, often in remarkable conjunction. Robert Ashworth of Carr in Lancashire, banksmen at a colliery, small farmer, lay-preacher and cellist, completed a session of sacred music and preaching at Winterburn Chapel by playing a hornpipe after the congregation left. Remonstrated with by a member for playing 'an idle tune' he replied that 'there were no idle tunes; it was all in the rendering'. John Newton, a hooker-on at a Bolton colliery and one of the premier Lancashire sacred tenors and singing teachers, was also famous for his rendering of 'Manchester Races'. But for the majority it was sacred music that generated the greatest enthusiasm and the music of the eighteenth-century composers Arne, Croft, Green and Boyce, and above all of 'their beloved Handel', formed the core of their musical culture.[49]

Handel's *Messiah* became almost a cultural icon. First performed in Dublin in 1742, it did not win any great popularity in London until 1750. Gradually it spread through the provinces and was received with remarkable enthusiasm in Yorkshire and Lancashire on its arrival in the 1760s.[50] Much has been written about the close relationship between *Messiah* and Methodist doctrine. It has been claimed that 'Handel gave musical expression to the very doctrines which those evangelicals [i.e. Methodists] rescued from neglect' and in particular to Wesley's doctrine of 'assurance'.[51] There is undoubtedly much in this, but it is tempting to suggest that for many the appeal was

doctrinal only in the limited sense that the work dealt with the essence
of Christian thought: prophecy, the coming of Christ, resurrection
and redemption. Here was a compendium of basic Christianity set to
music, exhilarating for both listener and performer. It is also important to appreciate that although local Methodists did much to encourage performances (normally selections rather than the full work),
some of its crucial early performances were held in Anglican establishments. In Yorkshire, for example, the first *Messiah* was held at
Halifax Parish Church in 1766. Joah Bates, son of the local parish
clerk and later to gain national prominence as the organiser of the first
Handel Festival in 1784, brought a manuscript copy from London
early in the year and the oratorio was eventually staged on 27 August.
Two years later the work received remarkable exposure, being performed on fifteen consecutive Fridays at Holbeck Chapel in Leeds,
another Anglican foundation.[52] It would be invaluable to know more
about the singing 'style' that carried these more serious compositions.
Roger Elbourne has suggested that an approach far removed 'from
severe classical style and high culture' was adopted, hinting at a style
not dissimilar to that of the church bands. While this might have been
true for the majority, the elite performers chosen to perform at
festivals around the country must have been able to employ the artistic
techniques of the day.[53]

It is significant that within Methodism at least, the popularity of
oratorio and compositions drawing inspiration from oratorio, proved
to be a source of tension between leadership and rank and file. While
John Wesley was appreciative of many eighteenth century works, in
general he felt the enthusiasm amongst chapel goers for what he called
'fugueing' music detracted from the spiritual message of the texts that
the music accompanied, thus eliminating their devotional value.

Our composers do not aim at moving the passions, but quite another thing – at
varying and contrasting the notes a thousand different ways. What had
counterpoint to do with the passions? It is applied to a quite different faculty
of the mind; not to our joy, or hope, or fear; but merely to the ear, to the
imagination, or internal sense . . . [now] this astonishing jargon has found a
place even in the worship of God![54]

At least until the third decade of the nineteenth century, the
Methodist Conference continued the attack on excessive
counterpoint, the introduction of anthems, and the use of instruments
other than the bass viol (theoretically the only instrument allowed),
but judging by how often these strictures had to be repeated, it seems

that local congregations ignored directives that interfered with their own taste. In cultural as well as theological matters, Wesley unleashed a popular tradition that he could not always control.[55]

From about 1820 – the chronology varies from region to region – two new themes emerge in the history of secular popular musical societies: the emergence of distinctive instrumental bodies in the shape of the wind band, and increasing levels of formalisation and organisation in all bodies. Throughout the eighteenth century instrumental and choral musicians had worked together, the instrumentalists accompanying the choir and then winning the limelight while the singers rested. 'A band of music' is occasionally encountered on its own in the late eighteenth century, but recognisable bands do not in general emerge until the next century. The early history of the wind band is extremely obscure and the holy grail of 'the first band' is as elusive as 'the first music-hall'. By 1820 a number of bands had emerged, mainly in industrial areas of England. Coxlodge Institute in Durham, Stalybridge Old (engaged to play at Peterloo but detained in a nearby pub, according to one story) and Besses o' th' Barn from Cheshire, Bolton Old from Lancashire and Queenshead from West Yorkshire, were all firmly established by that date. None of them were *brass* bands, most of them using an array of clarinets, bassoons, flutes and serpents. The identity of the first brass band is yet another awkward area, but the band founded in York in 1833 by Daniel Hardman is a serious contender for the honour.[56]

It has been suggested that wind bands were founded at this time partly as an extension of, partly in imitation of, the army and volunteer bands that proliferated during the Napoleonic Wars (1793–1815). There can be no doubt that many working men, either as soldiers, militia men or as inhabitants of industrial communities under something akin to military occupation during the unrest that permeated the period, had experience of performing in or listening to military bands. Once the wars were over, it is probable that many put their new musical experience to use. Bolton Old Band grew directly from the band of the Bolton Volunteers founded by Colonel Ralph Fletcher in 1803, for example, while there is evidence of other bands being trained by ex-military personnel.[57]

The little we know of the early band repertoire suggests that these early civilian bands saw themselves, much like military bands of the time, as providing a musical backcloth and a degree of colour, rather than as an artistic unit. By the 1840s many of these bands were performing selections from oratorio and opera to a very reasonable standard, but their early repertoire appears more functional. Besses o' th' Barn won an impromptu contest to celebrate the coronation of George IV in July 1821 with a rendition of 'God Save The King', which suggests that either they had a marvellous sense of occasion and/or that bands at this stage had only a limited repertoire suited to the enlivening of the local events which seem to have been their main source of activity at this time.[58] Significantly, they were frequent attenders at political demonstrations, an interesting example of working-class ability to adapt ruling-class institutions to their own ends. When military bands appeared in English industrial communities during the Luddite era (1811–1817), they were part of an apparatus designed to quell the working population into an acceptance of industrial 'progress' and the existing political system. When working people imitated these bands, they used them to give them heart during demonstrations for social reform and political change.

Useful as the concept of a military-civilian band link might be, it is, however, somewhat 'parochial' to view the band movement in isolation from other musical developments. The emergence of civilian bands needs to be looked at in conjunction with the second theme, the increased formalisation of amateur musical life and the question asked, why did bands and other formal musical societies, normally choral societies, emerge *at the same time*? From about 1820, crucial changes were taking place in the organisation of musical life. Of great significance, is the fact that societies now had *names*, which had been extremely rare in the earlier period. The clubs, classes, groups and meetings became the Huddersfield Choral Society, the Eton and Windsor Amateur Choral Society, the Gloucester Harmonic Society. By the 1840s there were dozens of 'named' societies scattered all over England. These new bodies had formal committees and increasingly rigorous rules. A system of fines featured prominently. Members of Huddersfield Choral Society were fined 3*d* for lateness, 6*d* for absence, intoxication or obscenity, 2*s* 6*d* for interrupting during the practice of a piece, and, under legislation introduced in 1843, suffered expulsion for attendance at the local Owenite Hall of Science.[59] These rules seem more stringent than those previously adopted by the local clubs. Perhaps most crucial of all, these new bodies gave regular public performances. This had happened before, but had normally tended to be part of a specific community ritual, such as the Sunday-school anniversary, rather than as a musical concert in its own right.

By the 1830s regular concert series were relatively common, with at least one society bankrupting itself in an attempt to meet the salaries of the professional singers that they hired.[60]

There has been surprisingly little attempt to explain this vital development, with most writers accepting the changes as a *fait accompli*. To some extent the new developments may have resulted from 'musical' factors. Some societies, notably the York Choral Society (1833) and Hereford Choral Society (1837), seem to have been attempts to keep together in regular practice the singers who performed in local cathedral choir festivals. Others represented a new response to the old problem of purchasing and distributing sheet music. The Bradford Musical Friendly Society, its mutual aid function clear from its name, was founded in 1821 as a music library for local musicians, although from the 1830s, under the name Bradford Old Choral Society, it also began to give concerts.[61] Especially in smaller communities, formal organisation may have resulted from the dissolution of church bands and the reform of the choirs, common from the 1830s. Displaced performers may well have looked for new outlets. A further possibility in the increased interest shown in amateur music by the growing group of professional musicians from this period, who had much kudos to gain from being associated with efficient, publicly-known organisations. William Weber, in his *Music and The Middle Classes*, has argued this point strongly, claiming that 'among the least affluent, informal music-making became transformed into formalised events governed by professionals'. However, important as professionals were to become, whether as choral conductors, band trainers or concert promoters, they were never as common as Weber suggests. Indeed, in the 1820s Joseph Bottomly, the first conductor of the Halifax Choral Society, was sacked for asking for a fee, a demand opposed to the determinedly amateur, democratic spirit of this and many other societies.[62]

While all these factors are of consequence, it is likely that the new formal emphasis owed most to social and economic change. The organised society, be it band, choir or orchestra, was both a response to new opportunities offered by a rapidly expanding and industrialising society and a defence against the dislocation emanating from the changes that expansion and industralisation created. The early decades of the nineteenth century offered the musical fraternity an unparalleled chance to parade their talents in public. Before about

1815, much music-making was informal simply because so few institutions existed which could generate public performance. But after that date, opportunities increased considerably. The concert became an increasingly common form of entertainment from the 1830s and 1840s as the expansion of industry and commerce increased the number of people with sufficient surplus income to allow enjoyment of leisure activity. Middle-class citizens in particular, looking for respectable, rational forms of entertainment, found the sacred choral concert much to their taste, and their support fuelled the growth of formal, concert-orientated choral societies. Similarly, the increase in size of towns in this period guaranteed a fairly sizeable audience for concerts and made them a less hazardous financial undertaking. The wind band movement was also encouraged, by the appearance of mill and mine owners and railway companies, anxious to jollify opening ceremonies and worker's 'treats', and by organisers of trade unions, temperance societies and political clubs seeking to dignify rallies and demonstrations. It became increasingly necessary for amateur musicians to abandon their anonymity, to adopt codes of conduct which encouraged efficiency and to embrace more sophisticated organisational structures, if they were to make the most of the new opportunities offered them.

As well as altering their mode of activity to meet the positive aspects of industrial change however, amateur musicians, especially less affluent ones, were reacting to its negative side. This was obviously most necessary in industrial districts, but the entrepreneurial mentalities, the 'rhythm of the clock', that so changed the nature of working-class existence, were absorbed by the middle classes all over Britain and had, therefore, the widest influence. The crisis passed through by so many workers in the textile districts of Lancashire and Yorkshire between approximately 1815 and 1848, has been more than adequately detailed by a host of scholars and only a generalised sketch is required here. A large section of the workforce was subjected to long hours of factory labour. Even the domestic workers, although sometimes still able to regulate their hours as they chose, worked increasingly long hours from about 1820 in order to compensate for the savage wage-cutting that stemmed at first from competition between masters and only later from mechanisation. The overall picture is of a large section of the working class working longer hours (certainly more regularly) and earning less than their eighteenth-century predecessors.[63] In such a situation, it is hardly surprising that the structure

and operation of leisure institutions had to change. Just as the population came to appreciate the need for sustained industrial and political organisation as opposed to traditional, sporadic forms of protest, it
was clear to them that in leisure too the time had come for united
action by the poorer classes of society.

It is probable that, for some, the changes in musical life after 1820
were often a strategy for survival, methods of husbanding precious
resources, as well as, or instead of, responses to new opportunities. If
every member paid a weekly subscription, then costs were shared out;
if people were fined for taking music, then they were less likely to
purloin a vital commodity when money for replacement was not
readily available; the weekly rehearsal at a set place and time was a
necessary replacement for the informal gatherings rendered less
common by the new work discipline. It must be stressed that for
several decades the older informal mode of music-making co-existed
with the new. Rates of social and industrial change were not uniform.
The cotton industry experienced substantial technological advances
before the woollen industry, while in turn, different sections of the
woollen trade altered at different paces. Handloom weavers plied
their trade late into the nineteenth century in some of the more remote
Yorkshire villages, and they could still adopt musical methods that
their great-grandparents would have recognised.[64] But in general,
industrialisation brought fundamental changes to the structure of
popular musical life.

To see that life survive and perhaps even progress during the early
industrial phase, is at first sight somewhat surprising to the historian
of popular recreation, so used to viewing the period c. 1780–1850 as
one of disaster for so many popular pastimes.[65] While numerous areas
of traditional recreation, such as football or bloodsports, came under
attack from the forces of evangelicalism and utilitarianism, the pattern of popular music-making was left altered, but substantially
unscathed. Firmly rooted in evangelical culture and carrying strong
overtones of moral health, it was allowed to continue and indeed
actually encouraged. While upper-class acceptance was essential to
survival, however, the resilience of the working population was arguably the most crucial factor. The early industrial age was far less a
recreational desert than some scholars have claimed because of the
inventiveness and determination of the working classes. William
Cobbett was both saddened and impressed by the determination of
the weavers he encountered in Halifax.

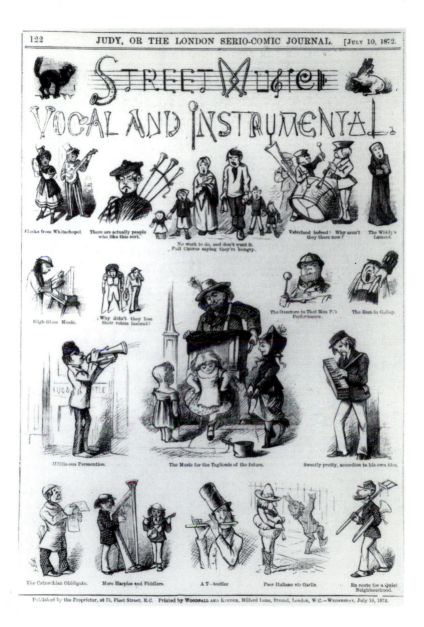

1 Street musicians were a favourite target of contemporary cartoonists. A considerable degree of venom lurks behind the quintessentially Victorian puns.

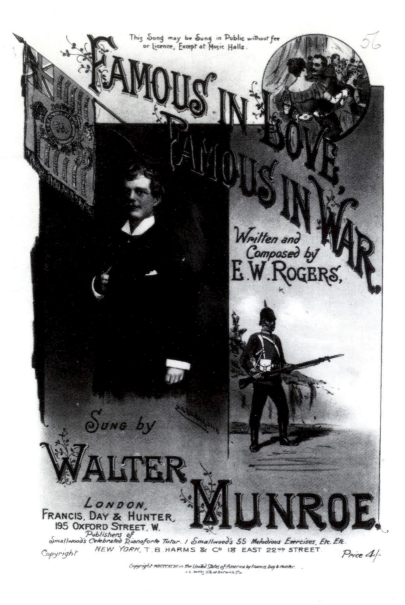

2   A song cover of 1893 glorifying military prowess and acknowledging in particular the bravery of Irish regiments.

3   London street musicians at the turn of the century.

4   Oldham Ringers in 1897, their Sunday best and embroidered cloth showing pride in their musical achievements.

5 'Besses' in 1860. The standardisation of brass band instrumentation was still not complete as illustrated by the clarinet (*front, far left*) and ophecleide (*back, far left*).

6 'Besses', c. 1903. Military uniform having long replaced dress suits, 'Besses', with conductor Alex Owen, seek to impress by posing with a host of trophies, including the Crystal Palace 1,000 Guinea Trophy (*immediately behind bass drum*).

7   William Atkinson (1851–1929), once a barman and ship's steward, later a respected violin-maker in Tottenham.

8   A violin class at Primrose Hill School, Pudsey, West Yorkshire, in the early 1900s, perhaps untypically, boys outnumbering the girls.

9   The family was of particular importance to brass bands as a unit of musical education. William Swingler was a prominent Halifax based trainer in the late Victorian and Edwardian periods.

FOUR SONS OF THE LATE MR. WILLIAM SWINGLER.

10   The specialist periodical press was an invaluable source of information for bandsmen: note the number of bands offering employment opportunities for soloists.

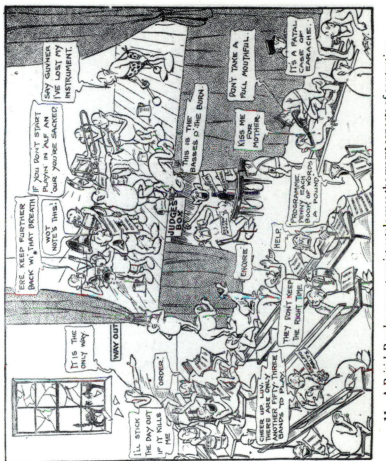

11   A *British Bandsman* cartoonist catalogues the worst aspects of contesting.

12 The problems of poverty as illustrated in the membership lists of the Leeds Philharmonic. Against the name of Paul Stott, a scavenger by trade, reads the annotation 'won't pay 2/6, man very poor, gave way paid 2/6'.

13 This letter from the secretary of Leeds Philharmonic chastising an errant member illustrates the commitment demanded by late Victorian choirs.

14 Popular music provided many social benefits.

15 Leeds Prize Musical Union, 1895, a male voice choir of artisans, clerks and commercial travellers.

It is truly lamentable to behold so many thousands of men who formerly earned 20 to 30 shillings a week, now compelled to live upon 5s, 4s or less. . . . It is the more sorrowful to behold these men in their state, as they still retain the frank and bold character formed in the days of independence.[66]

This refusal to bow down, expressed in the musical context by the willingness to walk thirty miles to a concert, or to sit up all night copying out music, even during a period of genuine economic and social crisis, ensured the survival of their musical culture. Perhaps in turn, this survival helped at least some of the community retain their spirit and independence. The nascent choral and band movements they had fashioned were now set to play an important role in popular social life. Born in a period of crisis and austerity, they were to flourish in the more sympathetic climate of the half-century that lay ahead.

Chapter 9

Brass bands

The brass band represents one of the most remarkable working-class cultural achievements in European history. The exact number of bands will probably never be known. Contemporary estimates vary alarmingly and are of little value. In 1889, for example, *Wright & Round's Amateur Band Teachers Guide* claimed that there were forty thousand amateur wind bands in Britain. A few months later the *Brass Band News*, also published by Wright & Round, put the number at thirty thousand, thus eliminating ten thousand bands and perhaps two hundred thousand bandsmen![1] The best that can be offered here is the impression that most communities of over a thousand people, and many a great deal fewer, managed some type of band at some time in the nineteenth century. The very best bands attracted crowds of seventy–eighty thousand to the national championships during the Edwardian period, went on national and even international tours and kept symphony orchestras supplied with a flow of talent. '*Das Land ohne Musik*' indeed!

References to bands in existing literature usually describe a 'movement' based in the 'towns' of the 'industrial North and Midlands'. While there is broad accuracy in such depiction, there is need for much greater precision when detailing the geography and structure of banding. Of prime importance is that bands were found in every part of England. One piece of research has detailed the existence of one hundred and forty-eight village bands in Oxfordshire alone between 1840 and 1914.[2] Many such bodies, especially in the south and west of the country, were not *brass* bands, often maintaining an instrumentation much closer to that of a military band. Again, some of them were fairly small. A late Victorian contributor to a band periodical, signing himself 'Sleepy Sussex', claimed that, 'our bands are all very small, ten and a drummer is the rule – five cornets, one horn, one baritone, one euphonium, one trombone, one piccolo and one drum – and there you are'.[3] Nevertheless, the widespread nature of amateur bands by late century adds a valuable corrective to the standard picture of popular music making: rural areas dominated by the 'folk' tradition, industrial areas by brass.

It is undeniable that the 'movement' was a northern phenomenon. The phrase, in contemporary parlance, referred to perhaps seven hundred to one thousand bands, each with twenty-four brass players and dedicated to *contesting*. Yet even here the use of blanket geographical term such as 'the North and Midlands' is misleading, for these bands were largely restricted to certain areas, of which the Nottinghamshire and Derby coalfields, the Lancashire coalfield and textile districts, the West Yorkshire coalfield and textile districts, the Durham and Northumberland coalfield, and, to a lesser extent, the Northamptonshire shoe towns, were the most important. The very best bands, the 'cracks', were drawn from an even more restricted area. Of the eighty-one bands winning prizes at the Belle Vue championships between 1853 and 1914, twenty-one came from Yorkshire (nineteen from the textile district) and fifteen from Lancashire, Cheshire bands accounted for the next highest total, a mere four. Only four of the eighty-one came from south of Staffordshire. The Championship class at the Crystal Palace contests between 1900 and 1914 displayed a similar pattern, despite the southern location, with eight of the twenty-seven prizewinners from Yorkshire and seven from Lancashire.[4]

Before exploring possible reasons for such a configuration, it is worth outlining the history of band contesting. Musical contests have been held in Britain from a very early period. The Welsh *Eisteddfod*, in particular, had a long lineage. During the second half of the nineteenth century, however, virtually every area of amateur musical life became imbued to some degree with the competitive ethos. The brass band contest is the best-known manifestation and certainly the first to become widely established. There appears to have been a type of impromptu contesting virtually from the moment amateur wind bands began to emerge after 1815. The first formal contest, however, took place in 1845 at Burton Constable near Hull, as part of a day of general merrymaking organised for the local populace by Sir Clifford Constable. The idea for a band contest stemmed from Sir Clifford's sister-in-law, who had encountered one in France. Five bands entered, Holmes Tannery Band with selections from Mozart's twelfth *Mass* and Wold Band with *Barber of Seville* tying for first place. The judge ordered the two to play again and eventually Wold's *Hallelujah Chorus* proved too much for the Tannery's *Der Freischütz* selection.

It was a small beginning but a highly significant one. That we know so much about such a relatively obscure event is due to the presence there of Enderby Jackson, a member of Sir Clifford's private dance band, whose memoirs, published in a musical journal in 1896, are an important, if not entirely objective, source of early brass band history.[5] Jackson claims that, impressed by what he had seen at Burton Constable, he and two other provincial bandsmen, James Melling and Tallis Trimmel, persuaded the manager of the Belle Vue Gardens in Manchester to hold a major contest there in 1853.[6] The exact origins of the contest and Jackson's role in its conception are unclear, but it was a resounding success. Held on the first Monday in September, to coincide with the local Gorton Wakes, it attracted eight bands, an estimated attendance of 16,000 and enthusiastic coverage by the regional press. The band contest was established.

Contesting grew steadily from this period, much of it in the 1850s and 1860s being sponsored by Jackson and his associate R.Alderson who organised contests, one imagines for essentially speculative as much as musical purposes, all over the North and Midlands. Apart from the Crystal Palace contests organised by Jackson from 1860–1863, and the National Championships found by J. H. Iles in 1900 at the same location, the band contest remained essentially a Northern and Midland phenomenon.[7] The National eventually grew to an enormous size, containing a number of sections including the one thousand guinea shield Championship class. Nevertheless, Belle Vue remained emotionally the bandsmens' Mecca, a venue which, in the words of *Musical Progress* in 1914, 'has won a place in brass band music which is held by no other place'. The peak period of contesting was the 1890s when some two hundred and forty contests were held annually throughout the country, with perhaps the most prolific areas being Lancashire and the coalfields of Durham and Northumberland.[8]

Many of the top bands enjoyed relatively brief periods of competitive success. Dominance of the field, of the type exerted by some football clubs for example, was unusual. Only Black Dyke Mills Band won prizes at Belle Vue in every decade between 1860 and 1910, and only four others in more than one decade between 1850 and 1910. The typical pattern (exemplified by Meltham Mills from Yorkshire in the 1870s, Littleborough Public from Lancashire in the 1880s and Kingston Mills from Cheshire in the 1880s and 1890s) was of short-term success followed by a slide into obscurity and, sometimes, dissolution. Economic depression, over-expediture on personnel and equipment, loss of key soloists to rivals and removal of entrepreneurial assistance (a theme returned to shortly), all played their part in this process. A successful band was a surprisingly fragile mechanism.

To an extent, the exalted position of Yorkshire and Lancashire bands stemmed from their proximity to the Belle Vue Pleasure Gardens, centre of the most important competition in the band calendar until at least 1900 and probably beyond. Although the choice of Belle Vue was in itself a reflection of the movement's initial geographical focus, there can be no doubt that this in turn gave increased stimulation to bands within relatively easy travelling distance. The history of the movement *might* have been different had the Crystal Palace contests of 1860–1863 continued. Although these were dominated by Yorkshire and Lancashire bands, Blandford Band from Dorset were winners in 1863, and more success of this type could have encouraged a deeper Southern and Western contesting tradition. Even bands in the more extreme Northern strongholds probably suffered from being at a distance from Belle Vue. Bands in Durham and Northumberland were amongst the keenest of all to organise competition, yet rarely made the relatively expensive trip to Belle Vue, and only appeared amongst the prizewinners with the emergence of St Hilda's Colliery Band in the years immediately before 1914.[9]

However, the strength of Yorkshire and Lancashire – and the other regions mentioned – seems to have owed most to the continued operation of the features already identified as crucial to the establishment of popular music-making. Especially noteworthy is the importance of smaller communities. In terms of both quantity, (meaning here musical institutions per head of population), and quality it was the large industrial village and the small town, settlements with populations of between three thousand and fifteen thousand, which usually enjoyed the most flourishing musical life. The picture is made clearer if broadened beyond the brass band world. Slaithwaite in West Yorkshire (population 4,763 in 1901) supported in the peak years of the 1890s and early 1900s a brass band, four choral societies and an amateur orchestra which was amongst the finest in the country. Cleckheaton (10,227, also in West Yorkshire, had two brass bands, two choral societies and an orchestra; Hucknall (15,250), a Nottinghamshire mining community, enjoyed, according to Eric Coates, one of its most famous sons, 'an excellent choir, an orchestra, a male quartet which made quite a name for itself in the Midlands and a first-class brass band which brought home many a coveted prize from competitions about the country'. The list could be extended to fill the rest of the chapter.[10]

Nowhere was this small town music-making more apparent than in the industrial settlements of the Colne and Holme Valleys, two regions immediately to the south and south-west of Huddersfield. Over the course of the nineteenth century and the first fifteen years of the twentieth, these two valleys, with a combined population of only fifty-five thousand in 1900, produced fifty-six musical societies. This is almost identical to the number founded in Leeds, twenty miles away, which had eight times the population. It is not merely the weight of numbers, but the quality of music that is so extraordinary. A list of the region's major organisations becomes a litany of all that was best in Victorian and Edwardian popular musical life. Meltham Mills brass band, which won the Belle Vue championship for three consecutive years between 1876 and 1878; Honley Band, champions in 1884; Linthwaite Band, which pioneered the inclusion of Wagner in the band repretoire; the Holme Valley Male Voice Choir, nationally famous within a few years of its foundation in 1910; Golcar Baptist Choir, with a far-reaching reputation in competitions from the 1890s; Crosland Moor United Handbell Ringers, who took handbell ringing to new levels of technical excellence in the Edwardian period, winning five consecutive Belle Vue championships in the process. Alongside these illustrious bodies were many others which won respect from both the national musical and the local communities.[11]

Successful brass bands were invariably from small communities, usually industrial villages, and, if they did emerge from a larger settlement, they were usually based on a specific institution or workplace. On occasions, the communities were extremely small. The case of Netherton Band from near Wakefield is particularly striking. 'Netherton Band is a wonder', claimed an enthusiastic observer. 'There are only about three hundred inhabitants in the place, and they have a band of twenty-two. Nearly every man in Netherton has been either a player or committee man.' Similarly, the village of Holme on the Yorkshire-Derbyshire border produced a band successful in several regional contests despite drawing on a population of only five hundred.[12]

The smaller community was bound to be the major focus of music-making, possessing the main social factors already defined as essential to musical 'spirit' in greater abundance than larger communities. At the same time, industrial villages and towns were often fiercely patriotic, determined to defeat their neighbours at whichever activity – be it bowls, rose-growing or collecting money for war widows – was currently the source of contention. In 1910 a brass band journalist located arguably the most important factor.

If the villagers could only be made to see it, they have infinitely better chances of forming good bands than the dweller in large towns, *for they have not so many counter attractions to cope with,* and most of their spare time can be profitably spent in practising together. All the best bands have been reared in small villages. Black Dyke, Besses, Wyke, Kingston Mills and Honley are, or were, all village bands which have risen to the top.[13]

The fundamental feature of small town recreational geography until the arrival of cinema in the years immediately before the First World War was the absence of an entertainment *industry*. Although local inhabitants could and did go into larger towns to visit music-halls, theatres and dancing-saloons, there is no doubt that the need to make one's own entertainment was paramount.[14]

The opportunities and advantages offered by the small community are made even clearer when set alongside a survey of banding in London. Bands from London, and indeed from the Home Counties in general, were a particular disappointment to many in the brass band movement. 'Citizen', the London correspondent of the *British Bandsman* lambasted local bandsmen after their poor showing in the 1911 Crystal Palace National Championship, in which only two southern bands had taken a prize from the six sections: 'it is the MATERIAL of our bands which is at fault, and no trainer can be successful with a band unless he has the full co-operation of every individual member of his band . . . we shall see no improvement while our men look upon banding as a hobby which may be taken up and dropped at their pleasure'.[15] The London and district bands in fact enjoyed few of the crucial social benefits underlying the northern tradition. The tight community spirit and ease of communication, so important in the smaller textile and mining centres, was lacking, especially in suburban areas. Men often had to commute considerable distances to practice, and rehearsal was made harder by the differing finishing times of the working day of individual members. Northern bands were unlikely to face these problems to anything like the same extent. Moreover, as some commentators pointed out, southern bandsmen had more musical rivals for their own time and that of their audience than those in other regions. Given the distribution of army barracks, the South had many more top-class military bands than the North while at the same time, especially in London, the music-hall was a powerful counter-attraction.[16] It is noticeable that those Home Counties bands which *did* enjoy a measure of success were based largely on imported northern expertise. The first three bands at the London and District contest of 1895 – Luton Red Cross, St Albans City and Olney Town – were all trained and conducted by northern bandsmen. The Luton band, to become a major force in the contest world in the inter-war years, rose from the obscurity of being mere Ashton Street Mission Band by appointing premier northern bandsmen, firstly, in 1894, J. T. Ogden of Kingston Mills and later Fred Mortimer of Hebden Bridge, as soloists and trainers.[17]

There is similar need for accuracy when detailing the institutional origins of bands. It is well known, for example, that a common starting place for the brass band was the place of work. There were essentially two types of works band: those actually founded by industrialists, and those given some form of assistance or sponsored after an approach had been made by an existing band or one in the process of formation. It is not always easy to detect workplace origins from band names. The origin of Black Dyke Mills Band is clear enough, but that of South Derwent Prize Band is not. In fact, they too were essentially a 'works' band, receiving substantial support from Dickenson and Company, a Durham colliery company. This problem makes the process of enumerating works bands extremely difficult and there may have been a greater number than initial research suggests. In general, however, it does seem that their number has been exaggerated in some popular literature. Ronald Pearsall, for example, has claimed that: 'Brass bands were . . . *primarily* works bands, supported by enlightened employers who wished to keep their operatives out of the gin palaces'.[18] In fact, the public subscription band, supported by the whole community, with local entrepreneurs being only one of many contributors, was always the most common form of band. The image of banding as employer-dominated probably results from the presence of a relatively small number of highly successful works bands whose elevated status was partially the result of financial advantages accruing to bands with particularly generous industrial patrons. Perhaps the real importance of the workplace was that it provided the initial focus for the friendships and discussions that led to formation of bands. Many bands started with half-a-dozen men who worked in the same pit, stone-dressing shop, weaving shed or engineering workshop.

There were also several important links between bands and temperance organisations with many bands – again exact numbers are not available – stemming from the Band of Hope, Church Missions, the Catholic League of the Cross and various other bodies. Bands from this source appear to have been most common in larger towns and cities, and although Miles Platting Mission (Manchester), Kingswood Evangelist (Bristol), or Tottenham Working Men's Mission and their counterparts only rarely made any notable contribution to the artisitic aspect of banding, they did play an important role in maintaining, perhaps even establishing, music-making traditions in these areas.

A significant addition was made to this cluster of supposedly 'morally reformed' bands by the Salvation Army. The first 'army' band was founded by Salisbury master-builder Charles Fry in 1878. Others soon followed and by March 1880 *War Cry* was urging 'soldiers' to learn instruments and build bands in order to attract crowds to meetings. In 1883 a music department was created and by July 1886 two journals, the *Salvation Army Brass Band Journal* and *The Musical Salvationist*, were in production.[19]

In no sense were Salvation Army bands part of the orthodox band tradition. In fact there was positive hostility between the two camps. 'Army' bands were hedged around with restrictions. Until 1901 no music was allowed that had not been originally created to accompany words. Even after this date, only music sanctioned by the 'army' could be performed. Literature such as the *British Bandsman* was proscribed and had to be obtained by interested salvationists with a furtiveness akin to the collection of socialist tracts in Tsarist Russia! The 'civilian' bands, for their part, were irritated by the salvationists' stranglehold on many promising young players and their position as rivals in public parks and parades. The movement's entrepreneurs, especially the publishers found the 'army's' musical self-sufficiency a further source of annoyance and took their revenge in the trade press, gleefully reporting salvationist 'defections' to the enemy. This movement of individual bandsman – and occasionally of entire bands – illustrates that the two traditions did have a meeting-point. For all the 'army's' supposed exclusiveness, it could not hold all its musicians and found itself an unwilling training ground for the secular band movement.[20]

Such behaviour was not the sole preserve of salvationists. Like many early football and cricket clubs, bands, especially those connected to religious or philanthropic bodies, showed only limited loyalty to their original sponsors, often declaring independence to escape restrictions placed upon them, and/or to widen their appeal. Here is yet another example of working-class capacity to extract the maximum benefit from rational recreation while ignoring or deflecting its ideology. The severence was sometimes painful, especially in the case of Brampton Total Abstinence Band from near Carlisle, sponsored by temperance advocate Lady Carlisle. While returning by train from a contest, the band spent the time filling and re-filling their newly-won trophy with alcoholic substances. On arriving at the local railway station where their patron waited eagerly, one of the bandsmen climbed out of the train and dropped the trophy ceremoniously at her feet, where it broke into two pieces. Strangely enough, the instruments were withdrawn and the band broken up![21] In 1904 the Reverend Kedwood of the Queen's Hall Mission, Hull, sacked the entire mission band because two of the men had been seen entering a public house. (They claimed that they had not drunk anything.) The band simply reformed themselves as West Hull Excelsior. On other occasions, the process was relatively amicable and based on more 'artistic' grounds, as with Ashton Street Mission Band, Luton, who, 'finding that the rules of the society somewhat retarded the progress of the band, severed their connection with the mission'.[22] Such secessions did much to reinforce the view of those evangelicals who believed that attempts to broaden the appeal of religion by recourse to recreational provision merely hastened the process of secularisation.

The membership of brass bands and indeed of civilian wind bands of all types was almost totally male – exclusively so in contesting bands – and solidly working class. There were, as noted earlier, a few manufacturers who played alongside their men in the earliest bands, but they were no longer present by 1850. The class divisions that had emerged in the first half of the century gave different musical performances and organisations definite class connotations. A member of the *haute bourgeosie* might encourage a band, for whatever motives, but would be anxious to define his superior social status by directing his own and his family's musical energies towards the choral society, the orchestra, the subscription concert and of course, the piano in the 'music room'. After 1850 a small number of lower-middle-class figures emerge. The bands in the Leeds-Bradford area included a road surveyor, a minor public health official and a number of publicans (including three ex-members of Wyke Temperance!), although these appear to have been soloists and trainers who had made enough money to *become* publicans, rather than this being their original trade. Such men were exceptions, however. Bandsmen always described themselves as 'working men', as did middle-class observers, whether friendly or hostile. The majority, judging by the evidence of oral testimony and the personal details that appeared in the brass band press, appear to have been from the skilled or semi-skilled sections of the working class. Hardly surprisingly, given the social and geographical base of the movement, many, perhaps a majority, were miners. Others simply reflected the occupational structure of their area.[23] The 'unskilled' members of the movement often turn out to be skilled craftsmen given a sinecure in return for playing in a works band. Willie Wood, by trade a wood-pattern maker, was employed to sweep up by Black Dyke whilst he was their solo cornet.[24]

There is more to understanding the brass bands, or indeed any musical society's social base, however, than analysis of its playing membership alone. In order to survive, bands had to forge links with a considerable body of people from outside the working-class community who could help in matters of organisation and finance, or, simply by listening to them, provide a *raison d' être*.

Bands offered three distinct types of performance, each requiring different degrees of commitment from the listener. These may be termed the 'enforced', at which the audience simply happened to be present at the same time as the band, for instance at a fairground or flower show; the 'non-committal' typified by the public park performance at which people could come and go as they pleased; and finally the 'chosen', the concert-hall performance and, above all, the contest, demanding from the listener financial outlay and often exposing him to technical elements of the repertoire.[25] The contest and the concert-hall audience seem to have been largely the preserve of the working class. A correspondent at the Belle Vue contest of 1888 described the audience as mostly 'of the artisan or respectable British workman class', again reinforcing the image of banding as an upper-working-class, male pastime.[26] In the 'non-committal style of concert, however, a wider audience was encountered. The park concert, although often conceived as a method of bringing wholesome entertainment to the poorest members of society, does not seem to have attracted that group to any extent, judging from the flimsy evidence available. The *Leeds Mercury*, reporting on Sunday band concerts in 1856, noted the absence of the 'unwashed, benighted, Sunday tippling denizens of our back slums, for whose sake these concerts were said to have been established'.[27] The *Mercury's* view was perhaps defined by its hostility to the secularist organisation behind the concerts, but its comments were endorsed by other observations over the country. Indifference towards, or ignorance of, philanthropic intention, or perhaps quite simply lack of suitable clothing, kept the 'submerged tenth' away. But the middle classes did come, especially if the concert was near to home. The performances in Manningham Park, Bradford, in the later nineteenth century attracted a highly respectable *clientèle*, according to the satirical magazine the *Yorkshireman*. Whether their time at the bandstand reflected musical interest or merely the desire to display their clothes probably varied from person to person, although, perhaps significantly, the *Yorkshireman* regularly criticised the 'swells' of Manningham for contributing less to the donation sheets than the 'humble frequenters' of other local parks.[28] Clerks, commercial travellers and others, usually in family groups, seem also to have been regular attenders in many towns. The band could, through its function as entertainer, reach out beyond the social class which produced it.

It was, however, in the field of organisation and financial support that middle-class (ranging from publicans to large-scale manufacturers) presence was at its most important. Many bands had an organising committee of some six to twelve people and local shopkeepers, clerks and other members of the lower middle class served on these quite frequently. Here again is what is probably an example of the social stratification of musical activity demanded by contemporary attitudes. For an insurance agent such as George Glover, secretary of Morley Borough Band, to be a playing member might be socially unacceptable, but an interest in banding could be satisfied by contributing 'expert' services. Local shopkeepers were also often called upon to be band trustees, standing surety for the band when they purchased instruments.[29]

A band's financial support had to come from the widest possible cross-section of the community. For the majority, the 'people's pennies', augmented by donations from shopkeepers and tradesmen, formed the basis of their income, but as the *British Bandsman*

informed potential backsliders: 'Nearly every band worthy the name
has a few good supporters in high social positions, who do their duty
loyally to the band by giving good support, also adding their name as
well as their presence at various functions'.[30] The most extreme and,
for some, the most sought after, manifestation of this patronage by the
rich was sponsorship by an industrialist. The motives for this have
already been discussed, but there can be no question as to the value to
the bands of such support, which made top-quality instruments,
tuition and soloists readily available. Some manufacturers simply
made financial contributions to bands. Between 1872 and 1883, one of
the partners of Jonas Brook and Company, cotton-spinners in the
village of Meltham Mills near Huddersfield, agreed to double the
prize money won by the local village band at any one contest per
season named beforehand. £390 was eventually obtained from this
source.[31] More strikingly, instruments, uniforms, employment for
suitable performers and, sometimes, the privilege of rehearsal during
work time, were provided by particularly enthusiastic employers.
The importance of entrepreneurial support was never more clearly
illustrated than when it was withdrawn. Saltaire Band, founded in the
1850s as a part of Sir Titus Salt's model community near Bradford,
won the Belle Vue competition of 1861, became one of the leading
bands in the country during the following decade and then declined
dramatically in status and efficiency as a new management withdrew
previous levels of financial assistance over the 1870s. Again, Leeds
Forge Band, founded by Samson Fox in 1882 and amongst the finest
in the country, was dissolved in 1892 when new management withdrew support. Saltaire eventually disappeared altogether in the 1890s,
while Leeds Forge re-emerged as a public subscription body, the
Armley and Wortley Band. However, the new band never recaptured
the heights made largely possible by Fox's generosity.[32]

    In the last analysis, the brass band movement's strength and quality
was derived from the working classes. Here were the 'common
people' entertaining themselves in exactly the manner so many
middle-class observers claimed to want. Nevertheless, it has to be
accepted that bands were forced to build links with the wider community. Many were helped through difficult moments, given
respectability –essential when purchasing instruments on HP – and
even given eminent status in the band fraternity, because of their links
with the wealthier classes. Whatever the motives of the more affluent
members of local society, without their assistance, it is questionable

whether the brass band movement would have obtained quite the size and quality that it did.

Making music

The earliest wind bands, as already noted, came in all shapes and sizes. Bands used whatever instruments the local community could lay claim too. At the first Belle Vue contest 1853 the eighteen-strong Bramley Band employed two D flat soprano cornets, three A flat cornets, two trumpets, two French horns, three trombones, two ophecleides and one unidentified instrument, called an A flat tenor cornet by the band's historian, but in probability a variety of tenor saxhorn. Dewsbury Band, however, had only eleven members who played three keyed bugles, two cornopeans, three trombones and three ophecleides.[33] Clarinets featured in some of the other leading bands of the day. As the structure of both bands show, there was as yet no related family of brass instruments to draw on and there was an absence of a really satisfactory bass instrument, the ophecleide with its rather limited range not always being suitable for the work it was called upon to do. Yet by 1860, in the North and Midlands at least, reed instruments had been largely superseded by a complete brass family, and by the mid-1870s a standardised brass band had emerged. Within twenty years' technical developments in the musical instrument industry, the impact of contesting and the influence of music publishing had created the brass band as we know it today.

The first important technical breakthrough came with the application of the valve to brass instruments. A joint patent was awarded to two Germans Heinrich Stölzel and Friedrich Blühmel in 1818, although each claimed his 'system' as his own, rather than a joint invention. It was soon applied by a number of brass instrument manufacturers to various instruments, solving as it did the problem of chromaticism – in other words, providing the performer with the means to obtain all twelve semitones within each octave with ease. By the late 1830s the *cornet-à-pistons*, normally termed simply the 'cornet', one of the results of this new technology, began to appear in Britain and to provide the nascent wind-band movement with what was to be its leading melodic instrument.[34] What was arguably the most important development took place in the 1850s with the widespread adoption of the first *family* of brass instruments, the saxhorns. The saxhorn was one of two complete and proportionately related sets of brass instruments, the other being the saxotromba, developed by Adolphe Sax, a Paris-based instrument maker in 1844 and 1845. The saxhorns were essentially 'improved bugles', the description Sax actually gave to them at first, rather than an entirely new concept such as his later 'saxophone'. The very first instruments had forward-pointing bells, although the upright bell was soon introduced. There were eventually seven members of the family; the high soprano, soprano, contralto, tenor, baritone, the B flat bass, usually known as the 'euphonium', and the E flat bass or 'bombardon'. The soprano and contralto horns, although extremely popular in France and Belgium, never became popular in England because of the established popularity of the cornet, but the remaining instruments, along with the cornet and trombone, became the basis of the British brass band.[35]

The saxhorns owe much of their popularity in Britain to the Distin Family, John Distin and his four sons, with wife on piano, who used the instruments in their highly successful concert tours in England from 1844. The family had seen Sax exhibit the instruments in Paris in that year at a concert organised by Berlioz, and had immediately asked Sax for a set. Distin senior claimed that 'we were the *first* who *successfully* introduced these instruments to the public'.[36] The 1851 Crystal Palace Exhibition, with its extensive musical exhibition, gave the saxhorn family a further boost. It is often claimed that Mossley Band from Lancashire was the first to be fully equipped with saxhorns, although if nomenclature alone is any guide, Fairbairn Lawson's Wellington Saxhorn Band, a Leeds-based works band founded in December 1851, may well have the honour. Nevertheless, it is indisputable that Mossley did much to advertise the saxhorn by winning the 1853 Belle Vue contest and thus inspiring other bands to begin the process of conversion.[37]

By 1860 standardisation had progressed a long way, as is illustrated by the composition of the massed band comprising the majority of competitors at the 1860 Crystal Palace Competition, which gave a concert at the close of the contests:

144	soprano	cornets
394	cornets	
205	tenor	horns
100	baritone	horns
74	tenor	trombones
75	bass	trombones

  80   ophecleides
155   bombardons
   2   BB flat   bassess
26 side drums, 1 giant drum and an organ

In order for this construction to be possible, the majority of competing bands must have adopted a recognisably 'modern' appearance.[38] Obviously not every band made the move towards the standard line-up at the same time. In 1860 Black Dyke still employed an E flat clarinet and a French horn. Such idiosyncracies were inevitable. Bands may have had expert musicians on older instruments and were unwilling to forgo old skills. There were also financial considerations. The 1850s was the most prosperous period for almost thirty years for the working community and this 'prosperity' helped make these substantial changes in instrumentation possible. However, the purchase of a new set of instruments was an arduous financial undertaking and forced several bands into bankruptcy and dissolution. Bass instruments were particularly expensive and this is perhaps the reason why the ophecleide, for all its faults, remained relatively common until the 1870s.

    The 1870s saw what was more or less the final phase of instrumental reform. The flugel horn, a later addition to the saxhorn family first used by Black Dyke in the 1860s, became popular in this period, while the phenomenal success of Meltham Mills Band, winners of Belle Vue in 1876, 1877 and 1878, led to imitation of their line-up by other competition bands. The following suggested line-up given by Thomas Wright and Enoch Round in their *Amateur Band Teachers Guide* (1889) was broadly that of Meltham Mills and of the majority of bands today. Flugel horns could be used instead of the repianos, second and third cornets if preferred.

1	E flat	soprano	cornet
3	B flat	solo	cornets
2	B flat	repiano	cornets
2	B flat	2nd	cornets
2	B flat	3rd	cornets
1	1st E flat	tenor	horn
1	2nd E flat	tenor	horn
1	3rd E flat	tenor	horn
1	1st B flat	baritone	horn
1	2nd B flat	baritone	horn
1	1st	tenor	trombone
1	2nd	tenor	trombone
1	bass	trombone	

2	B flat	euphoniums
2	B flat	bombardons
1	B flat	bass
1	BB flat	bass

drums (not used in contests)[39]

Various rather esoteric explanations have been put forward to explain the emergence of all-brass ensembles, usually focusing on some supposed link between the 'masculinity' of the brass sound and the self-image of the bandsmen.[40] This fails to take into account the continued use of reed instruments in many parts of the country by bands composed of equally 'masculine' individuals. The reasons are in all probability more prosaic. Competitive bands heard for themselves the value of building a band around a family of related instruments and saw this underlined by the success of bands like Mossley and Meltham Mills. Brass instruments were also easier to maintain than reeds and far less sensitive to the vagaries of the climate, which must have become an increasingly important consideration as bands took on more and more outside contest and engagement work. Perhaps most important of all were two further practical considerations. Brass instruments were relatively straightforward to learn, the three-valve action of most instruments presenting less problems to the beginner than, for example, the clarinet or bassoon. Moreover, the instruments (with the obvious exception of the slide trombone), were all fingered in virtually the same way, so that individuals could be moved onto other instruments in order to fill vacancies.[41]

Once established, the new instrumentation was cemented by the music publishing industry. The music of specialist band publishers was so cheap in comparison with the privately produced test piece that bands happily settled for their publications and the line-up that they suggested. Once publishers began to reap rewards, it became increasingly unlikedly that they would encourage new initiatives without being absolutely sure that there would be a market. In 1902, the *British Bandsman* gave clear expression to the publishers' standpoint.

The constitution [of the band] has, to a great extent, had the seal of efficiency placed upon it by publishers, who only issue parts for the present instrumentation. This of necessity renders any change in the present instrumentation one of serious import.[42]

There were, inevitably, attempts at reform. There was a substantial lobby, including William Rimmer, James Brier, Joseph Weston Nicholl and John Ord Hume, all major figures in the band world, in favour of introducing a quartet (in Brier's case a sextet) of saxophones in order to extend the tonal range. Ord Hume (1864–1932), perhaps because of a military band background, was especially interested in the topic and contributed several articles on the history and potential of the saxophone to the *British Bandsman* in 1902.[43] In fact only two British bands, Sirocco Lodge in Belfast and Perfection Soap Works, Warrington, added saxophones to their line-up before 1914 and there appears to have been no attempt to utilise any other non-standard instrument. Indeed, even in the seventy years since 1914, there have been only two major changes in the competition band: the addition of a second solo cornet in the 1950s in acknowledgement of the increasing difficulty of band music, and the allowing and subsequent encouragement of percussion at most competitions, beginning with the Belle Vue Championships of 1969.[44]

Certainly there were developments within the confines of the accepted instrumentation, most notably the great popularity of quartet playing which developed from the late nineteenth century. The traditional line-up comprised two cornets, tenor horn and euphonium, although Ord Hume noted ten other permutations. But the wider changes hoped for by the 'brass band chartists', as one writer dubbed them, never materialised. Expense, lack of expertise, conservatism and publishers' self-interest all contributed to maintain the *status quo*. This was not to the detriment of the brass band as an artistic force, however. As the period from 1914 showed, there was much for the existing combination to achieve without the addition of new instruments.

The key institution in the initial training of bandsmen was very often the family, and although this was true to an extent of all aspects of music-making, family connections appear to have been particularly strong in band circles. It was not unknown to find seven or eight members of a family in the same band. Interested parents and relations often began their young one's musical education at a very tender age, usually with little consultation with the infant in question. Harry Mortimer – who in no way regretted his father's efforts – began lessons at five. 'I don't think I was even asked if I wanted to learn – it was as much a matter of course as cleaning my teeth or polishing my boots'. John Paley, one of the finest cornet players this country has produced, began at four. His father, a publican in Shipley, West Yorkshire, and himself a cornettist and band trainer of distinction, would serve drinks with the bar-room door ajar so that he could hear his prodigy at work upstairs. Any untoward silence would be greeted with a yell of 'get back to that cornet'.[45] Excessive parental interest could lead to embarrassing and amusing situations. William Millington recounted the following tale of nervous parenthood, which actually involves the Lancashire tenor John Newton rather than a bandsman, but similar things happened at band events.

It seems he was singing a long tenor solo in an anthem, and in making a cadence at the end he got off the key. His father Samuel Newton, was parish clerk in Ellenbrook Chapel, and when he heard his son fail in making the cadence, he shouted out, 'Jack, thou art in the ditch; get out as soon as thou can'. Of course Jack got right again and made a good finish to the great delight of his father.

Certain sociologists have claimed that the nineteenth century, gave a 'freedom of choice' to individuals whose choices had previously been 'prescribed and defined' by local habits and customs in a pre-industrial early age. However, only when safely ensconced in adulthood did anything resembling genuine freedom of choice emerge.[46]

Not all potential musicians enjoyed the benefits, questionable or otherwise, of family support, but this was no block to band membership. A surprisingly large number of bands emerged from groups of absolute beginners. Irwell Bank, founded in 1875, was composed entirely of beginners, while only two of Bradford Postmen's Band could play a brass instrument when the band began in 1886.[47] These examples illustrate that banding could be taken simply as a hobby, like any other, and it is a reflection of the contemporary appetite for music that young working men should direct their energies in this way. A number of leading bands had junior sections to maintain a flow of recruits, although a more normal method was simply to 'poach' promising youngsters from lesser bands.

The amount of time devoted to the band depended upon its ambitions. A player might be asked to attend a weekly rehearsal backed up with a little practice at home, or he might find every available moment absorbed. In 1888, for example, Batley Band held fourteen practices in ten days before a major London competition! Most bands eventually hired or built their own bandrooms where they could practice, but, especially in the early period, they might be forced to stand in a field or other open space, a demanding activity, especially for bass players, after a hard day's physical labour. Rehearsal at home caused problems for those with unsympathetic parents and/or neighbours, and band folklore is replete with tales of young men driven onto rooftops, climbing into trees and occasionally taking refuge in privies in order to gain practice space.[48]

All bands had a bandmaster, whose job it was to coach and generally manage the other players. They were normally chosen by their fellow members in recognition of their possession of good musical knowledge, an appetite for hard work and, sometimes, patience. Top contesting bands would appoint a professional trainer to apply final polish and to conduct at the contest. Interviewed by the *Cornet* in 1898, B. D. Jackson commented rather acidly on his relationship with trainer John Gladney during Jackson's spell as Batley bandmaster around 1890. 'I spent much time with them before Mr Gladney came over to conduct. He got the praise and I got a lot of hard work;.[49] The 'trainer' was an important, although never common, figure in band circles. At the peak of the band movement in the 1890s there were probably no more than fifty or sixty, and nearly all were to be found in the North and Midlands. Most were probably semi-professional although some supported themselves from their banding activity alone. They began to appear first in Yorkshire and Lancashire in the 1850s. Biographical information on many is scanty, but the majority seem to have been professional musicians who had been drawn into the band movement rather than bandsmen who had worked 'through the ranks'. This was certainly true of Richard Smith who, as has been seen, was originally a musician with a menagerie band who had first met bandsmen when acting as a musical scribe. George Ellis, trainer of Accrington in the 1840s, enjoyed a similar background having played with Wombwell's Menagerie Band.[50]

Smith was probably the most successful of the early trainers, leading bands to sixty-two prizes between 1856 and 1861 alone. But the position gained its greatest importance from the 1870s, due to the efforts of three of the finest trainers of all time, the so-called 'Big Three' – John Gladney, Alexander Owen and Edwin Swift. They were associated with virtually every top-class band in the North of England in the period between 1875 and 1914. At the 1894 Belle Vue Championships, fourteen of the eighteen competitors were conducted by these three. Gladney (1838–1911) was born in Belfast, the son of a military bandsman. After a spell as militia bandsman he became a professional orchestral musician in the 1850s, eventually joining the Hallé as a clarinettist in 1861. He devoted himself to brass bands from the 1870s, moved, so he claimed, by a love of brass instruments, the desire to give working men a 'wholesome' recreation, and to bring 'good' music to the widest public. He taught over a hundred bands in Yorkshire and Lancashire, including both Meltham Mills and Kingston Mills, who managed hat-tricks at Belle Vue in 1876–78 and 1885–87 respectively. Overall, he conducted more first and second prize winning bands at Belle Vue than any other two conductors put together.[51]

Owen and Swift were both products of the band world itself. Owen (1851–1920) gained celebrity status as solo cornet with Meltham Mills in the 1870s and followed Gladney into trainership in 1877. He was most closely associated with Besses o' th' Barn, whom he took on a tour of France in 1905 (for which he was decorated by the French government) and on a world tour in 1906–1907. Swift (1842–1904) was born at Milnsbridge in the Colne Valley, son of a handloom weaver. By the age of sixteen he was solo cornet and assistant conductor of Linthwaite Band. A powerloom weaver by profession, he studied music extremely seriously, often working late into the night studying and transcribing orchestral scores, developing a particular appetite for Wagner. His *Bayreuth* selection for Linthwaite became a classic of the band repertoire. Eventually in 1875, having led Linthwaite to victory at Belle Vue the previous year, he decided to devote himself to training full-time. From then until his death, he taught thirty-four bands and won an enormous reputation for his skill as a teacher and arranger. His funeral, attended by several thousand mourners, and led by a massed band some eighty strong, was a moving testimony to his place in the late Victorian brass band world. New faces emerged, most notably, William Rimmer (1862–1936), Arthur O. Pearce (1872–1951) and William Halliwell (b. 1865–?), the latter being remarkably successful in the 1920s, but none of whom quite ever summoned forth the reverence that surrounded Gladney, Owen and Swift.[52]

Although there was doubtless some truth in Jackson's acid remark, the top trainers gave bands the subtleties that raised their music to the highest level. They achieved this by virtue of total understanding of their medium and by driving the bandsmen very hard indeed. The following description of a contest band at rehearsal illustrates the remarkable amount of effort involved – and many of the musicians involved would have just completed a day's work which had begun at 6.00 a.m.

Starting with the first chord, the selection is pulled to pieces; bar for bar and note for note; the whole combination of musical terms, attack, tune, precision, articulation, expression etc., are in every sense strictly observed and brought to bear upon each separate individual's part. . . . There is scarcely a bar in the whole of the selection, but what is played both sectionally and individually many times over, the result being that in two or three hours (time to retire) a fifteen-minute selection is scarcely ended.[53]

To the outside eye, especially that of the college trained musician, brass bands did not, despite such immense efforts, appear sophisticated or 'artistic'. Until as recently as 1965, bands used instruments set in 'high pitch' (A at 452.5 vibrations per second) as opposed to standard orchestral pitch (A at 440 vibrations per second). This was regarded as idiosyncratic in the extreme by many outsiders and also cut down the possibilities of interchange between bands and other 'orthodox' musical bodies.[54] Bandsmen used a musical vernacular unknown to outsiders. The word 'trainer' is a case in point, with its undertones of both the playing field and the circus, while players spoke of their performance as 'banding' or 'blowing'. Many could read music (albeit often only in the treble clef, tenor and bass being rarely used by publishers), but the majority were ignorant of musical theory and much terminology. The scale of B flat, for example, was more likely to be referred to as the 'scale of two flats'. Moreover, most bandsmen would have used dialect, which, for example, in the Huddersfield area, transformed 'soprano', 'trombone' and 'bass' to 'soprana' 'tram' and 'bass' (as in the fish or the beer, depending on one's taste) respectively. There was also a 'tap-room' feel to some of the goings-on, with shirtsleeves, pipes and tobacco-chewing. Ceres Jackson, Black Dyke's renowned solo cornet in the Edwardian period, was famed for spitting tobacco quids on to the floor at practices so that 'it looked as if a duck had shit all round' him.[55]

The most powerful element of what one commentator has referred to as the atmosphere of 'masculine gaiety' pervading the band world was brass band contest 'hooliganism'.[56] The word 'hooligan' was not given its current meaning until 1898 and it was in the years around 1900 that the issue of bad behaviour amongst bandsmen was most often debated in the trade press.[57] Nevertheless, displays of ill-feeling had long been a feature of contesting and indeed still occur, albeit infrequently. Such displays were usually triggered either by a band using an 'illegal' player (normally a paid soloist hired for the one contest) or by what was perceived as inept judging. However, these merely occasioned rather than caused the hooliganism and there were deeper-seated reasons for the bandsmens' behaviour.

First, there was undoubtedly a considerable amount of gambling amongst both players and supporters. The band journals saw the habit as abhorrent and attacked it regularly. The amounts wagered were probably small but obviously significant to those concerned. While gambling, allied with sheer aggressive competitiveness, explains much of the disorderly aspect of banding, it is possible that at least some outbreaks were inspired by sheer wounded pride. Much effort went into preparation for contests and what bands might see as the judges' lack of recognition for hard-won artistic excellence must have rankled.

What contemporaries termed 'hooliganism' did not always involve violence. A performance of the *Dead March* was a favoured method of showing disapproval after an unflattering or unpopular decision. Again, as in the Bradford Contest of 1858 described here, justice could be achieved through an expert display of 'peaceful' civil disobedience. The *Bradford Observer's* report is worthy of quotation in full.

The appearance of the Saltaire Band once again raised the disturbing elements. They were assailed by loud outcries, shouts of 'turn him out' etc. and counter-demonstrations from their friends, producing a disgraceful scene that utterly defies description. A brief subsidence of the noise, and the leader essayed to begin, his men blew their loudest and strongest but louder above all arose the yell of a mob of instrumentalists congregated at the end of the orchestra, and the brazen brass rung out the wildest notes, now shrieking from a trumpet or cornet and anon rising in the deep, gutteral tones of the ophecleides and trombones. The confusion was really 'most confounded' and very vexatious. This scene and others lasted perhaps half-an-hour, the leader of the Saltaire Band 'making faces' at his opponents, and trying to appear cool, 'sitting down to wait it out', and acting certainly in a most foolish and reckless manner. At length he made a desperate start, but his opponents started also, and there was another outrageous scene of tumult and noise, in the midst of which Mr Jackson (the judge) made his appearance from the tent and at once went to Mr Smith, leader of the Saltaire Band, and ordered the removal of the individual objected to, a trombone player, who, it appears, was a professional man, and not entitled to play in the contest. Mr Smith bowed to the referee's calm and dispassionate decision and the band was then allowed to play the tune in quietness.[58]

Physical force was, nevertheless, sometimes a final resort. Occasionally, fights broke out between bands, as at a Sheffield contest in 1860. More often it was the judge who fell victim. A judge at Ilkley in the late 1890s was thrown into a stream after a particularly unpopular decision.[59] A far worse fate would have befallen William Spark, the Leeds Borough organist, if we believe his description of the aftermath of a contest he had judged in the summer of 1888. 'As soon as one band found that they were unsuccessful, the members thereof launched out with a torrent of epithets which I doubt if the lowest riff-raff of Billingsgate and the East End of London could supersede or equal.' The unfortunate Spark then found himself on the same train as his critics, one of whom, 'was kind enough to say that he would tear me from limb to limb, an operation which I politely thanked him for and asked to postpone'. When, later in the journey, a change of train was necessary, another band had to surround him on the station platform to protect him from his pursuers.[60]

Spark was diplomatic enough not to name his would-be assailants, but implied very strongly that members of Wyke Temperance, one of the country's premier bands originating from an industrial village on the southern edge of Bradford, were responsible. Certainly the band was to be named in two further incidents in the next decade. In 1893, two of its members, the brothers Robert and Harry Bentley, were each fined £5 by Southport magistrates for offences arising out of a Whit Friday contest at the Lancashire resort. The contest judge, Howard Lees of Oldham, 'was alleged to have been severely kicked by the defendants about the lower parts of the body. He had to be locked up in a greenhouse for safety, and was eventually taken to the station in a cab to elude his assailants'. (The Bentleys denied the charges and the rest of the band clubbed together to pay the fines.) Again, at Scarborough in September 1895, police had to rescue the judge, Richard Stead, from an angry crowd, led, so Stead claimed, by members and supporters of the Temperance band.[61]

It must be stressed that such colourful incidents were relatively rare, the great majority of contests passing off without the threat or actuality of violence. Furthermore, problems seem to occur largely at relatively minor contests where organisation may have been lax, although both the Belle Vue championship of 1888 and the Crystal Palace contest in 1902 were marred by hooligans. At the former, the judge Charles Godfrey was 'hissed and hooted' and on leaving the hall 'found it necessary to secure the protection of a police constable'.[62] Nevertheless, it is significant that such problems should occur at all. Historians of nineteenth-century social life have broadly accepted the distinction between 'rough' and 'respectable' recreations. At first sight, brass banding was undoubtedly a 'respectable' pastime and was seen as such by many contemporaries. Yet some of these men with their smart uniforms, fondness for the music of

Wagner and their spirit of thrift and self-sacrifice could be equated with the 'lowest riff-raff of Billingsgate'. Even a temperance band could have members accused of assault and threatening behaviour. Rather than seeing the labels 'respectable' and 'rough' as absolutes, we should instead be aware that individuals could move through a variety of guises and types of behaviour. Human behaviour invariably transcends even the neatest categorisation.[63]

Band journals were extremely anxious lest such displays alienate middle-class sponsors and the professional musical establishment. It is uncertain how much damage was actually done, but it would be surprising if hooliganism, coupled with a reaction against the other overtly proletarian elements of band sub-culture described above, had not repulsed some sensitive spirits, ignorant of the fact that some fine musical performance was nurtured in this environment. It is to this performance that we now turn.

The band repertoire was remarkably catholic. This doubtless reflected popular taste, but it was also a function of the bands' musical position. They performed at an enormously wide range of functions and their music had to vary according to the situation. At the same time, given the relatively limited amount of music specifically composed for bands, bandsmen were forced to adopt material from any area of the musical spectrum that suited their formation and requirements. The result for the best bands was a large stock of material – in 1887 Besses o' th' Barn performed around one hundred pieces during a week-long engagement in Newcastle – forming the distinct blend of art and popular music that is still a feature of the band repertoire today.[64]

It is possible to divide the musical store into three broad categories: 'sacred', 'art' and 'light'. These classifications are not altogether satisfactory, but they serve as an approximate guideline.[65] Sacred music, in the form of oratorio selections and hymns, played a large part in the programmes of the early bands, especially in Lancashire and Yorkshire. This was inevitable given the essentially sacred foundation of much amateur music making at this stage. Most wind bands included a variety of choruses from the best known Handel and Haydn oratorios in their performances, and in fact some early band concerts drew almost entirely upon this genre. Similarly, sacred works were quite widely utilised as contest pieces. Wold Band performed the 'Hallelujah Chorus' at the Burton Constable contest of 1845 and, as late as 1858, Accrington won Belle Vue with two

movements from *The Creation*. Although largely displaced in the
contest field by the mid 1860s, such music remained essential for any
public performance at least until near the end of the century, sometimes taking up a quarter of the performance. A change appears to
have come in the late 1890s, according to a writer in the *British
Bandsman* of 1910, who claimed that a significant decline in the
performance of sacred music had begun 'about a dozen years ago'.
Certain occasions, such as Sunday-school anniversaries, demanded
appropriate music and preserved the continuance of a hymn playing
tradition still present today, but public concerts by the Edwardian
period were far more secular in content than previously. This was
partly a reflection of the lightening of religious mores and partly a
result of the increased availability of a wider range of music.[66]

The 'challenge' to sacred music in both the concert and contest
came initially from opera. The operatic selection and, to a lesser
extent, complete overtures, were the most typical form of 'art' music
in the brass band canon throughout the period. Arrangers wove
together, with varying degrees of skill, the main arias or even, in some
cases, simply parts of the main arias, into pieces graced with grand
titles like *Rossini's Works*. By the 1830s and 1840s opera, especially
Italian opera, was increasingly part of the popular musical repertory.
Theatres in larger towns offered operatic extracts, while the concerts
of the Distin Family and Jullien both included operatic selections.
Perhaps most important of all were the travelling menagerie and
circus bands, which were of a high standard and drew their music
from a wide area, including opera. These bands had a double importance in that their performances carried operatic airs fairly low down
the social scale and their musicians often acted as tutors to local
bandsmen, therefore allowing the transfer of their skills and music.
Italian opera, as well as being moderately familiar to some bandsmen,
was extremely well suited to the band structure. Its flowing, tuneful
melodies adapted well to the pattern favoured by most bands until the
1920s at least, whereby the soloists took up the melody with the rest
providing a simple accompaniment.[67] The compilers of the earliest
printed selections for brass bands were quick to grasp this. Macfarlane's *Cornopean Instructor*, published in 1837, included items from
Donizetti's *Anna Bolena* and *L'Elisir D'amore*, the latter having
reached the English stage only a few months earlier in December
1836.[68] It is not clear how many bands used such journals at this
stage, but their continued publication of operatic items doubtless

encouraged this form in the years ahead.

Throughout the 1840s and 1850s, operatic *pot-pourris* grew in popularity, especially as contest pieces, until, by 1860, they were a *sine qua non* in the competitive field. At a Bradford contest in 1862, twenty of the twenty-two test pieces were culled from opera.[69] Until about 1880, Italian opera, particularly Donizetti, Verdi and Rossini, with some assistance from French composers, especially Meyerbeer, and the British trio of Balfe, Bishop and Wallace, dominated contesting music. Even in 1914, although challenged by new genres, its popularity endured. Italian opera, mostly pre-1850, provided almost half the Belle Vue test pieces between 1853 and 1914, and a similar pattern emerged at other contests. In 1896, for example, forty-eight of the hundred and fifty-one British contests in which test pieces were set by the organisers featured works from the Italian school composed between 1833 and 1853.[70] Inevitably, these contest selections passed into the concert repertoire – three selections per public park concert was the average by the 1890s for the higher ranking bands – where they reached a wider audience. Some selections or overtures were used only once as test pieces; others endured throughout the century. Rossini's *William Tell*, Donizetti's *Lucrezia Borgia* and *L'Elisir D'amore* and Verdi's *Il Trovatore* were probably the most popular of all. Samuel Cope, editor of *British Bandsman*, went as far as to claim in 1907 that the aria 'Il Balen' from *Trovatore* was 'so well-known that every bandsman can whistle it from memory'.[71]

The first real innovation in the operatic repertoire came in the 1870s with the introduction of Wagner. It is possible that the earliest Wagner performance by a brass band was a selection from *Tannhäuser* arranged by J. Sidney Jones and performed by Stalybridge Band in 1875.[72] However, it was Edwin Swift who did the most to pioneer Wagner's music, particularly with Linthwaite Band in the late 1870s and 1880s. By the 1890s Wagner selections based almost exclusively on the early operas *Rienzi, Flying Dutchman* and *Tannhäuser* were extremely common in the concert repertory. The adoption of Wagner's music as early as the mid-1870s provides an excellent example of how closely the leading amateurs followed developments in the wider musical world. Wagner was almost unknown in Britain until the 1870s and yet, as soon as his music appeared in the opera house and concert-hall, musicians such as Swift absorbed it into their local tradition.[73]

Despite the broadening of horizons this had brought about, by the

end of the nineteenth century there were signs of disenchantment
with the existing repertoire, at least amongst some of the movement's
leading figures. There was a strong feeling that band music had
become outdated and ossified. The blame for this was attributed to
music publishers and contest organisers, both more willing to ransack
the more arcane areas of continental opera than to experiment with
music drawn from more varied sources. In 1914, long after criticism
had begun, *Musical Progress* launched a savage attack on that year's
Belle Vue test piece, a selection from Mehul's *Joseph*, a French opera
dating from 1808. It was said by its critic to be 'of the customary
ante-diluvian order, without a soul-stirring note in its composition
from start to finish – one of the most commonplace and insipid pieces
of rubbish we ever sat to hear'. There was also much criticism of the
whole concept of the selection. Calls for young composers to produce
original, discrete pieces specifically for bands became common. W. J.
Galloway drew a comparison between the transformation of choral
music brought about by the new competition repertoire, and the
band's stolid continuation of what he regarded as largely outmoded
musical practices, ending with a call to composers to 'enlarge the
limited musical interest of the bandsmen'.[74]

Changes did come gradually and much of the credit must be taken
by the organisers of the Crystal Palace championships. The guiding
spirit of the competition, J. H. Iles, both through the policy he
pursued there and through the pages of the *British Bandsmen*, which
he had purchased in 1898, made a serious effort to encourage exploration of alternative elements of the art music tradition.[75] Thus in
1906, 1907 and 1910, the previously neglected romantic composers
were embraced, resulting in *Gems of Chopin*, *Gems of Schumann* and
Gems of Schubert respectively. A *Daily News* correspondent gave a
detailed picture of the Schumann selection, which illustrates both the
range of material used by band arrangers and the artistic problems
posed by the need to hold the individual items together.

Nor could it be said that the music in which this interest was shown was of the
merely *ad captondum vulgus* type, for the test piece this year consisted of an
ingenious interweaving of extracts from the works of Schumann, presenting
many points of difficulty and no mean standard of appeal. A piece comprising
fragments from the *Hermann and Dorothea Overture*, the Fifth study for the
pedal piano, the songs *Widmung* and *Talisman*, the A minor concerto, the '*Fest*'
overture and the overture to *Genoveva* – even if these have suffered a certain
violence in extract – must still be regarded as claiming a larger culture than
goes to the general conception of popular musical interest in England.

Here at least, was one satisfied critic.[76]

The most crucial portent for the musical future of the British band movement, however, came in 1913. In that year the Crystal Palace test piece was a tone poem entitled *Labour and Love*, composed by Percy Fletcher (1879–1932), an aspiring composer and musical director at the Savoy Theatre, London. His enthusiasm for band music had been whetted by winning a fifty-guinea prize in a competition for military band composition, and he followed this up by composing *Labour and Love* and offering it to Iles's publishing company.[77] Iles decided not merely to publish it but to adopt it as a test piece. Here was the first piece of original music for brass band by a composer of any sort of standing which was intended as a serious 'artistic' work. Predictably, the *British Bandsman*, Iles's journal, was ecstatic about the work. Its editor described the work as a 'masterful production'. A writer in the rival *Musical Progress*, however, proclaimed it 'probably the easiest test piece by which the championship has been won. Here and there were pitfalls in a technical sense, but of subtleties none'. Irrespective of its merits, (it is still in the band repertoire, suggesting some value) it marked a major step forward. After the First World War, music specifically tailored for bands became increasingly common, and leading composers such as Elgar, Holst and Ireland were commissioned to produce it. In J. H. Elliot's words: 'It was a tentative beginning – but it marked the first important step in the emancipation of the brass band as a musical medium'.[78]

All this activity took place at the centre of the brass band stage and Iles was careful to give it maximum publicity. But there were others contributing to this mini-revolution and, in particular, the work of Joseph Weston Nicholl, conductor of Black Dyke for only a brief period from 1910–11, deserves far greater attention than it has ever received. Nicholl, born in Halifax in 1876, was an extreme rarity in the pre-war band movement – an academically trained musician and composer. He had studied organ, piano, violin and theory in Berlin before continuing organ studies under Rheinberger in Munich and Guilmant in Paris. He returned to England in 1901 to pursue a career as a violin and organ recitalist. His musical background, far greater than that of the traditional trainers, gave him the imagination and courage to challenge prevailing orthodoxy. His association was short because, always in poor health, he appears to have found the work too exacting and because in Black Dyke's tiny bandroom, 'the *ff* playing was a great strain on a sensitive ear'. However, in his short reign he instigated a policy of major reform, seeking to use contemporary compositions and to arrange them in a way which placed heavier demands on the whole band, not simply the soloists.[79] The extent of his achievement is probably best measured by comparing Black Dyke's concert repertoire of 1911 with their own repertoire of ten years previously when conducted by the highly influential Gladney, and also with that of Linthwaite in 1911, when Linthwaite were still a top-class band. All the following programmes took place at Greenhead Park, Huddersfield.

Black Dyke, 12 June 1901

March	*B. B. and C. F.*	Verner (pseudonym for J. Ord Hume)
Overture	*Poet and Peasant*	Suppé
Selection	*Cinq Mars*	Gounod
,,	*Spohr's Works*	Gladney (arr.)
,,	*Messenger Boy*	Monckton
,,	*Ruy Blas*	Lintz
Waltz	*Hydropaten*	Gung'l

Black Dyke, 26 June 1911

March	*Pomp and Circumstance*	Elgar
Selection	*Gems of Schubert*	Rimmer (arr.)
Largo	*New World Symphony*	Dvorak (arr. Nicholl)
Overture	*Magic Flute*	Mozart (arr. Nicholl)
Fugue	*in G Minor*	J. S. Bach (arr. Nicholl)
Tone Poem	*Finlandia*	Sibelius
Selection	*L'Africaine*	Meyerbeer
Scotch Patrol	*Jamie*	Dacre
Fantasia	*Rossini's Works*	Round

Linthwaite, 9 August 1911

Grand March	*Impregnable*	J. Ord Hume
Overture	*The Viking's Daughter*	Rimmer
Valse	*Casino Tanse*	Gung'l
Selection	*Sullivan No. 1*	
Euphonium solo	*The Village Blacksmith*	Weiss
Intermezzo	*In the Twilight*	Rimmer
Selection	*Meyerbeer's Works*	
Valse	*Septembre*	
Selection	*Duchess of Dantzig*	Monckton
Hymn	*Abide With Me*	

The 5/4 movement from Tschaikowsky's *Pathetique* Symphony, the slow movement from his Fourth Symphony and Guilmant's First

Organ Symphony were other important additions to the repertoire not included in this particular concert. The differences are striking. Nicholl had not merely introduced new composers and new works – this was almost certainly the first setting of Bach for brass bands – but he was pioneering the performance of entire pieces and movements in preference to selections, a feature not really developed by other arrangers until the 1920s and 1930s. While Black Dyke's programmes were exceptional, they reflect an extreme example of a fairly wide-spread change. Between about 1906 and 1914 the first movement from Schubert's *Unfinished Symphony*, Liszt's *Hungarian Rhapsody*, Grieg's *Sigurd Jorsfalfer* suite and Brahms's *Hungarian Dances* had all been performed by various bands. A certain spirit of adventure had undoubtedly penetrated a conservative movement.[80]

In bringing art music, albeit in an often truncated and ill-connected fashion, to a large audience, the band movement played a central role in the process of musical education. Many works, later to become in that dreadful, patronising phrase, 'popular classics', were given their initial place in the mainstream of musical taste by bands. The adop-tion of Wagner in the 1870s during the first period of popularity of his music in Britain has already been noted. The Belle Vue test pieces, which quickly passed into the general band repertoire, were often arrangements of music either recently composed or recently known in this country. Gounod's *Faust* was used in 1863, the year of its British premiere (in complete form). Similarly Verdi's *Un Ballo in Maschera*, first performed in Britain in 1861, formed the test piece in 1865, Meyerbeer's *L'Africaine*, first British performance 1865, was used at Belle Vue in 1866, while Verdi's *Aïda* was chosen in 1876, again the year of its British premiere.[81] This popularising process was more marked before 1875, although even even after this date, most notably in the exposure given to Tchaikovsky and Sibelius, there were plentiful examples in the later period. Significantly, this musical education was for the whole commuity and not just the working classes. The composer Sir George Dyson (1884–1964) remembered that he 'first heard Wagner on a brass band'.[82]

It has often been claimed that the bandsmen and many of their audience enjoyed only an arms-length relationship with art music, meeting it in selection form, but 'rarely [hearing] any of the pieces in their entirety or in their original orchestral or operatic form'.[83] Such a view does an injustice to the many musicians who keenly pursued all opportunities to watch professional operatic and orchestral performances. The *British Bandman's* Yorkshire correspondent drew attention to the large number of local bandsman at the Carl Rosa *Il Trovatore* at Bradford in 1907.

Il Trovatore seemed to be a great favourite among bandsmen, judging from the large numbers that attended the performance of this opera. I noticed Mr Heap, Mr Brier, Mr Phineas Ambler (who seemed to be enjoying himself), Mr Aked Haley (who was explaining to his friend Mr Pollard the intricacies of the French horn), Messrs Crowther and Simpson, the Wyke trombonists, and scores of other bandsmen.[84]

The *Bandsman* quite often gave biographical guides to composers and outlines of operatic plots, and on one occasions even printed a list of current London operas for the benefit of provincial bandsmen visiting the metropolis. For many bandsmen, art music was not something imposed upon them by publishers, bandmasters and contest committees, but a central part of their musical culture, a source of genuine artistic pleasure.

The 'art music' element of brass banding has been played up in this chapter, partly because much existing specialist literature ignores the key changes after 1900 and because it does much to challenge orthodox pictures of 'popular' musical culture. But all this should not obscure the fact that even the top bands played a considerable amount of 'light' music and that the majority of bands, especially those outside of the movement's heartlands, played almost nothing else. Big as the gap between Black Dyke and Linthwaite in 1911 might be, it is as nothing compared with the gap between Linthwaite's repertoire and the programme performed in the same year by Market Lavington Band in the vicarage gardens of their native village on the northern fringe of Salisbury Plain.

	God Save the King
March	*Monarch*
Selection	*Song Echoes*
Euphonium Solo	*Anchored*
Fantasia	*A Military Church Parade*
Entracte	*Evening Bells*
Hymn	*Sandon* ('Lead, Kindly Light')

Thousands of country bands would have been pleased to put together even this performance, based largely on the simpler works in Richard Smith and Company's catalogues.[85]

As with the sacred and art music repertoires, the range of light music changed and broadened throughout the period. Until the later nineteenth century the most common form was dance music. In the mid-century, bands often packed their programmes with schottisches, polkas and quadrilles, although it is unclear whether they were performing 'traditional' dance tunes, compositions by bandsmen themselves or the works popularised and/or written by Jullien. Significantly, most of the early brass band music publications, such as J. P. Parry's *The Brass Band*, published by D'Almaine between 1834 and 1848, consisted largely of dance music. By the 1870s there was an increasing amount of this type of music being published for bands with Henry Round's compositions becoming especially popular. As late as the 1890s, even quite eminent bands were sometimes engaged to play dance music at various functions and thus even their repertoire had its lighter side.[86]

By about 1900, although waltzes remained popular, the role of dance music in the repertoire was clearly diminishing. Two types of light music increasingly filled the vacuum: 'specialist' material such as marches, overtures and fantasias specially written for bands, and secondly, selections from light opera and musical comedy. Specialist music had always existed, but from the late nineteenth century, with the great increase in brass band music publishing, it appeared in great profusion. Some of the music, notably the fantasias of Henry Round, placed considerable technical demand upon the performers. His *Joan of Arc*, *Nil Desperandum* and *El Dorado* were popular test pieces in the late nineteenth and early twentieth century. Similarly, the skilfully constructed marches of William Rimmer and John Ord Hume became standard elements of the repertoire. A regular attender at band concerts would have become especially familiar with Rimmer's *Punchinello*, and *The Cossack* and Ord Hume's *B.B. and C.F.* (written in honour of the *British Bandsman and Contest Field Journal*), *Brilliant*, and *Monarch*. In a militaristic age, such lively works with their martial overtones found a wide and appreciative audience. Some of the newer 'custom' music was decidedly lighter in vein, such as the *Tone-Picture of Darkie Life*, included in the repertoire of the West Riding Military Band in the early 1900s. The synopsis is worthy of full quotation.

In the opening movement is heard the distant humming and singing of the 'darkies' as they march to camp meeting. After 'meeting' when the parson 'has done gone home', the 'old folks' join in an 'ole time' rollicking dance. Soon the 'young coons' join in and the pace becomes fast and furious, culminating in a wild 'Buck Dance' accompanied by shouting, laughing, and the rattle of the bones and the strumming of the 'ole banjo'. At last, tired out, they wend their way across the cotton fields to the well-loved strains of *The Old Folks at Home*. A lively finale brings the scene to a close.

Probably a good thing too![87]

The increased popularity of operetta and musical comedy once again illustrates the bands' ability to reflect the changing musical environment. Musical comedy, a creation of the 1890s, began to feature extensively in the band repertoire from about the turn of the century. As it gained more of a foothold in provincial theatres selections from the *Duchess of Dantzig* and *The Spring Chicken* appeared even on the programmes of such mighty organisations as Black Dyke. *Our Miss Gibbs* by Monckton and Caryll was a particular favourite, although this perhaps owed something to its storyline which partly concerned Tim, a Yorkshire bandsman, lost in London. (When Teddy Payne, the actor who portrayed Tim, died in 1914, the *British Bandsman* gave a relatively lengthy and appreciative obituary notice.)[88] The major new injection from the theatre, however, came not from musical comedy but from the music of Sir Arthur Sullivan. Band publishers poured out selections of his music, giving rise to such delightfully clumsy titles as *Gems from Sullivan, III*! These portmanteau works occasionally ventured beyond the Savoy operas to include his ballads, especially the ubiquitous 'Lost Chord', or extracts from 'serious' works such as *Ivanhoe*, but in general it was the melodies of *Iolanthe*, *Pirates of Penzance*, *HMS Pinafore* and the others that became so familiar to Edwardian audiences. There is perhaps no greater testimony to the catholicism of the bandsman's taste and that of his audience, than that in the decade when Tchaikovsky, Chopin, Schumann and even J. S. Bach made an entry into the band world, they were accompanied by the strains of 'Tit Willow' and 'When a Wooer Goes A-wooing'.

Other instrumental ensembles

The brass band was often referred to by contemporaries as the 'working man's orchestra' and in some senses this is a useful description. However, it should not be viewed as the *only* instrumental organisation to involve working-class musicians. Three other bodies deserve some investigation: the concertina band, handbell team and amateur orchestra.

The concertina was one of the most popular instruments of the nineteenth century. It was most often used as a solo instrument, either accompanying songs or performing dance music, but from the 1880s, in parts of the industrial North, it became an ensemble instrument. Wright and Round claimed to have over two hundred bands on their advertising lists in 1889, although no truly accurate count is available.[89] A strip of the Yorkshire textile district encompassing Halifax, Bradford and the towns of the heavy Woollen district, Batley, Dewsbury and Morley, seems to have produced the largest number, perhaps because one of the first successful bands, Wyke and Low Moor Model, was situated in the area and acted as a stimulus. Local imitation, however, could never become a more general 'colonisation', given the strength of the rival brass band movement, the limited size of the relevant musical literature and the scarcity of personnel available to coach and teach.[90]

The bands' social base seems to have been similar to that of the brass bands, as indeed was their repertoire. A typical band consisted of twenty-two instruments, and usually played arrangements based on brass band scores. Contests were held intermittently in the 1880s and then more frequently from the early 1900s, with a Belle Vue contest introduced in 1905 and one at Crystal Palace in 1908. Operatic selections dominated the contest repertoire with *The Caliph of Baghdad*, *Lucrezia Borgia* and *Bohemian Girl* amongst the most popular titles. Very little music was ever written specifically for them, although William Rimmer produced *La Belle Sauvage* for the 1908 Crystal Palace contest. Enthusiasts claimed the standards to be high, although the technical demands were not exceptional. Joe Haynes, an outstanding Bradford concertina player, left a local band after only one rehearsal, because there was too much 'one finger stuff'.[91] The majority of bands seem to have collapsed in the inter-war period and despite the revival of interest in the instrument since the 1970s, none have re-emerged.

The handbell ringers had both a longer pedigree and, to some extent, a broader geographical base than the concertina bands. Handbells were certainly used as secular instruments from at least the twelfth century. By the mid nineteenth century, handbell tune ringing seems to have become a relatively well-established working-class leisure pursuit in Lancashire and Yorkshire.[92] A contest was established at Belle Vue in 1855 (it continued until 1925) and Enderby Jackson organised one at Crystal Palace in 1859. Standards could be impressive. In the 1840s, a group calling themselves the Lancashire Ringers gave professional performances in northern cities. The circus entrepreneur P. T. Barnum was so impressed when he heard them in Liverpool that he took them on a tour of the United States, where, suitably attired, they appeared as the 'Swiss Bell Ringers'.[93]

There appears to have been an increase in activity from the late nineteenth century, although there is little evidence of ringing spreading beyond its traditional geographical confines. Many of the new teams of ringers that appeared in the late Victorian and Edwardian periods were associated with churches and chapels, although this was probably more a reflection of the increasing interest shown in recreational matters by organised religion than an extension of the historic link between churches and ringers. The teams, usually consisting of ten to twelve plus a conductor, stood behind a large table with a baize or felt top, upon which stood a peal of between a hundred and seventy and two hundred bells (novice teams might use only a hundred). Each player had charge of several bells which he would ring as required and then 'damp' on the table top. The bells could be extremely expensive equipment. Crosland Moor United Ringers from Huddersfield, who dominated contesting in the Edwardian period, had a hundred and seventy-two peal valued at over £100.[94] Their music was broadly similar to that of the brass bands and indeed the most famous of all Victorian handbell arrangers, William Gordon, was a band trainer from Stockport. *Il Trovatore* and *Norma*, both common brass selections, were popular contesting pieces along with selections from *Martha* and Hermann's *Le Diademe Overture*. Not all brass influences were beneficial, however. At a Yorkshire contest in 1907 the judge commented that *Tannhäuser*, chosen by the Lindley Ringers, 'did not adapt itself to performance on handbells very well'.[95] In general, however, their music seems to have been popular with Yorkshire and Lancashire audiences – a crowd of five thousand attended a park concert by a leading group on one occasion – although the limits imposed upon them by their mode of performance and their instrumental limitations prevented them from ever becoming a really major musical force.[96]

The amateur orchestra was far more of a national phenomenon than the concertina and handbell bands, and was also open to both sexes. It has traditionally been regarded as 'primarily a middle-class institution'.[97] Many contemporaries dismissed the idea that working people might possess instrumental talents beyond those needed by brass bandsmen. *The Times* informed its readers in 1902 'that the working man should learn to suit his stubborn fingers to the violin, at any rate with any success, is hardly to be expected'.[98] Certainly many amateur societies had a middle-class image, sometimes aggressively so. The London-based British Orchestral Association, founded in 1872, was 'composed of men of means who guarantee the expenses of a series of concerts they are about to give'. The social origins of the Stock Exchange Orchestral Society (1883) hardly requires a leap of imagination.[99] Nevertheless, there was a strong tradition of wind and string playing amongst working *men* dating back at least into the beginning the eighteenth century, a tradition most strongly apparent in the church and chapel bands. Despite the decline in these bands in the nineteenth century, the orchestral element in popular music-making remained strong, especially after about 1885, and there was a far greater working-class presence in amateur orchestras than has been assumed. The orchestras organised by many provincial choral societies contained a significant proportion of working men, and not merely on brass instruments. It is probable that in some areas, particularly from the 1880s when amateur societies began to appear in profusion, almost exclusively working-class societies existed. In October 1896, *The Orchestral Times and Bandsman*, pleased to discover that 'rough work and an artistic temperament are not incomparable', devoted considerable space to the twenty-six-strong Rothwell Orchestral Society, centred on a pit village south-east of Leeds, which included thirteen miners (four violins, viola, cello, double bass, two cornets, two horns, two trombones) and a quarry-man (first violin). Even in London, a number of working men's missions and institutes raised competent orchestras.[100]

Most of the orchestras which appeared from the late nineteenth century had problems obtaining a suitable balance. There were always a remarkable number of violinists present, a situation encouraged by the popularity of school violin lessons from the early twentieth century, but severe shortages occurred elsewhere, especially among the woodwind section. Many societies accepted the problem and operated purely as string orchestras. Repertoire and standard varied enormously according to circumstance. Many societies never graduated beyond waltzes, quadrilles and polkas with perhaps a stab at an early Haydn Symphony[101] or an overture; Herold's *Zampa* and Rossini's *Italiana in Algieri* were particularly popular. The leading societies, however, especially those who entered the orchestral classes at the competitive festivals after 1900, attained a standard only a little below that of a professional organisation. One such society was the Nelson Congregational Orchestral Band, founded in 1890 with a 1d a week membership amongst members of a local chapel. Its members were mostly 'young people who are chiefly employed in the manufacture of cotton goods. Most of them are weavers, and others are overlookers in weaving sheds, or mill managers'.[102] By the early 1900s the orchestra was enjoying considerable success in competitions and at the 1903 Morecambe Music Festival, in association with the orchestra from neighbouring Colne and a small leaven of professionals, were conducted by Elgar during performances of *Lohengrin* and his own *The Banner of St George*. Despite a few mishaps with the former, the standard, in view of the orchestra's social background, could, according to the *Musical Times*, 'only be considered astonishingly high'.[103]

Few amateur orchestras survived the gramophone and wireless 'revolution' of the nineteen twenties and thirties. The brass band and the choral society could co-exist with the new media because they had no professional rivals; choral singing and banding were almost exclusively amateur preserves. But the majority of orchestras had little chance of standing comparison with the musicians easily available from record shops and the BBC. Increasingly from the 1920s, only the school orchestra maintained this long established aspect of popular music-making.

Chapter 10

Choral societies

It is remarkable that while much has been written on the subject of choral music, almost nothing has appeared on the thousands of societies which performed that music. The following survey, while in no way definitive, suggests areas and arguments for debate.

By mid century, choral societies had been established in most English towns with a population of 20,000 plus, and in many of much smaller size. At first, most choirs were mixed voice and comprised anything from fifty to one hundred voices. By the late nineteenth century three basic forms were apparent. The mixed-voice choirs of medium size had been joined by the larger (sometimes over three hundred-voice) mixed oratorio choirs and by the smaller, male voice choir viewed so often as the archetypal choral unit, but in fact almost unknown in England until the 1880s and, even then, never reaching the popularity it attained in Wales.[1]

The choral society had much in common with the brass band. Its repertoire and audience (although rarely membership) often overlapped and joint performances were common. Nevertheless, there were clear differences between the two types of organisation. There was never, for example, a choral 'movement' and, therefore, little of the sense of common purpose and mutuality that was evident amongst bandsmen. Perhaps this was due partly to the late development of contesting amongst choirs, which meant that there was never an equivalent of the relatively homogeneous group of 'cracks' that were found in the band world. The choirs lacked the benefit of a specialist press to bind together their disparate activities. Finally, popular choralism had a broader geographical base than banding, a factor made possible by the historically wider spread of choral, as opposed to instrumental, technique. Within the competitive arena, there was admittedly a tendency for leading contests to be dominated by choirs within relatively easy travelling distance of the venue. The most prestigious mixed voice choirs of the Edwardian period, the Blackpool Glee and Madrigal, the Southport Choir and the Barrow Madrigal Society, owed part of their success to their proximity to the two major competitions, Blackpool and Morecambe.[2] Despite this, and the reputations of Yorkshire and Lancashire for especial excellence, choirs of above-average quality appeared in almost every part of the country. Even London produced some outstanding choirs and none better than Henry Leslie's choir, which between 1855 and 1880, was undoubtedly the finest mixed-voice choir in the country, raising the standard of part-song singing (and composition) to hitherto unsuspected levels.[3]

Choral societies emerged from all manner of backgrounds. In the mid century, especially in the North of England, they were mostly formalised versions of pre-industrial clubs. A few of the larger choirs, however, notably the Hereford Choral Society (1837), Birmingham Festival Choral Society (1845) and Bradford Festival Choral Society (1856), grew out of a desire to keep together in regular practice choirs created solely for local choral festivals.[4] By the late century, choirs came from every conceivable organisational background as the recreational penumbra of voluntary organisations increased massively. Temperance societies, chapels, Pleasant Sunday Afternoons, banks, mills, political parties and numerous other bodies spawned choirs.

At present, knowledge of the social base of choralism is in its infancy. However, it is certainly clear that choirs were not the proletarian institutions claimed by some authorities past and present. There has long existed an assumption, originating in the nineteenth century and still prevalent today, that a provincial accent, especially a Northern one, inevitably denotes working-class origin. Perception of the choral movement had certainly been shaped by this mentality. In 1889, the *Musical Herald* reported that Alfred Broughton, choirmaster of the Leeds Festival Chorus, 'had seen remarks by London critics to the effect that the 'Yorkshire Mill Girls' sing wonderfully. The chorus, however, is drawn from a higher class than this would seem to imply. He doubts if there is a single mill girl in it'. Many recent writers have reiterated Victorian misconceptions. A. L. Lloyd depicts the choral society as part of the nineteenth-century 'workers' movement', while Gareth Stedman Jones assumes the Northern choral movement at least was 'working class'. The reality was far more complex.[5]

There was certainly variation between regions and between choirs. In large cities, socially exclusive choirs occasionally appeared, such as the Bristol Royal Orpheus Glee Society, the Bradford Liedertafel, a glee club founded by the city's German merchant community, and the Leeds Musical Soirée, a society founded in the 1860s which, as its name suggests, had a membership list which read like a 'who's who' of mid-Victorian Leeds. In London, late Victorian and Edwardian choralism at least may well have had a rather lower-middle-class flavour with many of the better choirs based on the 'large commercial houses'.[6] The only really detailed material on social background stems from parts of the Yorkshire textile district in the 1890s. This suggests that popular choralism crossed class, taking in all levels of 'respectable' society from the skilled working class to the manufacturing and mercantile upper middle class.

Choral music in Yorkshire had always attracted a middle-class element, as has been seen, but at least until 1850 appears to have been essentially dominated by weavers, artisans and shopkeepers. By the 1890s, from which period detailed information becomes available, the base had broadened considerably, especially inside the larger choirs. What follows is an analysis of two large choral bodies, the Leeds Philharmonic and the Huddersfield Choral Society, and of one male-voice choir, the Leeds Prize Musical Union. The chorus roll-books of the three choirs, taken in conjunction with local trade directories, provide a suprisingly full picture of the choirs' social structure. Male and female singers have been analysed separately, because the directories only list the head of household and it is therefore not possible to discover any information relating to the occupation of the women. The information concerning women related here is, therefore, a record of their father's or husband's background, and affords only a general indication of their own social background. Nevertheless, a general indication is better than none at all.[7]

Occupations are listed here according to the nine-class categorisation developed by Guy Routh in his *Occupation and Pay in Great Britain, 1906–1960*, outlined overleaf:

1A	higher professional	Manual	
1B	lower professional	workers	
2A	employers and proprietors	5	skilled
2B	managers and administrators	6	semi-skilled
3	clerical workers	7	unskilled
4	foremen, inspectors, supervisors		

Like all attempts at classification, Routh's contains defects. 2A is a particularly awkward category, as it fails to distinguish between large-scale employers of labour and small businessmen. Similarly, the directory information being fed into this pattern can be problematic. If a person is described as a 'jeweller' or a 'baker' is he proprietor or employee? In any case, where an individual's circumstances are open to extremes of interpretation the person has been left out of the analysis. Despite these various problems, the information and categorisation taken together provide a valuable insight into musical life.[8]

Looking first at the Leeds Philharmonic in the concert season 1894–95, it is possible to discover the occupational background of just over half of the menfolk of the female singers. The material relating to the Huddersfield Choir is slightly less full, the background of some 40 per cent being discernible.

The data for the two societies are set out below.

Occupations of fathers or husbands of female members of the Leeds Philharmonic and Huddersfield Choral Societies in 1894–5

Category	Number	% parent's or husband's occupation known
Leeds Philharmonic		
1A	12	13.8
1B	7	8.0
2A	23	26.4
2B	6	6.9
3	19	21.8
4	4	4.6
5	14	16.1
6	2	2.3
7	–	–

Category	Number	% parent's or husband's occupation known
Huddersfield Choral		
1A	9	13.6
1B	4	6.1
2A	25	37.9
2B	2	3.0
3	12	18.2
4	–	–
5	14	21.2
6	–	–
7	–	–

As regards male singers, evidence for the Leeds society is again the fullest, with 60 per cent open to study as opposed to only 40 per cent in the Huddersfield choir. The next table records the relevant information.

Occupations of male members of the Leeds Philharmonic and Huddersfield Choral Societies in 1894–95

Category	Number[9]	% occupation known
Leeds Philharmonic		
1A	6 (5)	7.8
1B	5 (1)	6.5
2A	14 (4)	18.2
2B	6	7.8
3	19	24.7
4	2 (2)	2.6
5	24 (3)	31.1
6	1	1.3
7	–	–
Huddersfield Choral		
1A	5 (1)	7.6
1B	1	1.5
2A	19 (5)	28.8
2B	1	1.5
3	12 (1)	18.2
4	2 (4)	3.0
5	26 (2)	39.4
6	–	–
7	–	–

Before considering the broader issues arising from this material it is interesting to note the slightly differing structures of the two societies, as although a study of both organisations points to similar broad conclusions, individually they reflect the peculiarities of their respective town's economic environment. The Huddersfield Choral Society was clearly a more 'popular' society than its Leeds counterpart in the 1890s. The Huddersfield society had both a slightly higher percentage of both working class men (39.5 per cent as opposed to 32.5 per cent) and women (21.2 per cent as opposed to 18.4 per cent) compared with the Leeds Philharmonic and a slightly lower proportion of upper-middle-class men (23 per cent to 32 per cent) and women (42 per cent to 44 per cent). Further, although this is not apparent from the tables, the working-class contingents of the two choirs tended to come from slightly different occupational backgrounds. The typical working-man member of the Philharmonic was a skilled workshop craftsman, with perhaps as few as three of the twenty-five in the sample being factory operatives. Of the twenty-six working men in the Huddersfield sample, almost half were factory workers. This significant difference is partially explained by different occupational structure of the two towns. Huddersfield, barely a quarter the size of Leeds, had fewer outlets for men in such trades as bootmaking, cabinet-making, watchmaking and the like, and thus the skilled operative was more likely to be a factory worker.[10]

Overall, however, it is the similarities rather than the differences which are most apparent. What this body of data illustrates is that, far from being a part of 'worker's culture', these two choirs at least extended across class lines to embrace a broad span of local society. Working, lower middle and upper middle classes all made substantial contributions to these choirs. The extent of the social intermingling becomes even more striking if people replace statistics. J. J. 'Percy' Kent, MA (Cantab.) and gentleman of leisure, for example, had amongst his neighbours in the ranks of tenors at Leeds Philharmonic concerts R. J. Ellis 'hardware dealer', Benjamin Bray 'working jeweller' and Edwin Bramley 'machinist'; in Huddersfield, Miss M. B. Sykes of 'Roundfield', Imperial Road, Edgerton, daughter of a prosperous woollen manufacturer, rubbed shoulders with Mrs Hartley of 69 Prospect Street, Huddersfield, whose husband was a plumber.

It is the presence of people such as Miss Sykes that is perhaps most surprising, as our traditional image of late Victorian leisure institutions does not normally allow for the substantial presence of the upper echelons of local society within the same organisation as a considerable body of working men and their wives. Significantly, it was the wives and daughters of the *haute bourgeoisie* – more accustomed by 'philanthropic' role, perhaps, to dealing with the 'poor' socially – who were most likely to join in musical alliance with their social inferiors, although some eminent males found their way into the choral movement. In the mid 1890s both Sir John Barran, grandson of the founder of the Leeds Clothing industry, and Edward Kitson Clark, a partner of one of Yorkshire's largest engineering firms, were both members of the Philharmonic, along with several of towns leading clergymen and medical practitioners.[11]

Clearly, the presence of such people, remarkable as it might appear to those nourished on traditional histories of industrial England, should not obscure the fact that almost two-thirds of the choirs' members were drawn from the 'respectable lower classes', the lower middle and the skilled working class. Here may well lie the true social base of popular choralism. Similarly it is possible that this section of society had greater commitment to their art than their better-off counterparts. An analysis of approximately half of the Leeds Philharmonic's membership for 1908–09 (unfortunately, inadequate directories make it impossible to attempt a comparative study of Huddersfield Choral Society) illustrates a substantial decline in the number of singers from the higher reaches of the social scale.

Occupation of fathers and husbands of female members of the Leeds Philharmonic Society, 1908–09

Category	Number	% occupation known	1894–5 figures
1A	10	11.9	13.8
1B	6	7.1	8.0
2A	20	23.8	26.4
2B	1	1.2	6.9
3	16	19.0	21.8
4	2	2.4	4.6
5	27	32.2	16.1
6	2	2.4	2.3
7	–	–	–

N.B. The Society also had seven members of uncertain status but who were clearly of working-class origin.

Occupations of male members of Leeds Philharmonic Society, 1908–09

Category	Number	% occupation known	1894–5 figures
1A	1	1.2	7.8
1B	4	4.9	6.5
2A	15	18.3	18.2
2B	2	2.4	7.8
3	18	22.0	24.7
4	2	2.4	2.6
5	37	45.1	31.1
6	2	2.4	1.3
7	1	1.2	0.0

N.B. The society also had five members of uncertain status but who were clearly of working-class origin.

In 1894–95 approximately 41 per cent of the identifiable female membership consisted of women whose father's or husband's occupation can be placed in groups 1A, 1B, 2B and the upper echelons of 2B. By 1908–09 the figure had fallen to 32 per cent. Similarly, the proportion of males whose occupations came into these categories had fallen from 30 per cent to 17 per cent, a more striking decline. The lower-middle-class contingent remained steady and the working-class sector rose substantially. It remains to be seen whether such a pattern was in any way typical, although there is impressionistic evidence to suggest that it was.

It is apparent that, as with many other aspects of organised popular recreation, working-class involvement was restricted largely to members of the labour elite. To an extent, this was a matter of shillings and pence, with only skilled workers possessing the necessary surplus cash at the initial stage of membership. However, it was not simply lack of money or 'correct' clothing that proved a block to unskilled or semi-skilled workers. They remained largely outside the religious institutions which provided the key training ground for the choral movement. In Victorian England, the closing of one door, particularly this one, clearly closed many others.[12]

Significantly, it was skilled working *men* who formed the largest 'popular' element in the choral society's social structure. Both Yorkshire choirs studied here contained approximately twice as many working-class men as women. Paul Thompson has warned the historian against facile generalisation concerning the place of working-class women in social life at this time, stressing that a range of regional, social and personal factors could affect their lives. Nevertheless, the fact that women played a far smaller part than their menfolk does suggest that 'traditional' factors and, in particular, the assumption of a home-centred role by one or both partners, worked against them. Certainly, at least in the Leeds Philharmonic, there are signs of an increasing presence of women from working-class households by the Edwardian period (sixteen in 1894, thirty-six by 1909). Substantially increased female job opportunities in the local clothing industry may have been a peculiar local factor here, although it is possible that the general increase in 'white collar' employment by the Edwardian period, may have had a similar effect in other regions.[13] In general, however, it would seem that even in a leisure pursuit where specifically female attributes were needed, the potential for working-class women was decidedly limited.

The focus so far has been on the oratorio choirs, but, despite relatively scanty data, it is worth examining the structure of the smaller choirs. The cantata choirs almost certainly exhibited a social base similar to that of the two choirs discussed above. The competitive choirs, however, were almost certainly more 'popular' in complexion. Contemporary journalists portrayed both mixed and male voice choirs as largely working-class with impressionistic comments concerning 'mill, workshop and counter' occurring frequently. Almost certainly, the lower middle class played a far more significant role than such commentators assumed, but the broad social mix evident in the larger choirs was almost absent. The following table, listing twenty-five of the forty-nine traceable members of the Leeds Prize Musical Union, a male voice choir, between 1887–1896, illustrates an amalgam of skilled working men, clerks, travellers and shopkeepers.

Membership of Burley Glee Union[14] and Leeds Prize Musical Union, 1887–1889 and 1893–96

Category	Number	% occupation known
1A	1	4.0
1B	1	4.0
2A	2	8.0
2B	3	12.0
3	8	32.0
4	–	–
5	10	40.0
6	–	–
7	–	–

Only three singers can be described as 'middle class', and even they (two managers of small businesses and an architect only recently established in practice) hover uneasily at the less comfortable edge of the class. Obviously, the Leeds choir may not be typical – it would be interesting to obtain a detailed picture of a *mixed* choir – but significantly, no evidence of *haute bourgeois* presence has emerged from extant research. If it *was* typical, two explanations for the more 'humble' nature of competitive choirs suggest themselves. First, the idea of competition, especially that which involved financial reward, was essentially antagonistic to the middle and upper middle class ethos. It is possible that in the same way some middle class sportsmen eshewed the horrors of professionalism and took refuge in the purity of soccer's Arthur Dunn Cup (a tournament for ex-public schoolboys) or the Rugby Union, middle-class choralists preferred the purity of the oratorio choir to more 'sporty' habits of singing for £25 money prize plus gold medal.[15] Alongside this arose the issue of personal contact with subordinate social classes. Willing to sing alongside social inferiors in a large gathering, where social contact with them could be avoided unless they desired otherwise, the upper middle class were perhaps less willing to be forced into the intimacy demanded by the smaller numbers of the competition choir.

As with brass bands, it is necessary to look beyond the performers if we are to gain the fullest understanding of the social dynamics of choralism. Once again, there is much evidence of interest and involvement from a wide cross-section of the community.

Analysis of audiences suggests markedly that there were different social groupings according to the type of concert. The audience at oratorio concerts was almost certainly predominantly middle-class, a feature stemming from the practice, common by the 1880s, of issuing many tickets by subscription. Obviously, the subscription was vital from the societies' point of view, guaranteeing as it did an income with which to plan their season, but the rates were invariably too high for the pockets of working-class families. In 1897–98, for example, 1300 tickets for the Leeds Philharmonic season were purchased by some six hundred people, almost all of whome were drawn from the professional middle class and upwards. Many of the occupiers of the 'best' seats travelled by carriage from the villas of Northern Leeds or by first-class rail from Otley, Ilkley and Harrogate. For such people a Leeds Philharmonic concert was a central event in the social calender, and as much an excuse for a display of wealth as a musical event.[16] The remaining several hundred tickets were available at the door for 5s, 2s and 1s. Working men certainly purchased 1s tickets, but they were luxuries that could not be afforded particularly often. A privileged few could obtain the complimentary tickets given to members for their friends and families by some societies.[17] In the main, however, the oratorio choirs, although drawn most heavily from the lower middle and upper working classes, provided entertainment for those considerably higher in the social scale.

The smaller cantata choirs provided concerts at more popular prices, as did countless church and chapel choirs. Admission rates of 2d, 3d or 6d were very frequent, enabling them to draw sizeable audiences for such key social and musical events as the Christmas *Messiah*. Miss Pattie Smith, a violinist in a Halifax chapel orchestra, remembers how, at Christmas choral concerts, 'people came for miles and were sitting on the pulpit and up the staircase'.[18] In countless village halls, schoolrooms, mission halls and chapels, choral music reached those for whom the concerts of a Leeds Philharmonic were at best a luxury, at worst, an impossibility. Choral competitions too were relatively cheap to enter, although supporters of a particular choir would often have to find the extra expense of a train or tram fare.

As with the brass band, there was substantial middle-class input at organisational level. The larger societies, always anxious to better their rivals in terms of both technical excellence and status, often found it necessary to find a local benefactor. Thus, in 1897, Bradford Festival Choral Society were able to appoint the composer Dr Frederick Cowen as conductor and H. H. Fricker, the Leeds borough organist, as choirmaster thanks largely to the munificence of Henry Mason, a local industrialist. Harry Cawood Embleton, a mining engineer and shareholder in local mines who also had the good fortune to inherit £36,000 in his aunt's will, was another such benefactor. A small but useful proportion of his wealth was devoted to meeting the needs of Leeds Choral Union to whom he was secretary/treasurer from 1895–1930.[19] In general, Embleton seems to have been unusual in combining philanthropy with organisational work. The more mundane elements of committee work fell to figures who were less eminent, although still solidly middle-class. The Leeds Philharmonic committee in 1895–96 included a textile manufacturer, a bank manager, an estate agent, a vicar, a solicitor and two commercial travellers.[20] The choir's increasingly 'popular' face by 1910 had no reflection at organisational level, and indeed, working-class members

seem to have been loath to take administrative posts. The Leeds Prize
Musical Union's seven-man committee permanently contained a dis-
proportionately high number of white collar works.[21] Whether all this
resulted from an active assumption of their own suitability by those of
higher status and often higher levels of education, or from the passive
acceptance by working-class members that it was those of higher
social position who should organise, is unknown. However, this
situation, repeated in many soccer clubs and in the volunteer
movement, illustrates that the working classes could participate quite
happily in a recreational form without having much control over its
direction.[22]

Making music

In 1840, choral societies generally had less than a hundred members, a
preponderance of males, and were rooted firmly in the music of
Handel and Haydn (and by the end of the decade, Mendelssohn).
There was still a strong flavour of the social club about many of them,
with the members firmly in control of procedure and the professional
conductor only just emerging on the horizon. By the end of the
century, although some of these features persisted, choral music had
undergone some dramatic changes.

The most immediately striking feature of the oratorio choirs was
their increase in size. By the late nineteenth century, when the desire
for respectable, self-improving recreation was at its height, the largest
societies had memberships of up to 450. They rarely used their full
weight – although one suspects if they could have found stages large
enough, they would have done – but choruses of 250–300 were
common amongst the most prestigious northern choirs.[23]

Of greater importance, and affecting the smaller mixed and male-
voice choirs of the late century as well as the larger bodies, was the
increased role of women. In 1837, for example, only eight of the
Huddersfield Choral Society's fifty-four members were women. By
1895 they were a clear majority, comprising some 187 of the society's
330 members.[24] Indeed, probably as early as 1875, females were
numerically dominant in most societies, at least in most of Yorkshire
and Lancashire. (In mining areas, for example, where female job
opportunities and spare time were more limited, women may not have
had the necessary finances and leisure to become involved on such a
scale.)

Their presence obviously had a profound influence upon the musical structure of the choirs. In the earlier period, men occasionally took the treble part and male altos were almost universal. By the 1860s, however, female sopranos were fully established, and by the late nineteenth century the male alto, at least in mixed-voice choirs, was becoming a rarity – in 1877 Huddersfield Choral had fifty, by 1902 only twelve. The national picture was similar, perhaps even more dramatic. The Handel Festival choir, gathered from all over the country for a triennial celebration of Handel's music, had 419 male altos in 1859, but only 23 by 1903.[25] It is not clear why the male alto fell from grace. Did conductors and composers genuinely prefer the contralto, or was the change essentially the result of increasing pressure for entry from women seeking a fuller recreational life? Contemporaries are reticent on the issue, noting the change but rarely seeking to explain it. In all probability, musical and social factors coalesced in this instance. Composers preferred increasingly to give *solo* lines to contraltos in oratorio, a trend dramatically enhanced after Mendelssohn's use of the contralto Madame Sainton Dolby in *Elijah* (1847). Inevitably, the shift in taste affected choruses too and gradually 'composers now wrote oratorio alto lines much higher on average presupposing female voices. . . . The alto part was now unsuited and uncomfortable, sometimes even impossible, for the 'male' alto'. The cathedral choir and some male voice choirs were to be the last refuge for the male alto. It must be said, however, that the widespread fashion for using contraltos in chorus work was made possible by the increased female demands for 'improving' recreation.[26]

As with the brass band, the family was an important factor in a choral singer's initial education. Whereas most bandsmen graduated from a musical home straight into the band in order to continue their training, however, choristers usually passed through an intermediary stage, the church or chapel choir. Here basic techniques were refined and interests raised before a more senior member of the choir or the choirmaster might suggest the transition to a local society that he or she was connected with. For those unable or unwilling to join a church or chapel choir, there were the numerous tonic sol-fa societies already noted, which did much to contribute to the supply of choristers. The religious choir does, however, appear to have been the most important training ground. For some, the transition from choir to choral society had considerable personal significance. One singer defined passage into the male-voice choir as proof of 'having become a man and passed into mens' company.'[27]

The exact level of competence demanded of singers on entry to a choral society varied according to its standing. Some accepted anybody and did with them what they could; others were interested only in the best available talent. By the 1890s competition for entry to the societies was extremely fierce, especially for women. By this time, the Bradford Festival Choral Society, for example, had not only reduced the number of applicants they tested, but were regularly failing 50 per cent of the applicants they heard. Sopranos and contraltos had to face a selection panel, perform scales and a sightseeing exercise and answer questions on musical notation and general musical knowledge. Joining a first-rank choral society could be as much a test of nerve as an extension of musical horizons.[28]

Once in the society, the singer was usually faced with one two-hour rehearsal per week, more if a concert or contest was looming. The majority of societies were trained and conducted by a local musical enthusiast, normally (although not always) male, sometimes an individual who followed a non-musical career, sometimes a musician or music teacher. The larger societies were usually under the care of a chorus master, who prepared them in the early stages of rehearsal prior to the visits of a leading choral conductor. Most areas were dominated by one influential figure, who serviced the needs of most of the major choirs in the locality. Henry Coward conducted at least five choirs in Yorkshire, William Stockley five in Birmingham and the Black Country and Henry Watson eight in the Manchester region. In the 1890s Watson was reputed to be training a choir of some description every single night of the week from September to March.[29] A few wealthy societies were prepared to look outside their own region in order to make prestigious appointments. Coward was lured from his Sheffield home to conduct societies in Preston, Newcastle and Glasgow in the Edwardian period.

The nature of rehearsals obviously varied, but in general the atmosphere was strict and efficient. Persistent absentees were asked to resign, gigglers and chatterers chastised.[30] Most choirs did maintain some democratic control over their singing, however. The level of democracy was highest before the middle of the century. The Huddersfield Choral Society rules of 1836 allowed for every member in rotation to choose the music to be performed at monthly meetings. Discussion concerning the standard of performance at rehearsals and concerts was allowed, provided it was undertaken in a polite manner. By the 1840s most matters of organisation, policy and repertoire were passing into the hands of committees, a virtual necessity from this period because of the increased size of societies which made informal discussion harder, and the greater organisational load.[31] Crucially, these committees and all officers were elected, *including the conductor in many cases.* Some critics objected to this on artistic grounds, claiming that a society could too easily reject a conductor who attempted to stretch a choir by introducing unfamiliar music. This was certainly a danger, and the practice certainly waned by 1900, but the power of election occasionally proved invaluable. In 1887 a section of the Bradford Festival Choral's members launched an attack on their conductor Robert Senior Burton, an eminent West Riding choral conductor and organist from the 1850s, but a notoriously prickly and idiosyncratic man. The choir's spokesman, William Tate, claimed that rehearsals,

had not been nearly so instructive and interesting as formerly – that too much time was devoted to one branch of study, to the neglect of others of equal importance and urgency, and that members often separated without having advanced one step nearer to the realisation of the intentions of the composer.

The committee advised the critics to back down and Burton described the whole affair as 'scandalous' – but he lost the vote at the AGM and was asked to resign. The power of election was only rarely used, but it was vital if the choral movement was to remain a hobby for its members rather than fodder for ambitious professionals.[32]

Repertoire

The dramatic enlargement and diversification of the choral repertoire after about 1850 (even more so from about 1890) had three main causes. The changing religious climate led to acceptance both of new types of choir and of styles of choral music; the competitive movement of the late century generated a new repertoire; and composers and music publishers showed considerable skill in meeting the increasing demands of the choral market. To make sense of the musical developments that these influences set in motion, it is easiest to sub-divide the choral repertoire into four sections: that performed by the larger oratorio choirs, the smaller concert-orientated choirs, the amateur operatic societies and the competitive choirs.

Before beginning, it is critical to appreciate that much of the music under discussion would not have been written but for the existence of the British choral movement. Since the early nineteenth century the choral society has enjoyed the distinction of being perhaps the only amateur artistic institution which has generated the *creation* of art. Composers and publishers were acutely aware of the need to produce marketable commodities and would have turned to other areas had choral music not offered a guaranteed source of income. What was arguably the most important phase came between the late 1890s and 1914. Composers such as Elgar and Bantock would surely not have written, or even contemplated writing, the new part-song repertoire without the existence of choirs whose technical standards drove writers to produce more and more demanding works. Certainly, much Victorian and Edwardian choral music was of limited value, even by contemporary taste, but much of great value owed its existence to choirs in which the 'common people', so often assumed to have been excluded from traditions of 'high culture', played an important part.

There were undoubtedly regional variations in the repertoires of all types of choir as a result of local taste and habit, and loyalty to local composers. In general, however, broad national patterns can be established. Essentially, the larger choirs followed the pattern so well delineated by Scholes in *The Mirror of Music*.[33] Until the late 1860s the repertoire was still dominated by Handel, Haydn (although increasingly less so) and Mendelssohn (increasingly more so). *Messiah* was never superseded, and never has been in the public mind at least, as the premier choral work. By mid century it was firmly established as Christmas music, and not only the local prestige society but chapels, churches and Sunday-schools often organised their own performances, so that in larger towns at least, it became possible to hear several *Messiahs* in one week. Such slavish adherence to the dictates of modern taste upset many professional critics, Herbert Thompson speaking will ill-disguised annoyance on one occasion of 'the usual *Messiah* outbreak at Christmas tide'.[34] Many choirs agreed, but knew better than to abandon a guaranteed source of profit. Most northern choirs performed the work virtually every Christmas. A few other works also gained remarkable exposure in the third quarter of the century. Mendelssohn's *Elijah*, and, to a lesser extent, *St Paul*, gradually edged out Handel's *Israel in Egypt* and Haydn's *Creation* and *The Seasons*, from their place in popular esteem. *Elijah*, with its music, in the words of one twentieth-century critic, 'which felt familiar but which at the same time was just "new" enough', was eventually *Messiah's* closest rival.[35]

By the 1870s there was a veritable flood of new compositions to join these established works. Almost every composer was expected to produce at least one oratorio. *Grove's Dictionary of Music and Musicians* stated in 1889 that: 'The oratorio is to the musician the exact analogy of what the cathedral is to the architect – the highest art-form to the construction of which he can aspire'.[36] There was more at stake than simple artistic piety, however. Oratorio composition was an almost certain way of earning money and many pieces were commissions for the numerous civic and cathedral choral festivals that blossomed during the nineteenth century. Some were as ephemeral as the most trifling popular song – performed just once, occasionally twice, and then slipping away into oblivion. Scholes produced a list of several dozen such transient oratorios, including many festival commissions, produced between 1884 and 1893 alone. Swinnerton Heap's *The Maid of Astolat*, Joseph Smith's *St Keven*, Rosalind Ellicott's *The Birth of Song* and hundreds of other works now seem destined for eternal silence. Some inevitably found their way into the choral society repertoire and the record of many societies is littered with pieces performed only once. Leeds Philharmonic, for example, played some thirty compositions on only one occasion between 1870 and 1914. Irrespective of the quality, rarely can a society have had so much contemporary music thrown at it as did that of late Victorian England.[37]

Obviously, not all new additions can be so lightly dismissed. A small number of festival pieces, coupled with a steady influx of European (and occasionally American) material, also often produced for British festivals, gave choirs a rich choice. Bach's *Mass in B minor* and *St. Matthew Passion*, originally most enthusiastically greeted in London, gradually became known to provincial audiences in the late century, as did Berlioz's *Requiem* and Rossini's *Stabat Mater*. Gounod's *Redemption* (1882), Dvorak's *Stabat Mater* (1876/1880), Parry's *Job* (1892), Coleridge-Taylor's *Hiawatha* (1898) and, after a shaky start, Elgar's *The Dream of Gerontius* (1900), passed swiftly into the centre of the choral tradition.

This list points up the importance of the more tolerant theology of the period as a factor in the changing pattern of choral composition and dissemination. Increasingly, from the 1880s, audiences and performers were prepared to countenance both Roman Catholic and secular texts. Would the works by Dvorak, Rossini and Elgar have gained popularity in the High Victorian age? Even in 1900, *Gerontius* (based on Cardinal Newman's poem) was found offensive by many and one of the factors contributing to its unsatisfactory first performance at the 1900 Birmingham Festival was the religiously-inspired opposition of the Nonconformist chorusmaster.[38] Nevertheless, it was accepted relatively quickly. Secular oratorio was less controversial and not peculiar to the late nineteenth century. Schumann's *Paradise and The Peri* (1843), called by the composer 'oratorio, but for cheerful people', is a case in point. However, it became far more common from the 1890s, with such works as Coleridge Taylor's *Hiawatha* (1898) and Bantock's *Omar Khayyam* (1906). A society increasingly less well-versed in the scriptures came to accept, perhaps even expect, a broadened range of subjects. The fact that such works still *sounded* religious by association doubtless helped facilitate the change.

The secularisation of the repertoire was further aided from the 1890s onwards by the adoption of operatic selections by a few ambitious choirs. Concert performances by choral societies occasionally took place in the earlier period, but opera had for the most part been too closely associated with Catholicism, the theatre and the passions to be readily acceptable to some sterner spirits. By 1900, pieces of *Lohengrin, Tannhäuser, Der Freischütz* and even complete performances of *Maritana* and *Bohemian Girl* had been attempted and been well received.[39]

Not every community could sustain a choir of the size and skill required for adequate performance of oratorio and throughout the century, especially after about 1875, there was a growth of smaller mixed-voice choirs. These might usefully be called 'cantata' choirs because although they were willing to tackle *Messiah* and perhaps one or two other favourite oratorios, the cantata formed the basis of their repertoire. The output of cantata composition rose enormously in the late century, partly stimulating and partly stimulated by the rapidly expanding number of middle-sized choirs. Not only were these works produced for festivals, but scores of earnest provincial musicians produced them as part of the requirement for external Doctor of Music degrees. The development of the cantata repertoire is similar to that of the oratorio; massive production, a high 'mortality' rate, the dominance of a few pieces and an increased popularity of secular libretto from the late century. Alfred Gaul's *The Holy City*, composed for the Birmingham Festival of 1882, was probably the most commonly-performed of all cantatas. Its sacred theme and satisfying but technically straightforward music, when allied to the sales technique of Novello, proved perfectly suited to contemporary requirements. By 1914, one hundred and sixty-two thousand copies of the full score had been sold.[40] Sterndale Bennett's *May Queen* (1858), Sullivan's *Prodigal Son* (1869) and *The Golden Legend* (1886), and Stainer's *The Crucifixion* (1887) – as much a feature of a provincial Easter as *Messiah* was of Christmas – were other stock components of the repertoire.

As most cantatas did not last long enough to give audiences full value for money, most societies completed the programme – usually taking up the second half of the concert – with a miscellaneous selection. Favourite pieces from the Handel, Haydn, Mendelssohn oratorios, glees, madrigals, part-songs and vocal or instrumental renditions of such trusted pieces as 'Comin' Thru' The Rye' and 'Home Sweet Home' made up this portion.

In the late nineteenth century there appeared two new types of organisation which did much to broaden the base of popular choralism still further: the amateur operatic society and the competitive choir. The operatic society was a product of the very late 1890s and the Edwardian period. To some extent it fits uneasily in a section on choral music, for it was less concerned with the 'serious' aspect of music, gave opportunity to those as much or more interested in acting as singing, and, most obviously, was theatrical in mode of presentation. However, as a major new element of popular vocalism and one that, in terms of personnel at least, sometimes overlapped with the existing musical community, it cannot be ignored.

Gilbert and Sullivan provided the operatic societies with their *raison d'être*. The first amateur performance of Savoy opera took place at Kingston, Surrey in 1879, when the Harmonists Choral Society gave *HMS Pinafore*.[41] By the 1890s provincial performances were regular and popular events, and indeed may well have tapped audiences previously untouched by choral societies. An amateur Gilbert and Sullivan production at Hanley in Staffordshire in the mid-1890s attracted almost fifteen thousand people during its six days of performance. 'No choral society could do the same thing', an observer commented. In the Edwardian period when professional performances of Gilbert and Sullivan were increasingly rare – from

1910–1919, there were no London performances and only one D'Oyly Carte touring company operated – amateurs enthusiastically kept their works live. In 1909 the Bradford Amateur Operatic Society's *Mikado* made a profit of £350, 'a record for one week's performance of opera by any (amateur) society in the country'. This level of popularity suggests an audience extending some way into the working classes and indeed, Robert Roberts remembers a vogue for Gilbert and Sullivan amongst the skilled craftsmen of Salford and Manchester.[42] A few brave souls attempted imitation of the 'masters', although later generations do not remember Blatchford and Sykes of Halifax, Harwin and Akeroyd of Bradford or Oglesby and Grimshaw of Leeds! They enjoyed an albeit fleeting success in their localities, providing, if nothing else, a much-needed pause between the endless round of *Iolanthe*, *Penzance*, *Pinafore* and *Mikado*.[43]

In the long term, this enthusiastic adoption of Gilbert and Sullivan must rank as one of the most significant popular musical phenomena of the period to 1914. Their work has maintained its appeal quite remarkably, and is to this date a staple part of the musical culture of a broad social spectrum. At the time, however, the appearance of the competition choir was regarded as being of greater importance, at least in the artistic sense. The growth of the competition led to a remarkable blossoming of choral composition and a massive refinement of technique, and generally, played a significant part in the English musical Renaissance of the period.

It was not until the late 1880s and 1890s that the choral contest really emerged. There were two basic forms of choral contest. The first, its artistic and social philosophy explored in detail in an earlier chapter, was the so-called competitive music festival envisaged by organisers as a school of musical education, a place to learn and enjoy rather than to seek glory and financial reward. Medals and certificates were preferred to cash prizes. The second form of contest, usually a simple affair involving only a small number of choirs, was far more overtly competitive and was rooted in the choral strongholds of Yorkshire and Lancashire. Some of these contests did begin with educational intentions. The Hardraw Scar Brass Band and Choral Contest – founded in 1881 and held annually in a natural amphitheatre in the midst of beautiful Dales countryside near Hawes, North Yorkshire – was intended originally as an educational venture. The choirs who attended, however, although concerned with artistic standards, were quite clearly 'pot-hunting', as their critics termed their desire to win, and the organisers of this and other similar events which spread through Yorkshire and Lancashire in the 1890s made few of the missionary claims associated with the competitive festival movement.[44]

The competitive ethos had a profound effect upon musical life. Apart from the crucial impact of contesting upon both the repertoire and technical standards, it was responsible for much of the expansion and diversification that marked the period to the early 1900s. Competition actually brought societies into existence, a feature which was especially clear in the choral field. The Saltaire Prize Choir, one of the premier mixed-voice choirs of Late Victorian England, was founded in 1887 specifically to compete at Hawes. Encouraged by their success at the event, they became a permanent body.[45] New or previously rare types of choir were fostered by competition. The male-voice choir, regarded by many as the archetypal choral unit, was in fact little known outside Wales until the encouragement given to it by competition from the 1880s onwards. The competition also encouraged the 'nationalisation' of popular music, taking musical forms and organisation into previously unreceptive environments. It is doubtful whether, for example, the mixed-voice choir singing the part-songs of Elgar would have become quite so prominent a feature of the musical landscape of rural Westmorland, North Yorkshire or even Somerset without the stimulus given by contesting. While there were many who claimed a basic incompatability between art and competition, nineteenth and early twentieth-century musical life would have been altogether poorer without the competitive ethos.

At first, between about 1875 and 1895, competitive choirs drew on the existing repertoire. Male-voice choirs used the glees, madrigals and part-songs of the previous century. A small number of pieces gained particular popularity, and might well be sung three or four times by different choirs during the course of a contest. Webbe's 'Wanton Gales', Yarwood's 'Gentle Sighs The Evening Breeze', Spofforth's 'Hail, Smiling Morn', Battye's 'Child of the Sun' and Goss's 'O Thou Whose Beams' were amongst the most regularly-performed works. Mixed choirs showed more propensity toward sacred works, although secular part-songs were also popular. Sullivan's 'O Gladsome Light' from his *Golden Legend* and Pinsuti's 'The Sea Hath its Pearls' dominated mixed-voice classes.[46]

From the end of the century, and increasingly throughout the Edwardian period, an entire new part-song repertoire was called into being as competition organisers, publishers and composers hastened to meet the new demand. The best of this new material has been seen by many scholars as amongst the finest work in the British choral tradition. Competition organisers were determined that compositions should extend choral technique; some pieces took it almost beyond breaking point. Cornelius's *The Tempest* was described by a contemporary musical journalist as possessing 'abnormal difficulties', while many singers regarded sections of Delius's *On Craig Dhu*, the 1910 mixed-voice test piece at Blackpool, as physically impossible![47] More approachable, although challenging and highly regarded by contemporaries, were the songs of Elgar, who became closely associated with the Morecambe Festival as adjudicator and conductor from the early 1900s. 'O Wild West Wind' and 'Feasting I Watch' were performed with, especially in the case of the former, almost monotonous regularity. There was also a tentative exploration of previously neglected repertoires. Brahms, for example, began to feature on contest agendas from about 1908 while in the following year, a work by Palestrina appeared at the Morecambe Festival.[48]

The new repertoire was not for specialists alone. Choirs took their contest pieces into local concert-halls and gave them wide currency. Ambitious choirs such as the Halifax Madrigal Society, who offered local patrons concerts entirely devoted to Elgar and Bantock in 1905 and 1912 respectively, provided a quite remarkable level of musical education. Significantly, many competitive choirs still showed a remarkable catholicism in their concert programmes. The Madrigal Society, in its earlier guise as the male-voice Halifax West End Glee Union, once combined a programme of glees and madrigals with solo renditions of 'My Old Dutch' and 'Mrs 'Enery Hawkins'. Another choir in the Yorkshire area managed the glee 'Hail Bounteous May', Gounod's 'La Massagera d'Amor' and Harry Rickards's 'hilarious' 'Skippers of St Ives' on the same programme. English glee, French opera, music-hall song; only in Victorian England was such a mixture possible.[49]

To some extent, many of the changes outlined here led to the beginnings of a rift between choir and community, and indeed between choir and some members. Handel, Mendelssohn and perhaps a few of the new additions were quite adequate to meet some tastes, and new trends were not always popular. This point will be developed later, but it requires mention here. Nevertheless, irrespective of popular opinion, it is undeniable that by 1914 English choral societies were performing a far wider repertoire, dealing with a broader range of subject matter and singing with a greater degree of technical expertise, than would have seemed possible to the enthusiasts of the late eighteenth and early nineteenth centuries.

Chapter 11

Music and social change

A history of popular musical organisations must by definition focus upon music. It is impossible, however, to understand the appeal and influence of the amateur musical society without giving some attention to the many social and economic benefits which accrued to members.

At the most simple level, but of great importance, choirs and bands offered endless opportunity for basic sociability, and sometimes more. Rehearsals, concerts and competitions gave plentiful opportunity for talking, smoking and drinking in between and after the musical activities, while romance flourished over the tops of *Messiah* copies and down amongst the violins. By the late nineteenth century, a number of bands went as far as to establish social clubs, seeing this as a method of gaining the widest possible support from the local community as well as a chance to broaden members' social lives. Some grew to impressive proportions; by 1902 Shipley Brass Band, once a temperance band, had a social club with four hundred members who enjoyed access to a concert-hall, conversation-room, recreation-room and bar! The attachment of many bands to the volunteer movement, begun in 1859, added a range of military and sporting activities to bandsmens' recreational diet.[1]

Although all types of musical society offered plentiful scope for enjoyment, there was, as already implied, a difference between the social life of the smaller male organisations and the larger, mixed, choral and orchestral societies and the 'masculine gaiety' of the band movement already noted. This is not to accept the beery stereotype of bandsmen projected by many denigrators of popular culture, but it is undeniable that a visit to the Crystal Palace contest, for example, would have contained elements rather different from the Bradford

Festival Choral Society's presidential tea or the Barrow Madrigal Society's 'knife and fork supper'.

The prominence of alcohol in the band world was a crucial factor here. Public houses frequently acted as band headquarters, as well as providing rehearsal places and gathering points at contests and necessary refreshment after playing ceased. Even when supposedly enlisted to serve the temperance cause, some bandsmen were alive to the temptations of drink. A Leeds bandsman of many years' experience remembers one band, engaged to lead a Band of Hope demonstration, marching *en masse* into a pub during a pause in the activities.[2] Christmas was a particularly alcoholic occasion, with bands marching from street to street in villages and towns, their playing often rewarded with liquid refreshment. Some male-voice choirs also had reputations as prodigious drinkers. While much drinking merely reflects that playing and singing are thirsty work, the glass of ale was clearly a key item in the ritual of much male-centred musical life.

Beyond these relatively straightforward social activities, whatever the atmosphere that accompanied them, music held out richer prizes. For the best performers there was the pride of being trained by some of the finest musicians in the country. A frequent theme during interviews was the pleasure felt by musicians at having known Alexander Owen, Henry Coward or whoever. Much valued, and more generally experienced, was the opportunity music offered for travel. From the late eighteenth century onwards it become common for the best northern singers to be engaged at festivals all over the country, giving them the chance to 'see something of the world'. The potential for travel really widened from the mid-nineteenth century, however. Initially, it was the brass bands that benefited most, their talents being much in demand at seaside resorts, exhibitions, flower shows, Sunday-school outings and so forth. As early as 1851, Thomas Cook employed Idle Band from near Bradford to provide music for excursionists at the Great Exhibition. Isaac Murgatroyd, the band's conductor, regarded that week 'as one of the happiest of his life'.

Beside being boarded and treated generally like Lords and Dukes, the gentleman who employed us . . . was so pleased with our achievements that he gave us each five shillings a piece extra.[3]

As the century progressed, and particularly with the expansion of contesting, the chance to travel grew considerably. By the 1890s choirs regularly visited such pleasant spots as Hawes, Morecambe and

Blackpool (as well, of course, as less picturesque St Helens, Burnley and Batley!), while from 1900, the Crystal Palace band contests drew an annual pilgrimage of 60–70,000, mainly from the North and Midlands, to the capital. By this date visits to London were becoming almost commonplace, especially for bandsmen. The LCC was largely responsible for this, hiring Northern bands to improve the quality of their public park concerts.[4]

As the Edwardian period progressed, geographical horizons were widened still further for a fortunate minority with the introduction of international engagements. The pioneers in this respect appear to have been Besses o' th' Barn band. They had made a lengthy visit to the United States in 1891, but it was from 1905 that their touring began on a wide scale, visiting France in that year and then, from July 1906 to December 1907 undertaking a world tour which embraced the United States, Canada, New Zealand, Honululu, Fiji and Australia. Further foreign travel was undertaken by the band in 1909.[5] A similarly ambitious project was launched in 1911 when the Yorkshire Choral Union, drawn largely from singers from Sheffield, Leeds and Huddersfield, visited Canada, New Zealand, Australia and South Africa. There were other less grandoise but still significant visits; to the United States by Black Dyke in 1906 and the Horbury Handbell ringers in 1909, Australia and New Zealand by the Crosland Moor ringers in 1912, Germany by several choirs from 1906 and, above all, France. The most spectacular example of the musical entente was the entry of forty-six British choirs and bands in the gigantic three-day International Music Tournament organised by the Paris municipality in 1912.[6]

Much of this foreign journeying was rooted in the contemporary debate over Britain's role in international relations. Britain and its expanding population in the dominions was, in the period after 1902, increasingly driven by the threat of German naval expansion to seek new friendships and understandings with mainland Europe and indeed beyond. Many of these tours were the creation of musical enthusiasts who believed that their chosen art could cement better relationships between Britain and her European neighbours and, in the case of the visits to the Empire, to generate a sense of imperial consciousness amongst the performers, the hosts, and, perhaps most important, amongst politicians in Britain. One of the most aggressively political of these tours was that of the Yorkshire Choral Union in 1911, organised by Dr Charles Harriss and conducted by

Henry Coward. Harriss, professor of music at Ottawa University, conceived the tour as a method of building links between 'Motherland and Empire'. His financial position eased by marrying the widow of an iron magnate, he was able to spend £60,000 on the tour, organising a number of functions at which the ideological content of the tour could be publicised. Most notable in this respect was a concert before the Canadian Parliament. He could not have employed a better lieutenant than Coward, a fierce believer in the superiority of the white races and the virtues of empire.[7]

There were undoubtedly some 'successes' in all this activity. The French government thought highly enough of Besses' 1905 tour to decorate organiser J. H. Iles and conductor Alexander Owen with the *legion d'honneur* for their contribution to the *entente cordiale*. The response amongst the host population, especially in the dominions, could be extremely enthusiastic. Edwin Bleakley, first horn of Besses' world tour, recorded in his diary the reception received in Melbourne.

Thousands of people lined the streets and in Collins Street, traffic had to be brought to a standstill. Right the way to the town hall, every window en route was occupied – we never had such a reception before.[8]

Some of the surrounding political ethos may well have influenced the performers, particularly those on the most overtly imperial excursions. However, it seems probable that for the majority loftier perspectives were accompanied or superseded by the simple desire to utilise their musical talent in order to enable travel to areas of the world which, short of emigration, they could never conceive of visiting.

It is also probable that on occasions these events actually undermined attempts at international co-operation. The most spectacular example is provided by the Paris Festival of 1912. Noble hopes foundered as English competitors arrived to be greeted by inadequate accommodation, inedible food and non-existent travel arrangements. A minor riot erupted, resulting in the hospitalisation of two gendarmes who had attempted to move on a crowd of Parisians listening to an impromptu choral rehearsal in the Tuileries Gardens.[9] The disasters were reported in England with generous quantities of the very chauvinism the event was intended to avoid. *The Musical Times* bemoaned with venomous patriotism that they found it 'difficult to understand why the whole business was not handed over to Messrs Cook, a firm which British people can thoroughly trust'. Its rival the *Musical*

Herald agreed, announcing: 'British pluck emerged triumphant. We had to 'muddle through' because the French made the muddle.' Their correspondent also noted the 'cynicism and frivolity in the tone of the rabble in all references to the English'. All this was hardly indicative of the *entente cordiale* at grass roots level![10]

Journeys to far-off places only served to heighten the immense regard in which local musicians were held by their community. The respect which their efforts generated must have been one of the major benefits experienced by members of musical organisations. It was strongest in the smaller communities, although civic pride could be aroused even in larger towns outside the major musical centres. In 1910, when the Lincoln Malleable Iron and Steelworks Band took a major prize at Crystal Palace, a civic reception was held before the mayor, chief constable and sheriff of Lincoln in a packed local theatre.[11] In the smaller strongholds of amateur music, however, community respect was constant, sometimes, but by no means always, linked to contest success. Bandsmen were celebrities of their native village, idolised by young boys who regarded it as an honour to carry their instruments or turn the music at rehearsals. Their endeavours aroused remarkable enthusiasm. When Cornholme Band, from a textile village near Todmorden, reached the Belle Vue Championship in September 1893, all the mills shut for the whole day and most of the population de-camped to Manchester.[12] Some remarkably large crowds were attracted by the top organisations. An estimated 12–15,000 watched Leeds Forge at Eastwood Park, Keighley, in 1888 (the concert was in aid of a hospital charity which obviously raised the attendance); 12,000 saw Cornholme at Saltaire in 1895 and 10,000 Besses O' th' Barn at Halifax in the same year.[13] Even allowing for exaggeration by enthusiastic observers, these are impressive figures, especially when it is realised that all three bands were playing outside their own locality.

One of the finest pictures of community enthusiasm is to be found in the *School Music Review*'s description of Saltaire Prize Choir's triumphal homecoming from the 1896 Morecambe Competitive Festival. It deserves lengthy quotation because what it illustrates is not merely intense local pride, but an enthusiasm for choral music of almost epidemic proportion.

Some hundreds of friends had congregated at the railway station, and patiently awaited the return of the excursion train and the news it would bring. The time of waiting was relieved by singing glees, anthems, hymns, and comic songs – truly a miscellaneous programme (Purday's tune to 'Lead Kindly Light' being a chief favourite). An extempore choral contest was also conducted with great energy and zest by the younger spirits – representing, perhaps, future competitors in many a more serious struggle – and

THE HOUR OF 1.30 ON SUNDAY MORNING

saw undiminished the zeal and earnestness of the watchers.

At last the choir returned, triumphant.

Despite the fact that the rain had commenced to fall, time-honoured custom demanded a short concert on the bridge. Here the victorious songsters took their stand, and somewhat travel weary, sang Pinsuti's emotional part-song 'The Sea Hath its Pearls' and, considering the state of the weather, expected that this would suffice. But no! The audience would hear all, and 'Great God of Love' (madrigal in eight parts, by Pearsall) was sung splendidly – without copies and under the umbrella's canopy, for now the rain was coming down in torrents. Enthusiasm being somewhat quenched and curiosity satisfied, singers and audience dispersed and the little town resumed its state of normal respectability of demeanour.

The significance of such an event remains with us, however, and points to the deep and abiding love of music, more particularly choral music, in this district, and the hearty appreciation of effort in the direction of increased excellence, which is so great a factor of inspiration and energy alike to conductor and choir.[14]

The most moving displays of respect were reserved for funerals. Crowds estimated at several thousand were known to assemble to mourn the passing of local musicians. The bandsman's funeral was an especially sombre occasion with the band, instruments draped in black, marching at the head of the procession playing first the 'Dead March in Saul', followed by the deceased's favourite hymns by the graveside. Given the high proportion of miners in the band movement, funerals were occasionally given added poignancy by the cause of death. In December 1910, three members and four ex-members of Wingates Temperance Band were amongst the three hundred and fifty miners killed in the Pretoria Pit disaster near Atherton in Lancashire. One of the number was Albert Lonsdale, secretary and soprano cornet, and a figure of great standing in the movement, so disfigured in the explosion that 'his sorrowing wife was able to identify him (only) by the peculiar formation of his finger nails'. His funeral

was a most impressive one, marks of respect being shown by the whole village; drawn blinds, shops with shutters up, and many hundreds of people lined both sides of the road from the late residence of Mr Lonsdale up to the gates of the church . . . the coffin being completely covered with beautiful wreaths of

flowers, together with the cornet which the late Mr Lonsdale loved and played
so well.

For some, there were lasting memorials. In 1859, members of
Accrington Band subscribed for a headstone for Adam Westall, their
ophecleide player, producing eventually a draped ophecleide carved
in stone.[15]

More tangible than many of the benefits described above was
music's value as a source of financial support. This is not to suggest
that music offered great riches to its adherents: the majority of performers gained only the most modest of rewards. Moreover, money
earned from concert, contest or solo performance often only offset the
considerable expenses incurred on joining a musical society. By the
late nineteenth century the *Brass Band News* suggested that members
be charged 7s 6d on entrance, payable on entry, and then 6d a week.
The larger choral societies usually asked for a 5 s annual subscription,
although 7s 6d was common by 1914. Their preference for annual as
opposed to weekly payment – partly a reflection of their more
'respectable' social base – led to problems for working-class members
during periods of unemployment or if they could not save. In 1906 the
Leeds Philharmonic allowed free membership to an unemployed
warehouseman and to to a scavenger on grounds of his 'extreme
poverty'. Those too proud to advertise their plight simply left.[16]
Nevertheless, while these cautionary notes must be remembered,
music could provide a valuable source of additional income.

Music helped many in times of acute financial distress. Throughout
the period, choirs and bands operated as friendly societies, raising
money for aged, sick and injured members of their own and neighbouring organisations. Thousands were helped in this way. Similarly,
during strikes, periods of unemployment or trade depressions, musicians regularly went busking or gained short-term professional musical work in order to alleviate their difficulties.[17] In normal times
money could be raised through one's musical efforts in three main
ways: through contests and competitions, concert performances with
one's own society and through the application of skills learned in the
amateur environment in other areas of musical life.

In general, competitions did not provide any great levels of financial
reward as travelling expenses, broken time payments and general
running costs absorbed most of the prize money. The Todmorden
Male Voice Choir, for example, one of the most successful choirs of

the Edwardian period, won prizes to the value of £307 between 1906 and 1914 and yet made a profit of only £4.[18] Unsuccessful choirs and bands may well have lost money. The exceptions to this picture were the leading brass band soloists – probably never more than five hundred to seven hundred and fifty in number – who by the 1900s stood to gain as much as £2 per contest from bands willing to hire their services, thus in some cases doubling their normal income with one afternoon's work. Of more permanent benefit was that some bands provided soloists with regular full-time employment in a local industry in order to secure their services for a lengthy period. The practice of engaging paid players, especially for single engagements, was generally frowned upon and indeed illegal according to the rules of most contests. Except in exceptional circumstances, such rules were rarely enforced, however, too many leading soloists, training and bands stood to lose too much.[19]

Concert work was undoubtedly more lucrative, especially for smaller bodies. The large choral societies, with their high overheads, made little profit, but smaller choirs and instrumental bodies usually managed to generate a small 'surplus' which was divided amongst their members. The historian of Bramley Band remembered that 'In 1849, we bandsmen had some very good engagements and they helped us over the hard times'. Ten years later, the band took £230 from twenty-seven engagements, which must have left several pounds over for each bandsman. Rates of pay were often far from generous; in 1900 Manchester Corporation was offering a mere £2 per band for public park engagements.[20] Nevertheless, is some households the resultant coppers were valuable indeed. A few leading bodies, mainly brass bands, were regularly engaged in concert tours and during these the bandsmen became, in essence, professional musicians. Besses and Black Dyke were the most enthusiastic tourers and their members could expect rich rewards; Dyke's soloists received seven guineas a week during a six-month British tour in 1913. The only 'sacrifice' for such bands was that in years of major tours they were sometimes excluded from contests on grounds of professionalism.[21]

For the majority, however, the greatest rewards were to be found outside the confines of their own musical organisation. A whole class of semi-professional musicians grew up from the late nineteenth century as the musical environment expanded. For singers there were opportunities to strengthen the choir at provincial festivals or to sing solo parts in local church or chapel concerts. Opera companies were another, if less frequent, source of employment, swelling their choruses with local choristers. For those of broad mind, the music-hall and singing-saloon were promising areas for singers. Bradford saloons under threat of closure in 1902 offered this as proof of their respectability, claiming that 'many of the vocalists are members of church and chapel choirs'.[22] Instrumentalists had an even wider range of employment; theatres, concert-halls, music-halls, singing-saloons, public houses, dance-saloons, skating rinks, even some restaurants generated a massive demand for almost any musical formation, from solo piano to full orchestra. In any large town on a Saturday night in Victorian England there must have been hundreds of musical 'amateurs' adding to their weekly income.

The best musicians could obtain work that was both lucrative and prestigious. There was a constant flow into the best orchestras of the day, especially in the North. The Hallé, founded in 1857, drew heavily in its earlier years upon the native resources of Lancashire, making particular use of local brass musicians, although reed and string players sometimes gained positions. William Millington, whose study of popular musical activity in the Pendlebury area, *Sketches of Local Musicians and Musical Societies*, is such a valuable source for historians, combined daytime employment as a millwright with the bassoonist's chair for a considerable period. At least four other working-men musicians from the Pendlebury area alone had spells with the orchestra between 1860 and 1880. Theatre and music-hall orchestra pits were another favoured location. Harry Mortimer, while a clerk at Vauxhall Motors, earned a further 35 s a week (£4 after joining the Musicians' Union) at a theatre in Luton during the First World War.[23]

On occasions, musicians were criticised for abandoning the amateur world, to which they owed so much, in order to pursue financial gain. Harry Mortimer was chastised by his father for neglecting his obligations to his local band, Luton Red Cross, to which Mortimer senior was bandmaster. Again, an editorial in *The Cornet* of January 1910 complained that the current roller-skating boom was denuding many bands of their best players. While the situation may have seemed depressing to a (presumably) relatively affluent magazine editor, to a working man in financial need, however, the picture must have appeared somewhat different. There was also criticism from an entirely different direction. Amateurs, especially instrumentalists, came under constant attack from the 1890s from the newly-founded

Amalgamated Musicians' Union. The pages of its official publication. *The Musicians Report and Journal*, were full of references to 'unfair competition' from so-called amateur wind bands who, by accepting engagements at extremely low rates of pay, were denying professionals their rightful living. The word 'blackleg' was used on several occasions. The *Journal* was equally critical of those semi-professionals who took evening work in theatres and music-halls but refused to join the union. There is little evidence that such complaints were taken seriously. In an age when the battle for basic unionisation of the workforce was still extremely hard-fought, officials were unlikely to persuade amateur musicians of the need to apply union principles to their leisure hours.[24]

For a favoured minority, what had begun as a leisure pursuit could eventually lead not merely to semi-professionalism, but to a full-time career in music. This was probably of the greatest significance to musicians from a working-class background. Much detailed work work remains to be done before confident assertions regarding the social background of musicians can be made. Nevertheless, it seems clear that substantial numbers from working-class backgrounds found their way into the profession, thus embarking on a career which for the most part gave them a wage at least no lower than they had earned before, in some cases a certain degree of enhanced social status, and at least an element of the ingredient now termed 'job satisfaction'.[25]

Singers found plentiful opportunities in bodies as varied as cathedral choirs (Huddersfield alone produced thirty-four professional choristers between 1800 and 1874), opera companies and minstrel troupes. The employment potential of instrumentalists increased considerably throughout the century as the emergence of seaside orchestras provided a vital link between the end of the winter orchestral concert season in March and its re-opening in late September. Bandsmen were particularly fortunate, as their movement provided what was about the only source of professional brass players. Beginning with Louis Jullien's signing of ophecleide soloist Sam Hughes from the Welsh Cyfartha Band in 1850, most leading orchestras drew upon bands for professional as well as semi-professional personnel.[26]

Teaching, either as a full-time occupation or a supplement to other forms of professional work, was another major avenue for the aspiring musician. Although there are signs that there was an over-stocked market by 1900, teaching could be reasonably lucrative, especially if

combined with a range of other musical activities. This is well-illus-
trated by the career of Samuel Midgley. A miner's son from the village
of Bierley near Bradford, he followed his father into pit work at the
age of nine before a passion for learning, fed by attendance at a local
Mechanic's Institute, led him to become a pupil teacher. Always
extraordinarily fond of music, he decided to pursue it as a full-time
career, studying at Leipzig for a year in the 1870s before returning to
Bradford where, until his retirement in 1929, he taught, gave piano
recitals and sponsored chamber concerts. As a result, he acquired a
substantial villa in Bradford's most salubrious suburb and died a
respected and relatively wealthy figure.[27]

Self-employment in the musical service industry was yet another
option to amateurs alert to contemporary needs. Joshua Greenwood,
once a soloist with the Leeds Railway Foundry Band, set up an
instrument dealership and repair business in South Shields in the
1880s. His 'oil of lightning' lubricant for slides and valves was a
popular band accessory. Tom Kitchen, another Leeds bandsman,
opened a music shop still flourishing in the 1980s. Violin making, a
not uncommon hobby in the nineteenth century, also provided
potential. John William Owen (1852–1933), once an engineer in
Leeds, William Heaton (1827–1906), a cabinet-maker from Gomersal
in West Yorkshire and William Atkinson (1851–1929) from Stepney,
a barman, ship's steward and finally a joiner, were all individuals from
working-class backgrounds who turned a pastime into a full-time
business. (Heaton did not actually begin building full-time until his
retirement at age of sixty-five, with the bulk of his one hundred and
fifty-six instruments constructed between 1892 and 1906.)[28]

The majority of working and lower-middle-class musicians climbing the ladder from amateur to professional did so with relatively
limited aspirations. They knew that the heights of the profession were
in general only for those of more gentle birth, who had greater access
to education, training and the ear of the musical élite.[29] A tiny
number *did* attain at least regional and occasionally national fame,
however. It is significant that in almost all cases, they were involved at
least initially in either choral or brass band music, two areas traditionally neglected by professionals and thus allowing some opportunity for the generation of professional openings from within.
Between the 1830s and 1850s, Mrs Sunderland (1819–1904, *née*
Susan Sykes), daughter of a Brighouse gardener, progressed from
chapel soloist to an elevated position amongst the ranks of English

sopranos. She was a legendary figure in her native Yorkshire and nicknamed the 'Yorkshire Queen of Song' after a command performance before Queen Victoria. At her farewell concert in Huddersfield in 1865, the windows of the concert hall were opened to allow her to be heard by the hundreds in the street who were unable to gain admission.[30] In the Edwardian period, Leeds choral singer and bookbinder Charles Knowles began to build a career as an opera singer, while the early life of Harry Mortimer (son of a fustian weaver) between about 1910 and 1920 laid the base of a career as professional band trainer, trumpeter and professor at the Royal College of Music at Manchester that was to make him, in the age of the mass media, a household name.[31]

The most spectacular example – and probably the only one – of a passage to genuine stardom is provided by the career of Tom Burke, the so-called 'Lancashire Caruso'.[32] Born in 1890 in Leigh, Lancashire, son of an Irish immigrant, he was the eldest of nine children. At first a half-timer in a silk mill and later a 'lasher-on' in a local pit, he showed considerable musical gifts, earning a silver medal as solo cornet with Leigh Band in a junior section at Crystal Palace and gaining a reputation as a fine tenor singer in both a Catholic choir and the singing-rooms of local public houses, most notably the Pied Bull in Leigh. Eventually in about 1907, now a self-employed vegetable dealer, he began to attend a weekly singing class at Manchester College of Music, eventually attending full-time thanks to the intervention of Mrs Swarbrick, a local singer of some influence. In 1913 he was introduced by the conductor of the Hallé to the London impressario Hugo Gorelitz, who gained him work in ballad concerts which provided money for private tuition at the Royal Academy. Although Gorelitz was interned in 1914, Burke's career was kept alive by Mark Richardson Moore, a Bond Street tailor, whose financial help, although small, allowed Burke to work and study in Italy during the war. Picked by Melba as a leading tenor at Covent Garden in 1919, his career blossomed. By the late 1920s he had a Mayfair address, a butler and a Rolls Royce. Tragically, he soon added to the list a divorce on grounds of his adultery, several nervous collapses, a drink problem and, in 1932, bankruptcy. Although his career flickered during the 1930s and 1940s, his reputation for unreliability damned him. He eventually became a teacher of singing and died in 1969.

Burke's fascinating life is deserving of lengthy discussion because it points up the career problems faced by performers from poor back-grounds. He was seventeen before he received serious singing lessons. His full-time study from 1909–1918 had to be combined with a considerable amount of part-time manual work and was only possible because of the intervention of middle-class patrons – without Richardson Moore, the earlier stages of his career might not have been so dramatically successful. He succeeded because prodigious musical talent was combined with the necessary element of luck. He was born in the vicinity of a good college of music and he met suitable middle-class patrons. The majority of working-class musicians were less fortunate. The barriers imposed by working-class origin meant that, while music could facilitate a degree of economic and social mobility, even in their new position in the ranks of professional orchestras or choirs, most musicians from plebeian backgrounds remained socially 'inferior' to the soloists they accompanied and the conductors they sat before.

It is not intended to suggest that the musical fraternity offered its members an idyllic existence. The poorer members could never be entirely cocooned against the workings of society by the simple act of belonging to choir or band, while musical activity could breed its own problems, its own variety of bitterness, antagonism and mortification. Most organisations were beset at some time by unpleasant internal wranglings. Again, performances at concerts or competitions could be nerve-wracking and sometimes disastrous. It can have been little fun to have endured sleepless nights because of the 'snatches of *Golden Legend*, *Faust* and *Elijah* going through my brain the whole night'; or to read a judges' report which stated: 'commenced very much out of tune, and poor tone, no attack, and soft parts far too loud. Solos for trombone etc. a failure. Overture evidently too difficult for the band.'[33] William Millington's exquisite tale of one 'Billy Mull' (William Molineux) a collier and over-ambitious violinist, depicts perhaps the ultimate level of humiliation. At a concert in Walkden, Lancashire:

the late Daniel Timmins had to sing a song by Handel, entitled 'He was Brought as a Lamb to the Slaughter'. In playing the violin part 'Billy Mull' very soon got lost, and was playing wrong nearly all the way through. Mr Timmins seemed very much inclined to stop long before he got to the end of the song, but the violincello player kept him on to the end, and when the song was ended Mr Timmins turned round to the leader and, throwing a copy he was singing from at 'Billy Mull', cursed such leading as that. . . . During the progress of the song the greater part of the audience sat with their heads between their legs, like shot partridges.[34]

Equally, it should not be thought that the enthusiasm shown for music in the period to 1914 was based merely on a desire for riches and yearning for foreign climes – or at least, the seaside! For the majority, the desire to make music was paramount. The level of commitment in terms of time, money and energy which musical life demanded was too great to allow for self-seeking. 'It's rough to come home in your dirt, have a quick wash and change, grab your tea, and then go straight out to a gruelling two-hour practice; you have to be tough and you have to want to do it very much.' Henry Livings's succinct description of the brass bandsman's sacrifice might well be extended to the whole range of amateur musical activity.[35]

The significance of these social, emotional and economic elements is that, when wedded to the artistic pleasures on offer, they gave the musician a remarkably rich experience. To appreciate this is to grasp the fundamental importance of music, and indeed, of many recreational forms in the nineteenth and early twentieth century. Too often academics have viewed leisure in a rather negative way; it becomes in their eyes a means of 'escape', an antidote to more important aspects of life. Even Paul Thompson, in his remarkably sympathetic *The Edwardians*, informs us that: 'Music or literature helped to ease the monotony of many Edwardian lives".[36] This is surely too limited a view. It is clear from the level of self-sacrifice, the artistic pride it produced and the range of benefits that it offered, that music was not a way of relieving tedium, nor some fringe element, but a central feature of people's existence, more significant for some than their work, their politics and perhaps even their poverty. Until it is appreciated that recreation was more than mere ornamentation, its place in society will never be adequately understood.

Popular music and popular politics[37]

This brief section outlines possible links between the activities of bands and choirs and the popular political culture of the period, described in chapter one and typified by large-scale uninterest coupled with minority involvement in popular radicalism and, eventually, defensive Labourism. It is not easy to establish direct links between leisure experience and popular culture and much of what follows is speculative. Nevertheless, even tentative suggestions are worthwhile. Leisure and politics are, after all, not discrete entities but integral parts of the individual's life experience. Leisure pursuits, and in this instance popular musical life, were a central part of contemporary life and the opinions, interests and loyalties fostered during 'time off' must have played an important role in shaping attitudes toward many aspects of existence.[38]

Before commencing this investigation it is worth noting that the generally conservative role ascribed to musical societies by their middle-class supporters when funding bands or organising a tour in the interest of Empire unity received full blessing from what might be termed the popular musical 'establishment'. Indeed, on occasions its members added to the conservative ethos. Many of those connected with choral music hoped that a class consensus might flow from the mixed-class nature of many societies.[39] Spokesmen for the brass band publishing houses which made up a key sector of that establishment preached the need for political neutrality, lest important supporters should be alienated. In 1910 the editor of the *Cornet* argued that: 'It was not always good policy for bands to get mixed up in politics – as a band – for someone is to be offended. Bands cannot be too careful in this respect; there is so little to gain and often much to lose.' Similarly, bandsmen were encouraged to see themselves as 'bandsmen' above all else. Thus, the 1893 coal strike was viewed as a tragedy for the band movement, rather than an important moment in the history of organised labour.

The great coal strike has naturally spread its devastating influence among several brass bands in mining districts. From what we hear, the pinch of poverty has wrought sad havoc in many bandsmen's homes. A large number of bands, or at least a portion of them, have been compelled to utilise their musical abilities as a means of procuring the necessities of life for selves and families, causing them to leave home and invade the neighbouring towns and villages, playing about the streets and appealing to a sympathetic public for much-needed assistance. In consequence of this deplorable disagreement 'twixt masters and men', a large number of bands are unsettled and unable to do anything in the way of practice.[40]

In certain instances, even the repertoire was influenced by the idea of a non-contentious existence within capitalist society. This is well illustrated by Percy Fletcher's *Labour and Love*, the political significance of which has been largely missed by historians of music. The

piece expresses the changing mood of a working man, initially dissatisfied with a purposeless, physically exhausting job, but eventually
persuaded by his wife to view it as 'a labour of love'. In a final martial
movement, 'He smiles at his troubles, his heart swells with pride at his
work . . . he throws himself with determination into his task resolved
to improve his position by continued devotion to his daily task'. It
must be stressed that there is no direct evidence that either Fletcher or
J. H. Iles, who had chosen the piece for the 1913 Crystal Palace
contest, saw the work as overt propaganda. However, given the
enormous conservatism underpinning so many middle-class attempts
to encourage music-making, it is fitting that the first major work for
brass band by a composer of any standing should be a hymn to the joys
of hard work, loyalty, self-improvement and contentment.[41]

In exactly the way of the 'music for the people' movement examined
earlier, it is probable that choral societies and bands did help produce
something akin to the social and political climate desired by the
middle classes, although not necessarily in the way that had been
expected. Once again, music's capacity to influence society was more
complex a matter than the simple absorption by some working-class
musicians of the aspirations of their patrons.

Perhaps the one middle-class aspiration fulfilled almost as intended
was that choral societies may well have helped reduce class tension.
Obviously, the point should not be exaggerated; that a joiner and a
mill-owner were members of the same organisation did not necessarily
mean that they would like or even converse with each other. Furthermore, the very fact that singers from different social backgrounds
could come together in their leisure illustrates the existence of a
climate already conducive to a degree of cross-class social mingling,
and the choral society should not therefore be seen as the *initiator* of
collaboration. However, it is surely possible that mutual respect based
on an appreciation of technical skills exhibited by a 'better' or
'inferior', the unity of purpose that existed in most societies, and any
social contact that did take place, helped contain class antagonism.
Equally critical, popular choralism helped exacerbate divisions
within the working class by pulling the labour élite away from the
bulk of their class and perhaps even attaching them more firmly to
those of social substance.

'Unintended' contributions to the creation of a stable-class society
were more numerous. It is possible that the intense competitiveness
within much popular musical life exacerbated the already intensely

localised mentality, the *campanilismo*, of much northern industrial life. In West Yorkshire at least one distinguished commentator found such a 'territorial' outlook a major stumbling block to successful unionisation of the textile industry.[42] Secondly, it is at least worth considering that choirs and bands helped foster the mentalities required of workers in an industrial society. There is a certain superficial relationship between the order and regimentation of a choir at rehearsal or a band on the march and the discipline increasingly required by capitalism. Admittedly, supposedly 'disciplined' bands could lapse into hooliganism, or dissatisfied singers abandon rehearsal, and thus not all the habits learned were 'good' ones. Moreover, some features, such as the choral society's maintenance of some type of democracy, offered models of more radical forms of activity, and discipline was as valuable for socialist or trade union activity as it is in the workplace. Nevertheless, the sight and sounds of popular societies can hardly have been unpleasant to those involved in instilling factory discipline.[43]

There is also the possibility that membership of a band or choir created a tension between leisure and politics, thus diminishing the potential for individual involvement in political and industrial issues. In an important sense, leisure and politics were rivals fighting for the time, money and commitment of the working population. Many working people, while perhaps sympathetic to the ideals of trade unionism, independent labour or socialism, nevertheless devoted the bulk of their time and energy to other pursuits, of which music was undoubtedly one of the most important.[44]

This potentially de-radicalising aspect of music-making was further reinforced by societies' need to adopt almost a business mentality in order to maintain support from the widest possible clientèle. This was particularly true of wind bands, which were always more dependent upon 'engagements' than other bodies. It is sometimes presumed, for example, that bands were inextricably connected with the trade union movement. Undeniably, certain large union festivals, such as annual miners' galas, became major events in the band calendar and bands were often in evidence in strike processions and demonstrations. However, apart from the small number attached to specific socialist or trade union organisations, bands were never fully-fledged cultural adjuncts of organised labour. There is evidence to suggest that bands would not risk the consequences, in terms of financial and moral support from the wider community, of playing for strikers who did not have strong community backing. Strikers at a dyeworks in Sowerby Bridge in 1910, seeking to organise a procession, were rejected by several bands and only when local opinion hardened in favour of the strike was a willing band found.[45]

Furthermore, trade unions and socialist bodies were not alone in utilising local musical services. They were simply part of a chain of 'customers', many of whom preferred ideologies hostile to the labour movement. Bands played a prominent part in the numerous festivities – railway trips, teas, fêtes – with which employers tried to pull tighter the cords of paternalism and 'deference'. The Liberal Party as well as the Primrose League and other Conservative and Unionist associations regularly hired bands to perform at their open-air engagements.[46] Some bands showed a remarkable even-handedness in this respect. Perhaps the ultimate act of disinterest came during the 1839 general election campaign when *on the same day*, Bramley Band played for both Liberal and Conservative candidates. In June 1904, Brighouse Borough band came close to emulating this feat when in the same week they led an unemployed demonstration organised by the relatively militant Brighouse trades council as well as persuading Sir Thomas Brooke-Hitching, Conservative candidate for the local parliamentary constituency, to become their patron.[47]

Again, bands were invariably present to celebrate great events in the imperial calendar, their uniforms and martial music adding a suitably militaristic aura. The Queen's Jubilees, the coronations of 1902 and 1911 and the relief of Mafeking gave bands some of their busiest schedules of the whole period. During the earlier phase of the Boer war, bandrooms could become as jingoistic as the music-hall. *The British Bandsman* in conjunction with the *Daily Mail* organised a competition encouraging bands to collect for the *Daily Mail* war fund, as well as, for the same financial end, The Great Band Festival at the Royal Albert Hall in January 1900.[48] Suitable music, such as the cornet solo 'Comrades in Arms', the patriotic selection 'British War Songs' and the Grand Fantasia on 'God Save the Queen and Rule Britannia' offered by Smith and Co., enlivened proceedings across the country. There seem to have been few areas exempt from the patriotic enthusiasm of 1899–1900, with the *British Bandsman* delighted to note that even in pro-Boer Wales, bands came out on Mafeking night. Even in quieter moments, the association of many bands with the volunteer movement maintained the link between popular music and popular patriotism.[49]

The musical society's most potent contribution to the reinforcement of conservative elements within English culture, however,
stemmed from its capacity to offer members rich social, artistic,
emotional, even economic rewards. *Through their own musical experience*, not through blind acceptance of ruling-class platitudes, amateur
musicians discovered that society as it existed had much to offer them.
Music's ability to provide compensations in the shape of the benefits
outlined in the previous section, coupled with artistic satisfaction,
may have turned many working people, particularly those not politically motivated in the first instance, away from seeking political
solutions to their problems.

Avoidance of organised political activity has traditionally been
termed 'apathy' by contemporary observers and later generations of
scholars. Stephen Yeo has made a powerful assault on such interpretations. Writing of Reading between 1890 and 1914, but clearly
believing his words to have wider relevance, he suggests:

> that there was a kind of apathy few would deny from a 1975 vantage point,
> even if the reality behind the apathy should not be seen in the terms chosen by
> those who identified and deplored it at the time. Positive attitudes there were,
> even if not the attitudes observers wanted there to be. The holders of these
> attitudes, already emancipated from ties of deference to a local civic leader-
> ship, did not turn in new loyalty towards the organised structures of formal
> nationalised politics. Rather did they turn away from what is usually called
> politics altogether, towards realistic cynicism about 'them' up there in poli-
> tics, combined either with settling for satisfactions which could be had
> without involving 'them', or with deliberate attempts at by-passing politics
> via different forms of intermittent 'syndicalism'. What is called 'apathy' is
> often another name for positive, in certain circumstances militant, rejections
> of current structures and ideologies in politics.[50]

But even Yeo's analysis, helpful as it is, is perhaps too concerned with
the overtly 'political'. People did not necessarily 'turn away' from
politics: many never even contemplated it in the first place, preferring
to seek their pleasures and satisfaction from other areas of experience.
Leisure, and, in this instance, musical activity, was surely a major way
in which people 'settled for satisfactions' without recourse to the
political system and its exponents. The so-called political apathy of
many working-class people resulted to a considerable extent from the
fact that they often had 'better' things to occupy their minds.

All this is not to suggest a musical community seduced into
unquestioning acceptance of contemporary capitalism and its structures. Individuals could share in music's gifts and yet maintain a

radical stance. It was perfectly possible to be a choralist, violinist or bandsman yet remain a confirmed socialist or union activist. In 1915, twelve members of Foden's Motor Works Band, Cheshire, were prominent in picketing during a strike at the company's Elworth factory, the risk to their place in one of the premier Edwardian bands not sufficient to blunt their union consciousness. All of them were in fact sacked from the firm after the strike.[51] It was equally possible to inject radical standpoints into musical activities. In 1864, a section of the Bradford Festival Choral Society refused to sing at a concert in honour of a visit to the town by Palmerston, objecting to his opposition to parliamentary reform. (It was, however, as the society's historian proudly remarked in 1907, 'the only occasion when the harmonious working of the society has been disturbed by the introduction of either political or religious questions'.)[52] Similarly, musical activity could engender or, at least, reinforce class consciousness. In 1913, a contributor to the *British Bandsman* attacked the composer Josef Holbrooke for showing condescension towards bandsmen when discussing the Crystal Palace Championships of that year in a *Bandsman* article. It was nice, Holbrooke's critic claimed,

that at least one of the members of the great music aristocracy had looked down in the midst of our humble festivities and smiled benignly upon us . . . scores of humble working men, gifted in no little degree with the spark of divine genius (for, we would also say, we do not believe for one moment all the musical brains of the country have been showered upon the student who attends the Royal Academy of Music and similar institutions) have made their lives a living sacrifice for the brass band cause, and are doing it today.[53]

Here, the brass band stands as a proud symbol of popular artistic achievement. At a more mundane level, the determination with which many bands raised money for their own bandroom could be seen as an attempt to create their own space, away from the at time claustrophobic presence of employers and philanthropists.[54]

In general, however, the major thrust of much popular music-making was probably in a conservative direction. By building links, albeit often delicate ones, between classes, challenging the labour movement for precious resources of time and money, and by offering varied rewards to members, choirs and bands contributed to the reinforcement, perhaps even the establishment, of the less challenging elements of the political culture of Victorian and Edwardian England.

Popular societies in decline?

The self-deprecation that so marked Victorian musical writing had at
last begun to fade by the 1900s. The remarkable developments in
choral repertoire and technique, increased musical involvement by
the local state, the emergence of a new generation of composers, even
the improvement in the 'tone' of music-halls were all seen as evidence
of a resurgence in the nation's musical fortunes. Yet, at the very
moment when critics sensed a musical millenium at grass roots level
within the choirs and bands, there were disturbing signs of decline.
Membership fell, recruitment problems were experienced, audiences
dwindled and fewer new organisations were founded. The final years
of pre-war England saw the beginning of a process, still continuing
today, whereby the popular musical society, once the pride of a whole
community or at least a sizeable section of it, became a specialist
organisation catering for a diminishing minority.

A decline in numbers is of course in no way synonymous with
'decline' in a wider sense, and the period undoubtedly saw the
achievement of far higher technical standards than had been attained
before. (These two factors, may well be connected, however, as will
be seen later.) Neither were the problems peculiar to musical
societies. As Stephen Yeo has pointed out in his admirable *Religion
and Voluntary Organisations in Crisis*, the whole period from 1890 was
one of great difficulty for many voluntary bodies. Nevertheless, there
were sufficient problems to cause despondency amongst some figures
in the amateur musical community. Choral societies probably suffered the most. First, there was a serious shortage of male singers.
One authority claimed that, in all but the premier choirs, sopranos on
their own usually outnumbered the other parts. Choirs sometimes had
to borrow from each other to reach a reasonable standard for concerts
and contests. Equally critical was that audiences were falling and in
particular the number of subscribers to the concerts of the oratorio
choirs fell dramatically. *Musical Progress* recorded in 1914 that one
premier Leeds choir had seen its subscription list fall from 1,000 to
400 over the previous decade.[55]

Bands were not immune, however. In 1910, the Yorkshire correspondent of the *British Bandsman* bemoaned the attitude of local
youth in the Huddersfield area, traditionally a cornerstone of the band
movement: 'Can anyone account for the apathy of the younger
generation against becoming bandsmen?'. In January 1914, both

Bury Borough and Besses Junior Band were both disbanded because they could not find sufficient young players of suitable standard. If even the mighty Besses were experiencing recruitment problems, then important changes were indeed taking place.[56]

Crucial to those changes was the economic climate in which Edwardian musical societies existed. The great musical strides of the late Victorian period had been made in a period of increasing working-class 'affluence'. However, from about 1900, allowing for regional and occupational variation, real wage rates stagnated and from about 1908 may have actually fallen in some areas as increases in food import costs forced prices up. Whatever the reality of the economic situation, the degree of labour unrest in the period 1910–1913 suggests that workers *believed* their financial position was being eroded.[57]

Musical societies, as has been seen, had coped with economic slump, poverty and deprivation on many occasions in the past. In the later Edwardian period, however, economic problems had to be faced in a generally more hostile environment. Running costs had escalated considerably with the appointment of prestigious trainers and conductors. Transport too had become increasingly expensive. Brass bands suffered considerably from the decision by railway companies to abolish concessionary fares in 1900 and later to begin raising fares in some cases.[58] Choirs, although generally never favoured as much as bands by railways, also suffered from the price rises, with at least one major choir abandoning contesting because the increase in travel costs was not met by a commensurate increase in prize money. Contesting itself had become expensive for choirs, with more and more organisers demanding that societies should learn up to four test pieces, thus raising expenditure on music. The secretary of one choir informed readers of the *School Music Review* in 1912 that his organisation had recently entered a class at a major Lancashire festival at which they would have lost over £9 as a choir, plus half a day's wages as individuals, even if they had won first prize.[59] Critically, at the very moment when extra income was needed, the more monied elements, the middle-class subscribers and supporters, were deserting. Music was becoming an expensive pursuit and it is hardly surprising that new societies were not founded and existing members left. The rather plaintive atmosphere is well captured by the words of a choral singer, who, while walking home from a meeting that had just raised subscriptions from 5s to 7s 6d, remarked to his companion, 'Well I am afraid it's my last season – I just can't pay another half crown'.[60]

The economic problems were deepened – in some cases partially caused – by the ever-increasing availability of alternative leisure pursuits. There were now far more rivals for the money and time of the younger generation and those elusive younger *males* in particular. These new opportunities were made easier to enjoy by the development from about 1890 or cheap, regular systems of road transport, based on trams and buses, which by the early 1900s was even penetrating some relatively isolated areas, and thus increasingly drawing villages into the orbit of bigger population centres. Some of the new pursuits were of a voluntary nature. One of the great problems of Edwardian voluntary societies was that they were increasingly in competition with each other. Amateur football, cricket and rugby teams proliferated and newer sports, such as cycling, billiards and bowls, gained adherents. Youth organisations in the shape of the Scout Movement, Church Lads Brigade and others blossomed, particularly after 1910. Add to this list the fellowships, improvement societies, literary clubs, drama clubs and suchlike that continued to grow out of every form of religious, political and educational institution, and a powerful bloc of recreational pursuits can be seen.[61]

Of greatest importance were the new pursuits generated by various branches of the leisure industry. The music-hall began to penetrate those smaller towns previously regarded as uneconomic. The roller-skating craze, which reached epidemic proportions between 1909 and 1911, was one of a number of relatively short-lived pursuits that nevertheless reduced the viability of other activities during their short lifespan. Such developments, important as they were, were almost eclipsed, however, by the expansion of the cinema and of spectator sport.[62]

A novelty in the late 1890s, the 'moving pictures' had become a multi-million pound industry by 1914. By that date, over 3,500 cinemas existed in England, offering entertainment to an audience some thirty per cent of which was under eighteen. Even the smallest communities, previously largely untouched by commercial entertainments, now possessed or were within comfortable reach of an Electric Theatre, Theatre de luxe, or similarly glorified brick rectangle, wooden hut or church hall. The greatest expansion in cinema building seems to have come after 1908 at the very time when the first complaints about the musical tardiness of the younger generation were being expressed.[63]

Spectator sport, especially soccer, also enjoyed a boom in the

Edwardian period. The Football League had been founded as far back as 1888, but its geographical base had been restricted to the Midlands and Lancashire. From 1900 league soccer became almost a national phenomenon, and respectable crowds were attracted even to what now appear relatively insignificant fixtures. An end-of-season second division game between Bradford Park Avenue and Chelsea in April 1911 drew some 20,000, while in the same month, 6,000 people were prepared to see Huddersfield Town, sixteenth in the second division, play thirteenth-placed Glossop. Footballers and football teams were not mere entertainers; they were rapidly becoming the objects of intense civic loyalty and enthusiasm. The reception afforded to Bradford City's team when – with a little help from the Newcastle goal-keeper – they won the FA Cup in 1911, was fairly typical of the emotions sport could now generate.

Everybody appeared to be out in the street, and the centre of the city, turn where you would, was seething with an enthusiastic, excited throng. People of all classes, and well-nigh all ages, were there. . . . The multitude surged and swayed in Town Hall Square, Forster Square and Peel Square, and almost every street converging into those centres was so densely crowded as to be practically impassible. . . . The open space in front of the Exchange Station was a solid mass of people, some of whom perched on walls or swarmed up lamp-posts in order to catch a glimpse of the cup which Speirs, sitting beside the driver, proudly held up so that all who looked might see. The cheering swept through the street in waves, and the teeming populace seemed almost frantic with joy. It was an amazing scene which those tired players looked down upon in the course of their triumphal progress through the centre of the city, and one that will not easily be forgotten.

All that, and not a Yorkshireman in the side. Truly, important changes were taking place![64]

As early as 1893, a writer in the *Brass Band News* was expressing concern at the number of bandsmen watching football on winter afternoons instead of practising or collecting funds. The effect of the cinema was blamed by more than one choir or band for falling membership and attendances. Doubtless there was a degree of exaggeration in all this; dedicated musicians saw problems of recruitment facing them for the first time and inevitably turned their venom on the latest 'fads' of the younger generation. Undoubtedly many young men could, and did, visit the cinema, support a professional soccer team and remained committed members or supporters of a band or choir. Furthermore, old and new forged a relatively happy co-existence. Brass bands in particular regularly provided entertainment at football matches and occasionally even at cinemas. Nevertheless, the new leisure pursuits must have caused many a change of perspective. The cinema, football match and variety palace offered an excitement, freshness and novelty that band and choir could not always match. This was perhaps particularly true in the smaller towns and villages where commercial leisure was becoming available on a large scale for the first time, challenging the position previously held by the local musical community. There were now new focuses for loyalty, new heroes emerging. For the boys of Queensbury, would carrying Ceres Jackson's cornet ever again stand comparison against Tom Mix on the silver screen or Jim Speirs and his team mates at Valley Parade? Against such seductive opposition, there was perhaps not a great deal the musical society could do.

The choral movement had two other specific problems to deal with. Popular choralism as it existed by about 1890 owed much to two facets of Victorian society: the broad social mix of contemporary religion, especially Nonconformity, which allowed pan-class forms to emerge (the Liberal Party in politics, the choral society in music) and the strength of religious sensibility. By 1914 the class consensus was severely dented, and in some areas almost non-existent, at least in political terms, while at the same time the strength of organised religion was waning. Choralism suffered on both counts. It is at least possible that the middle-class defection from choral music was in part a rejection of the re-emergence of class politics and the increased organisation of industrial labour that took place after about 1890. Perhaps some middle-class males, especially now that new leisure forms were available, sought to distance themselves from the working class that they had previously been prepared to sing and perform with.

There can be no doubt about the impact of declining religious observance. In terms of sheer numbers, organised religion was in decline from the late nineteenth century.[65] When church and chapel lost members, choral societies so closely related to them did too. The process was only just beginning in the Edwardian period, but the implications were serious. Perhaps even more significant was the decline of much of the outward religious sentiment that inevitably accompanied the fall in numbers. While the choral *repertoire* may have been liberated by the erosion of some of the more claustrophobic religious moves, the choral *society* was bound to suffer from the secular drift. Choirs provided Victorians with respectable, religious or quasi-religious entertainment; in the altered atmosphere of

Edwardian England, such entertainment was no longer as necessary or as attractive.

The problems of the period were not accepted meekly. W. G. Rothery, a London schools inspector and one of several writers anxious to stimulate positive counterbalancing measures, exhorted societies to 'put their shoulders to the wheel', find out the root cause of the problem and find solutions.[66] In the last analysis, Rothery and many others felt that salvation must lie in the music they offered and it was hoped that the enhanced quality and variety of the Edwardian repertoire would stem the decline. It was not to be. Brass bands may indeed have failed to respond adequately. As has been seen, there were major changes, but there was a rather dated or overworked feel about some elements of the repertoire. Richardson's major publications for the 1911 contesting season, for example, were *Robert Il Diavolo*, *William Tell* and *Bohemian Girl*. Could such music really fend off the challenge of Lionel Monckton at the local theatre or, when it came in 1912, ragtime at the music-hall?

Even where, as in the case of the choral society, there *was* almost a revolution in repertoire, problems were still experienced. Indeed, it is possible that the new repertoire may have actually been a cause of difficulty. The old tradition had been rooted to some extent in community ritual; the music of Handel, Haydn and Mendelssohn expressed the sensibilities, real or assumed for respectability's sake, of the provincial, Nonconformist communities. Much of the newer work was 'specialist' music written for musicians and did not necessarily communicate to a wider public. This is clear from the reaction by singers and audiences to certain new compositions. The Keighley Musical Union, whose membership had actually risen during the period from 1904, saw it plummet from two hundred and nine to one hundred and thirty-eight during the 1912–1913 season. Much of the problem seems to have stemmed from the members' dislike of Hubert Bath's *Wedding of Shon MacClean*. Attendance at rehearsals for the work fell so low at one time that the committee contemplated abandoning the concert. Audiences too were often reluctant to support new works. The bond between music and community was breaking; the division between contemporary 'art' music and the mass of society, so noticeable today, had its roots in the Edwardian age. Both music and society were to suffer.[67]

It has to be stressed that the decline of the amateur choral and band tradition had only reached its earliest stages by 1914. In comparison with the late twentieth century, the number of organisations was vast and their place in local society far more central. But decline there was and it had begun, like many other changes often ascribed to the Great War, well before 1914. Even if the First World War had been avoided, even if the massive expansion of the electronic media had not taken place in the 1920s and 1930s, the popular musical society would have been a diminishing feature of cultural life.

That these events *did* take place made the situation one of genuine difficulty and, eventually, crisis. The First World War inevitably disrupted musical life. As musical bodies saw their menfolk leave in large numbers, some carried on – bands recruiting young boys, choirs accepting a major preponderence of women – others collapsed. It would have taken a lengthy period to recover. The crackle of the 'wireless' and the tones of Al Jolson and his counterparts emerging from numberless gramophones and cinema loudspeakers ensured that the period was not long enough.

Conclusions and epilogue

At 'grass roots' level, England (especially in the last two decades of the nineteenth century), was an intensely musical nation. There were considerable regional variations in terms of skill and taste, but a national musical culture was taking shape by the end of Victoria's reign. Musical organisations often reflected contemporary class divisions and tensions, but class lines could be crossed, as in some choirs and some music-halls, and there was a considerable sharing of repertoire amongst classes. In general a catholic taste prevailed. Enthusiasts in especially 'developed' musical regions such as the Yorkshire textile district could enjoy what was, by late twentieth century standards, a remarkable range of musical experience. In this context, working-class interest in what we now term 'art music' is especially noteworthy. Popular musical culture, like most aspects of contemporary social life, was essentially male-dominated, but to a lesser degree than, for example, sport. In the choral society, women gained a rare opportunity to obtain something approaching equal status to men. Much music was provided by philanthropists, even more by entrepreneurs, but despite the massive strides made by the music-hall and other branches of the entertainment industry in the late nineteenth century, it was the community itself that generated the bulk of musical entertainment, albeit entertainment drawing largely on the compositions emanating from the various branches of the musical profession. Music gave a variety of emotional, social and economic satisfactions to its adherents and, partly in recognition of its popularity and capacity to influence, was regarded by ideologues of varied persuasion as a major vehicle for the promulgation of 'correct' ideas and attitudes. Where music does appear to have exerted influence upon the popular imagination it probably did so in a 'conservative' manner, encouraging non-political activity and reinforcing popular radical rather than socialist attitudes.

At the risk of repetition, this final point does require a little development. The relationship between popular music and popular political mentalities has been a constant theme and an overview does seem appropriate at this stage. It is difficult to overstress the political significance of musical life in the Victorian and Edwardian periods. If nothing else, the material presented here should destroy any lingering vestige of belief in music, or the arts in general, as politically naïve, protected from the 'real' world by a coat of divinely-inspired creative genius. Whether the subject under scrutiny be the Leeds Philharmonic subscription concert as opportunity for reaffirmation of status by the local élite, the politically-motivated support of overseas choral tours or the patriotism of music-hall song, conflicts over class, power and ideology are always present.

To argue that popular music reinforced, perhaps helped generate, conservative tendencies is not to deny its potential as a radical force or its undoubted achievements when used to challenge dominant classes. The songs of Tommy Armstrong and Joe Wilson, the marches played by bands at union demonstrations and the hymns thundered at strike meetings must have given hope and inspiration. Neither is it to argue that performers and audiences alike fell simple and unquestioning prey to overt attempts at control through music. Undoubtedly some did, but much rejection and negotiation must have taken place.

Nevertheless, the weight of speculation in this work finds against the radicals. Music's contribution to the maintenance of what can justifiably be termed 'bourgeois hegemony' in the period after 1850 had four elements, all largely unforeseen by protagonists in the contemporary debate. At one level, ideas of dominant 'sectors' filtered into popular experience through a number of superficially ideologically innocent institutions. This has been discussed at length during consideration of the later Victorian music-hall where fatalism, suspicion of politics, passivity and even a simple imperialism were preached. The mid-Victorian opponents of music-hall would have been surprised by the de-radicalising service performed by the enemy. (Not all of whom, however, especially those of Liberal persuasion, would have approved.) The music-hall song, although perhaps the most potent vehicle for such ideas, was not the only one. Most so-called 'parlour ballads' were escapist in the extreme. Edwardian musical comedy glamourised the lifestyle of the rich and lacked any critical cutting edge. Pride in military and imperial achievement entered choral music overtly, through Stanford's *Revenge*, a setting of Tennyson, and the band movement covertly, through the marches and uniforms much loved by bandsmen. There was to a striking degree a unity of political sentiment in the whole field of popular music.[1]

More important, however, were the three factors already outlined in the analysis of choirs and bands but which can be extended to almost the whole field of popular music. First, music rivalled politics for the time, money and commitment of the working classes. Secondly, it could form an albeit uneasy link between potentially antagonistic social classes. This was probably clearest in the case of the choral and, to a lesser extent, the band movements, but there were other examples. Skilled workers, and their families on occasions, did 'mix' in music-hall and concert-hall in the sense that they found themselves in the same buildings listening to the same performers. In the music-halls, especially from the 1890s, it is also possible that artistes like Chevalier helped soften the image which the middle class might have of the 'dangerous classes'. Finally, and most importantly, music provided artistic, social, economic and emotional satisfactions which made existence under capitalism far richer than might otherwise have been the case. Obviously, the minority of dedicated musical 'activists' stood to gain the most, but the majority of the population could gain great pleasure from a night in the gallery at a music-hall or people's concert, or even from a hard bench at the chapel institute's *Messiah* or *Crucifixion*.

To argue this is not to eulogise the urban social life of Victorian and Edwardian England. A lengthy session with the writings of Edwin Chadwick or Charles Booth soon mutes the hallelujahs and brings one back to more painful realities. Nevertheless, the fact that music and, in all probability, leisure pursuits in general brought satisfaction, thereby enriching the popular experience and making working class subordination within capitalism a process at times cheerful, is vital. This is not profound: indeed, such a belief is almost a truism of much sociology. But it deserves to be placed more firmly amongst the many factors historians have used to explain the political development of the working class after the later 1840s. It must be seen as only *one* possibility, but one which, if nothing else, serves as a useful antidote to interpretations based on crude models of social control, in which the working class dance like well-schooled puppets, and even to neo-Gramscian approaches centred on the concept of cultural hegemony. The ideas of Gramsci, as applied by writers such as Robert Gray, have provided a subtle and, to an extent, satisfying picture of class relations in Victorian England. However, such an approach is still somehow patronising, concerned, in the final analysis, despite all the potential for negotiation and counter-hegemony, with the *downward* flow of ideas, with small minorities and with the failure of the working class to fulfil its supposed historical mission. Certainly, any attempt to make sense of the political ramifications of popular musical culture must allow for the downward percolation of ideas, as the section here on music-hall illustrates. Nevertheless, the greatest emphasis has to be upon the capacity of large numbers of ordinary people to *discover for themselves*, upon their ability to work out their own destinies.

The particular musical culture that reached its zenith in the 1890s and was already altering by 1914 has long since disappeared. Most of the elements that created it still exist in various degrees, still recognisable but suitably tailored to meet changed times. The 'philanthropic' element discussed at length in Part One is still present. The State at national and local level – through local education authorities, Regional Arts Associations and the Arts Council – has become the guiding spirit, replacing almost completely the individual benefactors of the Wakefield, Collings and Meakin type. Motives (at least explicitly) have also changed. The emphasis in public statements is far more upon the enjoyment of the arts for their own sake than the repression of unhealthy and dangerous elements of popular culture, although echoes of the 'control' mentality are still sometimes present. In general, latterday musical philanthropy probably offers a more solidly 'serious' musical diet to the public and has extended the opportunity to see professionals of the highest calibre. Whether as wide an *adult* audience (children do receive some outstanding musical opportunities) is reached in the 1980s when compared with the 1880s is less certain. Perhaps the Arts Council might invest in a horse and cart?

The major community-based institutions also still exist, but in new guises. The brass band, now with so many rivals for the time and energy of the younger generation, has become, with a few exceptions, a minority pursuit rather than the focus of a whole community. Nevertheless it has survived because of a willingness to adapt. In recent decades, bands have absorbed many more middle-class members and, more importantly, many more females, into their ranks in an attempt to offset the changing habits of working-class males. The brass band movement certainly still retains much of its proletarian, masculine atmosphere, although whether this will remain the case is questionable. As well as changing its social and sexual base, the movement has shown artistic flexibility. Beginning with Fletcher in 1913, progressing through works from Elgar, Holst, Ireland and others in the inter-war period and embracing Malcolm Arnold, Gilbert Vintner and Harrison Birtwistle more recently, bands have shown a willingness to adopt new, challenging music. Most important of all for its long-term survival, the band movement has learnt both to co-exist and co-operate with the electronic media that might otherwise have destroyed it. Indeed, television and radio performance, coupled with recording work, have brought the leading bands into contact with a potentially larger audience than ever before and provided vitally-needed income.[3]

Choral societies have fared less well. Even the leading societies suffer from a shortage of males and there is a decidedly middle-aged flavour about many organisations. The movement is above all else a victim of the increasing secularisation that has taken place in English society. A phenomenon so closely linked with organised religion will inevitably suffer when the parent body diminishes in influence. The choral movement will not die, but by the twenty-first century it will surely be even more of a minority pursuit than is currently the case.

New forms of 'community' musical life have emerged to supplement or supersede the older forms. Piano sales have increased in recent years, organs become a more common piece of living-room furniture. Most striking of all is the spread of the guitar. A remarkable number of people seem to own one even if they cannot play it! Much late twentieth-century community music is made in a manner markedly different from that described in this book. It is more 'privatised', with much of the activity revolving around the individual pianist or guitarist in lounge or bedroom, although most aspiring guitarists have found themselves, however briefly, members of a 'band'. It is also more closely linked with the media and the entertainment industry; amateur musicians are now more likely to draw their material, ideas, inspiration and ambition from figures in the popular music industry than from older generations of their family, a local band trainer or a choral conductor.

Almost certainly, the *general* level of musical knowledge and technical expertise is lower now than in the Victorian and Edwardian periods. Moreover, the breadth of individual taste has probably also diminished, or at least divided quite markedly along lines of generation. If so, the emergence of radio, television, the cassette recorder and, most recently, video, taken in conjunction with the decline in the role of the family as an institution of musical training and cultural socialisation, is absolutely central here. Increasingly private and/or solitary listening habits based on this technology have helped encourage the development of musical sub-cultures. It is now possible to subsist on a perpetual diet of Beethoven, rock n' roll, reggae or whatever. Locked away with one's favourite music, it is easy to forget that other types exist. This was much less likely to occur before 1914, when son followed father into the band or families gathered around piano or concertina on Sunday evenings. In such circumstances each generation could pass some of its taste and culture to the young. Obviously there were generational conflicts before 1914. Flora Thompson's well-known description of an Oxfordshire village singing session, with the old men singing 'old' country songs and the young music-hall numbers, is testimony to this.[4] In general, however, the gaps in taste between some parents and some children that have emerged in the mid 1950s, for example, do not appear to have been so strong.

We must be careful not to dismiss the new musical cultures, however, as inferior to that which existed before about 1914. While it is possible to admit to individual artistic preferences, the cult of the Hammond organ or a current trend in musical youth culture must be looked at with the same detachment and scholarship as any other manifestation of popular musical life.

The one major 'casualty' amongst the musical forms studied here is the music-hall. Whatever its many devotees may claim, as an *institution* it is dead and has been since the 1950s.[5] Radio, cinema and television have long undermined its position. Its *influence*, however, is still felt in many ways. The songs of the halls are much sung by the forty-plus age group and a few are well known by younger audiences. Many comedians have strong music-hall elements in their perform-ance while a few, notably Roy Hudd, actively seek to rediscover the best material from the early period. Moreover, something very similar to the atmosphere and style of early music-hall can be found in some working men's clubs. It is, however, quite probable that these influ-ences will diminish. Young people are not exposed to the popular musical tradition of previous generations to anything like the extent they used to be, and it is essentially through the family and community oral network that the songs of the halls persisted. It is likely that by the mid twenty-first century the pop 'standards' of our time will have superseded those of one hundred years ago.

We should not be sad to lose the world that created the musical life of 1840–1914. But in my opinion at least, many aspects of that musical life were worth preserving and the passing of many of them is surely a matter for regret. Whether a society more humane that that of Victorian and Edwardian times, yet still capable of generating the active, broad-based and catholic culture of those times can be created, is impossible to predict. It is most certainly to be hoped for.

Appendix

Working-class composers

As well as disseminating and stimulating 'establishment' musical composition, surprisingly large numbers of the amateur musical community sought to compose music of their own, occasionally for profit, but usually for pleasure. This practice was perhaps most common in the period before 1850 when published works were scarce and expensive, although many examples can be found from the later period. Most of this music is long forgotten, but brief exploration seems justified, as a further illustration of both the musical skills found amongst the 'common people' and the limits social factors placed upon the development of some of those skills.

Clearly working-class composers were restricted by lack of time, formal education and, most critically, money. As Stephen Banfield has pointed out, 'a private income, however small' was an essential pre-requisite for Victorian and Edwardian composers.[1] In response to these constraints, just as working-men *literati* tended to write poetry or dialect stories rather than full-length novels and plays, aspiring plebeian composers generally concentrated on shorter forms.[2] The hymn was probably the song type most frequently chosen. Innumerable local musicians produced hymns, many of which have been lost, although a surprisingly large number continue to emerge during the spring cleaning of attics and organ lofts, invariably lovingly copied out and bound in leather-backed books. Often these hymns would be little known outside the composer's immediate locality, although before the 'nationalisation' of church music began around mid century with publication of, for example, *Hymns Ancient and Modern* in 1861, the best would have gained considerable currency locally. A very few composers did reach a wider audience, if not always in their own lifetime. Accepted Widdop (1749–1801), a woolcomber from the village of Illingworth near Halifax, wrote a large number of hymns, many of which were published after his death in order to raise money for his family. Three of his tunes, *Birstal*, *Widdop* and *Ossett*, became especially popular, the former still featuring in the official Methodist hymnbook in the early years of the twentieth century. James Leach, a handloom weaver from Wardle near Rochdale, enjoyed greater immediate success, eventually becoming a full-time musician and hymn writer, advertising his work in the *Arminian Magazine*.[3]

Short works for brass bands, particularly marches, were another element produced in significant quantities. Such composition generally held out better financial reward than sacred pieces. Edward Newton, a textile worker from Silsden in West Yorkshire, wrote over three hundred marches during the nineteenth century, many of which were published and assimilated into the repertoire of 'crack' bands. Similarly George Wadsworth, a monumental stone mason from Holmfirth, again the the West Riding, composed almost all of the marches and dances published by the Rochdale firm of J. Frost and Son in their *Manchester Brass (& Military) Band Journal*.[4]

More ambitious composers ventured into the sometimes treacherous field of 'art' music. For bandsmen, this was likely to involve them in arrangement of the existing stock rather than the creation of new material, as they grappled with operatic and, less often, symphonic scores, seeking to present their bands with suitable contest pieces. Edwin Swift, whose work on Wagner has already been noted, William Short, responsible for *Gems of Chopin* and *Gems of Schumann* at the 1906 and 1907 Crystal Palace Championship, and, above all, the prolific Southport-based arranger William Rimmer, eventually chief editor for Wright & Round, were probably the best known. A few brave musicians, like the Bradford draper and violinist Stephen Scholey who completed at least one symphony attempted original orchestral composition, but in general simple lack of technical expertise made such efforts rare.[5]

Experts on vocal music had more opportunity to compose art music through the medium of the glee and part-song as these were easier to produce than a full-scale instrumental work and, probably more important to an aspiring composer, more likely to be performed. Representative of such figures was William Hollingworth (1840–1905) of Great Horton near Bradford, originally a textile worker later a 'machinist' and eventually in later life a publican/ professor of music. Although unable to play a musical instrument (he was *un*representative in that sense) he wrote over five hundred hymns, two masses, one of which featured in Black Dyke's repertoire in the early 1890s, and a large body of glees and partsongs, many of which were published by Novello. His glee 'Here's Life and Health to England's Queen' (1887) was a particular favourite with Yorkshire male-voice choirs. Such writers enjoyed considerable, if parochial, reputations. When the eminent singing teacher Randegger came to Bradford to organise a Jubilee concert in 1887, he was unwilling to include 'Here's Life' because of his total unfamiliarity with both song and composer. (He eventually relented and dutifully told the delighted Bradford populace how the piece impressed him.) Similarly in 1898, Sullivan, when given an impromptu concert by the Leeds Musical Union which included the piece, had to admit that he had never heard of Hollingworth but praised his composition. The local musical community thought highly of him, whatever his reputation or lack of it, and he became a minor Yorkshire celebrity in his last years.[6]

Of all the working men composers (no working *women* have come to light) writing before 1914, only two, Havergal Brian and Edmund Rubbra, attained national or international eminence. Peter Pirie would add a third, for he claims Elgar, son of a pianotuner/music shop owner, to be 'working class', but this seems to stretch late Victorian class definition well beyond breaking point.[7] Neither Rubbra nor Brian achieved major success within the period under study – Rubbra was of course only born in 1901 – and their early careers underline the problems faced by working-class composers, especially the vexed question of finance.

Rubbra was born in Northampton into what the *New Grove* calls 'a poor working-class family', his father being employed in a shoe factory. His basic musical education was at the hands of his mother and his uncle, who owned a music shop. On leaving school in 1915, he took a small step up the social ladder by becoming a railway clerk, by which time he had gained a reputation as an outstanding pianist. His path into the musical establishment was eased in 1920 when he gained a composition scholarship to Reading University, an early example of the importance of an expanding higher education system to the artistic progress of people from poor homes. This scholarship, however, was at least partially secured by the efforts of the composer Cyril Scott, whose piano pieces Rubbra played so expertly. Even at this stage, an element of patronage was required if a working-class composer was to build even the beginning of a career.[8]

Havergal Brian (1876–1972, actually William Brian at birth) became something of a cult figure in the 1960s and 70s, hardly surprising given the discovery that here was a man entirely forgotten by the musical world and with no prospect of hearing his work performed, who had nevertheless written twenty symphonies between his seventy-third and ninety-second years.[9] His early career in outline sounds at first like the plot of a sub-Lawrence novel, but gradually reveals how economic reality combined with family pressure restricted artistic potential, with, in this case, disastrous consequences for Brian and those around him. He was born in Dresden, Staffordshire, son of a potter's turner, keen chrysanthemum grower and brass bandsman. The young Brian very quickly showed great musical promise and expressed the desire to be a professional composer and musician. His family, however, viewed music as only a pastime rather than a career and he pursued a number of jobs – truck weigher in a pit, apprentice joiner, railway clerk – all of which he hated, all of which he did badly and all of which he lost. His apprenticeship ended after he took a day off work to play the church organ in the company of an older workmate who had befriended him.

As soon as he [the boss] had turned his back – he was supposed to be out for the day – I rushed off for the key of the parish church organ, and took my soldier-piano-pub player to the church to blow for me. We were there for hours. . . . [The soldier would shout] 'Lets have that again, this time with all the bloody stops out'. Sadly, the boss returned early.[10]

He regularly took time off work to study, read and compose, desperately trying to create the necessary lifestyle in a hopeless situation.

By 1899, he married a girlfriend, Isobel, who was already three months pregnant, but this did little to alter his pattern of existence. Increasingly, he became alienated from his family, especially his mother, who resented what she saw as his rejection of his working-class origin, his poor treatment of Isobel, his adulterous relationships and, eventually, his decline into heavy drinking. In 1910, Herbert Robinson, a local pottery manufacturer, gave him the patronage, to the amount of £500 a year, that should have strengthened a career that had promised much despite all these pressures. A *Musical Times* critic, for example, after hearing his *English Suite* in 1907, claimed there to be 'a freshness and significance in his music which indicates creative power'. However, patronage merely led to indolence and heavier drinking and it was a long time indeed before his talent re-emerged.[11]

The re-discovery of Brian fifty years later gives his story a happy ending. One wonders how many other happy endings there might have been if the economics of Victorian music had been different. Admittedly, most working-men composers had relatively low expectations. Some of them, like the weaver composer William Hesling, whose brass band piece of 1856 'contained many plagiarisms' according to the *Leeds Intelligencer*, were not very good.[12] But there can be no denying the existence, within the working-class musical community, of a real desire not merely to consume, but to produce music, to make a contribution to musical culture. Much of what resulted contained, at least by contemporary standards, a certain merit and some lasting value.

Notes

Foreword

1 *School Music Review*, November 1897. *Musical Times*, 1975, pp. 439, 625, 877 discusses the origins of this phase.
2 R. Middleton & D. Horn (eds.), *Popular Music*, 1, Cambridge, 1981, is an excellent starting point for detailed reading.
3 Nettel's *Music in the Five Towns*, Oxford, 1944, is still one of the few serious studies of the social aspect of choral singing.
4 Two forms I feel especially disappointed to have cast aside are the drum and fife bands associated with various youth groups from at least the 1850s, and the working-class dance-halls of the later Victorian period.

Chapter 1: Introduction: music and society 1840–1914

1 Rounded version of the figures given by C. Ehrlich, *The Music Profession in Britain Since the Eighteenth Century: A Social History*, Oxford, 1985, table one; *The Brass Band Annual*, F. Richardson, Sibsey, 1897, p. 13; *British Bandsman* 4 October, 1913. It is not clear whether this figure includes all visitors to the Palace, some of whom were presumably not attending the contest; C. Ehrlich, *The Piano: A History*, 1976, p. 97.
2 William Cudworth, *Condition of the Industrial Classes of Bradford and District*, 1887, p. 58.
3 W. J. Galloway, *Musical England*, 1910, p. 17.
4 *Musical Times*, July 1903.
5 For Armstrong, A. L. Lloyd, *Folk-Song in England*, 1967 ed., pp. 377–86. For Holme Valley Beagles, Ian Russell's notes to the LP, *A Fine Hunting Day: songs of the Holme Valley Beagles*, Leader LEE 4056.
6 R. Pearsall, *Victorian Popular Music*, Newton Abbot, 1973, pp. 89–91. F. Richardson, *Annual*, 1897, pp. 68–71.
7 Fifteenth edition, London 1888, p. 547.
8 January 1868. My italics.
9 J. S. Curwen, 'The progress of popular music', *Contemporary Review*, August 1887.
10 K. Cook (ed.), *Oh, Listen to the Band*, 1950, pp. 13, 16, 36–7, 57–63.
11 Dave Harker, *Fakesong*, Cambridge, 1985, is most useful on the issue of 'mediation'.
12 William Morris, 'The society of the future', quoted in A. L. Morton (ed.), *Political Writings of William Morris*, 1973, p. 193; quoted in E. P. Thompson, *William Morris, Romantic to Revolutionary*, 1955, pp. 771–2.

It may be, of course, that Morris regarded much Victorian 'Art' music as 'banal'.

13   S. Hall & P. Whannel, *The Popular Arts*, 1964, p. 52; D. Thompson (ed.), *Discrimination and Popular Culture*, 1968, p. 172; H. Raynor, *Music and Society Since 1815*, 1976, p. 152.

14   T. Staveacre, *The Songwriters*, 1980, pp. 11–31, 33–55; H. Mortimer with Alan Lynton, *Harry Mortimer on Brass*, Sherborne, 1981, p. 41; interview with Mrs Anne-Marie Wagstaff.

15   *Bradford Observer*, 26 June 1871; *Bournemouth & Boscombe Amusements*, 5 July 1897.

16   R. Hoggart, *The Uses of Literacy*, Penguin ed. 1973, p. 163.

17   E. Hobsbawn, *Industry and Empire*, 1968, p. 158.

18   G. Crossick (ed.), *The Lower Middle Class in Britain, 1870–1914*, 1977, pp. 18–19.

19   D. Lockwood, *The Blackcoated Worker*, 1958, p. 21.

20   H. Perkin, *The Age of the Railway*, 1970, is still the best simple introduction.

21   R. Middleton, 'Popular music of the lower classes', in N. Temperley (ed.), *Athlone History of Music*, V, 1981, p. 66.

22   Historians have in general stressed class conflict in the field of leisure and the tendency for different classes to develop their own recreational patterns and institutions. Common ground, however, whether genuinely sought or mere convenience, was more frequently shared than is sometimes believed. B. Harrison, 'Religion and recreation in nineteenth-century England', *Past & Present*, XXXVIII, 1967, has exercised great influence over my thinking on this issue.

23   H. Cunningham, 'Leisure' in J. Benson (ed.), *The Working Class in England 1875–1914*, 1985, pp. 134–7 provides an excellent introduction to these issues. M. Bienefeld, *Working Hours in British Industry*, 1972, is a key text.

24   It is no coincidence that popular musical culture, and indeed so many other aspects of popular recreational life (most notably seaside holidays and professional sport), reached maturity first in the textile districts of Lancashire and Yorkshire. Here, amongst other things, the early introduction of the shorter day and the opportunity for regular, family employment, led to the demand for and expansion of facilities, earlier than in any other part of the country. In general, Yorkshire lagged a little behind Lancashire in the development of 'commercial' leisure and this may account for its slightly more developed tradition of community music in the late century. J. K. Walton, 'The demand for working-class seaside holidays in Victorian England', *Economic History Review*, XXXIV, 1981, is obligatory reading for students of time and money in the nineteenth century.

25   B. Harrison, *Religion*, is a good starting point.

26   D. Russell, 'The Leeds Rational Recreation Society, 1852–59; 'music for the people' in a mid-Victorian City,' *Publications* of the *Thoresby Society*, LVI, 1981, pp. 141–3.

27   George Gissing, quoted in H. Cunningham, *Leisure in the Industrial*

Revolution, 1980, p. 104.

28 W. Spark, *Musical Memories*, 1888, p. 403; F. J. Crowest, quoted in R. Myers, *Handel's Messiah*, New York, 1948, p. 238.

29 Interview with Miss Annie Smith.

30 The section entitled 'The Chaos' in H. McCleod, *Religion and Class in a Late Victorian City*, 1974, is an outstanding introduction to this process.

31 S. Yeo, *Religion and Voluntary Organisations in Crisis*, 1976, is a stimulating analysis of the churches' response to the problems of late Victorian and Edwardian Britain.

32 *Leeds Mercury*, 2 December 1895.

Chapter 2: Music and morals, 1840–1880

1 Quoted in R. Pearsall, *Victorian Popular Music*, Newton Abbott, 1973, p. 119.

2 *School Music Review*, February 1907.

3 *Yorkshire Daily Observer*, 20 August 1907.

4 George Hogarth, 'A village oratorio' in *Mainzer's Musical Times*, 15 November 1834, pp. 131–3.

5 The phrase, sometimes with capitals, sometimes without, gained currency in the 1880s. See, for example, 'Music for the people', *Musical Times*, September 1881.

6 G. Stedman Jones, *Outcast London*, 1971, provides some striking examples of politically motivated philanthropy.

7 B. Harrison, *Drink and the Victorians*, 1971, pp. 66–9.

8 L. Faucher, *Manchester in 1844*, Reprint, Newcastle, 1969, p. 49; *Bradford Observer*, 15 February 1849.

9 G. Wilson, *Alcohol and the Nation*, 1940, p. 335.

10 *School Music Review*, November 1909. See also R. Newmarch, *Mary Wakefield, A Memoir*, Kendal, 1912, p. 86; W. J. Galloway, *Musical England*, 1910, p. 184.

11 F. Manders, *A History of Gateshead*, Gateshead, 1973, p. 246.

12 P. Bailey, *Leisure and Class in Victorian England*, 1978, pp. 161–2.

13 P. Summerfield, 'The Effingham Arms and the Empire', in E. & S. Yeo (eds.), *Popular Culture and Class Conflict 1590–1914*, Brighton, 1981.

14 D. Farson, *Marie Lloyd and Music-Hall*, 1972, pp. 62–9.

15 S. Pollard, 'Factory discipline in the industrial revolution', *Economic History Review*, 2nd series XVI, 1963–64, remains an excellent introduction.

16 J. L. Scott, 'The Evolution of the Brass Band and its repertoire in Northern England' (unpublished Ph.D. thesis, University of Sheffield, 1970) pp. 113, 115; E. MacKerness, *A Social History of English Music*, 1964, p. 130. Attitudes toward rational recreation musical or otherwise were not always straightforward, however. Music-lover Joseph Strutt is traditionally supposed to have started the controversial and non-rational Derby street football match that was to cause so much conflict between classes in the 1840s. Indeed, his support of the game may well have given it protection against 'rational' attack. A. Delves, 'Popular recreation and

social conflict in Derby 1800–1850', in E. & S. Yeo (eds.), *Popular Culture*, p. 104.

17   MacKerness, *Social*, p. 131.
18   J. F. C. Harrison, *Robert Owen and the Owenites in Britain and America*, 1968, for an introduction to Owen.
19   MacKerness, *Social*, p. 130; Scott, 'Evolution', p. 112; Anon., 'The Origins and Progress of the Caminando Band with a Few Short Accounts of the Most Striking Incidents in Connection with its Formation etc.', MS in records of R. V. Marriner & Company, box 117 (held in special collection, Brotherton Library, University of Leeds).
20   J. Spencer Curwen, *Music At the Queen's Accession*, 1897, pp. 17–18.
21   B. Rainbow, *The Land Without Music*, 1967, pp. 30–52 is a useful introduction.
22   *Musical Times*, July 1887.
23   MacKerness, *Social*, p. 165; Rainbow, *Land*, p. 57.
24   P. Scholes, *The Mirror of Music*, I, 1947, p. 14. Scholes implies that this work was still sold in the 1930s.
25   For the non-historian, E. Royle, *Chartism*, 1980, provides a good general orientation, a balanced view and a copious bibliography.
26   Scholes, *Mirror*, pp. 3–10; *Mainzer's Musical Times and Singing-Class Circular*, 1842–44.
27   *Mainzer's Musical Times*, 1 August 1842 and 15 July 1842.
28   *Ibid.*, 23 December 1842.
29   *Ibid.* 1 February 1843.
30   *Ibid.*, 15 April 1843; *Leeds Intelligencer*, 11 January 1845.
31   Scholes, *Mirror*, pp. 11–13.
32   Quoted in B. Rainbow, *The Choral Revival in the Anglican Church*, 1970, pp. 46–7.
33   R. Pearsall, *Victorian*, p. 113.
34   Scholes, *Mirror*, pp. 13–17; W. Shaw, 'John Curwen' in K. Simpson (ed.), *Some Great Music Educators*, 1976, provides a clear exposition of his theories in non-technical language. The keen might try J. Curwen, *The Standard Course of Lessons and Exercises in the Tonic Sol-fa Method of Teaching Music*, 1872.
35   Working men, even radical ones, saw people's concerts as central to any recreational scheme. *Four essays by Working Men of Bradford on the Most Practicable Means of Promoting Rational Recreation Among the People*, Bradford 1858, pp. 5–6.
36   W. Weber, *Music and the Middle Class*, 1975, is obligatory reading.
37   *Mainzer's Musical Times*, 15 April 1843; H. Cunningham, *Leisure and The Industrial Revolution*, 1980, pp. 102–3; J. Sutcliffe Smith, *The History of Music in Birmingham*, 1945, p. 117.
38   In the Leeds district, for example, *Leeds Intelligencer*, 6 November 1852, 30 June 1855.
39   *Leeds Mercury*, 13 December 1851. For a detailed study of the Leeds Society see D. Russell, 'The Leeds Rational Recreation Society 1852–9: 'Music for the People' in a mid-Victorian city', in *Publications of the Thoresby Society*, LVI, 1981.

40 Free concerts appear to have been extremely rare in this period.
41 *Leeds Intelligencer*, 23 April 1853. There were other songs which the newspaper did not record.
42 Quoted in *The Star Folio of The Hundred and One Best Songs*, London, n.d., pp. 98–9.
43 Rev. G. M. Conder in a letter to *Leeds Intelligencer*, 1 May 1852.
44 H. Hird, *Bradford Remembrancer*, Bradford, 1972, pp. 179–87; S. de B. Taylor, *Two Centuries of Music in Liverpool*, 1976, p. 99; H. Meller, *Leisure and the Changing City*, 1870–1914, 1976, p. 57.
45 *Bradford Observer*, 1 September 1853.
46 Official programme in Hailstone Collection, York Minster Library; A special cheap concert – minimum entry 1s – was offered during the festival week. *Morning Chronicle*, 5 September 1853.
47 *Halifax Guardian*, 18 February 1852.
48 Quoted in P. Razzell & R. W. Wainwright (eds.), *The Victorian Working Class*, 1973, p. 172; *Leeds Intelligencer*, 6 May 1854.
49 The 1850s had, of course, been remarkably free from the social and political conflicts which had been so much a feature of almost the whole period from the 1790s, but one senses that by about 1860 some Victorians really believed that social peace and stability was to be long lasting.
50 Quoted in *Musical Times*, June 1879. 'Water' is only marginally less problematic.
51 *School Music Review*, April 1896.
52 S. de B. Taylor, *Liverpool*, pp. 93–5.

Chapter 3: Music and morals 1880–1914

1 *Musical Times*, December 1883.
2 S. Yeo, *Religion and Voluntary Organisations in Crisis*, 1976, has much of value on the withdrawal of what he calls the 'vice-presidential' stratum from civic life.
3 D. Harker, 'May Cecil Sharp be praised?', *History Workshop Journal*, XIV, 1982, p. 46; F. Marshall, 'Music and the people', *Nineteenth Century*, December 1880, pp. 922–32.
4 For the Kyrle Society see Octavia Hill, 'Colour, space, and music for the people', *Nineteenth Century*, XV, 1884; *Musical Times*, July 1883.
5 *Ibid.*, February 1903.
6 *Musical Herald*, April 1899.
7 *Yorkshire Daily Observer*, 27 August 1910.
8 In a sense musical 'philanthropy' reflects the more flexible, more realistic (more 'humane'?) face of much English philanthropy in general from the late nineteenth century. For a useful introduction and bibliography, see D. Fraser, *The Evolution of the British Welfare State*, 1984 ed., Chapter six.
9 R. Roberts, 'The corporation as impressario: the municipal provision of entertainments in Victorian and Edwardian Bournemouth' in J. Walton & J. Walvin, (eds.), *Leisure in Britain, 1780–1939*, Manchester, 1983, pp. 149–50.

10 W. J. Galloway, *Musical England*, 1910, pp. 49–65 is a useful source for
    the study of municipal funding. Galloway, a Conservative MP, moved a
    bill in support of a state-sponsored national opera company in 1903. See
    J. Minihan, *The Nationalisation of Culture*, 1977, pp. 149–50.
11 E. Fricker, 'Herbert Austin Fricker, 1868–1943', MS in Leeds Public
    Library, p. 2.
12 The programmes for the Leeds concerts are held in bound volumes in
    Leeds Public Library. This programme was for 6 February 1904.
13 *Yorkshire Post*, 21 January 1905; 14 January 1907; programme 8
    December 1906.
14 Roberts, *Impressario*, p. 150.
15 *Yorkshire Post*, 27 November 1911.
16 *Yorkshire Evening Post*, 27 January 1909.
17 *Ibid.*, 4 February 1909. Wilson argued that the poor behaviour of the
    'gangs of rabble' that were attracted to park concerts undermined the
    musical value of such events and made them a mere nuisance.
18 For an informative, if partial, account of her life and philosophy see R.
    Newmarch, *Wakefield, passim*.
19 *Musical Times*, March 1884; R. Newmarch, *Wakefield*, p. 80.
20 *Musical Times*, June 1904; August 1914.
21 *Ibid.*, August 1906.
22 *Ibid.*, November and December 1910.
23 *Musical Times*, June 1904. This report on the foundation of the AMCF is
    an important source; *Competition Festival Record*, July 1910.
24 *Musical Times*, June 1904.
25 *Musical Times*, June 1905; *Competition Festival Record*, June 1910,
    December 1911. For a helpful introduction to the Girls Friendly Society,
    B. Harrison. 'For Church, Queen and Family: The Girls Friendly
    Society 1874–1920', *Past & Present*, 1973.
26 *Yorkshire Post*, 8 May 1905. The protegé in question was almost cer-
    tainly C. H. Kitson.
27 For further details of the tournaments, J. Sutcliffe Smith, *A Musical
    Pilgrimage in Yorkshire*, 1928, pp. 255–6.
28 *Competition Festival Record*, December 1910.
29 J. Spencer Curwen, *Accession*, p. 17.
30 For those musicians or others seeking a brief guide to the 1870 Act, J.
    Lawson & H. Silver, *A Social History of Education in England*, 1974, pp.
    314–22.
31 *School Music Review*, June 1892.
32 Scholes, *Mirror*, II, p. 625.
33 R. Colls, 'Oh happy children of the poor', *Past and Present*, 1976.
34 *School Music Review*, August 1892.
35 V. Gammon, 'Folk song collecting in Sussex and Surrey, 1843–1914',
    History Workshop Journal, VII, 1980, p. 74. Gammon's article along with
    D. Harker, *Fakesong*, 1985, part 3 make excellent starting points for a
    discussion of folk-song, although 'traditionalists' will be appalled by
    Harker's critique of Sharp's methods.
36 Gammon, *Collecting*, p. 80.

37   *School Music Review*, November 1903.
38   *Ibid.*, March 1904.
39   Scholes, *Mirror*, II, p. 621.
40   *School Music Review*, June 1892.
41   *Ibid.*, July 1907.
42   *Ibid.*, May 1909.
43   The thirty-six-strong band at Hanson Boys' School in Bradford, highly regarded by the inspectorate, included twenty-nine stringed instruments. *Ibid.*, July 1904.
44   *Ibid.*, June 1906.
45   *Ibid.*, September 1898. It is uncertain whether the gender difference resulted from the pupils' attitudes or from a stronger emphasis being placed upon music in girls' as opposed to boys' schools.
46   *Ibid.*, November 1903; February 1910.
47   For amateur orchestras see below, chapter nine.
48   *School Music Review*, August 1902; Jim Bullock, *Bowers Row*, East Ardsley, 1976, pp. 99–100.
49   John Taylor, *From Self-Help to Glamour: The Working Men's Club*, History Workshop pamphlet, 7, 1972. pp. 61–2.
50   J. A. Harrison, *A West Riding Childhood*, Guiseley, 1967, pp. 111–12.
51   *School Music Review*, October 1896.
52   *Ibid.*, December 1905; July 1904.
53   *Ibid.*, April 1905.
54   W. Shaw, in Simpson, *Educators*, pp. 94–5.
55   For some interesting comments on recent musical education in schools, G. Vulliamy, 'Music as a case study in the 'New Sociology of Education', in J. Shepherd *et al.*, *Whose Music?*, New Jersey, 1977.
56   See, for example, the chartist philosophy quoted in M. Vicinus, *The Industrial Muse*, 1974, p. 107.
57   A. L. Lloyd, *Folk-Song in England*, 1967, ed., pp. 343–4. For North-Eastern pit song see D. Harker, *One for the Money*, 1980, pp. 159–90.
58   I. Watson, *Song and Democratic Culture in Britain*, 1983, p. 22.
59   J. Wigley, *The Rise and Fall of the Victorian Sunday*, Manchester, 1980, is an excellent study of the sabbatarian issue.
60   E. Royle, *Victorian Infidels*, Manchester, 1976, p. 237.
61   J. Wigley, *Sunday*, p. 70.
62   *Leeds Mercury*, 17 June 1856.
63   *Ibid.*, 24 May 1856; 27 May 1856.
64   In Bradford, as in many Northern towns, the campaign for Sunday band concerts was still being fought strongly in the Edwardian period. *Bradford Pioneer*, 19 December 1913. The paper, the journal of the local ILP, listed some twenty towns which had established Sunday concerts.
65   For this cluster of socialist activity see S. Yeo, 'A new life: the religion of socialism in Britain', *History Workshop Journal*, IV, 1977.
66   *Yorkshire Factory Times*, 2, 9 and 16 July 1897; *Bradford Labour Echo*, 18 and 25 May 1895.
67   For Blatchford, see L. Thompson, *Robert Blatchford: Portrait of An Englishman*, 1951. For Clarion and other socialist leisure groups see D.

Prynn, 'The Clarion clubs rambling and the holiday associations in Britain since the 1890s', *Journal of Contemporary History*, July 1976.

68   The articles appeared on 1, 15 and 29 September. The first, 'on striking the lyre', is the most important. For further biographical information see M. Blatchford's obituaries in *Clarion*, 22 April 1910 and *Yorkshire Factory Times*, 19 May 1910.

69   For full details of chorus by 1910, see *Clarion*, 4 February 1910. For his comments on competitions *ibid.*, 21 December 1895.

70   *Keighley Labour Journal*, 26 June 1897. I am indebted to David James for this reference.

71   *Clarion*, 12 January 1895.

72   *Ibid.*, 12 December 1895.

73   *Keighley Labour Journal*, 10 December 1895.

74   The best brief introduction to the nineteenth and early twentieth-century co-operative movement is S. Pollard, 'Nineteenth century co-operation from community building to shopkeeping' in A. Briggs and J. Saville, *Essays in Labour History*, 1, 1967 ed. The Huddersfield choir is dealt with in some detail in O. Balmforth, *Huddersfield Industrial Society Ltd.*, *Jubilee History*, Manchester, 1910, pp. 213, 215, 217–20.

75   *Clarion*, 9 April 1898.

76   *Ibid.*, 4 May 1906. 'Comrades' could be sung both as an expression of socialist fellowship or, simply, of mutual friendship.

77   *Competition Festival Record*, May 1914.

78   J. Bennett and J. Baldwin, *City of Bradford Co-operative Society Ltd, 1860–1910*, Bradford, 1911, pp. 235–6.

79   *Yorkshire Daily Observer*, 25 September 1904; *Co-operative News*, 21 September 1907. It must be said that the British 'radical' choral movement appears fairly insubstantial when compared with its German equivalent. The difference is presumably largely explained by the far greater strength of socialism in Germany, but the fact that the British labour movement did not normally need 'front' organisations to disguise illicit political activity, a common function for German choirs, was also a contributory factor. See D. Dowe, 'The workingman's choral movement in Germany before the first world war', *Journal of Contemporary History*, XIV, 1978.

80   The popular rejection of a 'patronising' approach is a constant theme of Victorian leisure. It was especially evident in the working men's club movement. See J. Taylor, *Glamour*, and P. Bailey, *Leisure*, chapter five.

81   B. Harrison, *Drink and The Victorians*, 1971, p. 347.

82   S. Yeo, *New Life*, p. 38.

83   The phrase is T. Tholfsen's in his *Working-Class Radicalism in Mid-Victorian England*, 1976, p. 205.

84   For music and the Wesley family see E. Routley, *The Musical Wesleys*, 1968.

85   *Bradford Observer*, 20 February 1891. For similar mixtures see also *ibid.*, 8 and 16 January 1891.

Chapter 4: The popular music industry

1 Mayhew's findings are usefully summarised in D. Cohen and B. Green-wood, *The Buskers*, Newton Abbot, 1981, pp. 135–7.
2 *Leeds Intelligencer*, 18 July 1857.
3 *Musical Herald*, December 1899.
4 D. Cohen and B. Greenwood, *Buskers*, p. 143; R. Pearsall, *Edwardian Popular Music*, Newton Abbot, 1975, pp. 147–8; E. Mackerness, *Somewhere Further North*, Sheffield, 1974, p. 83.
5 F. Crowest, *Phases of Musical England*, 1881, p. 119.
6 D. Cohen & B. Greenwood, *Buskers*, p. 141.
7 R. Pearsall, *Victorian Popular Music*, Newton Abbot, 1973, pp. 189–94.
8 M. T. Bass, *Street Music in the Metropolis*, 1864.
9 H. R. Haweis, *Music and Morals*, 1888 ed., pp. 533–40 gives a surprisingly sympathetic view of street music.
10 R. Roberts, *The Classic Slum*, 1973 ed., p. 124.
11 P. Scholes, *The Oxford Companion to Music*, 1955 ed., pp. 226–35, is a useful outline of the concert's history on a world scale. W. Weber, *Music and the Middle Class*, 1975, is obligatory reading for those seeking an understanding of music's social function in the nineteenth century.
12 M. Kennedy, *The Hallé Tradition*, 1960, p. 30.
13 S. de B. Taylor, *Two Centuries of Music in Liverpool*, 1976, p. 83.
14 E. Lee, *Music of the People*, 1970, pp. 95–6.
15 *Ibid.*, pp. 110–12.
16 What follows is largely based on A. Carse, *The Life of Jullien*, 1951.
17 Anon. 'Origins of Caminado Band etc.' MS in R. V. Marriner & Co. Records, Box 117, Special Collection, Brotherton Library, University of Leeds, p. 67.
18 *Yorkshire Daily Observer*, 30 January 1926; *Bradford Pioneer*, 23 May 1913. The writer was possibly the very young J. B. Priestley.
19 C. E. Hallé and M. Hallé (eds.), *Life and Letters of Sir Charles Hallé*, 1896, p. 143.
20 E. MacKerness, *Somewhere*, p. 43. Bradford was visited by at least seventeen companies between 1856 and 1912. See J. Handby, *History of Opera in Bradford*, Bradford, 1922, *passim*.
21 M. Lubbock, *The Complete Book of Light Opera*, 1962, pp. 65–6, 268.
22 J. Rodgers, *Dr Henry Coward, The Pioneer Chorus-Master*, 1911, p. 11.
23 *Bradford Observer*, 13 January 1890.
24 For Cardus on cricket see B. Dobbs, *Edwardians at Play*, 1973, pp. 119–25.
25 N. Cardus, *Autobiography*, 1947, pp. 16, 247.
26 Based on study of programmes in J. Handby, *Bradford*.
27 See comments in *Yorkshire Daily Observer*, 10 December 1912.
28 For a brief attempt to outline the standing of opera as popular entertainment in the period 1840–1914 see D. Russell, 'Tuppenny opera' in *Opera*, March 1985.
29 A useful general outline in provided by R. Pearsall, *Edwardian*, pp. 17–45, and R. Mander & J. Mitcheson, *Musical Comedy*, 1969.

30   R. Mander & J. Mitcheson, *Comedy*, pp. 12–14.
31   *Ibid.*, p. 15 for plot of *A Gaiety Girl*. The *Era* described it as 'always light, bright and enoyable'. A true product of a changing moral climate.
32   Tony Staveacre, *The Songwriters*, BBC, 1980, pp. 33–55, for Monckton; R. Pearsall, *Edwardian*, p. 19 for the marriage statistics.
33   R. Middleton, 'Popular music of the lower classes' in N. Temperley (ed.), *The Athlone History of Music*, V, 1981, p. 80.
34   Report from the Select Committee on Theatres and Places of Entertainment, 1892, Irish University Press edition, p. 204. The 'definitive' history of the halls is not yet written, although the researches of Peter Bailey should soon bear fruit and provide the academic work historians have long needed. A contemporary work, C. D. Stuart & H. J. Park, *The Variety Stage*, 1895, coupled with D. Cheshire, *Music-Hall in Britain*, Newton Abbot, 1974, provide the best starting-place. Essential bibliographical and reference tools for would-be researchers are D. Howard, *London Theatres and Music-Halls*, 1970, and L. Senelick, D. Cheshire & U. Schneider, *British Music-Hall 1840–1923*, Connecticut, 1981.
35   For origins of London halls see C. D. Stuart & A. J. Park, *Variety*; D. F. Cheshire, *Music-Hall*, pp. 11–20; H. Scott, *The Early Doors*, 1946.
36   Most of this paragraph is in fact based upon that work, W. H. Morton & H. Chance Newton, *Sixty Years' Stage Service*. 1905, especially pp. 1–12.
37   P. Bailey, *Leisure and Class in Victorian England*, 1978, p. 30.
38   *Ibid.*, pp. 30–1.
39   P. Razzell and R. Wainwright (eds.), *The Victorian Working Class*, 1973, pp. 280–2.
40   For Birmingham, *Ibid.*, pp. 318–19. The pattern of growth was not, however, consistent across the country. See K. Barker, 'The performing arts in Newcastle Upon Tyne, 1840–1870' in J. Walton & J. Walvin (eds.), *Leisure in Britain, 1780–1939*, Manchester, 1983, p. 60 for a comparison between 'underdeveloped' Newcastle and 'developed' Sheffield.
41   H. Scott, *Early Doors*, pp. 55–6.
42   *Leeds Mercury*, 20 December 1851.
43   Report from the Select Committee on Theatrical Licences and Regulations, 1866, Irish University Press ed., pp. 44–5.
44   *Ibid.*, p. 38.
45   H. Cunningham, *Leisure in the Industrial Revolution*, 1980, pp. 169–70.
46   There is as yet no 'academic' study of provincial halls, but G. J. Mellor, *Northern Music-Hall*, Newcastle, 1971, is a useful starting-place.
47   H. Cunningham, *Leisure*, p. 170.
48   *Ibid.*; W. McQueen-Pope, *The Melodies Linger On*, 1951, p. 287. The *Lions comiques* were the first music-hall stars, their distinctive imitations of upper-class swells beginning around 1863–64. C. Pulling, *What They Were Singing*, 1952, pp. 183–7.
49   Based on Mellor, *Northern*. Halls were sometimes established in smaller communities than this, but in general they appear to have been the older

singing-saloon type. For a decidedly temporary hall in a small community – it fell down – see the description of Russell's Theatre of Varieties, Maryport, *Era*, 30 March 1889.

50   Such tours can be followed in the pages of the music-hall press, especially the *Era*.

51   For an excellent case study see P. Summerfield, 'The Effingham Arms and the Empire: deliberate selection in the evolution of music-hall in London' in E. & S. Yeo (eds.), *Popular Culture and Class Conflict 1590–1914*, Brighton, 1981.

52   G. Mellor, *Northern*, contains much on syndication. F. Barker, *The House that Stoll Built: The Story of the Coliseum Theatre, 1957*, is also helpful. Here, surely, is a major field for economic historians?

53   P. Honri, *Working the Halls*, Farnborough, 1973, p. 43.

54   *Magnet*, 1 February 1902.

55   *Music-Hall & Theatre Review*, 31 January 1902. Some large halls, however, did undoubtedly use singing-saloons as training grounds.

56   C. D. Stuart & A. J. Park, *Variety*, p. 168; C. MacInnes, *Sweet Saturday Night*, 1967, p. 21.

57   The interviews and obituaries in the music-hall press provide a mass of material.

58   P. Razzell & R. Wainwright, *Victorian*, pp. 280–2; P. Bailey, *Leisure*, pp. 154–5; *The Historical Development of Popular Culture in Britain*, unit 5, 'The Music-Hall', Open University U203, 1981, p. 62.

59   C. B. Hawkins, *Norwich: A social study*, 1910, p. 310; *Musical Herald*, April 1899. Of course, those with little money could find entry nevertheless. For an example of nine people entering a hall on three tickets, P. Thompson, *The Edwardians*, 1977, p. 177.

60   F. Anstey, quoted in R. Mander & J. Mitcheson, *British Music-Hall: A Story in Pictures*, 1965, p. 23. Penny Summerfield, 'Patriotism and Empire: music hall entertainment 1870–1914' in J. Mackenzie (ed.), *Imperialism and Popular Culture*, Manchester, 1986, pp. 22–4 is useful on admission prices and audience structure.

61   Select Committee, 1866, pp. 46–7.

62   *Ibid.*, p. 169.

63   *Ibid.*, p. 260.

64   I mean by this vague term a fairly broad range encompassing superior clerks, teachers, managers and perhaps even some professionals, along with their families. I have been told, though, of a Merseyside accountant who as late as the 1930s disguised himself in 'workingmen's clothes' to avoid being recognised at the Argyll, Birkenhead.

65   The cycling craze is the one most fully documented at present. D. Rubinstein, 'Cycling in the 1890s', *Victorian Studies*, XXI, 1977.

66   D. Cheshire, *Music-Hall*, p. 39.

67   See the splendidly self-congratulatory A. Chevalier & B. Daly, *Albert Chevalier: A record by Himself*, 1895.

68   G. Mellor, *Northern*, pp. 145, 160; A. Chevalier, *Himself*, p. 120.

69   For Marie Lloyd, D. Farson, *Marie Lloyd and Music-Hall*, 1972; G. Mellor, *Northern*, pp. 131–2. It seems to have been fairly common for

managers to 'censor' performances from the 1890s. Even in the repertoire of 'safe' singers, however, a remarkable degree of *double entendre* was allowed.

70   Transcript, anonymous, in author's possession. Essentially, the theatre of variety was of *provincial* origin, designed to capture a new audience.
71   G. Mellor, *Northern*, p. 143 is very informative; *Variety Artistes' Time-Table*, 26 February 1906. The provincial estimate is a personal guess.
72   On attendance, see T. E. Dunville, *Autobiography of an Eccentric Comedian*, 1912, p. 26. Skelmerdine's testimony appears in Select Committee, 1892, p. 244.
73   *Era Almanack*, 1913, pp. 199–208. I had several conflicting results. *Era Almanack*, 1899, quoted in R. Mander and J. Mitcheson, *Music-Hall*, p. 27.
74   *Times*, 24 January 1910; *Illustrated London News*, 15 August 1914. The establishments of the Royal Command Variety performance in 1912 was perhaps the greatest symbol of changing times.
75   *Era*, 30 September 1877.
76   P. Bailey, *Leisure*, p. 153.
77   *Ibid.*, pp. 164–8.

Chapter 5: The music-hall and its music

1   In an albeit extreme case, the programme at the York Empire in the first week of January 1911 contained no singers at all. *York Evening Press*, 10 January 1911.
2   Select Committee, 1866, p. 259.
3   D. Farson, *Marie Lloyd*, p. 25; P. Scholes, *Mirror of Music*, 1, 1944, pp. 90–91; H. Scott (ed.), *English Song Book*, 1926, p. XI.
4   The ubiquitous *Il Trovatore* was one of the most popular choices. It should be noted, however, that at least one commentator claimed that the selection often led to a 'rush to the bar'. *Musicians Report and Journal*, September 1900.
5   *Bradford Telegraph*, 24 March 1914.
6   Charles Coborn, *The Man Who Broke the Bank*, 1928, p. 88. Coborn's is one of the most informative music-hall autobiographies.
7   J. Rodgers, *Coward*, p. 6; R. Nettel, *North Staffordshire Music*, Rickmansworth, 1977, dustjacket autobiography.
8   R. Middleton, 'Popular', in N. Temperley (ed.), *Athlone*, V, pp. 81–7, is an excellent introduction to the origins of distinctive music-hall styles.
9   C. Hamm, *Yesterdays: Popular Song in America*, 1979, pp. 284–325.
10   C. MacInnes, *Saturday*, p. 21; G. Stedman Jones, 'Working-class culture and working-class politics in London, 1870–1900: notes on the remaking of a working class'. *Journal of Social History*, VII, 1974, pp. 481, 490.
11   Quoted in R. Mander & J. Mitcheson, *Music-Hall*, p. 23.
12   For 'On Guard' see H. Scott, *Early Doors*, p. 215. For Godfrey's other material, *Variety Stars*, 1906, pp. 16–18.
13   A. Chevalier, 'On costers and music-halls', *English Illustrated Magazine* (n.d. copy in author's possession), p. 484 and C. Coburn, *Bank*, pp. 63–4

both provide examples of performers making little effort to change their material on provincial tours. Coborn's efforts were not successful in one instance where, in a Kent singing saloon, he sang in praise of coastguards in a village famed for smugglers!

14   *Music-Hall Artists Association Gazette*, 11 May 1887; *Era*, 6 April 1889.
15   A. Chevalier, *Costers*, p. 400. For example of censorship of political material, P. Honri, *Working*, pp. 187–8.
16   This particular song was written to revive a career blighted by Coborn's involvement in early attempts at unionisation of the music-hall 'profession'. See *Bank*, pp. 173–87. Bob Weston and Bert Lee, who came together in 1915, worked office hours and agreed to produce a song a day. M. White, *You Must Remember This*, 1983, p. 240.
17   *Era*, 17 March 1894; 10 February 1894.
18   *Ibid.*, 10 March 1894. My italics.
19   McGlennon's work is very well represented in the British Museum sheet music collection.
20   Better known perhaps as 'My old man said "follow the van" '.
21   Quoted in MacInnes, *Saturday*, p. 55.
22   For the majority, wages were not exceptional, although the £4 per week Coborn was earning as a supporting act in the larger provincial halls by 1878 must have been appealing to entertainers from a working-class background. Stars, however, could receive spectacular reward. Mac-Dermott earned £1250–£1500 a year at his peak in the early 1880s. By the early twentieth century, Harry Lauder may well have been earning £100 per week for brief periods.
23   For Stratton, T. Staveacre, *Songwriters*, pp. 21–2.

Chapter 6: Social and political comment in music-hall song

1   Unless another source is given, all songs discussed here were consulted in the British Museum Music Library. The name in the text refers to the *singer* unless otherwise stated.
2   P. Davison, *Songs of the British Hall*, 1971, pp. 16–19. For more on the *Lions* see C. Pulling, *Singing*, pp. 183–7.
3   *Ibid.*, pp. 58–9.
4   OU, U. 203, Unit 5, pp. 62–8 is informative on women and images of women in the halls. For Hunt's 'girl swindler' songs, folio H. 1257 in British Museum Music Library. Sara Maitland, *Vesta Tilley*, 1986, was published as this book was going to press, and has not been used here as much as it deserves. Maitland ultimately takes a 'progressive' view of Tilley, stressing that she had a special rapport with working class women, perhaps because she 'offered a model of where the New Woman might be going'. However, the intense conservatism, with capital and lower-case 'c's, that runs through Tilley's public and private life, and which is so well documented by Sara Maitland, suggests that the opposite argument is equally tenable.
5   *Era*, 30 September 1877.
6   A. L. Lloyd, *Folk-Song in England*, 1967, Chapter 4.

7   C. MacInnes, *Saturday*, pp. 62–3. One wonders how far music-hall artists were creating regional stereotypes which 'home' audiences imitated.

8   G. S. Jones, *Working class*, p. 497 makes this point beautifully.

9   W. Morton and H. Chance Newton, *Sixty Years*, pp. 9–10; S. McKechnie, *Popular Entertainments Through the Ages*, 1951, p. 145.

10 A. L. Lloyd, *Folk-song*, p. 371–2. For Tyneside songs in general see D. Harker, introduction to *Allan's Tyneside Songs*, Newcastle, 1972 ed., and his 'The making of the Tyneside concert-hall', *Popular Music*, 1, Cambridge, 1981. Harker contrasts the radicalism of the early halls and saloons with the escapism of the later ones.

11 P. Davison, *Songs*, pp. 26–9.

12 For popular attitudes to the police, see especially R. Storch's articles 'The plague of blue locusts: police reform and popular resistance in Northern England, 1840–1857', *International Review of Social History*, XX, 1975 and 'The policeman as domestic missionary: urban discipline and popular culture in Northern England, 1850–1880', *Journal of Social History*, IX, 1976. S. Humphries, *Hooligans or Rebels*, Oxford, 1983, is also invaluable.

13 C. MacInnes, *Saturday*, pp. 96–7.

14 'The Parrot and the Parson' by Frank Archer and Tom Richards, noted above, suggests the mildest of anti-clerical sentiment? Certainly, what Bernard Waites has called 'preachy liberalism' and excessive moralising, whether by clerical or lay moral reformers, was a target for music-hall singers. See 'And Her Golden Hair was Hanging down her Back', P. Davison, *Songs*, p. 85, and G. W. Hunt's 'I am not Such a Saint as I Look'.

15 MacInnes, *Saturday*, pp. 130–1; G. S. Jones, *Working-Class*, p. 492. Jones could not have found a less authentic voice than Chevalier.

16 Anon, *Variety stars*, 1906, pp. 16–18; E. R. Pennell, 'The pedigree of the music hall', *Contemporary Review*, 1892, p. 582.

17 £3,612 8s 4d to be exact. *Era*, 17 April 1912. The song was the first published song produced by the prolific Bob Weston whose last hit was 'What a Mouth' for Tommy Steele in 1960. To produce successful songs over such a period is a remarkable achievement. M. White, *You Must*, pp. 238–42.

18 Composed in 1896 by Oswald Cuthbertson and A. Myers. I have not been able to ascertain its intended audience.

19 P. Davison, *Songs*, pp. 46–9.

20 A. L. Lloyd, *Folk-song*, has many examples of this starting point.

21 MacInnes, *Saturday*, p. 57; Quoted in D. Cheshire, *Music-Hall*, p. 90. In the 'variety' phase after 1900, there does seem to have been a marked decline in material dealing with social and political issues, thus muting the entertainment still further.

22 K. Robbins, *The Eclipse of a Great Power: Modern Britain, 1870–1975*, 1983, is a good introduction.

23 For MacDermott's standing as top comedian, see *Era*, 27 May, 1877. He went bankrupt in 1885, eventually becoming a manager. Of all the stars

of the 'middle' period of music-hall, he is perhaps most worthy of a full-scale biography.

24 The song was ' 'E Talks Just Like a Picture Book' (1894).

25 Collette claimed there had been only one complaint; *Era*, 23 March 1889.

26 Lyrics by Sidney Bourne. This *may* have been intended as a pantomime song, as it does not follow the normal music-hall convention of being published with the name of the singer who had popularised it on the song cover.

27 St Clair later specialised in hymns to bravery such as 'The Skipper's Farewell'. See folio H. 3981 in British Museum Music Library.

28 *Era*, 6 April 1889. In general the music-hall press, anxious to encourage respectable, non-controversial entertainment, was critical of the political song, *Era* 28 November 1885 dismissing them as 'the opinions of the daily papers reproduced in ungrammatical and vapid verse'. Individual managers did sometimes allow strikers to hold meetings in music-halls, however.

29 Laurence Senelick, 'Politics as entertainment: Victorian music-hall songs', *Victorian Studies*, XIX, 1975, p. 165.

30 *Bradford Telegraph*, 24 March 1914.

31 This is forcefully argued by Bernard Waites, *OU U203*, Unit 5, p. 48. In musical culture, Waites posits a split between a Liberal, progressive choral movement and the Conservative, fatalistic music-hall. As a very broad generalisation this seems justifiable. One of the first 'Tory' songs was a direct response to the Licencing Act, composed by Gus Leach, 'I'd Tell You, If I Were a Little Fly'. It is noteworthy, however, that this song attacks the act for closing pubs but not West End clubs.

32 T. H. S. Escott quoted in G. S. Jones, *Working-Class*, p. 490.

33 J. Wolff, *The Social Production of Art*, 1981, is indispensable for those seeking an entry to the arcane world of cultural theory and literary criticism.

34 The consensus, if there is one, amongst media sociologists would still seem to echo Joseph Klapper's contention that 'persuasive man's communication is in general more likely to reinforce the existing opinions of its audience than it is to change such opinions'. Quoted in J. Tunstall (ed.), *Media Sociology*, 1970, p. 22.

35 It is hardly surprisingly that many – although not all – socialists were hostile to the halls. See I. Britain, *Fabianism and Culture*, 1982, pp. 223–52, 259–61. Many objections were 'moral', but the fantasy world of music-hall was not appreciated.

Chapter 7: Patriotism, jingoism and imperialism

1 J. A. Hobson, *The Psychology of Jingoism*, 1901. Henry Pelling in 'British labour and imperialism', *Popular Politics and Society in Late Victorian Britain*, 2nd ed., 1979, pp. 87–8, manages to reach a tentative conclusion on the evidence of one song. Senelick *Entertainment*, gives serious consideration to the issue, as does P. Summerfield, 'Patriotism and empire: music-hall entertainments 1870–1914' in J. Mackenzie (ed.), *Imperialism*

and Popular Culture, Manchester, 1986.

2   H. Cunningham, 'The language of patriotism, 1750–1914', *History Workshop Journal*, XII, 1981, p. 25. If space permitted analysis of sketches here as well as songs, the weight of patriotism would be even more striking.

3   J. Hobson, *Jingoism*, p. 1.

4   R. Price, *An Imperial War and the British Working Class*, 1972, sees popular enthusiasm for the Boer War as essentially a lower-middle, rather than a working-class, phenomenon. J. Mackenzie, *Propaganda and Empire*, Manchester, 1984, along with many of the contributors in his *Imperialism and Popular Culture*, argues for the existence of a deep-seated, cross-class imperial consciousness for much of the period 1880–1960.

5   See advertisement for Albert in *Era*, 15 April 1877.

6   R. T. Shannon, *Gladstone and the Bulgarian Agitation*, 1963; R. Blake, *Disraeli*, 1969 ed., pp. 570–654.

7   The full text can at present be found only in the British Museum. P. Summerfield, *Patriotism*, p. 25 gives the first verse and chorus. It is of course possible that in performance, the song, especially when MacDermott was being encouraged by a vociferous audience, gained a far more aggressive tone than is suggested by its opening phrase.

8   See advertisements in *Era*, June 1877 to July 1878.

9   G. S. Jones, *Working Class*, p. 493; *Era*, 6 May 1877, suggests the song was first performed at the Sun on 2 May. One singer remembered Saturday audiences at the Forresters as 'a rough crowd'. Ada Reeve, *Take it For a Fact*, 1954, p. 28. For the song in provinces see MacDermott's *Era* advertisements 21 October, 2 December.

10 See report on People's Palace, Bristol, *Music-Hall and Theatre Review*, 4 January 1895.

11 See also L. Senelick, *Entertainment*, p. 176. Certainly, after 1870, with occasional exceptions, the Irish in Britain were less often viewed as a 'problem'.

12 MacInnes, *Saturday*, p. 77.

13 'The Last Good-bye', sung by Florrie Forde.

14 B. Porter, *The Lion's Share*, 1975, is the best general introduction to the British Empire. For a brief but excellent guide to the economic issues and a full bibliography, P. J. Cain, *Economic Foundations of British Overseas Expansion, 1815–1914*.

15 See R. Hyam, *Britain's Imperial Century, 1815–1914*, 1976, p. 27. Admittedly, the really significant shift away from the USA does not begin until about 1900.

16 'If England to herself be true', quoted in P. Summerfield, *Patriotism*, p. 27–8.

17 See MacInnes, *Saturday*, p. 81.

18 Quoted in C. Pulling, *Singing*, p. 78. *Music-Hall and Theatre Review*, 21 December 1900, when discussing pantomime 'big scenes' told readers they would 'see much symbolism of the new Imperial spirit, as shown in the splendid way in which the sons of the Empire have come to the

assistance of the Motherland'.

19 Quoted in MacInnes, *Saturday*, p. 116.

20 Transcribed from the LP *Oh, What a Lovely War*, WRC SH130.

21 B. Gainer, *The Alien Invasion*, 1972; J. A. Garrard, *The English and Immigration, 1800–1900*, 1971.

22 On German immigration, H. Kellenbenz, 'German immigrants in Britain' in C. Holmes (ed.), *Immigrants and Minorities in British Society*, 1978. For attitudes to Jewish immigrants, J. Garrard, *Immigration*, especially pp. 75–9, and N. Deakin, 'The vitality of a tradition' in C. Holmes, *Immigrants*, pp. 161–3.

23 This was the infamous Jameson Raid.

24 *Times*, 6 January 1896.

25 Quoted in *Era*, 20 February 1909.

26 *Era*, 17 April 1909. The hall in question was the Euston.

27 *Encore*, 20 August 1914.

28 *Yorkshire Evening Press*, 29 December 1914.

29 *Encore*, 8 October 1914.

30 Published by a small Hastings company, Placette, this may not have been a widely-performed number, but it does illustrate the extremes that were on offer.

31 'We're going to fight for you'; 'Now you've got your khaki on'.

32 T. Pakenham, *The Boer War*, 1979, for a general history.

33 *Music-Hall and Theatre Review*, 25 May 1900 gives a nationwide picture of Mafeking celebrations.

34 'The heroes of Mafeking' (1900); 'The Only Way' (1900).

35 *Music-Hall and Theatre Review*, 20 December 1901.

36 MacInnes, *Saturday*, p. 80.

37 'Dear Old Bobs' (1900).

38 MacInnes, *Saturday*, p. 80.

39 *Era*, 28 November 1885. When George Mozart, manager of the Chiswick Empire, made a recruiting speech in 1914 one of the audience interrupted to suggest that if it was so worthwhile why hadn't he gone? *Encore*, 1 October 1914.

40 H. Pelling, *Politics*, p. 88. Writers were quick to realise which overseas episodes were not the object of strong public interest. See *Music-Hall and Theatre Review*, 21 December 1900 on the public's lack of interest in the Boxer Rebellion and managements' subsequent response. This does suggest that material included in performances did reflect the 'public mood'.

41 R. Roberts, *The Classic Slum*, 1973, p. 182; 'Tommy' in *Barrack Room Ballads*, 1892.

42 *OU, U203*, 5, pp. 71–2.

43 J. Taylor, *From Self-Help to Glamour*, History Workshop pamphlet, VII, 1972, p. 49.

44 'I don't want to fight' (1878). The song also attacks war-mongering newspapers and politicians quite powerfully; Quoted in W. MacQueen–Pope, *The Melodies Linger On*, 1951, p. 320.

45 P. Davison, *Songs*, p. 110–13. For historians playing up the element of

parody see B. Waites, *OU 203*, unit 5, p. 71; H. Cunningham, *Patriotism*, pp. 25–6; S. Maitland, *Tilley*, p. 125.

46 'I wonder what next they will do', by V. Davis and C. Merrion. Penny Summerfield also suggests possible professional rivalry between Campbell and MacDermott. *Patriotism*, p. 39.

47 'The Seventh Royal Fusiliers' (1893); 'The Gordon Highlanders' (1898).

48 See I. F. Clarke, *Voices Prophesying War*, Oxford, 1966. J. Mackenzie, *Propaganda* includes an excellent survey of modes of popular imperial expression at this time.

49 *Ibid.*, pp. 145–6.

Chapter 8: The emergence of a popular tradition

1 N. Temperley, *The Athlone History of Music, V*, 1981, p. 4. Only in London *might* this have been true.

2 Anonymous press cutting dated 21 January 1904 in Huddersfield Glee and Madrigal Society collection, Kirklees Archives Department.

3 See Barker's advert in *Cornet*, January 1898; *ibid.*, November 1898.

4 D. W. Krummell, 'Music publishing' in N. Temperley, *Athlone*, p. 49. It should also be remembered that lyrics (and sometimes tunes as well) reached a wide public from beyond the confines of what is normally termed the publishing 'industry'. Broadsides remained an important source well into the nineteenth century, while pages of *The People* and the *News of the World*, and even the backs of ½d 'Lucky Bags', proved useful sources for singers of popular song.

5 The 'official' history, from which much of this is taken and which has greatly influenced some later writers is Anon., *A Short History of Cheap Music*, 1887. For a recent survey, M. Hurd, *Vincent Novello and Company*, 1981.

6 Anon., *Cheap*, p. 51.

7 See below.

8 P. Young, *A History of British Music*, 1967, p. 423.

9 J. Scott, 'The Evolution of the Brass Band and its Repertoire in Northern England', unpublished PhD thesis, Sheffield University, 1970. *Brass Band News*, March 1890.

10 J. Scott, *Evolution*, p. 250.

11 *Ibid.*, p. 249 for Wright and Round; see the list in the *Brass Band Annual*, Sibsey, Lincs., 1899, p. 32.

12 *Brass Band News*, January 1890.

13 W. Cudworth, *Condition of the Industrial Classes of Bradford*, 1887, p. 58.

14 C. Ehrlich, *The Piano: A History*, 1976, pp. 98–105; F. R. Spark, *Memories of My Life*, Leeds, 1913, p. 159.

15 F. Crowest, *Phases of Musical England*, 1881, pp. 200–1.

16 Kay Pearson, *Life in Hull: From Then Till Now*, Hull, 1980, p. 32.

17 The best introduction to the concertina is the two-part article by N. Wayne, *Folk Review*, March and April 1974. Interestingly, it was originally conceived as a concert-hall instrument.

18 On the emergence of brass instrument makers, J. Scott, *Evolution*, p. 86.

For Boosey and Bessons, see V. & G. Brand, *Brass Bands in the Twentieth Century*, Letchworth, 1979, pp. 21, 30; and A. Rose, *Talks with Bandsmen*, 1895.

19   The best introduction to the band service industry is simply to work through the advertisements in the trade press. For Beever see J. F. Russell & J. H. Elliot, *The Brass Band Movement*, 1936, p. 165.

20   E. Coates, *Suite in Four Movements*, 1953, pp. 8, 28.

21   J. Craven, *A Bronte Moorland Village and its People: A History of Stanbury*, Keighley, 1907, p. 129.

22   Many of the bandsmen 'biographied' in band journals appear to have been pianists.

23   C. Ehrlich, *Piano*, p. 109; F. J. Crowest, *Phases*, p. 191; R. Roberts, *The Classic Slum*, 1973, p. 153.

24   J. Bullock, *Bowers Row*, East Ardsley, 1976, p. 54.

25   *Yorkshire Observer Budget*, 11 March 1911; 18 March 1911. Sheffield United supporters favoured the more menacing 'Rowdy Dowdy Boys'. See R. Palmer (ed.), 'The Minstrel of Quarry Bank: reminiscences of George Dunn', *Oral History*, XI, 1983, p. 66.

26   *Yorkshire Daily Observer*, 30 January 1902; H. Cunningham, 'Leisure' in J. Benson (ed.), *The Working Class in England, 1875–1914*, 1985, p. 142.

27   Carole Pegg, 'Factors affecting the musical choices of audiences in East Suffolk, England', *Popular Music*, IV, Cambridge, 1984; G. Dunn, *The Fellowship of Song*, 1980.

28   *Musical Home Journal*, 10 March, 1908.

29   A Hutchings, *Church Music in the Nineteenth Century*, 1967; N. Temperley, *The Music of the English Parish Church*, Cambridge, 1979.

30   V. Gammon, ' "Not appreciated in Worthing?" Class expression and popular song texts in mid-nineteenth century Britain', *Popular Music*, IV, 1984, pp. 19–20 especially, for Burstow; B. Pegg, *Folk*, 1976, pp. 58–60.

31   In January 1978, I taped the playing of Joe Haynes, a Bradford concertina player, then in his mid-eighties. His repertoire, largely learned between 1906–1930, included 'Salut d'amour', an extract from overture to *Don Giovanni*, 'In a monastery garden' and several hymns. This gives a good insight into the 'typical' mixture enjoyed by the most competent players.

32   R. Nettel, 'The influence of the Industrial Revolution on English music', *Proceedings of the Royal Musical Association*, 1945–46, p. 27; J. Sutcliffe Smith, *The Story of Music in Birmingham*, 1945 p. 13.

33   K. H. MacDermott, *Sussex Church Music in the Past*, Chichester, 1923; V. Gammon, 'Babylonian Performances: the rise and suppression of popular Church music, 1666–1870, in E. & S. Yeo, *Popular Culture and Class Conflict*, 1590–1914, Brighton, 1981.

34   *Ibid.*, p. 76.

35   *Ibid.*, pp. 79–80.

36   S. Baring-Gould, *Old Country Life*, 1895, p. 244.

37   Quoted in E. MacKerness, *A Social History of English Music*, 1964, p. 113. One of the most striking examples of musical enthusiasm in these

regions was the habit of naming people, and less often, streets, after musicians. For Mendelssohn Fawcett *et al.*, see D. Russell, 'The Popular Musical Societies of the Yorkshire Textile District, 1850–1914', unpublished D.Phil thesis, University of York, 1980, appendix 4.

38   E. Routley, *The Musical Wesleys*, 1968.
39   Quoted in J. S. Curwen, *Studies in Worship Music*, 1881, p. 31.
40   *Ibid.*, p. 26.
41   W. Cudworth, *Music in Bradford*, 1885, pp. 7–15.
42   G. Wright, *The Fawcetts of Eccleshill and Horsforth*, 1974; S. Baring-Gould, *Yorkshire Oddities*, 1, 1877, pp. 109–16; W. Watson, *Idlethorpe*, Bradford, 1950, pp. 451–3.
43   W. Millington, *Sketches of Local Musicians and Musical Societies*, Pendlebury, 1884 pp. 16–17; R. P. Elbourne, *Music and Tradition in Early Industrial Lancashire, 1780–1840*, pp. 40–1. These books are obligatory reading for this period. Similar patterns existed even until quite late in the nineteenth century in other parts of England. W. Bush, 'A family of shoemakers and musicians: The Billinghams of Kislingbury', *Northamptonshire Past and Present*, 11, 1954–59. See note 53 for festivals.
44   E. P. Thompson, *The Making of the English Working Class*, 1968 ed., pp. 321–5.
45   J. Spencer Curwen in *Leisure Hour*, January 1891 reprinted in *Bradford Observer*, 2 January 1891; W. Smith, *Old Yorkshire*, V, 1884, p. 235–8.
46   Bradford Brass Band Treasurer's Book 1854–56, Bradford Archives, shows 'settled in county court' against the name of four unfortunate members; J. Sutcliffe, Smith, *The Life of William Jackson*, Leeds, 1926, pp. 24–5; R. Elbourne, *Music and Tradition*, p. 163.
47   J. S. Curwen, *Music at the Queen's Accession*, 1897, pp. 29–30.
48   Keighley Choral Society minute book, Keighley Public Library, 8 February 1848. The Society gave him five shillings as a 'present'.
49   R. Elbourne, *Music and Tradition*, pp. 120–1; W. Millington, *Sketches*, pp. 24–5.
50   For a general background see R. Myers, *Handel's Messiah*, New York, 1948.
51   *Ibid.*, p. 229.
52   *Halifax Courier*, 2 December 1920; E. Hargrave, 'Musical Leeds in Eighteenth Century', *Publications of the Thoresby Society*, XXVIII, p. 329.
53   R. Elbourne, *Music and Tradition*, p. 42. Choral festivals, usually held in parish churches and intended to raise money for local charities and especially hospitals, were a common feature of provincial life by the late eighteenth century. For a full history see B. Pritchard, 'The music festival and the choral society in England in the eighteenth and nineteenth centuries', unpublished Ph.D thesis, University of Birmingham, 1968.
54   E. Routley, *Wesleys*, pp. 17–18.
55   J. T. Lightwood, *Stories of Methodist Music, Nineteenth Century*, 1928.
56   A. Taylor, *Brass Bands*, Manchester, 1979, pp. 10–23.
57   *Ibid.*, p. 17.

58   *Ibid.*, p. 8.
59   W. K. Wilmhurst & S. Crowther *The Huddersfield Choral Society*, Hud-
     dersfield, 1961 pp. 8–9, 13–14. Like many early societies they met in a
     public house, on a night near the full moon so that they could find their
     way home.
60   W. Cudworth, *Bradford*, pp. 10–11.
61   *Ibid.*, pp. 6–7.
62   W. Weber, *Music and the Middle Classes*, 1975, p. 116. In fairness he is
     probably referring to music in capital cities; *Halifax Guardian*, 3 April
     1869.
63   J. Rule, *The Experience of Labour in Eighteenth-Century Britain*, 1981; E.
     P. Thompson, 'Time, work-discipline and industrial capitalism', *Past
     and Present*, XXXVIII, 1968.
64   E. Sigsworth, *Black Dyke Mills*, Liverpool, 1958, pp. 4–72 provides an
     invaluable outline.
65   R. Malcolmson, *Popular Recreations in English Society, 1700–1850*, Cam-
     bridge, 1973, is especially pessimistic. For a partial counter-balance, H.
     Cunningham, *Leisure and the Industrial Revolution*, 1980.
66   Quoted in E. P. Thompson, *Working Class*, p. 314.

Chapter 9: Brass bands

 1   *Brass Band News*, November 1889.
 2   A. Howkins, *Whitsun in Nineteenth-Century Oxfordshire*, History
     Workshop pamphlet, No. 8, Oxford, 1973, p. 30.
 3   *Brass Band News*, July 1895.
 4   Based on analysis of championship results in A. Taylor, *Brass Bands*,
     Appendix One.
 5   E. Jackson, 'The Origin and Promotion of Brass Band Contests',
     Musical Opinion, March 1896; A. Taylor, *Brass Bands*, pp. 33–59.
 6   See V. & G. Brand, *Brass Bands in the Twentieth Century*, Letchworth,
     1979, pp. 72–91, for the full history of contesting at Belle Vue.
 7   Almost 90 per cent of English contests in 1895 were held in the North
     and Midlands. Only seven were held south of Luton. Based on *Brass
     Band Annual*, Sibsey, 1896, pp. 49–70. For the National, J. F. Russell
     & J. H. Elliot, *The Brass Band Movement*, 1936, pp. 171–6. *British
     Bandsman*, 5 October 1907, includes a large number of press reports on
     the previous week's national which communicate something of the
     flavour of the event.
 8   Thirty-one contests in Durham and Northumberland, thirty-seven in
     Lancashire. *Brass Band Annuals* 1896, *loc. cit.*
 9   A. Taylor, *Brass Bands*, Appendix One.
10   E. Coates, *Suite*, p. 13. It is significant that the Staffordshire mining
     district did not produce any particularly strong banding tradition,
     unlike other mining areas. The fact that local miners did not normally
     live in separate mining communities but in larger towns, may well have
     been crucial here. For Staffordshire miners, P. Razzell & R. Wain-
     wright, *The Victorian Working Class*, 1973, pp. XXXII–XXXIII.

11   For further detail D. Russell, Yorkshire Textile District, pp. 88–92.
12   *Cornet*, January 1894; *Brass Band Annual*, 1898, Sibsey, p. 32.
13   *Brass Band News*, February 1910.
14   The furthest reaches of the Holme Valley, for example, were not touched by public transport until the 1920s, which made access to commercial entertainment difficult.
15   *Brass Band News*, 7 October 1911.
16   *Ibid.*, January 1888 and January 1889.
17   *Brass Band Annual*, Sibsey, 1896, pp. 35–6.
18   R. Pearsall, *Victorian*, p. 199.
19   B. Boon, *Play the Music Play*, 1966, is the standard history of Salvation Army bands.
20   For a defection see *Brass Band Annual*, Sibsey, 1897, p. 31.
21   H. Mortimer with A. Lynton, *Harry Mortimer on Brass*, Sherborne, 1981, p. 67.
22   T. Cooper, *Brass Bands of Yorkshire*, Clapham, 1974, pp. 81–2; *Brass Band Annual*, Sibsey, 1896, p. 35.
23   For fuller details, D. Russell, Yorkshire Textile District, pp. 56–8.
24   A. Taylor, *Labour and Love: An oral history of the brass band movement*, 1983, p. 16.
25   Park concerts could be very unsatisfactory events. *Keighley Labour Journal*, 5 June 1897, remarked: 'The selection abounded with hidden melodies – hidden by the noise of the children playing round the bandstand'.
26   *British Bandsman*, October 1888.
27   *Leeds Mercury*, 10 June 1856.
28   *Yorkshireman*, 3 August 1878, 17 August 1878, 12 September 1878.
29   D. Russell, Yorkshire Textile District, p. 61.
30   *British Bandsman*, 1 January 1910.
31   *Brass Band Annual, 1896*, pp. 19–23.
32   *Manchester Guardian*, 25 July 1861, claimed that the band cost Salt 'more than £1,000 per annum, besides constant treats and tea-drinkings'. The band did not finally fold until 1895. Anon, *Shipley Through the Camera*, Shipley, 1902. The dissolution of Leeds Forge is dealt within *Brass Band Annual*, 1898, p. 29.
33   J. Scott, *Evolution*, p. 136.
34   *Ibid.*, pp. 21–106 is an excellent guide to band instrumentation and technical development. For valves see also, P. Bate, *The Trumpet and Trombone*, 1972, pp. 141–82.
35   W. Horwood, *Adolphe Sax 1814–1894*, 1980, is an excellent guide.
36   A. Taylor, *Brass Bands*, p. 31.
37   *Leeds Intelligencer*, 27 December 1851.
38   R. Marr, *Music and Musicians at the Edinburgh International Exhibition*, Edinburgh, 1887, pp. 131–2.
39   *Amateur Band Teachers Guide*, Liverpool, 1889, p. 2.
40   J. Scott, *Evolution*, p. 124.
41   It is likely that the solo instruments, especially the cornet, were dominated by younger players. Good teeth and firm gums are an aid to brass

playing and obviously the younger element would tend to be best equipped! More work needs to be done on the age structure of popular music in general.

42 *British Bandsman*, 12 July 1902.
43 *Ibid.*, 16 and 23 August, 20 September 1902.
44 Many bandsmen are still critical of the inclusion of percussion. Certainly, percussionists do have a tendency to use every single part of their equipment even in the shortest pieces.
45 H. Mortimer with A. Lynton, *On Brass*, p. 15; I am grateful to Harry Lambert for the story of the Paleys and also for many helpful hints and encouragements at the early stages of my work.
46 W. Millington, *Sketches*, p. 24; M. Marrus (ed.), *The Emergence of Leisure*, New York, 1974, pp. 5–6, 8–9.
47 *Brass Band Annual*, 1895, p. 29; *British Bandsman*, June 1888.
48 *Cornet*, July 1893. Much of the 'folklore' has a factual base.
49 *Ibid.*, December 1898.
50 A. Taylor, *Brass Bands*, p. 25. Wombwell's Band had a remarkably high reputation especially in the early and middle part of the century and was an undoubted inspiration to bandsmen.
51 For Gladney, *British Bandsman*, May 1909; P. Hammond and R. Horricks, *Music on Record, 1, Brass Bands*, Cambridge, 1980, p. 69. For Owen, J. Russell & J. Elliot, *Movement*, pp. 144–6, 178–80.
52 *Cornet*, March 1904; J. Russell & J. Elliot, *Movement*, pp. 147–9. P. Gammond and R. Horricks, *Record*, give good biographies of Rimmer, Pearce and Halliwell, pp. 72, 87–8, 86.
53 *British Bandsman*, April 1891. This is a description of Besses o'th' Barn at work, but most top bands had a similar approach.
54 V. & G. Brand (eds.), *Twentieth Century*, p. 39.
55 A. Taylor, *Labour and Love*, p. 18.
56 The phrase is from E. MacKerness, *Social*, p. 166.
57 For a splendid history see G. Pearson, *Hooligan: A History of Respectable Fears*, 1983.
58 *Bradford Observer*, 2 September 1858. The *Dead March* appears to have been used quite frequently as a mode of expressing disapproval. For use by a football crowd, see R. Palmer ed., 'The Minstrel of Quarry Bank: reminiscences of George Dunn; *Oral History*, XI, 1983, p. 66.
59 Interview with Cecil Dowling. Transcript in author's possession.
60 *British Bandsman*, July 1888.
61 *Cornet*, July 1893; *Brass Band News*, July 1893; *Ibid.*, September 1895.
62 *British Bandsmen*, October 1888.
63 For a stimulating appraisal of rough and respectable see P. Bailey, ' "Will the real Bill Banks please stand up?" Towards a role analysis of mid-Victorian working-class respectability', *Journal of Social History*, XII, 1979. See also D. Russell, Yorkshire Textile District, note 45, p. 402.
64 A. Taylor, *Brass Bands*, p. 87.
65 For lengthier, if equally inconclusive, discussion over terminology, see D. Russell, Yorkshire Textile District, pp. 232–4.

66 *British Bandsman*, 2 April 1910. It was still sometimes necessary to indulge in a little subterfuge, especially at Sunday afternoon concerts where sacred music was normally required, sometimes actually stipulated by local by-law. In September 1900, *The Musicians Report and Journal*, noted the overture to *Maritana* being played under the title *The Fall of Babylon*.

67 J. Scott, Evolution, p. VII.

68 *Ibid.*, p. 195.

69 *Bradford Observer*, 9 August 1860.

70 *Brass Band Annual, 1897*, pp. 68–71.

71 *British Bandsman*, 2 February 1907.

72 *Ibid.*, 4 April 1914.

73 For a general introduction to Wagner in Britain see P. Scholes, *Mirror of Music*, 1, 1947, pp. 251–6.

74 *Musical Progress*, August 1914; W. J. Galloway, *Musical England*, 1910, p. 206.

75 For Iles (1871–1951), who discovered brass bands in 1898 when killing time on a Manchester business trip by visiting Belle Vue, see especially J. Russell & J. Elliot, *Movement*, pp. 173–80; P. Gammond & R. Horricks, *Record*, pp. 76–7.

76 *British Bandsman*, 5 October 1907.

77 *Ibid.*, 6 September 1913; P. Gammond & R. Horricks, *Record*, p. 58.

78 *British Bandsman*, 27 September 1913; *Musical Progress* October 1913; J. Russell & J. Elliot, *Movement*, pp. 180–1.

79 He received a lengthy and sympathetic obituary in *Halifax Courier*, 2 May 1925.

80 D. Russell, Yorkshire Textile District, p. 214.

81 Details of testpieces from A. Taylor, *Brass Bands*, Appendix One, of first performances from A. Lowenberg, *Annals of Opera*, 1943.

82 G. Dyson, *Fiddling While Rome Burns*, 1954, p. 11.

83 J. Scott, *Evolution*, p. 259. See also J. Russell and J. Elliot, *Movement*, p. 129.

84 *British Bandsman*, 12 January 1907. For a bandsman at a Wagner orchestral concert in Leeds, *Musical Progress*, January 1914. As will be seen later band soloists were often hired by travelling opera companies.

85 *British Bandsman*, 17 June 1911.

86 D. Russell, Yorkshire Textile District, pp. 216–17.

87 Greenhead Park concert programme, 22 July 1903, Kirklees Central Library.

88 *British Bandsman*, 11 July 1914.

89 *Brass Band News*, October 1889. I discovered twenty-two in the Yorkshire textile district between *c.* 1885–1914.

90 For the early history of bands in this area, *Cornet*, August 1903; *British Bandsman*, 8 June 1907.

91 *Ibid.*, 3 August 1907; transcript of interview in author's possession.

92 Ernest Morris, *The History and Art of Change Ringing*, Wakefield, 1974 ed.; P. Bedford, *An Introduction to English Handbell Ringing*, Chemsford, 1974, and N. Poore Tufts, *The Art of Handbell Ringing*,

1962, provide good introductions to an undeservedly neglected area.

93   P. Bedford, *Introduction*, p. 6; N. Poore Tufts, *Art*, p. 20.

94   *British Bandsman*, 3 September 1902.

95   P. Bedford, *Introduction*, p. 20, J. Scott, Evolution p. 155; For a detailed breakdown of Crosland Moor United's repertoire, *British Bandsman*, 12 August 1903; Lindley & Wagner, *British Bandsman* 13 July 1907.

96   *Ibid.*, 20 July 1907.

97   P. E. P., *Arts Enquiry*, 1949, p. 113. See also H. Meller, *Leisure and the Changing City*, 1870–1914, p. 224.

98   *Times*, 18 October 1902.

99   P. Scholes, *Mirror*, 1, p. 405.

100 See, for example, the report of the Battersea branch of the Peoples' Entertainment Society, *Musical Times*, July 1883.

101 The 'Surprise' was a particular favourite.

102 *Musical Times*, June 1902.

103 *Ibid.*, July 1903. It is probable that the professionals did make a substantial difference, for things were less happy the next year in their absence. *Ibid.*, June 1904.

Chapter 10: Choral societies

1   More limited work opportunities for women, with consequent curtailing of economic freedom, may be a factor in the continued dominance of male-voice choirs in Wales to 1914.

2   The Blackpool Glee and Madrigal Society took fifteen prizes at these two contests between 1900 and 1910.

3   P. Scholes, *Mirror*, 1, pp. 23–38 provides a good outline of London activity; pp. 28–30 for Leslie. However, as with bands, some commentators felt that the easy availability of professional performance limited public interest in amateur performance. See *Musical Herald*, August 1896, 'A symposium on choral societies'.

4   J. Sutcliffe Smith, *The Story of Music in Birmingham*, 1945, p. 57; G. F. Sewell, *A History of the Bradford Festival Choral Society*, Bradford, 1907, p. 45.

5   *Musical Herald*, March 1889; A. L. Lloyd, *Folk Song in England*, 1967 ed., p. 316; G. S. Jones, 'Working-class culture and working-class politics in London 1870–1900', *Journal of Social History*, VII, 1974, p. 498. Weber's data on the London-based Sacred Harmonic Society in the 1830s and 1840s does suggest a picture not dissimilar from that developed below, although his social categories are rather awkward. W. Weber, *Middle Class*, p. 103.

6   W. J. Galloway, *Musical*, p. 133.

7   The remainder of this section is based on D. Russell, Yorkshire Textile District, pp. 66–86.

8   See G. Routh, *Occupation and Pay in Great Britain, 1906–1960*, Cambridge, 1965, pp. 3–6, 155–7.

9   Given the limitations of trade directories, it is not possible to give the

occupation of male singers living in the parental home. The figures in brackets refer to the head of household's occupation and are *not* included in the final percentages.

10 See D. Russell, Textile District, Appendix Two.

11 D. Ryott, *John Barran's of Leeds*, 1951; E. K. Clark, *Kitsons of Leeds*, 1938. P. Branca, *Silent Sisterhood*, 1975, p. 18, notes the restricted role of married middle-class women. Even choral societies, if Leeds and Huddersfield were typical, offered more opportunity to single middle-class women than to married ones. In 1894 about three quarters of the Leeds Philharmonic sopranos and contraltos in social groups 1–3 were unmarried.

12 In general the working class, especially the unskilled, seemed to have a well-honed hostility towards organised groupings of *any* sort.

13 P. Thompson, *The Edwardians*, 1977, pp. 81–90; on clothing industry opportunity, P. Stearns, 'Working-class women in Britain, 1870–1914', in M. Vicinus, *Suffer and Be Still*, 1972, p. 110. Teaching was an especially important 'white collar' avenue.

14 The two choirs have been conflated because the Leeds Prize Musical Union grew out of the Burley choir.

15 B. Dobbs, *Edwardians at Play*, 1973, pp. 37–64, 89–96 makes a good introduction to the amateur professional split. A. Mason, *Association Football and English Society 1863–1915* 1980, and E. Dunning and K. Sheard, *Barbarians, Gentlemen and Players*, 1979, for more detailed accounts.

16 A number of Edwardian choralists when interviewed remembered the fashionable glitter of city centre concerts. Leeds Philharmonic subscription ledgers in Leeds City Public Library.

17 G. F. Sewell, *Bradford Festival*, p. 243.

18 M. Hartley & J. Ingilby, *Life and Tradition in West Yorkshire*, 1976, p. 94.

19 Bradford Festival Choral Society minutes, 1 March 1897; *Yorkshire Evening Post*, 7 February 1930.

20 Leeds Philharmonic concert programmes in Leeds City Public Library, in conjunction with trade directories.

21 Leeds Prize Musical Union minutes, 21 September 1895 in conjunction with local trade directories.

22 For control of soccer clubs see especially S. Yeo, *Religion and Voluntary Organisations in Crisis*, 1976, pp. 189–96; H. Cunningham, *The Volunteer Force*, 1975.

23 The Victorians had an obsession with 'monster choirs', numbers symbolising success. These were usually associated with religious or charitable events. Thirty thousand Sunday-school teachers and pupils formed a 'choir' at the 1852 Halifax Sunday-school jubilee. *Leeds Intelligencer*, 5 June 1852.

24 Huddersfield Choral Society rollbooks.

25 P. Giles, *The Counter-Tenor*, 1982, p. 52.

26 *Ibid.*, pp. 52–70 is excellent on the musical changes.

27 Interview with James Petty, transcript in author's possession.

28 Bradford Festival Choral Society minutes, 17 December 1890; interview with Annie Smith, transcript in author's possession.
29 J. Rodgers, *Dr. Henry Coward, The Pioneer Chorus Master*, 1911; W. Stockley, *Fifty Years of Music in Birmingham*, Birmingham 1913; *Musical Herald*, December 1896, *British Bandsmen*, 21 January 1911.
30 Leeds Philharmonic Letter Books, 29 January 1896, 25 March 1901, 12 March 1913.
31 W. Wilmhurst and S. Crowther, *Huddersfield Choral*, p. 9.
32 Bradford Festival Choral Society minute book, 3 February 1887 and *Bradford Observer* 4 February 1887.
33 See *Mirror*, 1, Chapter Three.
34 *Musical Times*, February 1896. As a member of Leeds Philharmonic he would have to sing the work too.
35 T. Finney, 'The oratorio and cantata market: Britain, Germany, America *c*. 1830–1910' in A. Jacobs (ed.), *Choral Music*, 1963, p. 219.
36 Quoted in R. Pearsall, *Victorian*, p. 143.
37 *Mirror*, 1, pp. 143–4.
38 C. Reid, 'Britain from Stanford to Vaughan Williams *c*. 1880–1939' in A. Jacobs, *Choral*, p. 272.
39 G. F. Sewell, *Bradford Festival*, p. 184 and p. 261; *Musical Times*, April 1894, *Bradford Observer*, 6 March 1901.
40 P. Scholes, *Mirror*, 1, p. 115.
41 L. Baily, *Gilbert and Sullivan and their World*, 1973, p. 59.
42 *Musical Herald*, August 1896; *Yorkshire Daily Observer*, 1 February 1910; R. Roberts, *Slum*, p. 151.
43 *Musical Times*, November 1891; January 1892; April 1891.
44 The event has recently and successfully been revived as a brass band contest. For a criticism of 'pot-hunting', *Yorkshire Post* 18 June, 1894.
45 B. Lonsdale, *History of Saltaire Methodist Church*, Bradford, 1968, p. 8.
46 This is based on reading of the programmes and press cuttings in minute books of Leeds Musical Union.
47 *Competition Festival Record*, November 1908; November 1910.
48 *Ibid.*, July 1909.
49 *Halifax Guardian*, 25 February 1909; *Competition Festival Record*, July 1909; *Halifax Guardian*, 23 February 1895; *Ibid.*, 14 February 1895.

Chapter 11: Music and social change

1 See, for example, J. H. White, *A Short History of Bramley Band*, 1906, p. 25.
2 Interview with Cecil Dowling, transcript in author's possession.
3 W. Watson, *Idlethorpe*, p. 457.
4 *British Bandsman*, 16 August 1902 gives an account of King Cross Band from Halifax spending nine days in London during the coronation celebrations.
5 *British Bandsman* June 1891 and J. Russell & J. Elliot, *Movement*, pp. 178–80.
6 H. Coward, *Round the World on Wings of Song*, 1933; *Yorkshire Observer*,

30 June 1906; C. M. Cudworth, *Photographs of Old Horbury*, p. 45 (my pagination); M. Hartley and J. Ingilby, *Life and Tradition in West Yorkshire*, 1976, p. 152; *Competition Festival Record*, May and June 1912.

7   H. Coward, *Wings*, pp. 1–7, 13–15.

8   A. Taylor, *Labour and Love*, p. 14.

9   *Bradford Weekly Telegraph*, 31 May 1912.

10 *Musical Times*, July 1912; *Musical Herald*, June 1912.

11 *British Bandsman*, 21 October 1911.

12 *Cornet*, October 1893.

13 *British Bandsman*, October 1888; *Brass Band News*, September and July 1895.

14 *School Music Review*, June 1896.

15 *British Bandsman*, 7 January 1911; *Bolton Evening News*, 30 December 1910. See also for funerals of Charles Auty and Willie Lee, *Brass Band News*, June 1888 and April 1890; A. Taylor, *Brass Bands*, p. 28.

16 *Brass Band News*, August 1889; Leeds Philharmonic, chorus roll book, 1904–1905, margin comment.

17 See article on Emley Band, *Huddersfield Weekly Examiner*, 9 February 1957.

18 *Competition Festival Record*, February 1914.

19 V. & G. Brand, *Brass Bands*, pp. 71, 76.

20 *The Musicians Report and Journal*, August 1900.

21 A. Taylor, *Labour and Love*, pp. 16, 18.

22 *Magnet*, 1 February 1902.

23 W. Millington, *Sketches* p. VI. Fifty-one of the one hundred and thirty-eight singers and musicians discussed in detail seem to have been involved in at least semi-professional activity at some stage; H. Mortimer, *On Brass*, p. 41.

24 C. Ehrlich, *The Music Profession in Britain since the Eighteenth Century; a Social History*, Oxford, 1985, pp. 142–85 for unionisation battles.

25 *The Musicians Report and Journal*, September 1900, claimed that musicians were mostly, 'the sons of humble mechanics or small storekeepers'. Rates of pay, of course, could be very low. See C. Ehrlich, *Profession*, pp. 173–9 provides some statistics as did most copies of the *Report and Journal*.

26 R. Mellor, *Memoirs of a Veteran Organist*, Huddersfield, 1874, pp. 33–4; J. Scott, Evolution, p. 211.

27 S. Midgley, *My Seventy Years' Musical Memories*, 1934.

28 *Cornet*, January 1904; *The Strad*, February 1900, September 1900, November 1900.

29 A considerable number of singers, at least before 1900, did, admittedly, come from what might be termed a 'lower-middle-class' background.

30 W. Smith (ed.), *Old Yorkshire*, 11, 1890, pp. 235–8; R. Brook, *The Story of Huddersfield*, 1968, p. 215.

31 E. Hick, Leeds Press Cuttings, VIII, Leeds City Reference Library, p. 60; H. Mortimer with A. Lynton, *On Brass*.

32 This paragraph is built upon John D. Vose's splendid, *The Lancashire Caruso*, Blackpool, 1982.

33   Quoted in E. MacKerness, *Somewhere Further North*, 1974, p. 97; *Brass Band News*, June 1889.

34   W. Millington, *Sketches*, p. 63.

35   H. Livings, *That the Medals and Baton be Placed on View*, 1975 p. 36.

36   P. Thompson, *The Edwardians*, 1977, p. 198. At times during my research I have wondered if historians are too deeply imbued by the work ethic?

37   Much of this section first appeared as 'Popular music and popular politics in the Yorkshire textile district, 1880–1914' in J. Walton & J. Walvin (eds.), *Leisure in Britain, 1780–1939*, Manchester, 1983.

38   'Work', broadly defined to include the whole apparatus that grew out of it, especially in the factory towns of the North, was probably the *central* determinant. See P. Joyce, *Work, Society and Politics*, 1982 ed.

39   See letter from Samuel Midgley, *Yorkshire Daily Observer*, 15 August 1907; *Musical Herald*, January 1891 claimed that 'gentle and simple stand side by side in the pursuit of art' in the Huddersfield Choral Society.

40   *Cornet*, October 1893.

41   *British Bandsman*, 6 September 1913, for the full programme.

42   J. H. Clapham, *The Woollen and Worsted Industries*, 1907, p. 207.

43   Leisure 'discipline' if nothing else reinforced work discipline?

44   Is it significant that Fountain Byers, killed in the Pretoria Pit disaster of 1910, 'an ardent and enthusiastic worker in the labour cause, [who] did yeoman service for Mr Wilson at Wingates during the last election' had become an *ex*-member of the Wingates Temperance Band by the time of the election? In this case, politics may have been the 'victor', and for many, there was probably not space for active involvement in two demanding areas. See *Bolton Evening News*, 27 December 1910.

45   *Yorkshire Factory Times*, 2 and 23 June, 1910. Even during the Manning-ham Mills strike in Bradford, 1890–91, which generated considerable popular support, bands charged for their services. See M. Haynes, 'Strikes', in J. Benson, *Working Class*, p. 110.

46   *British Bandsman*, September 1891; *Brighouse Echo*, 15 and 29 July, 19 August 1904.

47   J. H. White, *Bramley Band*, p. 73; *Brighouse Echo*, 10 June 1904.

48   V. & G. Brand, *Brass Bands*, pp. 24–5; *British Bandsman*, 10 June 1904.

49   *Ibid.*, June 1900, for Mafeking celebrations.

50   S. Yeo, *Religion*, p. 273.

51   A. Taylor, *Brass Bands*, p. 119.

52   G. Sewell, *Bradford Festival*, p. 88.

53   *British Bandsman*, 18 October 1913. For Holbrooke's article, in which after a remarkably patronising introduction he admitted to being 'astonished in a powerful degree' by the overall quality', *ibid.*, 4 October 1913. His *Clive of India*, was the 1940 Belle Vue testpiece.

54   Although, was the entrepreneur's hold ever *so* choking as Patrick Joyce makes it seem in *Work, Society and Politics?* Building on the ideas of the Centre for Contemporary Cultural Studies, especially S. Hall and T. Jefferson (eds.), *Resistance Through Rituals*, 1975, it might be possible to

push the idea of music, and leisure in general as a 'radical' force, further than has been done in the last couple of paragraphs. The use of art music by popular organisations was perhaps to an extent a militant 'we're as good as you are' statement to the leisure class, a type of symbolic resistance. At present, however, I prefer empirically, as opposed to theoretically, rooted speculation.

55   *Musical Progress*, August 1914.
56   *British Bandsman*, 30 April 1910; *Cornet*, January 1914.
57   H. Cunningham, 'Leisure' in J. Benson (ed.), *Working Class*, p. 137.
58   *Orchestral Times*, February 1901.
59   *School Music Review*, January 1912.
60   Interview with Anne-Marie Wagstaff, transcript in author's possession.
61   One wonders if in fact voluntary organisations were in 'crisis' because of their 'health'.
62   Brighouse, for example, a small Yorkshire town with a population of source 30,000, supported two rinks in 1909.
63   For early cinema, M. Chanan, *The Dream that Kicks*, 1983. G. J. Mellor, *Picture Pioneers*, Newcastle, 1971, is useful on Northern cinema.
64   *Yorkshire Daily Observer Budget*, 29 April 1911.
65   A. D. Gilbert, *Religion and Society in Industrial England*, 1976, Chapter Two.
66   *School Music Review*, January 1910.
67   Keighley Musical Union chorus roll books, 1904–1923, Keighley Public Library; *Keighley News*, 26 April 1913.

Conclusions and epilogue

1   C. Reid, 'Britain from Stanford to Vaughan Williams c. 1880–1939' in A. Jacobs (ed.), *Choral Music*, 1963 ed., p. 268, for *Revenge*.
2   See especially, R. Gray, 'Bourgeois hegemony in Victorian Britain', in J. Bloomfield (ed.), *Class, Hegemony and Party*, 1977.
3   For an excellent general overview of bands since 1914 see A. Taylor, *Brass Bands*, 1979, pp. 121–254.
4   F. Thompson, *Lark Rise to Candleford*, 1945 ed., pp. 62–9.
5   By which stage it was most decidedly 'variety'. In a sense, music-hall was dead by 1914.

Appendix: Working-class composers

1   S. Banfield, 'The artist and society' in N. Temperley, *Athlone, V*, p. 28.
2   For working-class literature, M. Vicinus, *The Industrial Muse*, 1974.
3   For Widdop, undated cuttings in A. Clay, Press-Cuttings Book, Calderdale Archives Department, and J. Sutcliffe Smith, *A Musical Pilgrimage in Yorkshire*, Leeds, 1928, p. 225. For Leach, J. T. Lightwood, *Methodist Music*, pp. 20–2.
4   *Cornet*, October 1903; *Ibid.*, November 1898.
5   A Symphony 'in the manner of Pleyel'. *Bradford Old Choral Society Centenary Souvenir*, Bradford, 1921, p. 4.

6 *Bradford*, 8 February 1896; Leeds Musical Union minute book, 8 October 1898.
7 P. Pirie, *The English Musical Renaissance*, 1979, p. 26.
8 *New Grove*, XVI.
9 I found K. Eastaugh, *Havergal Brian: The Making of a Composer*, 1976, particularly useful.
10 *Ibid.*, p. 29.
11 *Musical Times*, November 1907.
12 *Leeds Intelligencer*, 5 July 1856.

Bibliography

This listing is not a detailed record of the sources consulted during the writing of this book. The footnotes provide adequate bibliographical detail for those seeking to pursue specific points. Rather, this is an introductory bibliography of secondary material intended to guide those commencing research into the field of popular music, 1840–1914.

General works on popular culture and popular leisure

Books
I. Appleyard, *Leisure Research and Policy*, Edinburgh, 1974.
P. Bailey, *Leisure and Class in Victorian England*, 1978.
T. Bennett, G. Martin, C. Mercer, & J. Woolacott (eds.), *Culture, Ideology and Social Process*, 1981.
M. Bienefeld, *Working Hours in British Industry*, 1972.
C. Bigsby (ed.), *Approaches to Popular Culture*, 1976.
A. Briggs, *Mass Entertainment: The Origins of a Modern Industry*, Adelaide, 1972.
P. Burke, *Popular Culture in Early Modern Europe*, 1978.
J. Clarke, C. Critcher & R. Johnson (eds.), *Working Class Culture*, 1979.
A. Clayre, *Ideas of Work and Play*, 1974.
H. Cunningham, *Leisure in the Industrial Revolution*, 1980.
S. Hall & T. Jefferson, *Resistance Through Rituals: Youth Subculture in Post-War Britain*, 1975.
S. Hall & P. Whannel, *The Popular Arts*, 1964.
T. Hawkes, *Structuralism and Semiotics*, 1977.
R. Hoggart, *The Uses of Literacy*, 1973 ed.
L. James, *Fiction For the Working Man*, 1974.
R. Malcolmson, *Popular Recreations in English Society, 1700–1850*, Cambridge, 1973.
M. Marrus (ed.), *The Emergence of Leisure*, New York, 1974.
H. Meller, *Leisure and the Changing City*, 1976.
S. Parker, *The Sociology of Leisure*, 1976.
J. H. Plumb, *The Commercialisation of Leisure in Eighteenth Century England*, Reading, 1973.

K. Roberts, *Leisure*, 1970; *Contemporary Society and the Growth of Leisure*, 1978.

C. Rojek, *Capitalism and Leisure Theory*, 1985.

M. Smith, S. Parker, C. Smith (eds.), *Leisure and Society in Britain*, 1973.

R. Storch (ed.), *Popular Culture and Custom in Nineteenth-Century Britain*, 1982.

A. Swingewood, *The Myth of Mass Culture*, 1977.

D. Thompson, *Discrimination and Popular Culture*, 1968.

E. P. Thompson, *The Making of the English Working Glass*, 1968 ed.

M. Vicinus, *The Industrial Muse*, 1974.

J. Walton & J. Walvin (eds.), *Leisure in Britain, 1780–1939*, Manchester, 1983.

J. Walvin, *Leisure and Society, 1830–1950*, 1978.

R. Williams, *Culture and Society*, 1971 ed.; *The Long Revolution*, 1971 ed.

J. Wolff, *The Social Production of Art*, 1981.

E. & S. Yeo (eds.), *Popular Culture and Class Conflict, 1590–1914*, Brighton, 1981.

S. Yeo, *Religion and Voluntary Organisations in Crisis*, 1976.

Articles

P. Bailey, ' "Will the real Bill Banks please stand up?" Towards a role analysis of mid-Victorian working-class respectability', *Journal of Social History*, XII, 1979.

H. Cunningham, 'Leisure', J. Benson (ed.), *The Working Class in England 1875–1914*, 1985.

R. Gray, 'Bourgeois hegemony in Victorian Britain', J. Bloomfield (ed.), *Class, Hegemony and Party*, 1977.; 'Styles of Life: The "labour aristocracy" and class relations in later nineteenth-century Edinburgh,' *International Review of Social History*, XVIII, 1973.

B. Harrison, 'Religion and recreation in nineteenth-century England', *Past and Present*, XXXVIII, 1967.

G. Stedman Jones, ' "Class expression versus social control?" A critique of recent trends in the social history of "leisure" ', *History Workshop Journal*, IV, 1977.

H. Perkin, 'The social tone of Victorian seaside resorts in the north-west', *Northern History*, XI, 1975.

S. Pollard, 'Factory discipline in the Industrial Revolution', *Economic History Review*, XVI, 1963–64.

R. Price, 'The working-men's club movement and Victorian social reform ideology', *Victorian Studies*, XV, 1971.

D. Prynn, 'The Clarion Clubs, rambling and the holiday associations in Britain since the 1890s' *Journal of Contemporary History*, 1976.

D. Reid, 'The decline of Saint Monday, 1766–1876', *Past and Present*, LXXI, 1976.

R. Storch, 'The plague of blue locusts: police reform and popular resistance in Northern England, 1840–1857', *International Review of Social History*, XX, 1975.; 'The policeman as domestic missionary: Urban discipline and popular culture in Northern England, 1850–1880', *Journal of Social History*, IX, 1976.

'The problem of working-class leisure: some roots of middle-class moral reform in the industrial North, 1825–1850', A. P. Donajgrodski (ed.), *Social Controls in Nineteenth Century Britain*, 1977.

K. Thomas, 'Work and leisure in pre-industrial society', *Past and Present*, XXIX, 1964.

E. P. Thompson, 'Patrician Society, Plebeian culture', *Journal of Social History*, VII, 1974.; 'Time, work-discipline and industrial capitalism', *Past and Present*, XXXVIII, 1967.

'Work and Leisure in industrial society: conference report', *Past and Present*, XXX, 1965.

M. Vicinus, 'The Study of Popular Culture', *Victorian Studies*, XVIII, 1975.

Popular Music

Books

T. Adorno, *Introduction to the Sociology of Music*, Seabury, 1976.

Anon., *A Short History of Cheap Music*, 1887.

P. Bate, *The Trumpet and Trombone*, 1972.

P. Bedford, *An Introduction to English Handbell Ringing*, Chelmsford, 1974.

B. Boon, *Play the Music Play*, 1966.

V. & G. Brand, *Brass Bands in the Twentieth Century*, Letchworth, 1979.

J. Brattan, *The Victorian Popular Ballad*, 1975.

N. Cardus, *Autobiography*, 1947.

A. Carse, *The Life of Jullien*, 1951.

D. Cheshire, *Music-Hall in Britain*, Newton Abbot, 1974.

E. Coates, *Suite in Four Movements*, 1954.

C. Coborn, *The Man Who Broke the Bank*, 1928.

D. Cohen & B. Greenwood, *The Buskers*, Newton Abbot, 1981.

K. Cook (ed.), *Oh, Listen to the Band*, 1950.

T. Cooper, *Brass Bands of Yorkshire*, Clapham, 1974.

P. Davison, *Songs of the British Music Hall*, 1971.

M. Willson Disher, *Victorian Song*, 1955.

C. Donakowski, *A Muse for the Masses*, Chicago, 1977.

G. Dunn, *The Fellowship of Song*, 1980.

K. Easthaugh, *Havergal Brian*, 1976.

C. Ehrlich, *The Music Profession in Britain Since the Eighteenth Century*, Oxford, 1985.; *The Piano, a History*, 1976.

R. Elbourne, *Music and Tradition in Early Industrial Lancashire, 1780–1840*, 1980.

D. Farson, *Marie Lloyd and Music-Hall*, 1972.

P. Gammond & R. Horricks, *Music on Record 1, Brass Bands*, Cambridge, 1980.

P. Giles, *The Counter-Tenor*, 1982.

C. Hamm, *Yesterdays: Popular Song in America*, 1979.

D. Harker, *One For the Money*, 1981.

D. Harker, *Fakesong*, 1985.

P. Honri, *Working the Halls*, Farnborough, 1973.

D. Horn & P. Tagg (eds.), *Popular Music Perspectives*, 1982.

W. Horwood, *Adolphe Sax, 1814–1894, His Life and Legacy*, Bramley, 1980.

D. Howard, *London Theatres and Music-Halls 1850–1950*, 1970.
C. Humphries & W. Smith, *Music Publishing in the British Isles*, Oxford, 1970.
A. Hutchings, *Church Music in the Nineteenth Century*, 1967.
A. Jacobs (ed.), *Choral Music*, 1963.
J. Kerman, *Musicology*, 1985.
E. Lee, *Music of the People*, 1970.
J. Lightwood, *Stories of Methodist Music: the Nineteenth Century*, 1928.
H. Livings, *That the Medals and the Baton be put on view*, Newton Abbot, 1975.
A. L. Lloyd, *Folk Song in England*, 1967.
A. Lowenberg, *Annals of Opera*, Cambridge, 1943.
K. Macdermott, *Sussex Church Music in the Past*, Chichester, 1923.
C. MacInnes, *Sweet Saturday Night*, 1967.
E. MacKerness, *A Social History of English Music*, 1964.; *Somewhere Further North*, Sheffield, 1974.
S. Maitland, *Vesta Tilley*, 1986.
R. Mander & J. Micheson, *British Music-Hall: A Story in Pictures*, 1965.; *Musical Comedy*, 1969.
W. Mellers, *Music and Society*, 1946.
G. Mellor, *Northern Music-Hall*, Newcastle, 1971.
H. Mortimer (with A. Lynton), *Harry Mortimer On Brass*, Sherborne, 1981.
R. Myers, *Handel's 'Messiah'*, New York, 1948.
R. Nettel, *Music in the Five Towns*, Oxford, 1944.
R. Palmer, *A Touch on the Times*, 1974.
PEP, *Arts Enquiry: Music*, 1949.
A. Peacock & R. Weir, *The Composer in the Market Place*, 1975.
R. Pearsall, *Edwardian Popular Music*, Newton Abbot, 1975.; *Victorian Popular Music*, Newton Abbot, 1973.
M. Pickering, *Village Song and Culture*, 1982.
P. Pirie, *The English Musical Renaissance*, 1979.
C. Pulling, *What They were Singing*, 1952.
B. Rainbow, *The Land Without Music*, 1967.
H. Raynor, *Music and Society Since 1815*, 1976.
E. Routley, *The Musical Wesleys*, 1968.
J. F. Russell & J. H. Elliot, *The Brass Band Movement*, 1936.
S. Sadie (ed.), *The New Grove Dictionary of Music and Musicians*, 20 vols., 1980.
P. Scholes, *The Mirror of Music*, 2 vols., Oxford, 1947.; *Oxford Companion to Music*, Oxford, 1970 ed.; *The Puritans and Music*, 1934.
H. Scott, *The Early Doors*, 1946.
L. Senelick, D. F. Cheshire & U. Schneider, *British Music-Hall 1840–1923*, Connecticut, 1981.
T. Staveacre, *The Songwriters*, 1980.
J. Sutcliffe Smith, *The Music of the Yorkshire Dales*, Leeds, 1930.; *A Musical Pilgrimage in Yorkshire*, Leeds, 1928.
A. Taylor, *Brass Bands*, 1979.; *Labour and Love: An Oral History of the Brass Band Movement*, 1983.

S. de B. Taylor, *Two Centuries of Music in Liverpool*, 1976.
N. Temperley (ed.), *The Athlone History of Music*, vol. V, 1981.
M. Turner & A. Miall (eds.), *The Parlour Song Book*, 1974.; *The Edwardian Song Book*, 1982.
J. Vose, *The Lancashire Caruso*, Blackpool, 1982.
W. Weber, *Music and the Middle Class*, 1975.
I. Whitcomb, *After the Ball*, 1973 ed.
K. Young, *Music's Great Days in the Spas and Watering Places*, 1968.
P. Young, *The Choral Tradition*, 1962.; *A History of British Music*, 1967.

Articles
P. Bailey, 'Custom, capital and culture in the Victorian music-hall', R. Storch (ed.), *Popular Culture and Custom in Nineteenth Century England*, 1982.
D. Dowe, 'The workingmens' choral movement in Germany before the First World War', *Journal of Contemporary History*, XIII, 1978.
R. P. Elbourne, 'Singing away to the click of the shuttle: musical life in the handloom weaving communities of Lancashire', *Local Historian*, XII, 1976.
V. Gammon, ' "Babylonian performances": the rise and suppression of popular church music, 1660–1870', E. & S. Yeo (eds.), *Popular Culture and Class Conflict, 1590–1914*, Brighton, 1981.; 'Folk-song collecting in Sussex and Surrey, 1843–1914', *History Workshop Journal*, X, 1980.; ' "Not appreciated in Worthing?" Class expression and popular song texts in mid-nineteenth century Britain', *Popular Music*, IV, 1984.
D. Harker, 'May Cecil Sharp be praised?' *History Workshop Journal*, XIV, 1982.; 'The making of the Tyneside concert-hall', *Popular Music*, I, 1981.
A. Howkins, 'The voice of the people: the social meaning and context of country song', *Oral History*, III, 1975.
G. Stedman Jones, 'Working-class culture and working-class politics in London, 1870–1900: notes on the re-making of a working class', *Journal of Social History*, VII, 1974.
E. Mackerness, 'Sources of local musical history', *Local Historian*, II, 1975.
R. Nettel, 'The influence of the industrial revolution on English music', *Proceedings of the Royal Musical Association*, 1945–46.
C. Pegg, 'Factors affecting the musical choice of audiences in East Suffolk, England', *Popular Music*, IV, 1984.
D. Russell, 'The Leeds Rational Recreation Society, 1852–9: "music for the people" in a mid-Victorian City', *Publications of the Thoresby Society*, XVII, 1981.
L. Senelick, 'Politics as entertainment: Victorian music hall songs', *Victorian Studies*, XIX, 1975.
P. Summerfield, 'The Effingham Arms and the Empire: deliberate selection in the evolution of music-hall in London', E. & S. Yeo (eds.), *Popular Culture and Class Conflict, 1590–1914*, Brighton, 1981. 'Patriotism and Empire: music-hall entertainment, 1870–1914,' J. Mackenzie (ed.), *Imperialism and Popular Culture*, Manchester, 1986.
N. Wayne, 'The concertina revival, parts 1 and 2', *Folk Review*, March and April 1974.
R. Woods, 'The church bands', *Folk Review*, February 1975.

Index